Praise for previous editions of

100 BEST CRUISE VACATIONS

"During my 15 years of covering the cruise industry, I have met no one more knowledgeable about the cruise ships and vacations at sea than Theodore W. Scull. His latest book, 100 Best Cruise Vacations, *seems destined to be both the perfect companion for armchair travelers dreaming of a cruise and the ideal guidebook for active cruisers planning their next voyage. Ted's 'Top 100' include my favorite cruises, and likely will include yours, too."*

—Charles Doherty
Managing Editor, Cruise Travel *magazine*

"From historic tall ships to river cruisers, Ted Scull tells you where to find the unique cruises that make lifelong memories. His research and presentation are first-rate."

—Steve Blount
Editorial Director, World Publications,
Caribbean Travel & Life

Help Us Keep This Guide Up to Date

Every effort has been made by the author and editors to make this guide as accurate and useful as possible. However, many things can change after a guide is published—phone numbers change, itineraries vary, ships come under new management, etc.

We would love to hear from you concerning your experiences with this guide and how you feel it could be made better and be kept up to date. While we may not be able to respond to all comments and suggestions, we'll take them to heart and we'll also make certain to share them with the author. Please send your comments and suggestions to the following address:

The Globe Pequot Press
Reader Response/Editorial Department
P.O. Box 480
Guilford, CT 06437

Or you may e-mail us at:

editorial@GlobePequot.com

Thanks for your input, and happy travels!

100 Best
CRUISE
VACATIONS

Third Edition

THE TOP CRUISES
THROUGHOUT THE WORLD FOR
ALL INTERESTS AND BUDGETS

THEODORE W. SCULL

The
Globe
Pequot
Press

GUILFORD, CONNECTICUT

Text design by Nancy Freeborn
Photo layout by Sue Preneta

ISSN 1546-0789
ISBN 0-7627-2817-5

Manufactured in the United States of America
Third Edition/First Printing

The schedules and rates listed in this guidebook were confirmed at press time. We recommend, however, that you call before traveling to obtain current information.

TO MY DEAR WIFE, SUELLYN,

WHO HAS ALSO TAKEN A COTTON TO CRUISING.

—TWS

AUTHOR'S THANKS

100 Best Cruise Vacations is now in its third edition, and revising, deleting, and adding to the entries was a daunting, if highly pleasurable task, but one that could not have been accomplished without the help of friends and fellow cruisers who suggested and wrote up their favorite shipboard experiences.

Bill Mayes, European traveler and generous B&B provider in England, helped update several chapters and wrote completely new ones for ferry cruising to the islands north of Scotland and through the Adriatic between Venice and Greece. Ben Lyons, merchant marine officer, contributed to the *Queen Mary 2* and the *Star Flyer* chapters and helped out with several others. Jane Lyons related tales of her Canmar container ship crossing from Le Havre to Montreal. David King-Wood, my former colleague in teaching, shared his Costa Rica to Panama adventure aboard Lindblad's *Sea Voyager.*

Others who have contributed in many ways are Stephen Card, Brad Hatry, Andy Kilk, Jonathan Siskin, and Vincent Messina, the last named a great friend who, sadly, died before publication.

Cruise writer Heidi Sarna, both colleague and friend, provided invaluable help based on her numerous shipboard experiences and, equally important, a timely sense of humor when needed via e-mail between the East Side and West Side of Manhattan. Matt Hannafin, another West Sider, also aided in checking many facts and itineraries.

My brother Sandy and I left our wives at home to cruise the Inside Passage aboard the pretty little *Spirit of '98* and aboard the landmark *Delta Queen* in the Deep South as our parents had done forty years ago.

Finally, my dear wife, Suellyn, accompanied me on about half of these cruises, including recent ones aboard the *Seabourn Pride,* our honeymoon ship; Holland America's *Prinsendam;* NCL's *Norwegian Dawn;* the European riverboats *Mozart* and *Frederic Chopin;* and perhaps best of all, a couple of Atlantic crossings and a cruise aboard the *Queen Elizabeth 2.* In addition, she has given me great moral support over the months of rewriting and has scanned the copy for errors and suggested adjustments. Lastly, thanks to Heather Carreiro at The Globe Pequot Press for editing this third edition.

Queen of the North

Niagara Princess

Seabourn Pride

R/B River Explorer

L'Abercrombie

Alaska/
Norwegian Sky

American Queen

Sun Boat III

Star Flyer

Queen of the West

Endeavour   Tobermory on the Isle of Mull/ Hebridean Princess

Spirit of Endeavour   Spirit of '98

Grand Caribe   Reef Endeavour

Queen Elizabeth 2   Sea Cloud

Olympia Voyager   Clipper Adventurer

Sea Cloud

Sea Cloud

Pacific Explorer

Sea Cloud

The World

Dawn Princess

CONTENTS

ATLANTIC OCEAN

THE BAHAMAS AND CARIBBEAN ISLANDS

LATIN AMERICA

PACIFIC OCEAN

EUROPE

AFRICA AND THE MIDDLE EAST

SOUTHEAST ASIA AND THE FAR EAST

POLAR REGIONS

CIRCUMNAVIGATIONS

INTRODUCTION

The popularity of cruise vacations has increased more than 300 percent in the last ten years. By the end of 2003, 8.5 million Americans—up from a little more than five million in 1998—had embarked. Cruises are increasingly seen as affordable, great fun, romantic, and a relaxing, hassle-free way to visit many parts of the world. To both meet and fuel the demand for cruise vacations, more than two dozen large cruise ships are on order for completion between 2003 and 2005, joining the several hundred oceangoing ships that currently sail the high seas. Additional fleets of coastal and inland-waterway vessels, with many more under construction, explore inshore waters, rivers, and canals.

A traveler's cruising options have become mind-boggling, with so many different lines and respective reputations. The multitudinous decisions to be made include the specific type of cruise, itinerary, optimum ship size, whether it's a brand-new one or a fast disappearing classic liner, how much to spend on a cabin (and if to pay extra for a private veranda), the best time to go, and the relative personal importance attached to food, service, entertainment, and activities. Who are the other passengers going to be, mostly Americans? Or will there be persons of several nationalities aboard? What's the age range? And is this a cruise for children?

100 Best Cruise Vacations will help sort out the options by selecting the top ships, taking into account a fair balance between a ship's particular ambience, standards, and itineraries. Some of my choices will be obvious and others may seem quirky or head scratchers.

Oceangoing ships come in sizes from 150,000 gross tons down to a little more than 2,000 tons, with passenger lists from less than one hundred to more than three thousand. The very largest may qualify as

destinations themselves, where the itinerary is secondary to the rich shipboard experience, whereas others may offer a new port every day. Some people like lots of time at sea, so perhaps a voyage with ports spaced out every few days or a transocean crossing will fill the bill.

Enrichment cruises accompanied by top lecturers in a variety of fields may take in the great sites of the ancient world, while expedition-style voyages explore remote regions with a team of naturalists to lead passengers ashore. Some of the latter take you to places that may be hard, even impossible, to get to any other way, such as remote sections of Australia's Great Barrier Reef, South Pacific, the Galápagos Islands, Chilean fjords, and the white continent of Antarctica. Voyaging under sail through the Greek islands and along the Turkish coast or among the Caribbean's Leeward and Windward Islands may seem a romantic concept, and terrific choices are happily expanding. If you like water sports, some ships fold out their own marinas, with all sorts of boating, snorkeling, and diving equipment available for use.

To celebrate Americana, listen to great jazz and big-band sounds, and dine on Southern and Cajun cuisine, board a stern-wheeler for a river cruise in the antebellum South, along the Upper Mississippi, or the Ohio up past Cincinnati. European river journeys ply the Rhine, Moselle, Elbe, and Danube to visit timeless medieval towns, hunting castles, and great Romanesque and Gothic cathedrals; and exotic inland trips penetrate deep into the Amazon Basin or into the heart of China. The pokiest cruises are aboard luxury barges, where the distance covered takes second place to savoring the passing countryside, biking into a nearby village, and sharing wonderful food and wines with a passenger complement of two dozen or fewer.

A cruise can be as short as an overnight crossing between the Scandinavian capitals, but more typically lasts a week to ten days. Vacationers with time and money can sail for several weeks around the bottom of South America or along the African coast, or go all the way, taking three to four months to circumnavigate the globe. Anyone remotely interested in taking a cruise vacation, or looking for something different, will find several that should appeal.

In this book, the cruise vacations are grouped into logical geographical regions beginning in North America and then casting a wider net overseas.

Defining the Best

What is terrific to one person may not appeal to someone else, and I am sure there will be lots of agreement and disagreement about the ships and the cruise itineraries I have chosen. Right up front, each cruise is entirely my own selection. After spending more than four years at sea since I made my first crossing to Europe as a teenager aboard the dear-departed French Line, I have come to thrive on the increasing diversity of available cruise experiences. I can be equally happy crossing the Atlantic, cruising around Britain, navigating Alaska's Inside Passage, exploring the Upper Amazon, or transiting the Panama Canal. For me the cover has long since blown off such clichés that cruises attract only old people, are nonstop drinking parties, or that they are stuffy, regimented, dull, crowded, and claustrophobic.

The best cruise vacation might imply the most expensive, and although some of the highest-rated boutique ships can cost upward of $500 to $1,000 a day per person, this need not be the case at all because there are excellent cruises at a third of that price and great values for even less. You will find itineraries at all fare levels.

The best cruises may involve the tangible and intangible features of a particular ship. The biggest ships on the high seas have always had a following, and I have picked those that truly excel in design and layout, have a pleasing or delightfully offbeat decor, provide lots of things to do aboard all day and well into the night, and have sound reputations for serving, feeding, and handling a small city of passengers and crew. If a midsize ship is more appealing, I have chosen these on the same but scaled-down basis. Remember, this is a selective guide, not inclusive of every best cruise vacation on the high seas, so if your favorite is not listed here, you already know about it.

Many of the finest ships, in terms of food and service, have passenger capacities that range from one hundred to about four hundred, and some cruisers choose the ship first, then one of several itineraries, and return again and again to the same ship or sistership.

The itinerary may be paramount. For the popular Panama Canal cruise, I offer several choices with different Caribbean and Pacific ports and a variety of onboard lifestyles and prices. Alaska and the Mediterranean also offer several alternatives.

Not all cruises should stand alone as the total travel experience, so for the islands north of Scotland, the Inside Passage of Alaska, and others, I have suggested land extensions.

I happen to be partial to older liners, and, in some cases, knowledgeable cruisers will wonder why I have included an over-the-hill ship, but she may offer something unique, giving readers the chance to sample what sea travel used to be like, before it's too late. It is fading fast.

The Itinerary

Some Caribbean ships may cruise year-round to the same set of ports, whereas others move seasonally to the Mediterranean or Alaska from late spring to early fall. I might suggest a ship for one itinerary and then make reference to another region where the same ship or a fleet mate cruises. Several top ships may get more than one full entry, as they cruise in many different parts of the world during one calendar year.

A few ships may not repeat itineraries from one year to the next, and a set of ports for one Mediterranean or South American cruise might change the following year. While this muddies the waters, if the ship seems attractive to you, there will likely be some draw for a different itinerary. Cruise lines typically announce their schedules a year in advance, but then a ship gets sold or transferred elsewhere and another ship comes on line to take its place. Cruising is always in a state of flux, especially in these uncertain times, so please don't expect to be able to exactly duplicate every cruise vacation listed here. Rather use this book, literally, as a guide to what's out there—then get the latest news from your travel agent, the Internet, or the cruise line.

Specialized destinations, such as the Galápagos and Antarctica, sometimes include two ships making more or less the same cruise, and although their relative merits may be treated separately, the itineraries will be combined to save reading unnecessary repetition.

Every chapter will have a reference section that lists the following useful information:

Address/Phone: This listing includes the line's name and address, phone numbers, fax number, e-mail addresses, and Web sites, when available. Some lines do not take direct bookings because they sell cabins only through travel agents, tour companies, or over the Internet, so the phone numbers may be for information and brochures only. Cruise-line Web sites vary from excellent to you-wonder-why-they-bother because the information is so thin or out of date.

The Ship: The vital statistics are the year of build and previous names, if any; gross tonnage and length to give an indication of size; and draft (how deep in the water the ship sits), with a larger figure generally indicating more stability in heavy seas when matched with tonnage. Coastal ships and riverboats naturally have shallow drafts, so

an exact figure is not always important, but it is likely to be 8 feet or less.

Passengers: This figure is usually for double occupancy, two to a cabin, whereas the maximum capacity may be higher as some cabins have third and fourth beds, perhaps a sofa bed or upper foldaway berths. The average age and nationality of one's fellow passengers are key points of information. Generally, the shorter the cruise, the younger the passenger, and average age increases markedly when the cruise begins to exceed a week. You can enrich the experience by sailing with Europeans or South Americans, or you may prefer to keep it simple and travel with passengers from your own country.

Dress: As most people increasingly seem to balk at getting dressed up, it is important to note what a line suggests for a particular evening, hoping that most passengers will comply to maintain the ambience. A little dressing up is part of the cruise experience for special occasions. I have used male evening dress codes, as they tend to be less understood and they can act also as a guide for women. "Formal" here means a tuxedo, dinner jacket, or a dark suit for men; "informal" means jacket with or without a tie; and "casual" means collared shirt and long pants. Daytime wear is even more casual. For women formal would be a gown or cocktail dress; informal, a dress or pants suit; and casual, a skirt or pants. You will not find me using terms such as "casually elegant" and telling people no T-shirts or tank tops in the dining room. If this is your style when the suggested dress at dinner is otherwise, you're on your own.

Officers/Crew: Some ships trade on the nationality of their officers and crew, so here we find out who's in charge and who does the serving.

Cabins: In addition to the accommodation information in the text, the number of cabins is listed, plus the number that are outside (with portholes or windows) and the availability of verandas, those private cabin balconies that let you step outside, found on many of the newer and largest ships. Few ships have dedicated single cabins, but if they do, this information is listed.

Fare: The $ signs are designed to give approximations for comparative purposes and are cruise brochure rates per person, double occupancy, per day for a standard outside cabin: $ = $100–$150; $$ = $150–$250; $$$ = $250–$400; $$$$ = $400–$600; $$$$$ = $600 upward.

Cruise-line fares are all over the map, even with the same ship on different itineraries. It's really no different from the yield management of the airlines. An empty cabin is lost revenue not only for its fare but also for what passengers will spend for shore excursions, drinks, shopping, gambling, spa treatments, and so on. Except for some small expedition ships and riverboats, the brochure rate is usually only the starting point for determining what you will ultimately pay. Nearly all lines have early booking discounts and may offer deals for departures selling poorly, which could occur months out or announced just before sailing. There are many ways to find the best-value fare, and it may be through a travel agent, a cruise-only specialist, a newspaper ad, the Internet, or directly from the line.

What's included: The $ to $$$$$ is based on what's normally included. A separate listing for what's not included specifies the extras. Most fares are cruise only, but increasingly the port charges are bundled into the fare. When they appear as a separate line item, they may add $100 to $200 to a typical seven-day cruise. Airfare to and from the ship is usually not included, but the line may have special add-on rates that are less than you can get on your own. Remember, if the line books the air travel,

they can route you any way they want, but they are more likely to help you catch up to the ship if the flights are delayed or cancelled than if you have made your own arrangements, including the use of frequent-flyer mileage. Some expedition cruises include shore excursions in the cruise fare, but most lines do not. A few upscale lines offer complimentary wine with meals, and fewer still include drinks and stocked minibars. For most lines tipping is your responsibility, but they will also almost always tell you what's expected, usually about $10 to $13 per day per person. The bottom line is to see what's included and what's not—the $ to $$$$$ may be skewed upward for a few lines because so much is already built into the fare.

Highlights: A summary of what makes this ship and/or cruise worth writing home about.

Other itineraries: If you like what you read but want to take a particular ship or the cruise line somewhere else, you will find references to other itineraries.

Ships Have Personalities

Some ships come from the same mold, but as they mature, they begin to show distinctive characteristics and differences from those of their fleet mates. Hundreds of passengers and crew help make a ship a living, breathing, seagoing community. A few ships have souls, and this special aspect will usually come across whether you are looking for it or not. All ships have personalities, and the best ones are happy ships, important not only to you as a paying passenger but also to the officers and crew who live aboard for months on end. Their time onboard may eventually add up to years, more than they spend ashore.

I hope you find your ship. I have, and it is present in these pages in great variety.

NORTH AMERICA

CRYSTAL CRUISES'
Crystal Symphony
New York via New England to the St. Lawrence and Montreal

 Upscale, classy, and much larger than all other high-end cruise ships, the *Crystal Symphony,* sister *Crystal Harmony,* and larger and newer *Crystal Serenity* provide lots of space, amenities, and activities for Crystal's far-ranging itineraries. During a relatively short fall season, the *Crystal Symphony* visits New York, New England, and eastern Canada.

Crystal Cruises, owned by Japan's NYK Line, offers European-style service to a largely American clientele. The *Crystal Symphony,* built in Finland rather than Japan as was the *Harmony,* is designed for worldwide cruising and spending happy days at sea. (The third ship of the line, the *Crystal Serenity,* was completed at a French yard in 2003.)

The primarily European and Filipino hotel and dining staff provides top service throughout the ship in the restaurants, bars, lounges, and on deck. The most popular gathering spot is the Palm Court, on this ship, one large wraparound room that serves as the venue for sight-seeing in cool northern climes, reading, and enjoying formal afternoon tea and drinks before and after dinner. On this same Lido Deck, there's an outdoor lap pool, a second indoor-outdoor pool, adjoining Jacuzzis, lots of deck chairs in a wide variety of groupings, a snack and ice-cream bar, and indoor-outdoor buffet. The deck above has one of the largest oceanview spas at sea with an elaborate fitness center, saunas, steam rooms, aerobics, and body treatments, plus a paddle tennis court, golf driving range, and putting green. The jogging/walking teak deck at the promenade level runs the full length of the superstructure, and you can walk the perimeter of the Sun Deck.

Tiffany Deck 6 houses most of the public rooms radiating off the two-deck-high central atrium, understated compared to the Caribbean megaships. Aft of the all-the-way-forward Galaxy Show Lounge, for large-scale shows that are not a feature of the smaller upscale ships, are Caesar's Palaces at Sea casino, a proper cinema for screening films and hosting lectures on theme cruises, several boutiques surrounding the atrium, the Bistro for coffee and pastries, a nightclub, library, computer center, and card room.

Dining is a delight, and the two special dinner options by reservation are Prego, a smartly decorated Italian restaurant, and the Jade Garden, Chinese/French fusion on this ship rather than Japanese/Asian as aboard the *Harmony.* The main dining room has two seatings, unusual for a ship of this caliber, but the food is excellent and the wine list, emphasizing California, is fairly priced. The Crystal Cove is a popular rendezvous for drinks outside the Crystal Dining Room.

All cabins are outside with well over half having private verandas, and the vast majority are laid out the full lengths of Decks 7 to 10. Amenities include sitting area, queen or twin beds, desk, TVs and VCR, Internet access, refrigerator, safe, and bathrooms with stall showers and tubs, some not full length in lower categories. Room service from an extensive menu is available twenty-four hours, and penthouses have butlers in attendance.

The Itinerary
Following a summer season in Europe, the *Crystal Symphony* comes to New York for a brief series of seven- and eleven-day New England and Canada cruises. The short

ones are round-trips from New York while the more lengthy voyages are one-way, originating either in New York or Montreal.

The cruise featured here departs from the Big Apple for Montreal, and as the ship progresses northward to the Canadian Maritimes and the St. Lawrence Valley, the autumn colors will dramatically change. Sailing from **New York** is always a treat with its majestic skyline, the Statue of Liberty, the passage beneath the Verrazano-Narrows Bridge, and ultimately out to sea.

The next morning the ship anchors off **Newport, Rhode Island,** and you can explore the elegant "summer cottages" along the Cliff Walk or stroll downtown Newport, a major East Coast sailing center. Be sure to go inland beyond the tourist shops along Thames Street to historic Newport, established well before the late-nineteenth-century new rich came to show off their wealth along Bellevue Avenue.

The *Symphony* exits Narragansett Bay and skirts Cape Cod to approach **Boston** through its harbor islands. From the Black

Falcon Cruise Terminal, good walkers can reach the center of the city in about twenty minutes and access the T to take you by subway and trolley to wherever you wish to go—Boston Common, Beacon Hill, Faneuil Hall and Quincy Market, Back Bay, Cambridge, or the museums. Salem and its Witch Museum is less than an hour away. Then it's an overnight sail to **Bar Harbor, Maine,** for another look at an upscale summer resort, a lobster bake, and a great view of the surrounding seascape from atop Cadillac Mountain in **Acadia National Park.** Then after a full day at sea, the call at **Sydney,** a Cape Breton Island port in northern Nova Scotia, provides access to the scenic coastline.

The *Symphony* then leaves the North Atlantic and passes into the mouth of the St. Lawrence where the river is at first too broad to see the opposite shores. En route to **Quebec City,** the river becomes more defined, and it is possible to see whales, especially at the mouth of the Saguenay River. Docking beneath the Citadel, again

Address/Phone: Crystal Cruises, 2049 Century Park East, Suite 1400, Los Angeles, CA 90067; (310) 785–9300; (800) 446–6620; brochures: (800) 820–6663; fax: (310) 785–3891; www.crystal-cruises.com

The Ship: *Crystal Symphony* was built in 1995, has a gross tonnage of 51,044, a length of 781 feet and a draft of 25 feet.

Passengers: 940 double occupancy; mostly North Americans fifty-five plus

Dress: Fit to kill. Formal nights, jackets and ties on informal nights

Officers/Crew: Norwegian and Japanese officers and European and Filipino crew

Cabins: 470 cabins, all outside, and 276 with private verandas

Fare: $$$$

What's included: Cruise fare, port charges, bottled water, soft drinks, specialty coffees

What's not included: Airfare, alcoholic drinks, shore excursions, tips

Highlights: Alternative Chinese/French fusion and Italian restaurants, excellent waiter/bar service, lots of onboard amenities

Other itineraries: In addition to these seven- and eleven-day New England and Canada cruises, which operate from late September to early November, the *Crystal Symphony, Crystal Harmony,* and *Crystal Serenity* make Panama Canal trips and cruise northern Europe, the Mediterranean, and, indeed, cruise most of the world.

you can tour on your own, first in the lower older city, then by funicular or on foot to the upper city. Have a drink and a great view at the Marine Bar in the Chateau Frontenac, one of the great castle-style hotels built by the Canadian Pacific Railway. The city has a distinctive French flavor, and with an overnight stay you can enjoy dinner out on the town in an atmosphere not unlike that of a Paris bistro.

The St. Lawrence narrows considerably when approaching **Montreal,** and the *Symphony* will tie up overnight opposite Old Montreal, another fine historic district to explore on foot with a walking tour map and to have a meal out at numerous restaurants within easy distance of the ship. The city's Metro is simple to use for reaching the commercial and shopping centers and perhaps for the gentle climb up through wooded Mont Royal Park.

This cruise also operates from Montreal to similar ports, and often adds **Halifax,** noted for its maritime flavor and coastal drives. A waterfront path connects the cruise terminal and the immigration museum with the attractions of the city's center.

HOLLAND AMERICA LINE'S
Maasdam
New England and Canada from Boston

 Holland America, one of the world's oldest shipping companies, has long had a solid reputation of friendly service and beautiful, well-run ships. The 55,451-ton *Maasdam*, built in 1993, is the second ship in the *Statendam*-class series.

Two levels of public rooms, punctuated by a glass sculpture rising dramatically through the three-deck atrium, run the length of the ship along Promenade and Upper Promenade Decks, creating a rhythmic flow as passengers seek out their favorite spots and pass to and from the two-story dining room. An impressive double staircase links the two levels, and a Filipino orchestra serenades diners from a raised platform, with sound quality well distributed. HAL perpetuates its tradition of good, uncomplicated food and service by an attentive Filipino and Indonesian staff. A Pinnacle Grill has been added to the ship (and now the entire fleet), featuring a Pacific Northwest theme admirably suited to this East Coast itinerary and which includes salmon and crab cakes as well as steaks and chicken dishes. For informal dining, the well-laid-out lido restaurant has picture windows and seating inside and under cover near the pool, and it gets dressed up for dinner at night.

The bi-level show lounge, designed with good views except from the rear balcony, presents elaborate Broadway-style entertainment. A band plays for listening and dancing in the attractive Ocean Bar, the ship's principal social center. The Crow's Nest provides an indoor perch for viewing the coastal scenery, afternoon tea service, and a disco at night.

The roof of the central pool retracts in good weather, and sandwiches, pizza, and satay are informally served here. A gym, massage and steam rooms, saunas, and a juice bar look over the stubby bow, and a jogging track encircles the mezzanine above the lido. Constitutional walkers will enjoy circuits of the Lower Promenade Deck, also a favorite spot for stretching out in a wooden deck chair.

Cabins are arranged over five decks, with those on the topmost two having verandas. To provide as many outside cabins as possible, the rooms tend to be long and narrow, with small sitting areas, TVs, VCRs, and minibars.

The Itinerary

These one-week cruises are repeated throughout the warm-weather months and depart from Boston's Black Falcon Terminal, located within sight of downtown. Pre- and post-cruise hotel stays are offered to take advantage of this culturally rich and easily walkable city.

Sailing from **Boston,** the *Maasdam* slides past the end of the main runway at Logan Airport and out through the Harbor Islands into the Atlantic to round the tip of Cape Cod en route to **Martha's Vineyard.** A full day is spent at sea to help passengers find their way about the ship and to prepare for the six consecutive days of port visits.

Anchoring off **Oak Bluffs,** passengers tender ashore, where they can choose between organized shore excursion programs or independent touring using an inexpensive day bus pass that gives access to most points of interest. Oak Bluffs was established first as a Methodist summer campground, and the narrow lanes of tiny, colorful gingerbread Victorian houses are the result of the tented camp growing into a permanent resort. Larger summer homes face the green fronting onto the anchorage and Nantucket Sound.

Edgartown is a short bus ride away and a quieter and more upscale summer retreat. The town is largely residential and free of the day-tripper commercial trappings of busy Vineyard Haven or the peripheral sections of Oak Bluffs. From a landing at the foot of Main Street, you can ride the Chappaquiddick ferry *On Time* for the short distance to and from the island, best known for its great beaches.

Address/Phone: Holland America Line, 300 Elliott Avenue West, Seattle, WA 98119; (800) 426–0327, fax: (206) 281–7110; www.hollandamerica.com

The Ship: *Maasdam* was built in 1993, has a gross tonnage of 55,451, a length of 719 feet, and a draft of 25 feet.

Passengers: 1,266 passengers, double occupancy; mostly Americans forty-five and up on these short cruises

Dress: Formal, informal, and casual nights

Officers/Crew: Dutch officers and Indonesian and Filipino crew

Cabins: 632, of which 502 are outside and 150 have verandas

Fare: $$$

What's included: Cruise only and gratuities included, but most tip extra

What's not included: Airfare, port charges, shore excursions, drinks, extra tips

Highlights: A port-intensive itinerary available for the complete season, and convenient Boston embarkation for New Englanders

Other itineraries: In addition to these one-week New England and Canada cruises, which operate from May through October, the *Maasdam* also makes one-week Boston to Montreal trips and vice versa, and the *Rotterdam* takes longer ten-day voyages between New York and Montreal. The large Holland America fleet makes cruises in the Caribbean, South America, through the Panama Canal, to Hawaii and Alaska, Europe, and around the world.

After an overnight sail, **Portland, Maine** reveals a once hard-working waterfront transformed into a balanced combination of commercial and recreational uses. Have a lobster lunch or New England clam bake. The waterfront is easily walkable, and the downtown is just up the slope. For American art lovers, the Portland Art Museum has a collection of paintings by Andrew Wyeth, Edward Hopper, and Winslow Homer.

Organized excursions head south to **Kennebunkport,** the Victorian and Federal-style summer retreat for the Bush family, out to Portland Head Lighthouse at Cape Elizabeth, and to **Freeport** for some L.L. Bean and major outlet shopping.

Saint John, New Brunswick's main port, gives access to inland destinations such as the curious Reversing Falls, where the Bay of Fundy's high tides cause the Saint John's River to flow backward, and **St. Andrews-by-the-Sea** for the Algonquin, a classic summer hotel setting for an afternoon tea with scones and clotted cream.

Sailing north along the Nova Scotia coast, **Halifax** is a walkers' paradise. The waterside path leads straight from the cruise terminal and immigration museum to the downtown waterfront with its great fish restaurants and Maritime Museum of the Atlantic, featuring exhibits on the *Titanic* and the Halifax Explosion, which leveled much of the city during World War I. Walk up a steep hill to the Citadel and stroll through the pretty adjacent Public Gardens and upscale, leafy residential neighborhood. A taxi is advisable for a visit to the cemetery, where 150 of the *Titanic's* passengers and crew are buried. A car rental agency on the pier is available for independent touring south along the rugged Lighthouse Route in the direction of **Peggy's Cove,** a tiny picture-postcard fishing port.

Returning south, the *Maasdam* anchors off **Bar Harbor,** the main town on **Mt. Desert Island.** Many of the grand summer homes were destroyed in a great fire in the late 1940s, and today's town is more down to earth, while Northeast Harbor has gained ascendancy but has never showed off in the Newport sort of way as Bar Harbor did. A drive around the island perimeter reveals the multilevels of summer residential life.

On a clear summer's day Cadillac Mountain, set in deeply wooded **Acadia National Park,** offers a delightful view of the nearby islands and coastline. The *Maasdam* then weighs anchor and sails overnight to Boston for disembarkation.

One-way seven-day Boston–Montreal cruises are offered regularly throughout the season, calling at Bar Harbor, Halifax, Sydney, Charlottetown (Prince Edward Island), and Quebec City in both directions.

NORWEGIAN CRUISE LINE'S
Norwegian Dawn
Year-round Cruising from New York to the Sun

Breaking the mold once again, Norwegian Cruise Line has tarted up one of its newest ships to catch the eye, with portraits of a dolphin playing in Technicolor waves on one side of the hull and a depiction of the Statue of Liberty and signatures of Impressionist artists on the other. The colorful artwork calls attention to the *Norwegian Dawn's* innovative year-round operations between New York, Florida, and the Bahamas.

Completed in late 2002, the 91,740-gross-ton giant offers cruisers every imaginable attraction to please the young and young at heart. For the active, facilities include a combination basketball and volleyball court, a golf driving range, gym and spa, swimming pools, Jacuzzis, a kids' wading pool, and jogging track. For entertainment, the list includes a three-level show lounge for major productions, sports bar, video arcade, Internet center, casino, a disco for adults and another for teens, and fanciful play areas for young children. For a cluster of quiet retreats, high up there's a library, separate reading and writing room, and a card room.

Cabins range from inexpensive insides and lots of oceanview cabins with private balconies up to NCL's signature garden villas. The pair of three-bedroom, 5,350-square-foot suites boasts a living room furnished with a grand piano, an entertainment center, a kitchen, butler and concierge services, an outdoor dining area, a private Italian garden for relaxing, a Jacuzzi, and a roof terrace. Some families and friends move into one of these extravaganzas and disappear for the whole week.

Aboard the big new NCL ships, it's the dining options that set them well apart from other popularly priced lines. For foodies and those who like to sample as many new venues as possible, this ship has got what you want. Some eateries are open only for dinner but with extended hours— 5:30 P.M. to midnight. A few have a cover charge or à la carte menu, but most come with no additional charge at all.

The three main dining rooms are Aqua, a modern restaurant with a healthy and light contemporary menu; the traditional, European-style Venetian with arrival via a grand staircase and big windows facing aft; and Impressions, offering a varied menu in a sophisticated Paris circa 1900 setting with Impressionist painting reproductions on walls of burl-wood paneling.

Three restaurants carry cover charges that range from $10 to about $25 per person. Le Bistro, a signature French restaurant also offered on the *Norwegian Sky* and *Sun,* serves both traditional French and nouvelle cuisine in a formal yet colorful setting enhanced by original Impressionist paintings from four artists—Matisse, Monet, Renoir, and Van Gogh. The adjacent Wine Cellar is an annex for Le Bistro that also hosts wine tastings.

Bamboo, a sprawling Asian restaurant, has three sections: a sushi, sashimi, and sake bar where the plates arrive on a conveyor belt; an eighteen-place Japanese teppanyaki room, where diners watch the food being prepared; and the main dining area with a long Chinese-Japanese-Thai menu.

The third, Cagney's, well away from the others on Deck 13, is an open-kitchen steakhouse serving sumptuous Angus beef for prime ribs and filet mignon, lamb, fish, and grilled chicken in a setting of wood and brick–style walls and newspaper wall clippings.

The most casual dining takes place at Salsa, a Tex-Mex-Tapas-Spanish-Middle Eastern–style restaurant overlooking the central atrium that also serves sangria and chips for those listening to the house band; diner-style Blue Lagoon, serving fish and chips, hamburgers, stir fries, and snacks round the clock; and the Garden Café for typical buffet food at breakfast and lunch, such as omelets, pastas, soups, and salads. One section, which gets a bit more ethnically dressed up in the evening as La Trattoria, offers pastas, pizzas, Italian desserts, and espresso. The bar here has a great beer selection from England, Scotland, and Australia. Lastly, the Bimini Bar & Grill dishes up simple fare such as hot dogs, burgers, and fries all day long.

The Itinerary

The *Norwegian Dawn* began offering year-round itineraries from **New York** in May 2003, the first ship to do so in many years. The upside for many Northeasterners is not having to fly to meet the ship, and instead being able to drive or take the train or a bus to New York or directly to the pier. The downside for some in winter might be the cool, even cold, and sometimes rough weather conditions for the first twenty-four hours after leaving New York, but with so much going on inside the ship, the fast passage into warmer weather should seem a relatively brief one. And the sail away from Manhattan cannot be topped.

Two nights and a day after leaving New York, the ship will dock at **Port Canaveral, Florida,** and the long port call permits ample time to tour the nearby Kennedy Space Center or travel one hour inland to spend the day at **Walt Disney World** for the Magic Kingdom, Epcot, Disney-MGM Studios, and Animal Kingdom or to its rival, **Universal Orlando,** with working motion-picture and TV studios and a theme park for thrilling roller-coaster rides and water slides.

Following a South Beach disco party and an overnight sail to **Miami,** many will head to South Beach's art deco district for a walking tour, a meal, or just to ogle the local characters who flock here. For a visit to a flamboyant villa, Vizcaya Museum and Gar-

Address/Phone: Norwegian Cruise Line, 7665 Corporate Center Drive, Miami, FL 33126; (800) 327–7030 or (305) 436–0866; fax: (305) 436–4126; www.ncl.com

The Ship: *Norwegian Dawn,* built in 2002, has a gross tonnage of 91,740, a length of 965 feet, and a draft of 27 feet.

Passengers: 2,224, mostly American of all ages, especially during school holiday sailings

Dress: Casual or as you wish

Officers/Crew: Officers are Norwegian and the crew international

Cabins: 1,112, of which 759 are outside, and 509 have balconies

Fare: $$

What's included: Cruise fare

What's not included: Airfare, port charges, excursions, drinks, tips

Highlights: For New York region residents, a year-round cruise option without the need to fly; a ship with ten dining choices

Other itineraries: Besides this weekly cruise by the *Norwegian Dawn* that operates year-round from New York, the *Dawn* will offer several longer January and February ten- and eleven-day sailings from New York to the deep Caribbean; a sample itinerary includes calls at St. Thomas, Antigua, Barbados, Grenada, Dominica, and Tortola. NCL ships cruise from many U.S. ports to Canada and New England, Bermuda, the Caribbean, South America, the Panama Canal, Alaska, Hawaii, and in Europe.

dens is a spectacular Italian Renaissance–style mansion. Kids will want to go to the Miami Seaquarium to watch Flipper, the TV dolphin, and Lolita the killer whale perform, plus see sea lions, manatees, and sharks feeding. At the Monkey Jungle, it's the performing primates that roam free while the visiting humans walk through caged passages.

Arriving in **Nassau** in the morning, you can travel by foot, horse-drawn carriage, jitney, taxi, moped, scooter, rental car, or ferry for a day at the beach, snorkeling, or scuba diving; take a historic tour to the Queen's Staircase to see upscale houses; visit Paradise Island for a tour of the Cloister and Versailles Gardens; head out to Crystal Cay for the aquariums and underwater observa-tion towers; or just hang around town and explore the British colonial connections and modern shopping district.

For the last call, spend the morning and early afternoon at NCL's private Bahamian island of **Great Stirrup Cay,** a tranquil palm-fringed beachfront that turns into an all-day party when passengers disembark. Facilities include barbecues and bar with live or broadcast music, hammocks for a read or snooze, massage treatments, and water activities such as paddleboats, Sunfish, parasailing, banana boats, and snorkeling. Leaving the NCL playground, the *Norwegian Dawn* turns northward for New York with two nights and a day to make the final rounds of favorite or not-yet-sampled restaurants.

SCOTIA PRINCE CRUISES'
Scotia Prince
An Overnight Ferry Cruise: Maine to Nova Scotia

 Scotia Prince Cruises has operated this service since 1970, using a succession of ships until 1982, when the present *Scotia Prince* arrived. Built in 1972 and enlarged in 1986, the stabilized eight-deck ship can take up to 1,200 cabin and deck passengers.

The public rooms include the forward Dolphin Lounge, used as the principal entertainment venue, a bar with TV sports channels, and a quiet nonsmoking lounge. In addition, there is a popular casino with blackjack, roulette, Caribbean stud poker, craps, and 200 slot machines, as well as a duty-free shop offering liquor, perfumes, and jewelry. A newly added Sky Deck features a tiki bar and grill, hot tubs, dance floors, exercise area, and observation perch. For late-evening diners on the 8:00 P.M. night sailing from Portland, there's a full buffet from 7:30 P.M., but give yourself a Down East treat and enjoy a sit-down dinner served in the Concorde Dining Room. The à la carte menu features broiled or steamed lobster, plucked alive from the tank, prime rib special with shrimp cocktail, grilled haddock, succulent steaks, and vegetarian dishes. Prices, including wines, are reasonable, and service is attentive.

On the day crossing from Yarmouth, leaving at 9:00 A.M., the dining room offers an à la carte lunch menu, and from 3:00 to 6:30 P.M. the Bountiful Buffet includes salads, hot dishes, and a carvery with roast turkey and roast beef. A prix-fixe menu includes two starters, four entrees including lobster and prime rib, and two desserts. A kids' menu is also available, and a coffee shop serves hot meals including breakfast.

Accommodations range from suites with sitting rooms to simple two-, four-, and even six-berth family arrangements that comprise 199 upgrade cabins with private facilities and 115 standard cabins without shower but with at least a washbasin and sometimes a toilet. Although there is no pool for this cool-weather crossing, the hot tubs and ample deck space can be enjoyed on the Yarmouth to Portland day crossing.

The Itinerary

There are lots of creative ways to use this service with or without a car. The shortest is a twenty-three-hour round-trip, overnight from Portland to Yarmouth, with a sixty-minute stopover and an eleven-hour day-light return. Departing **Portland** in the summer and on the way back, you will see the pretty Casco Bay Islands and Portland Head lighthouse. As you approach the rocky Nova Scotia coastline, an impressive solitary lighthouse marks the narrow entrance to **Yarmouth**'s inner harbor.

Entertainment aboard includes Broadway, country, rock and roll singers and dancers, and a six-piece band that stages a show at 10:00 P.M. on the night crossing and 4:30 P.M. on the day return. Other daytime activities include a feature film, karaoke, bingo, horse racing, trivia quiz, and country line-dancing lessons. During the summer vacation period, kids can enjoy supervised activities such as face painting, a scavenger hunt, arts and crafts, and cartoons and videos.

You may also choose to stay at a nearby Yarmouth hotel for a couple of days and, of course, take along your car for a driving tour through Nova Scotia to Prince Edward Island or by two major ferry routes to Newfoundland. While cruise ferries abound in Europe, the *Scotia Prince* is the only game on the U.S. East Coast. For some vacationers, the crossing is an all-night party, while for others, it is a comfortable way to avoid many driving miles.

Address/Phone: Scotia Prince Cruises, P.O. Box 4216, Portland, ME 04101-0416; (207) 775–5616 or (800) 574–8250; fax: (207) 773–7403; www.scotiaprince.com

The Ship: *Scotia Prince*, first built in 1972 as the *Stena Olympica*, then enlarged in 1986, has a gross tonnage of 11,968, a length of 485 feet, and is stabilized.

Passengers: 1,052 in berths and up to 1,200 on day crossings; 200 vehicles

Dress: Casual at all times

Officers/Crew: International

Cabins: 324; simply furnished, insides and outsides, some with upper and lower berths; most with shower and toilet, some standard cabins without

Fare: $ (day), $$ (with cabin)

What's included: Cruise only, including port charges unless buying one of the many packages, including the twenty-two-hour minicruise

What's not included: Transportation to the ship, tips, meals, drinks

Highlights: A chance to sample a European-style overnight ferry cruise; lobster dinner

Itineraries: Daily crossings depart Portland, Maine, at 8:00 P.M., and Yarmouth, Nova Scotia, at 9:00 A.M. between early May and mid-October. In winter the ship operates as the *Yucatan Express* from Tampa, Florida, to Mexican ports. (866) 286–4532; www.yucatanexpress.com

HOLLAND AMERICA LINE'S
Ryndam and *Statendam*
Alaska's Glacier Discovery Cruises and Alaska/Yukon Land Tours

 Holland America Line dates back to 1873, operating transatlantic passenger service for the first hundred years. Now owned by the Carnival Corporation, Holland America runs one of the largest and most modern fleets, combining classical interiors with up-to-date amenities.

The *Statendam,* the first in the new series, and the *Ryndam,* the third, both offer ten decks of accommodations for 1,266 passengers. The Crow's Nest on Sports Deck is a delightful sight-seeing lounge during the day and an intimate nightclub in the evening. The Lido Deck offers health and fitness facilities and a large pool area that can be covered by a retractable dome during Alaska's cooler weather.

The buffet restaurant amidships is designed to keep the queues short and provides a great selection at both breakfast and lunch and a semi-served buffet dinner. The aft dining room's two-level space offers decent food in a beautiful setting, with such regional specialties as baked Alaska, cod fillet, steamed king crab legs, and sesame-roasted king salmon fillet. For an extra charge, the Pinnacle Grill features a Pacific Northwest menu, including Dungeness crab cakes, seared duck breast, and Washington and Oregon wines. The show lounge has both balcony and orchestra levels for cruise-ship-style extravaganzas. The Ocean Bar, a Holland America Line trademark, is the social center for drinks and dancing, while the Explorer's Lounge provides a similar, though quieter, venue. Both ships have attractive, understated three-story atriums that lead to the Java Café and the Wajang theater as well as to the lower level of the show room forward and the dining room aft.

The 633 cabins and suites range from 187-square-foot inside cabins to four-room penthouse suites measuring 1,126 square feet. Avoid cabins above the theater if you retire early. Both ships have lots of open deck space for viewing the scenery, and the Lower Promenade is fully teaked for the constitutional walkers.

The Cruise Itinerary

Holland America offers more than one hundred departures each season, and presented here will be a one-week northbound cruise embarking at **Vancouver.** The ports will vary slightly depending on the departure.

Following two nights and a day cruising between Vancouver Island and the mountainous British Columbia coast, the *Ryndam* or *Statendam* will call at **Ketchikan,** where the active might kayak the fishing harbor's waterfront or take a drive out to see the world's largest collection of totems depicting legends of Native Alaskans. Next, at **Juneau,** you can see the Mendenhall Glacier from the road or a small plane, or by helicopter that lands on the glacier. The capital is worth a look on foot as is the once raucous, now tame Red Dog Saloon, Alaska's most famous entertainment bar. Pay a visit to the Alaska State Museum for exhibits on the state's history, wildlife, and Native culture, or ride the Mount Roberts Tram for a 2,000-foot-high view.

At **Sitka,** passengers go ashore by tender, arriving within walking distance of many attractions. The New Archangel Dancers perform a show worth seeing in the Centennial Hall, which also houses the visitor center. Nearby stands St. Michael's Russian Orthodox Cathedral, rebuilt after a fire in 1966. At the edge of town, the Sitka National Memorial Park has the most finely carved totems in the state.

Sailing across the Gulf of Alaska with the Wrangell–St. Elias National Park forming a backdrop, the ship turns to cruise up to the **Hubbard Glacier**. Enter **Prince William Sound** cruising **College Fjord,** with sixteen glaciers named after eastern colleges and universities, before sailing overnight to **Seward** for disembarkation. Some cruises spend a half day in Glacier Bay instead of visiting Hubbard Glacier.

The Land Itineraries

Holland America Westours provides nearly three dozen escorted pre- and post-cruise options. The following eight-day tour includes the most popular destinations, but there are shorter and less expensive offerings.

The tour begins with a scenic drive across the **Kenai Peninsula** to **Anchorage** for the night and a visit to the Alaska Native Heritage Center, followed by a rail cruise, including a full meal, aboard the **McKinley**

Explorer dome cars, which seat sixty-six in a lounge and at tables. Overnight at a lodge on the Nenana River is followed by a drive into **Denali National Park** to look for caribou and grizzly bears beneath 20,320-foot Mount McKinley (Denali). Rejoin the McKinley Explorer for the rail trip to **Fairbanks.**

From Fairbanks there's a short river cruise, then a drive along the Alaska Highway to **Tok** for an overnight. The next day, a 102-mile **Yukon River** cruise from Eagle travels to the preserved former boomtown of **Dawson City.**

The Alaska-Yukon Explorer coaches, equipped with a lounge and galley, travel to the **Yukon Wildlife Preserve** for sightings of moose, musk oxen, caribou, and Dall sheep. Both Dawson City and **Whitehorse** provide spirited Follies-style entertainment. From Whitehorse, drive to the summit of the White Pass to join the **White Pass and Yukon Railroad** for a vintage train ride spiraling down along the Trail of '98 to **Skag-**

Address/Phone: Holland America Line, 300 Elliott Avenue West, Seattle, WA 98119; (800) 426–0327; brochures: (800) 626–9900; fax: (206) 281–7110; www.hollandamerica.com

The Ship: *Statendam* was built in 1992 and the *Ryndam* in 1994, and they share a gross tonnage of 55,451, a length of 719 feet, and a draft of 25 feet.

Passengers: 1,266; mostly Americans, age fifty-five and up

Dress: Formal, informal, and casual nights

Officers/Crew: Dutch officers; Indonesian and Filipino crew

Cabins: 633; 502 outside and 150 with verandas

Fare: $$$

What's included: Cruise only unless a fly-cruise-land package is purchased, basic tips

What's not included: Airfare, port charges, shore excursions, drinks, extra tips

Highlights: Most attractive ships on which to spend time at sea; lots to do on shore excursions during the cruise and on land tours in Alaska

Other itineraries: In addition to this seven-night Glacier Discovery cruise, which operates between early May and mid-September, there are seven-night Inside Passage cruises round-trip from Vancouver and longer fourteen-night voyages from San Francisco to a wider range of ports. The *Statendam* cruises to Hawaii, and both ships sail through the Panama Canal to the Caribbean. Holland America's large fleet pretty much covers the globe, including the *Prinsendam*'s round-the-world cruises.

way, the main port of entry for the gold prospectors. The last stage is a daylight cruise along the Lynn Canal, a natural waterway leading to **Juneau** and flights south to the Lower 48.

PRINCESS CRUISES'
Dawn Princess and *Sun Princess*

Big-Ship Cruising and Touring the Inside Passage, Gulf of Alaska, and National Parks

 Princess Cruises, based in Los Angeles, is owned by Carnival Corporation, the world's largest shipping line. Here the *Dawn Princess* is the featured ship, but sister *Sun Princess* is so similar in design, layout, and services that it may be considered inter-changeable. Completed in 1997, the *Dawn Princess* is 77,499 gross register tons and has ten principal passenger decks. The four-story Grand Plaza is the main social center, with public spaces, shops, cafes, and the two dining rooms radiating from it. The marble foyer offers connecting circular stair-cases, glass elevators, and a stained-glass dome.

The two attractively decorated main restaurants, using wood-grain paneling and etched glass, are located aft, one atop the other, with the tables arranged in small groupings on different levels to avoid a large-room feeling. The menus are typically varied and the quality and presentation average. The twenty-four-hour Horizon Court (the cruise industry's first) has a bistro menu for dinner, a bar, dance floor, and sweeping panoramic views over the bow. A pizzeria serves excellent, freshly prepared varieties, and there's a steak house, a caviar and wine bar, a hamburger grill, and a patisserie for pastries and special coffees. Two show rooms offer lavish productions in a Broadway-style theater and in smaller-setting cabarets. All shows are repeated for both sittings in both dining rooms. Dining options include open sittings.

There are pools in three locations, five whirlpools, and a huge amount of outside deck space with bars nearby. A paddle-tennis court located by the ship's funnel can be used for basketball and volleyball. Other amenities are a two-level spa with pool and whirlpools, a movie theater, a disco, a casino, a library, a card room, a beauty salon, and children and teenage rooms.

Two-thirds of the cabins are outside, and about 70 percent of these have private verandas. Standard features include queen-size or twin beds, decent storage space, phones, TVs bringing in CNN and ESPN, refrigerators, safes, and bathrooms with showers.

The Cruise Itinerary

Northbound the *Dawn Princess* sails from **Vancouver** out under the Lion's Gate sus-pension bridge. Threading through the fast-flowing Seymour Narrows, the ship may encounter Pacific swells for several hours before returning to the protection provided by the Queen Charlotte Islands.

Ketchikan, reached on the second morning, was Alaska's salmon capital and is now oriented to tourism, especially along the once-bawdy Creek Street and at the two splendid totem pole parks. The active might canoe on a lake or go mountain bik-ing or fly fishing. **Juneau,** the state capital, provides a walkable visit, although expect steep streets and steps, as the city is set against a mountainside. The Alaska State Museum is a good bet, and tours that drive and fly out to the **Mendenhall Glacier,** include a guided alpine walk and sea kayaking in nearby Auke Bay. Departing late evening, the ship sails overnight to **Skagway,** a town that trades entirely on its historic link with the Klondike Gold Rush. The best excursion is on the White Pass and Yukon's vintage train that climbs out of Skagway to the top of the White Pass.

For many people **Glacier Bay** is the high point of the cruise, where the *Dawn Princess* enters at about dawn to cruise amid floating ice. Mount Logan can be seen rising nearly 20,000 feet as the *Dawn Princess* crosses the **Gulf of Alaska.** Twenty-four hours later, the ship passes through **Prince William Sound** to reach **College Fjord,** where sixteen long glacial tongues slide into the sea. The cruise ends at **Seward,** where you can fly home from Anchorage or stay to enjoy one of the land extensions.

The Land Itineraries

Three- to nine-night land tours are very popular before or after the week's cruise. They comprise several mix-and-match ingredients, lodge and hotel stays, train rides, river excursions, rafting, fishing, hiking, and flightseeing. Most tours begin with a drive from Seward through the Kenai Mountains to **Anchorage,** Alaska's largest city, for the night.

The **Midnight Sun Express,** using Princess Tours rail cars, provides a scenic daylight ride to **Denali National Park.** The bi-level dome cars offer lounge seating with bar service beneath glass windows on the upper level and a dining room and open platforms below. **Mount McKinley** (Denali), North America's highest peak at more than 20,000 feet, is the centerpiece of the park where Princess operates two wilderness lodges. Tours may continue by Midnight Sun Express to **Fairbanks** for gold-mine tours, a paddlewheel excursion, visits to an Athabascan Indian village, and a flight to **Fort Yukon** above the Arctic Circle.

The **Kenai Peninsula** extension provides stays at the wilderness lodge and sport-fishing trips, rafting through the Kenai Canyon, naturalist hikes, horseback riding, and a wildlife cruise. Additional tours penetrate into the more remote regions of Alaska into the Yukon Territory. Many land itineraries can be taken without the cruise through Princess Tours (800–835–8907).

Address/Phone: Princess Cruises, 24305 Town Center Drive, Santa Clarita, CA 91355; (661) 753–0000 or (800) PRINCESS; brochures: (888) 478–6732; fax: (661) 259–3108; www.princess cruises.com

The Ship: *Dawn Princess* was built in 1997, *Sun Princess* in 1995. They share a gross tonnage of 77,499, a length of 856 feet, and a draft of 26 feet.

Passengers: 1,950; mostly Americans, all ages in summer, but mainly forty-five and up

Dress: Formal, informal, and casual

Officers/Crew: British and Italian officers; international crew

Cabins: *Dawn* (1,050); *Sun* (975) with more than 400 veranda cabins

Fare: $$$

What's included: Cruise only

What's not included: Airfare, port charges, shore excursions, drinks, tips

Highlights: Spectacular glacier and mountain scenery, creative optional tour programs

Other itineraries: In addition to these seven-day cruises between Vancouver and Seward, which operate from the middle of May to late September, Princess offers many other Alaskan, Caribbean, Bermuda, and European itineraries, and elsewhere.

NORWEGIAN CRUISE LINE'S
Norwegian Sky
Freestyle Cruising from Seattle to Alaska

 Like its namesake, the *Sky* is a bright and sunfilled ship with an abundance of floor-to-ceiling windows. Surrounding the central atrium on several levels, you will find a bar, a pianist, and clusters of chairs creating relaxing pockets. All total, there are nearly a dozen watering holes, including a dark and cozy cigar club with the most comfortable thick leather chairs and couches imaginable, Gatsby's wine bar, a sports bar, Checkers nightclub/disco, two large poolside bars, and a coffee bar connected to the Internet cafe.

For kids, the *Sky*'s huge children's area includes a sprawling playroom with high ceilings, a teen center with a large movie screen, a pair of foosball games, and a video arcade. For the active adult, the well-stocked gym may be on the small side for a ship of this size, but, like the large adjacent aerobics room, it has floor-to-ceiling windows that make workouts a pleasure and a convenient location abutting the main pool deck. Nearby, the attractive spa and beauty salon are ocean-view too, with lovely gilded Buddha statuary dotting the area. Out on deck, there are four hot tubs clustered between a pair of pools. There's a fifth hot tub and kids' wading pool sequestered at the aft end of the Sports Deck above. Here you will also find the combo basketball/volleyball court, a pair of golf driving nets, and shuffleboard.

The *Sky*'s cabins are pretty, done up in wood tones and pastels, but they're small and there's scant stowage for your clothes. All cabins, even suites, have only a two-panel closet and a small bureau with four slim drawers. The 252 suites with balconies measure 202 square feet, including the veranda, and the vast majority of standard outside and inside cabins measure about 150 square feet (compared to Carnival's standard 188 square feet). All cabins have a small sitting area, a mini-fridge (not stocked), a hair dryer, robes, TVs, and a desk and chair. Bathrooms are compact, with tubular shower stalls and slivers of shelving. A note of interest: The ship was originally designed for Costa Cruises with large cabin portholes and no balconies, but after the shipyard went bust, NCL took it over and worked around the existing portholes and added balconies, resulting in an odd door-and-porthole combination.

But what really stands out is the line's "freestyle cruising" concept, where you choose what to wear and where and when to dine. In all five dining venues, dinner is served anytime between 5:30 P.M. and midnight. In the French-inspired Le Bistro, the most elegant and cozy venue on the ship, try the warm goat cheese spinach salad and sautéed salmon in sorrel sauce. In summer 2004 the *Norwegian Star,* featuring no less than ten restaurants, will begin cruising to Alaska, and after October 2004 the *Norwegian Sky* will move to Hawaii and be renamed *Pride of Aloha* to operate under the U.S. flag for NCL America's new three-, four-, and seven-day cruise program.

Ciao Chow, a pan-Asian alternative restaurant, operates twenty-four hours a day and is great for the Firecracker Chicken Wrappers (chicken satay) and Oriental soup with fresh ingredients like turnips and tofu. The Garden Café buffet restaurant serves grilled burgers and chunks of fresh salmon and California rolls until 1:00 A.M., and twenty-four-hour room service includes pizza delivery, in a cardboard box just like at home. Because passengers move around from restaurant to restaurant, tips are now automatically added to passengers' accounts, to the tune of about $70 a person a week, which may be adjusted upward or downward.

The Itinerary

At present, the *Norwegian Sky* is one of the few ships sailing regularly from the U.S. port of **Seattle,** offering better air connections from some gateway cities. On a clear evening upon sailing, the route taking the ship through the **Puget Sound** is flanked by Mount Baker and Mount Rainier to the east and the Olympic Peninsula Range to the west.

After two nights and a day cruising along the highly scenic **Inside Passage,** the first port of call is **Ketchikan** for its two collections of tall totems and Creek Street souvenir shopping, then **Juneau,** the Alaska state capital, wedged into the side of steep Mount Juneau and Mount Roberts. One tour uses a converted school bus for a twenty-minute ride out to Auke Bay for a guided kayaking excursion and a great

workout. On the day we went, we saw a glimpse of **Mendenhall Glacier** from sea level, lots of eagles feeding along a far shore, and a couple of seals bobbing in and out of the water. Cruise Sawyer Glacier en route to Skagway.

In **Skagway,** the Red Onion Saloon offers a lively scene with live period music and barmaids dressed in turn-of-the-century prostitute garb. Upstairs, $5.00 tours are given by one of the maids, in character, a fun and informative way to learn about late-nineteenth-century life for a woman living in a rough gold prospecting town like Skagway. For something active, go for the downhill 15-mile bike ride along the scenic **Klondike Road,** outfitted with helmets, gloves, and rain gear. Snowcapped mountains are all about, and the bonus is a ride into Canada.

This ship calls at **Victoria,** British Columbia, and the treat here is to have tea (make reservations) at the famed Empress Hotel facing the inner harbor. From here it's a short overnight sail back to **Seattle.**

Address/Phone: Norwegian Cruise Line, 7665 Corporate Center Drive, Miami, FL 33126, (305) 436–0866 or (800) 327–7030; brochures: (800) 323–1308; fax: (305) 436–4126; www.ncl.com

The Ship: *Norwegian Sky* was completed in 1999 and has a gross tonnage of 77,104, a length of 853 feet, and a draft of 26 feet.

Passengers: 2002; mostly Americans of all ages in Alaska during the height of the season

Dress: Informal at all times, unless you wish to dress up for the captain's night

Officers/Crew: Norwegian officers; international crew

Cabins: 1001; 574 outside and 252 with verandas

Fare: $$$

What's included: Cruise fare

What's not included: Airfare, port charges, tips, drinks, and shore excursions

Highlights: Freestyle dining with a wide choice of restaurants and Alaska's scenery

Other itineraries: Besides this one-week cruise from Seattle that operates between late April and late September, NCL offers other Alaska itineraries and cruises in Hawaii, the Caribbean, along the East Coast, South America, and Europe.

CELEBRITY CRUISES'
Infinity
Alaska Round-Trip from Vancouver

this ship is same as the one that cruises from LA to Alaska. Includes Sitka

Beautiful surroundings, intimate recesses, and subtly lit lounges. The *Infinity* is as finely decorated and elegant as a mega-ship can be, full of burled woods, dark velvets, golden brocades, ornate topiaries, intriguing art, and ample ocean views. The 91,000-ton ship is the second in Celebrity's four-ship *Millennium* class; she's not at all graceful to look at from the outside, but within she pleases and excels.

Dining is an event at tables in the Trellis restaurant, where a grand staircase and a two-story wall of glass facing the ship's wake create a glamorously retro backdrop to sample dishes like broiled king salmon in an orange sauce and roasted pork loin stuffed with sun-dried tomatoes. But for the ultimate dining experience, and an extra charge, sample the superb menu and the service in the SS United States restaurant.

Sophisticated and featuring original etched glass panels from the 1950s Blue Ribbon liner of the same name, one is looked after by a team of the most professional waitstaff I've ever seen at sea. They come to the table to toss salads and drizzle hollandaise sauce on asparagus spears. The maitre'd carved a Long Island duckling, an SS United States specialty dish, right in front of us with theatrical finesse. Afterward, a waiter wheeled over a cart with a most impressive selection of cheeses and crackers. The intimate restaurant experience is nothing short of nirvana, well worth the cover charge and dressing up for an occasion. Make your reservations early.

At the opposite end of the dining scale, for informality at breakfast, lunch, and dinner, the windowed buffet restaurant allows you to eat while Alaska floats by.

For a drink to lighten the mood in the evenings, the Rendezvous lounge attracts a good crowd each night before dinner; sit in the oversized golden bucket seats and have a twirl around the dance floor. Following dinner, take in a Vegas-type show in the three-level Celebrity Theater—perhaps it's a *West Side Story* medley—and then check out the sprawling and airy Constellation observation lounge-cum-nightclub, high on the topmost deck. Theme nights include a '50s sock hop party, and gentleman hosts are on hand to circulate, dance, and chat with single ladies. Sip a cappuccino in the rich Venetian-style Cova Café, and browse the shops for high-end clothing, accessories, souvenirs, and Michel Roux cookware.

The standard inside and outside cabins measure a roomy 170 square feet, and more than 200 of the ship's staterooms in the premium and deluxe category measure 191 square feet with a 41-square-foot balcony. Decorated in shades of terra-cotta and butterscotch, they have a sitting area with a reclining couch, lots of storage space, TV, safe, and a stocked minibar.

In the suite categories, butler service operates twenty-four hours a day, and rooms measure from 251 to 538 square feet, with the largest having separate bedrooms, whirlpool bathtubs, and oversize verandas. At the top, the 1,423-square-foot penthouse suites are among the largest at sea with marble foyers, wood floors, a piano, computer stations, and oceanview bathrooms with full-size hot tubs.

When not ashore, you can spend an hour pounding away tension on a step machine in the large, oceanview gym, another bobbing up and down in the spa's thalassotherapy pool, surf the Web at the Internet center, don headphones in the twenty-four-hour music library, attend a wine-tasting seminar or an art auction, and watch a slide show on Alaska wildlife by a guest lecturer to prepare you for the scenic itinerary.

The Itinerary

As you cruise the Inside Passage round-trip from **Vancouver,** the thick green forests of British Columbia and icy-blue mounds of southeast Alaska's glaciers form the backdrop. The cruise begins with two nights and a day en route to **Juneau,** the state's capital. Here, take the Mount Roberts Tramway up some 2,000 feet above the city for spectacular views of the snowy Chilkat mountain range and the arteries of the Inside Passage. Afterward, shuffle across a sawdust floor and settle down with a pint in the rustic Red Dog Saloon.

Continue north along the Lynn Canal, a natural waterway between steep mountain ranges to the top end of the Inside Passage, where the ship can go no farther. You can easily take in the main drag of tiny **Skagway** and have a free National Parks Service walking tour to hear about the gold rush days when this town was alive with men seeking their fortune. For a little excitement, stop at the Red Onion Saloon, a bordello during the Klondike's gold rush days. For the more active, join a small group and bicycle through a gorgeous field of wild irises and into a forest of spruce trees to examine the ruins of another gold-mining town at Dyea.

Then it's out to sea and up the coast to the **Hubbard Glacier** hanging down from the great St. Elias Range. Listen for the crack and quickly look for calving ice. Sailing south to **Ketchikan,** have a simple meal ashore, such as a halibut sandwich, the bright white meat as tender as tofu, at a small café on the boardwalk of shops lining Creek Street, where fisherman and call girls crossed paths a century ago. Re-energized, paddle a kayak across the Tongass Narrows by booking one of the ship's shore excursions.

Finally, it's a relaxing two nights and a day south between the British Columbia coast and Vancouver Island for disembarkation at the mainland city of Vancouver.

Address/Phone: Celebrity Cruises, 1050 Caribbean Way, Miami, FL 33132; (305) 539–6000 or (800) 327–6700; fax: (800) 722–5329; www.celebrity-cruises.com

The Ship: *Infinity*, completed in 1991, is 91,000 gross tons, has a length of 965 feet, and a draft of 26 feet.

Passengers: 1,950, mostly Americans, forty-five and up, including all ages during school holidays

Dress: Formal, informal, and casual

Officers/Crew: Officers are Greek and the crew international

Cabins: 975 cabins, of which 780 are outside and 590 have balconies

Fare: $$$

What's included: Cruise fare only

What's not included: Airfare, port charges, extra tariff restaurant, drinks, excursions, tips

Highlights: Classy ship; restaurant ambience and the special evening in the SS United States restaurant

Other itineraries: Besides this seven-night itinerary that operates weekly between May and September, Celebrity offers other Alaskan itineraries, land tours, and cruises to and from Hawaii, Mexico, Central America, the Caribbean, South America, Bermuda, and Europe.

SEVEN SEAS CRUISES'

Seven Seas Mariner

Inside Passage from Vancouver to Alaska

The newest Seven Seas' ships represent the line's future, offering all-suite accommodations and worldwide itineraries. The 50,000-gross-ton *Seven Seas Mariner,* completed at Chantiers de l'Atlantique in France, became the world's first all-balcony ship; the 2003-built *Seven Seas Voyager* became the second, and the earlier 1999-built, 28,550-ton *Seven Seas Navigator* is not far behind with 90 percent private verandas. Balconies are an ideal way to enjoy the Inside Passage scenery, now just a step from the bedroom.

Although most passengers are well-heeled, well-traveled Americans, the line also attracts other nationalities, mostly Europeans. The top officers are French and the staff is European and Filipino.

The *Mariner*'s roominess has pluses and minuses, and the latter becomes evident in the public lounges and bars, where except for the cocktail hour and meals, the ship often seems rather quiet. After dinner, the show lounge is a draw, but otherwise, many passengers retire to their suites.

The Observation Lounge, located two decks above the bridge, offers comfy rust- and tan-colored seating to enjoy hot hors d'oeuvres and soothing piano music before dinner, while taking in the grand 180-degree view. From a perch along the horseshoe-shaped bar, the space takes on a magical quality at night. The semicircular Horizon Lounge, facing aft on one of the lowest passenger decks, is the handsome setting for a served afternoon tea with music and light after-dinner entertainment. Additional covered outdoor seating is little used and makes a quiet daytime reading spot. Nearby, the Connoisseur Club is a sophisticated tan-leather-chair and electric-fireplace setting for smoking Cuban and Dominican cigars and sipping liqueurs and wines.

The liveliest venue is the Mariner Lounge, drawing a crowd before dining in the adjacent Compass Rose or Latitudes restaurants. The curvy art deco design is highlighted by deep blue chair fabrics and glass tabletops, embedded with a translucent star pattern and framed by raised wooden rims.

Stars Nightclub cum disco, decorated with black-and-white celebrity photos of Fred Astaire, Ingrid Bergman, and Katharine Hepburn, is an oddly designed space with a spiral staircase in its midst that links to the midsize casino above. The semicircular two-level Constellation Lounge, with continuous brushed blue cotton banquette seating and joined by a symmetrical pair of two stage-flanking staircases, presents full shows and cabaret acts under a starlit ceiling of changing colors. A terrific Welsh comedian was the highlight on my cruise.

It's the choice of dining venues that gives the *Mariner* its most distinctive quality. Two restaurants are open seating with no reservations, and two take reservations for specific tables, and there is never a cover charge. Complimentary wines are served with dinner in all four restaurants. The large Compass Rose is the main dining room, most attractive and spacious with a recessed arched ceiling and faux light-wood columns topped with banded stainless steel capitals. The daily changing menu may offer homemade crab cakes as an appetizer, cream of asparagus soup, two salad selections, a pasta dish, and main courses such as sauteed jumbo prawns and Black Angus beef. The choices also include well-being, vegetarian, and a Menu Degustation, a sampler of dishes appropriate to the cruising region. For dinner, a portion of La Veranda, also open seating, is a Mediterranean bistro with a tapas, mezze, or antipasti buffet, then a served soup of the day, salad, pasta, main course, and dessert trolley.

Le Cordon Bleu of Paris offers Signatures, a reserved-table restaurant. With a much wider choice of entrees and main courses, it is worth revisiting several times on a long cruise. Marinated fillet of red snapper and roast breast of quail with turnips in a morel sauce are two examples from the list of six choices. One appetizing dessert included warm chocolate tart with cinnamon ice cream.

Latitudes, with a set sampler menu, includes a fois gras mousse, crab and avocado in a light curry sauce, tomato bisque, pan-fried lobster in a lemongrass gravy, and beef tenderloin in salsa. The setting is South Seas oriental with black lacquer chairs, large side windows with slatted venetian blinds, and walls decorated with wooden masks and headdresses.

For breakfast and lunch, Compass Rose offers table service and La Veranda a buffet with sheltered outdoor seating aft at wooden tables and chairs set under an awning. An outdoor grill is sited here. The latter's buffet stations are far too cramped and limited in selection compared to the company's other ships.

The open-shelf library offers a generous selection of hardbacks, reference books, and videos with tables to spread out an atlas and comfortable seating for reading newspapers and magazines. Club.com is the very plainly decorated Internet center with fourteen terminals plus three more in the adjacent library.

Deck space centers around the lido pool, three whirlpools, slatted wooden tables and chairs, a ten-stool outdoor bar, and a mezzanine above and forward and deck space aft. Outdoor sports include paddle tennis, shuffleboard, and golf nets.

The all-suite, all-veranda accommodations measure from 301 square feet to 1,580 square feet with veranda included. Paneling is light-wood surfaces and the fab-

---

Address/Phone: Seven Seas Cruises, 600 Corporate Drive, Suite 410, Fort Lauderdale, FL 33334; (954) 776–6123 or (800) 285–1835; brochures: (800) 477–7500; fax: (954) 772–3763; www.rssc.com

The Ship: *Seven Seas Mariner* was completed in 2001, has a gross tonnage of 50,000, a length of 709 feet, and a draft of 21 feet.

Passengers: 700, mostly Americans, some Europeans, forty-five and up

Dress: Formal, informal, and casual nights

Officers/Crew: French and European officers, European stewardesses, and international crew

Cabins: 350, all outside suites with balconies, with twins that convert to king-size beds

Fare: $$$$

What's included: Cruise fare, gratuities, wines with dinner, soft drinks and juices, stocked minibar

What's not included: Port charges, airfare, alcoholic drinks

Highlights: Unusually spacious ship, top European service

Other itineraries: In addition to these seven-day cruises northbound from Vancouver and southbound from Seward that operate between late May and early September, the Seven Seas fleet covers the world. Note that the Radisson name has been dropped in the cruise line's name.

ric colors are gold, orange rust, and a light green. The deluxe suites are the most numerous and have slightly partitioned and curtained bedroom and lounge, walk-in closets, and marble baths with tubs and showers. Curiously, the baths and closets are smaller than on the *Navigator*, something that got rectified aboard the *Seven Seas Voyager*.

The next up, the penthouse suites, somewhat misnamed, are larger at 449 square feet but not all are located on a higher deck as the designation might warrant. They feature a roomy partitioned lounge with L-shape couch, two lounge chairs, and a glass-top table. The 73-square-foot teak deck balcony has rather ordinary white plastic chairs and a low table. Accommodations increase in spaciousness in the higher categories, and these offer butler service. Some suites will take a third person, and the two-bedroom master suites accommodate up to five.

All accommodations have TV/VCR, bathrobes, hair dryers, personal safes, telephones, in-suite bar set up upon embarkation, and complimentary replenished bottled water, soft drinks, and beer. Expanded tabletops make in-room meals a pleasure, and a full meal may be ordered from the Compass Rose restaurant or twenty-four hours a day from an in-suite menu. Suite meals are a very popular feature, especially at the end of a busy day ashore. People who like an enticing choice of top restaurants, roomy veranda suite accommodations, and a large element of privacy will love this ship.

The Itinerary

The Alaska cruises embark in **Vancouver** for the northbound itinerary and Seward for the southbound trips. The voyage north follows the Inside Passage between Vancouver Island and the British Columbia coast, with two nights and a day en route to a side trip into **Misty Fjords National Park,** a narrow steep-side waterway that the largest ships do not penetrate. Later that same day, the first port call at **Ketchikan** offers the standard totem park and town tour or a nature hike through a coastal rain forest, perhaps including a light drizzle. At **Juneau,** there are many choices over water such as an ocean kayak trip, a twelve-person traditional Native American canoe ride into Mendenhall Lake, and some gentle white-water rafting near the glacier. Nosing into **Tracy Arm,** there is an excellent chance to see sea lions and a possibility of whales cavorting near the mouth.

At the north end of the natural Lynn Canal, the **Skagway** tours offer a bike ride to **Dyea,** now a partial ghost town but once boasting 10,000 inhabitants, and a trip on the **White Pass and Yukon Route** rail line to the top of the pass and back. At the edge of the Pacific Ocean, **Sitka,** once the Russian American capital, reveals its colorful past on a town center walking tour or more energetically on a bicycle ride along a winding path between mountains and sea. The totem collection here is much finer than at Ketchikan.

Northward into the Gulf of Alaska, the *Mariner* sails up to **Hubbard Glacier,** located in the shadow of the Wrangell-St. Elias mountain range. Listen for the crack of calving ice, then be quick with your camera. Later in the morning, the ship crosses the Gulf to dock at **Seward,** where there are land extensions to **Denali National Park, Anchorage,** and **Fairbanks.**

CRUISE WEST'S
Spirit of '98
Small-Ship Cruising Alaska's Inside Passage

 Following my first big-ship Alaska cruise a few years back, I came home very happy, and then I returned to sail aboard Cruise West's wee *Spirit of '98*. It was an altogether different experience. I communed with nature—the stupendous landscape, variable weather, birds of all sorts, wildlife galore in the water and on shore, and sweet scents and pungent smells (those Steller sea lions!)—in an almost spiritual way.

Unlike many small coastal ships, the 100-passenger *Spirit of '98* has character. She exhibits the graceful profile of an early twentieth-century American steamer with a rounded superstructure, upward sheer to the decks, straight stem, and a tall black stack embossed with Cruise West's white bear logo. The *Spirit of '98* began life on the East Coast in the mid-1980s as the *Pilgrim Belle,* and I made one of her very first trips in Long Island Sound, and then I followed her under different owners to the Chesapeake Bay and along the St. Lawrence River and Seaway. Now based in the Pacific Northwest, the *Spirit of '98* looks as if she might have headed north to the Klondike Goldfields in 1898, but the happier reality has her taking modern-day explorers in search of wildlife, scenery, and a good time.

The *Spirit of '98*'s plush interiors are Victorian and Edwardian with pressed-tin ceilings, square mirrored columns, overstuffed furniture, an elaborate dark wood bar, and mirror-backed dining room buffet. Heads turn when she passes or approaches a dock, and her passengers soon develop a deep affection for their conveyance and the young, all-American crew.

Meals take place in the big-windowed, open-sitting dining room at large round tables and cozy banquettes. A buffet breakfast displayed in the lounge draws early risers and light eaters, and an on-deck barbecue features spare ribs, fresh coho salmon, sausage, and burgers. Dinner menus offer just one soup, two salads, fresh hot breads, a choice of six main courses, and a featured dessert plus sherbets. For the cocktail hour set, the pre-dinner hot hors d'oeuvres serve as appetizers. Cooking is straightforward American style and uniformly very good, better and more varied than expected, with memorable entrees such as Dungeness crab, grilled halibut, and prime rib.

Cabins are all outside and small but not cramped, the majority opening onto one of two covered promenades. The announcement of a humpback whale sighting means just a quick step out the door. TVs, unusual for most small ships, have VCRs for screening freely selected videos. Cabins windows drop open, a big plus, allowing the sound of the sea to lull one to sleep, and it is not an exaggeration to report that I slept better here than at home.

Enrichment includes Native American oral traditions, costumes, and dancing; talks by Cruise West expedition leaders and National Park Service personnel; much socializing and bonding; and the great state of Alaska.

The Itinerary

As the 192-foot *Spirit of '98* sails from **Seattle**'s Pier 69, she makes an early-evening tour of Seattle's active recreational and commercial waterfront before heading north along the Inside Passage on a relaxed schedule that allows the captain to dawdle and diverge from the set course when there is good reason.

The first such opportunity arises on the

second day, when we encounter a large pod of Pacific white-sided dolphins that our interpreters estimate to number one hundred. Once in their midst, those standing one deck above the waterline look directly down as the dolphins play in our bow wave, and a few yards away others roll on their sides and even breach. On day three, the *Spirit of '98* slips into Green Inlet, and ringing "dead slow," the little ship silently eases up to within a few hundred yards of four brown bears, a sow and three cubs, grazing on the sedge grass and pawing at rocks encrusted with succulent caches of mussels.

In **Misty Fjord,** most aptly named for an almost constant drizzle, the ship negotiates narrow waterways flanked by steep cliffs, and then in **Tracy Arm,** we pass through rafts of floating ice to within 400 yards off **South Sawyer Glacier,** remaining for an hour to ogle the massive formations and varied shades of greens and blues. On the way out, we nose up to a waterfall, and those standing at the bow get showered in spray.

Shore trips are offered at Ketchikan, Skagway, and Haines, many similar to those offered by the big ships, but there are differences. On the big ships with 1,500 to 2,500 passengers, you may have more choices, and you may get preferential time slots for the helicopter and float plane trips, but apart from these two examples, Cruise West contracts its own excursions and, with fewer than 100 passengers, the groups are smaller when spread over three to five tours.

At **Ketchikan,** one trip goes out to the totems at Saxman Indian Village, and the more independently minded can walk to the Totem Heritage Center and visit the shops along Creek Street, which include an excellent first- and second-hand bookstore with lots of titles reflecting Alaska and the Pacific Northwest.

At **Skagway,** several **White Pass and Yukon Route** trains back down to the piers, and *Spirit of '98* passengers occupy

---

Address/Phone: Cruise West, 2401 Fourth Avenue, Suite 700, Seattle, WA 98121; (800) 426–7702; fax: (206) 441–4757; e-mail: info@cruisewest. com; www.cruisewest.com

The Ship: *Spirit of '98* was built in 1984 as the *Pilgrim Belle* and later traded as the *Colonial Explorer* and *Victorian Empress,* and has a length of 192 feet and a shallow draft.

Passengers: 96 passengers, mostly Americans and Canadians in their forties and up

Dress: Casual, morning, noon, and night

Officers/Crew: American

Cabins: 49, all outside with windows, some opening onto the side deck and one large owner's two-room suite

Fare: $$$

What's included: Cruise fares, port charges, and some excursions

What's not included: Airfare, optional shore excursions, drinks and tips

Highlights: Glorious mountains, fjords, and glaciers seen close up; intimate atmosphere on a very special ship

Other itineraries: In addition to this eight-day cruise, including a one-night hotel stay in Juneau, between Seattle and Juneau, which operates between May and August, Cruise West operates many additional variations along the Inside Passage, in South Central Alaska, the Bering Sea, plus overland extensions, and cruises along the Columbia and Snake Rivers, in California Wine Country, the Sea of Cortez, and Central America. All Cruise West ships fly the U.S. flag except the *Spirit of Oceanus* (Bahamas) and the *Pacific Explorer* (Honduras).

their own private railway coach for the climb paralleling the arduous trail the prospectors followed in 1898. A few years later, they traveled far more comfortably over this very rail line. The narrow-gauge train whistles out through town, then twists and turns up to the summit for long-range views back down to Skagway and west to the distant St. Elias Range. In Skagway, the National Park Service runs a free town tour with the interpreter relating stories of hardship, the Canadian government's requirement that prospectors carry a year's supply of provisions before being permitted to cross the border, the terrible toll of 8,000 horses dying along the trail, rampant lawlessness, and greed.

By contrast, the adjacent port of **Haines** is a sleepy little place, and some passengers go birding in the "Valley of the Eagles" aboard a white-water raft, while others take a walking tour of Fort Seward, a former early-twentieth-century U.S. Army base, and its line of fine wooden hillside houses looking across a village green to the main channel leading from Skagway south to Juneau.

The most anticipated event comes on the final day, when the ship enters **Glacier Bay** at 6:30 A.M., not to exit until 8:30 P.M. While waiting for the big ships to leave, our captain takes us close to tufted puffins' and pigeon guillemots' rookeries on North and South Marble Islands.

In Tidal Inlet, we have black and brown bear sightings in four different directions, a bull moose on the beach, a rare wolverine peering at us from the brush, and a humpback whale feeding close to shore. In South Sandy Cove, we watch mountain goats

cavort and yet manage to maintain footing on a seemingly 90-degree slope. At the waterline, a pack of Steller sea lions, mostly males, give off guttural grunts and an odor that sends one reeling aft in search of fresh air.

Moving up through the bergie bits to Margerie and Grand Pacific glaciers, the ship stands off watching the calving ice, and when one sizeable blueish white tower collapses, the captain aims the ship's bow into the oncoming waves. On the last evening in **Icy Strait,** there is not a cloud in the sky, a light ashore, or another vessel in sight. A full moon rises in the east, and the sun sets over the St. Elias Range in the west. As we slowly drift, the sea first reflects patches of pinkish purple, then takes on a golden hue, and the calm waters ripple from diving ducks and a lone humpback whale. Dozens of sharp snowcapped peaks envelop us in a complete circle, and without a chart, one wonders which way Captain George Vancouver might have chosen to seek the open ocean in 1795. No one wants to leave the decks, even at midnight, the last night before landing in Juneau.

Juneau, Alaska's capital, is set against a sheer mountain wall, easily demonstrating why there is no road to the outside world. Steep streets promise a good workout, and busy waterfront streets host plenty of shops selling local handicrafts and souvenirs. The Alaska State Museum, a short walk from the center, is a most worthwhile visit for great exhibits on how native Alaskans lived, dressed, hunted, and used the sea for fishing. On a clear day, take the cable car of Mount Roberts for a mountain and sea view from on high.

ALASKA MARINE HIGHWAY'S
Columbia, Malaspina, Matanuska, Taku, **and** *Kennicott*
The Inside Passage: On Your Own

 The Alaska Marine Highway, with its present fleet of nine blue-and-white ferries, was established in 1963 to serve Alaskan Panhandle communities, including the state capital of Juneau, that have no road access to the outside world. Three principal services are of interest for cruise passengers: They begin at Bellingham, Washington, just north of Seattle; at Prince Rupert, British Columbia; and at Juneau, the state capital. You may make one-way or round-trip voyages on all of them.

The *Columbia, Malaspina, Matanuska, Taku,* and *Kennicott,* all named after Alaskan glaciers, share many of the same offerings such as a forward observation lounge, a cocktail bar, and hot and cold meal cafeteria-style dining with big window viewing. The food, pay-as-you-go, is good American fare, and entrees include Alaskan salmon and halibut, chicken teriyaki, and New York strip steaks. The *Columbia* also has a dining room. The topdeck, heated solarium gives protection and warmth and has seating facing aft. The ship provides films, informal on-deck talks, and an easy social atmosphere in which to meet Alaska residents, other cruisers, backpackers, motorists, and commercial drivers.

The cabins, sold as a unit, are plainly furnished and comprise two-, three-, and four-berth insides and outsides incorporating private showers and with configurations and capacities unique to each vessel. Cabins book up fast for the summer months, and the ships carry deck passengers who find space to sleep in the lounges and the solarium. If making stopovers, some of the connecting daylight passages do not require a cabin. As the ferries serve a basic transportation function, all carry cars, recreational vehicles, and trucks that are driven on and off during port calls. These occur at all hours of the day and night, but stops are short in duration, from one to four hours, so elaborate excursions require a stopover. The scenery en route is never-ending beauty, and some passengers find it satisfying to simply make a round-trip.

The Itineraries

Bellingham to Skagway: Taken as a continuous round-trip voyage, the weekly trip (twice weekly in summer) departs **Bellingham,** Washington, located north of Seattle, on a Friday evening aboard the 500-passenger *Matanuska,* the *Malaspina,* or the 625-passenger *Columbia.* The initial two nights and a day are spent cruising north along the British Columbia coast. Vancouver Island, off to port, provides protection from the Pacific swells for much of the way. The scenery is mountainous, forested, and deeply incised with bays and narrow arms of the sea penetrating far inland. The narrow passage through the fast-flowing, and once dangerous, **Seymour Narrows** is particularly dramatic. Most commercial traffic travels on barges and ferries, and in summer you also encounter some of the two dozen cruise ships that ply the **Inside Passage.**

The ferry's first call is at **Ketchikan,** Alaska. As this is a purposeful ship, it remains long enough to load and unload passengers, vehicles, and cargo, giving through passengers time for a quick visit to the town center. **Wrangell** and **Petersburg** come later that same day, and only Marine Highway vessels and small cruise ships treat passengers to the **Wrangell Narrows** passage, where seventy channel markings require several hours of constant course changes. **Juneau's Auk Bay** terminal is reached on Monday morning, and persons wishing to see something of the capital, excellent state museum, and Mendenhall glacier should disembark for a day or two, then continue northward on the daily summer ship to Haines (5.5 hours) and Skagway (6.5 hours). Passengers remaining aboard are rewarded with a beautiful daylight sail up the Lynn Canal, flanked by high mountain peaks and an occasional glacier, to call at **Haines,** where many vehicles leave for the trip through the Yukon Territory to Alaska over the Haines and Alaska highways. An hour later the ship docks at **Skagway,** the most northerly Inside Passage port, remaining three hours before returning south. Consider leaving the vessel here to explore the restored gold rush entry point for prospectors bound overland to the Klondike from 1898

onward. A road runs inland to Whitehorse, Yukon Territory's capital, and the **White Pass and Yukon Route** operates excursion trains alongside the old Chilkat Trail, which the railroad replaced, to the top of the White Pass and back.

The southbound Marine Highway ferry will leave Skagway early Monday evening, call briefly at Haines, sail overnight to Juneau, then negotiate the twisting Peril Strait route (too narrow for the big cruise ships) to **Sitka.** The island town was Russian Alaska's capital until the United States took possession in 1867. Sights are St. Michael's Russian Orthodox Cathedral and a rain-forest walk through the Sitka National Historical Park to see the great collection of tall totems and an early nineteenth-century fort. The ship retraces the route south, calling on Wednesday at Petersburg, Wrangell, and Ketchikan, then spends two nights and

Address/Phone: Alaska Marine Highway, 1591 Glacier Avenue (P.O. Box 6858), Juneau, AK 99801; (907) 465–3941/42 or (800) 642–0066; fax: (907) 277–4829; www.dot.state. ak.us/amhs or www.akferry.com, or www.north-to-alaska.com for Alaska and British Columbia information.

The Ships: *Taku*, built in 1963, length 352 feet; *Matanuska* and *Malaspina,* built in 1963, then enlarged, length 408 feet; *Columbia*, built in 1974, length 418 feet; *Kennicott*, built in 1998, length 380 feet. The first four have shallow drafts, and the *Kennicott* is deep draft.

Passengers: Total capacity including berths and deck: *Taku* 450, *Matanuska* and *Malaspina* 500, *Columbia* 625, *Kennicott* 748; all ages and mostly North Americans

Dress: Casual at all times

Officers/Crew: Alaskan

Cabins: Number of berths: *Taku* 106, *Matanuska* 247, *Malaspina* 272, *Colum-*

bia 294, *Kennicott* 320, all in two- to four-berth cabins sold as units

Fare: $

What's included: Fare, port charges, and cabin (if purchased)

What's not included: Transportation to and from ports, meals, drinks, excursions

Highlights: Great scenery; social life aboard ferries; ease of stopovers, variety of routes

Other itineraries: Alaska Marine Highway also operates several smaller ferries, without cabins, to a half dozen other ports in the Alaska Panhandle. Ferries with and without cabins operate between South Central and Southwest Alaska. The sixty-eight passenger *Tustumena* (two- and four-berth cabins) makes monthly, five-day round-trips from Kodiak Island to the Aleutian Islands, a seagoing adventure with potentially some of the roughest sea conditions in the world.

a day cruising through Queen Charlotte Sound and Strait of Georgia for an early Friday morning arrival back at Bellingham, Washington.

Prince Rupert to Juneau: Ferry service sails north to Alaskan Panhandle ports from **Prince Rupert,** two to six times a week, increasing from one- to the three-ship maximum strength in summer. If you're not driving, there are two creative ways to reach Prince Rupert, one by rail and one by sea. From Jasper Via Rail's domeliner the *Skeena* provides a two-day scenic mountain, lake, and valley ride west to Prince Rupert for the Alaska ferry north. From Vancouver and Victoria on Vancouver Island, bus connections to Port Hardy, near the top of the island, connect to the BC Ferries' *Queen of the North* for a highly scenic ferry cruise to Prince Rupert.

Some Marine Highway ferries departing Prince Rupert call at **Ketchikan,** pass through the Wrangell Narrows, then stop at **Wrangell** and **Petersburg,** turning around at **Juneau** for a twenty-seven-hour one-way transit. Sailings to Juneau take two nights and a day if the route diverts via Sitka. Once a week this latter route is extended to **Haines** and **Sitka** aboard the seagoing *Kennicott.* All ships return to Prince Rupert via the same set of ports, so it is relatively easy to transfer between ships, but remember, cabin space for the overnight portions is at a premium in the summer months.

Prince Rupert to Juneau, Valdez, and Seward: In 1998 Alaska Marine Highway took delivery of its seagoing ferry *Kennicott,* a deep draft vessel, whereas the rest of the Inside Passage fleet have flat bottoms and shallow drafts. The *Kennicott* is designed to handle the rough waters sometimes encountered when crossing the Gulf of Alaska. For the first time in about a half century, it is now possible to sail from the Lower 48 and Inside Passage ports to South Central Alaska with onward road and rail connections to Anchorage, Denali National Park, and Fairbanks, avoiding the long Alaska Highway route.

While the *Kennicott* leaves from Prince Rupert for the direct sailing, persons coming from Bellingham can transfer to it at **Ketchikan** or **Juneau.** The *Kennicott* then sails directly to **Valdez,** in Prince William Sound, a thirty-seven-hour passage, or onto **Seward** in two nights and a day, or about fifty hours. Valdez is connected by road to the interior, and Seward has both road and Alaska Railroad links. Transit time from Prince Rupert to Seward is four nights and three days. For the return trip the *Kennicott* sails from Seward and Valdez to Juneau, Ketchikan, and Prince Rupert, the full elapsed time taking three nights and three days.

BC FERRIES'
Queen of the North and *Queen of Prince Rupert*
The Canadian Inside Passage and Queen Charlotte Islands

 BC Ferries, a British Columbia provincial company, operates a forty-vessel fleet providing the missing links in the BC highway system. The routes are complex, so a good map will help when planning itineraries around the two featured ships with cabin accommodations.

The *Queen of the North*, reflecting her Scandinavian origins, is newer, larger, and sleeker than the simpler but no less comfortable Canadian-built *Queen of Prince*

Rupert. In the main summer season, the *Queen of the North* holds down the scenic daylight run between Port Hardy at the northern tip of Vancouver Island and Prince Rupert, while the *Queen of Prince Rupert* sails between Prince Rupert and Skidegate on Queen Charlotte Island. Both ships have a lounge, a licensed bar, and cafeteria, and the *Queen of the North* has, in addition, an elaborate prix-fixe buffet for breakfast, lunch, and dinner. These meals may be pre-paid at the time of booking, resulting in savings and convenience when making the two-day round-trip. The deck space is well designed for viewing, and both ships have video arcades for children. On the *Queen of the North's* daylight sailings, entertainment includes films, live music, and informal talks by naturalists and creative artists.

Simple double and quad cabins have lower berths that become sofas during the day, and the uppers fold away. All inside and outside cabins have washbasins and toilets, and those above the vehicle deck have showers, too. The least expensive cabins below the car deck will be claustrophobic for some. On the *Queen of the North's*

fifteen-hour daylight sailings, cabins may be booked for the day, or if making a round-trip, they may be occupied that turnaround night. If you are joining at either port early in the morning, you must stay ashore the night before sailing. In the off-season the Port Hardy–Prince Rupert route changes to a longer twenty-two-hour overnight run, making one to three intermediate calls en route. The *Queen of Prince Rupert* may be substituted when the other ship is undergoing drydocking.

The Itineraries

Port Hardy to Prince Rupert: Port Hardy is an obscure little place that really only exists for the ferry. To connect to the sailings without a car, there is regular bus service from Victoria with pickup stops along the way, which take most of the day, and another equally long ride from Vancouver using the ferry to Nanaimo to reach Vancouver Island. A creative way is to take Vancouver Island's railway, which operates 1950s diesel-powered railcars from Victoria to Courtney, about halfway to Port Hardy, then switch to the bus. Motels in Port Hardy

Address/Phone: BC Ferries, 1112 Fort Street, Victoria, BC V8V 4V2; (250) 381–1401; fax: (250) 388–7754; www. bcferries.bc.ca or www.bcferries.com

The Ships: *Queen of the North*, built in 1969 as the *Stena Danica* and rebuilt for BC Ferries in the 1980s, has a gross tonnage of 8,889 and a length of 410 feet. *Queen of Prince Rupert* was built in 1966 and has a gross tonnage of 5,864 and a length of 332 feet.

Passengers: *Queen of the North* 750 (210 berths); *Queen of Prince Rupert* 458 (90 berths); all ages and some non–North American passengers

Dress: Casual

Officers/Crew: Canadian

Cabins: Both ships have two- and four-berth outside and inside cabins with

showers, and some are below vehicle deck with washbasin and toilet only

Fare: $

What's included: Cruise fare, port charges, and if booked, cabin and a meal plan (*Queen of the North* only)

What's not included: Transport to and from piers, drinks, meals not purchased in advance

Highlights: Some of the world's most beautiful scenery; lots of creative itineraries

Other itineraries: In addition to these two short getaways, which operate year-round with varying schedules, short ferry routes exist throughout coastal British Columbia, some incorporating through intercity buses between Vancouver-Victoria and Vancouver-Nanaimo.

look close to the ferry landing across the harbor, but a transfer is required.

In summer the *Queen of the North* leaves at 7:30 A.M. every other day for the 275-mile, fifteen-hour, nonstop passage. The first portion crosses a 50-mile stretch of open water called Queen Charlotte Sound, then enters Fitz-Hugh Sound to remain in protected waters for most of the balance of the day. The scenery is fjord land with mysterious arms that head inland, some traversed by a secondary BC Ferry service in summer. In the off-season the *Queen of the North* or *Queen of Prince Rupert* makes a few calls at towns without any road access, with **Bella Coola** being the exception. The coastal range will have snowcapped peaks during the early part of summer, and the deck temperatures may vary from being quite warm to chilly. En route you should see bald eagles, and you can expect to see some killer whales (orcas), porpoises, and seals. Many keen eyes will help you spot the wildlife.

Arrival at **Prince Rupert** is 10:30 P.M. for most summer sailings, and except late in the season, there should still be light in the sky. The landing is shared with the *Queen of Prince Rupert* and adjacent to the Alaska Marine Highway, but same-day connections are rare. Prince Rupert's motel district is about 1.5 miles away, and some motels overlook the harbor.

Sleep onboard if you are returning the next day to Port Hardy, or, as an alternative, take Via Rail's domeliner the *Skeena* to Prince George, spend the night, and continue on the *Skeena* eastward to Jasper.

Prince Rupert and Skidegate to Queen Charlotte Islands: On this shorter route, sailings are usually during the day to the Queen Charlotte Islands, a six-and-a-half-hour run, with return to Prince Rupert overnight. Turnaround time is five and a half hours (Monday sailing from Prince Rupert is mostly overnight; Monday and Tuesday sailings from **Skidegate** are day).

The mystical **Queen Charlotte Islands** are largely undeveloped, with wonderful misty forests, a rugged landscape, and the strong culture and artwork of the coastal Haida people. For more than a superficial visit, some sort of personal transportation is required, as there are no bus services.

AMERICAN CANADIAN CARIBBEAN LINE'S
Grande Caribe
Erie Canal, St. Lawrence Seaway, and Saguenay River

The *Grande Caribe* is the creation of Luther Blount, a Yankee shipbuilder and shipowner who has been launching small cruise vessels since 1966, and at 185 feet it is ACCL's longest vessel ever. The one hundred passengers are mainly well-traveled American retirees ready to do without luxuries but not without camaraderie, which they share in rather tight quarters with a score of young American crew members.

The lounge, which also serves as theater and lecture hall, is forward on the upper of two accommodation decks. The dining room, one deck below, doubles as a card room and reading area. The American fare is fresh, well prepared, and served family style at one open sitting. Lunch is soup, salad, pasta, or sandwiches. Alcohol is not sold, but the ship has storage for passengers' own stock and provides setups gratis. The Sun Deck extends nearly the ship's full length and has a protected viewing area. The pilot house collapses approaching low bridges, and the patented bow ramp lowers for dry landings.

The fifty cabins—forty-one are outside with windows (some slide open) and portholes—have twin or double beds, and a few reduced-rate units have triple berths. Each cabin has air vents, limited hanging and shelf space, and minuscule bathrooms with handheld showers. ACCL has a loyal clientele, thanks to the owner's innovative itineraries and moderate fares.

The Itinerary

The complete twelve-day Erie Canal to Saguenay cruise described here is altered in the fall to Erie Canal to Quebec City only (also twelve days), as sailing farther downriver is also north and nippy. Both fall foliage and the onset of snow come early to the lower St. Lawrence Valley.

Embarking at **Warren,** Rhode Island, the *Grande Caribe* sails overnight, arriving in **New York** about dawn and passing down the East River within 2 blocks of my apartment; then, with a loop by the Statue of Liberty, it turns up the **Hudson River,** stopping at **West Point.** At **Troy** the pilot house is lowered for "low bridge on the Erie

Canal." At **Waterford** the ship climbs 150 feet in a set of five locks to enter the canal proper, making stops and tying up at night, allowing the young American crew some freedom and passengers a chance to explore the delights of a small canal town. By breakfast the ship may already be under way, and from the open top deck, you can commune with the locals ashore, who are watching the unusual sight of a passenger vessel gliding by their front yards.

Turning into the **Oswego Canal,** the vast expanse of **Lake Ontario** is ahead, and soon one is threading among the beautiful **Thousand Islands.** Stops are **Clayton**'s Antique Boat Museum and splendid **Upper Canada Village,** with houses, churches, and public and farm buildings spanning one hundred years of Canadian architecture and small-town life. The tiny *Grande Caribe* shares the **St. Lawrence Seaway** with huge lake carriers and locks through to **Montreal** for a stop and a bow landing at Bay of Eternity in the dramatic **Saguenay Fjord.** From here the ship sails upriver to disembark at **Quebec City.** Passengers return to Rhode Island by bus in one day, and others come up to join the ship at Quebec.

Address/Phone: American Canadian Caribbean Line, P.O. Box 368, Warren, RI 02885; (401) 247–0955 or (800) 556–7450; fax: (401) 247–2350; e-mail: info@accl-smallships.com; www.accl-smallships.com

The Ship: *Grande Caribe* was built in the company's shipyard in 1997, has a tonnage of 99, a length of 183 feet, and a shallow draft of 6.5 feet.

Passengers: 100; age fifty-five and up and mostly Americans

Dress: Casual at all times

Officers/Crew: American

Cabins: 50 cabins, quite small; 9 inside; smoking on outside decks only

Fare: $$

What's included: Cruise and port charges, soft drinks, and setups for BYOB

What's not included: Airfare, shore excursions (very reasonably priced), tips

Highlights: The company's most popular route; social experience for passengers

Other itineraries: In addition to this twelve-day inland-waterways cruise, which operates June to October, ACCL offers many summer options in New England, eastern Canada, Great Lakes, Mid-America, Intracoastal Waterway, and winter cruises in Belize, Panama Canal, Caribbean, Orinoco River, and the Bahamas.

MID-LAKES NAVIGATION'S
Emita II
Cruising the Canals of New York State

 Mid-Lakes Navigation, run by five sons and one daughter of the company's founder, Peter Wiles Sr., has its home base in Skaneateles, New York. In three decades this small operation has brought due recognition to the state's treasured recreational waterways.

At first sight at the dock in Troy, just north of Albany, the 65-foot *Emita II*, a former Maine coastal passenger ferry, appears not much larger than a cruise-ship launch. The boat's top viewing deck, half protected by a new canopy, is attractively furnished with deck chairs and cushioned wooden benches. Mahogany trim accents the pilot house, and stairs lead down to the forward open deck and interior cabin. The dining room is aft, arranged with long, custom-built wooden tables, banquettes, and chairs. Oriental-patterned scatter rugs, a red deck, and orange life preservers in the overhead racks give the room and the forward library section both color and warmth.

All meals are taken aboard, and nights are spent ashore in nearby hotels and motels. Breakfast and lunch are buffet style, and dinner is served by waiters. One night features an outdoor summer supper, and entrees run to roast beef and Virginia baked ham; lunch is soup, salads, and sandwiches.

The Itineraries
While the Erie Canal from Albany (Troy) west to Syracuse and Buffalo is by far the best-known waterway, the company's forty-passenger packet boat, *Emita II*, also navigates the **Champlain Canal** from Albany (Troy) to Whitehall, from early June to mid-October. On the three-day Champlain Canal cruise, boarding begins in the morning at

Troy, and Captain Dan Wiles sets the tone for the come-what-may trip with a short talk before departure.

Within minutes the boat comes to the first of a dozen locks that divide the Hudson River and the Champlain Canal into a series of controlled pools. The *Emita II* plows ahead at a leisurely pace of 8 miles per hour between wooded shores and rolling farmlands, where cows and children come down to the water's edge for a look. Powered yachts gather to share the transit through the toll-free locks. At Fort Edward the boat ties up for the night, and passengers spend two nights at a motor inn in **Glens Falls,** where the captain gives a slide-illustrated talk on canal history and current preservation efforts. On the second day the *Emita II* continues north along the pretty Champlain Canal to **Whitehall,** the turnaround point. The town's Skenesborough Museum recalls the city's past as the birthplace of the U.S. Navy and Marine Corps and as a once-important canal and rail center.

Besides the Champlain Canal trip, the *Emita II* makes three-day **Erie Canal** cruises from Albany (Troy) to Syracuse along the Mohawk River. The highlights are the **Waterford Flight** of five locks, which lift the boat 150 feet, old factory towns such as **Amsterdam** and **Little Falls,** and the 22-mile Oneida Lake crossing. From **Syracuse** to Lockport, near **Buffalo,** the *Emita II* passes through **Montezuma Wildlife Refuge** for possible sightings of bald eagles and Canada geese, restored canal towns such as **Fairport** and **Pittsford,** and the original canal's small locks and stone-arched aqueducts. These last structures were built by Frederick Law Olmsted of Central Park fame. In places the bridges are so low that the crew has to remove the boat's pilot house, and passengers have to crouch. On this stretch the boat docks at a canal park for the first night, and the hotel is just steps away. Both Erie Canal trips are one-way, with each night ashore in a different hotel and bus return to the port of embarkation.

Address/Phone: Mid-Lakes Navigation Company, Box 61, 11 Jordan Street, Skaneateles, NY 13152; (315) 685–8500 or (800) 545–4318; fax: (315) 685–7566; e-mail: info@midlakesnav.com; www.midlakesnav.com

The Ship: *Emita II* was built in 1953 and then modified for day cruising. She has a gross tonnage of 65, a length of 65 feet, and a shallow draft.

Passengers: 40; mostly age fifty and up and many repeaters and whole-boat charters

Dress: Casual at all times

Officers/Crew: American

Cabins: Stay ashore in hotels/motels

Fare: $$

What's included: Cruise fare, port charges, all meals on boat, hotel stays, and transfers

What's not included: Drinks, tips

Highlights: Cruising historic canals while passing through rural and industrial landscapes

Other itineraries: In addition to the *Emita II*'s three above itineraries, operating between June and mid-October, the boat makes several Syracuse-Waterloo two-day cruises. The company also charters out Lockmaster English-style narrow boats for self-operated New York State canal cruising.

AMERICAN CRUISE LINES'
American Eagle
Coastal Ship among the New England Islands

 Cruise ships don't come much less populated than forty-nine passengers, a full-ship figure for the *American Eagle*. Completed in April 2000, she is a product of the owner's own Chesapeake shipyard in Salisbury, Maryland.

There are five cabin categories, all outside, and the second grade up, the AAs, measure 192 square feet, larger than what is found on the small-fry ship competition. The six AAV cabins spread out to 249 square feet including verandas, and seven more are dedicated single cabins priced at about a 50 percent premium over the AA category. The cane-style couches are comfortable for an afternoon's read and watching satellite TV, and the windows slide open to allow salt air to gain supremacy over the processed kind.

Four decks may not sound like much ship, but the public spaces are especially roomy. The forward-facing Nantucket Lounge seats all passengers, and amidships, a shipwide foyer offers additional comfy couch seating. A library, occupying a cabin-size space, offers TV, VCR, and books. The decor is a bit plain with utilitarian-looking walls and ceilings, but the carpets and fabrics help to dress things up.

The three-sided, glass-enclosed dining room operates on an open seating plan at large round tables. The ship does not have a liquor license, but there is a complimentary bar instead at the very popular cocktail hour and carafes of chardonnay and burgundy on the table at dinner. Sumptuous pre-dinner hors d'oeuvres may be jumbo shrimp, beef sate in peanut sauce, or melted brie on French bread.

Set dinner menus, with a choice of two entrees, include delicious grilled artichoke hearts, hearts of palm in balsamic vinegar, Cornish game hen with all wild rice, grilled catfish, sliced breast of duck, boiled live lobster, and desserts such as pecan peanut butter pie and whipped chocolate mousse in a pastry shell. Lunch is much lighter fare, such as crab cakes and chicken Caesar salad with garlic croutons.

The fourth or Sports Deck is both covered and open to the sky with deck chairs for everyone plus tables and chairs and a putting green. Additional covered deck space faces aft, and the open deck forward of the lounge is excellent for viewing ahead.

That's the ship, plain and simple, and delightfully *sans* casino, health spa, shops, staff pitching expensive drinks, fake-friendly celebratory dining room events, and the like. Cruising can be different, and this style adds up to a most pleasant vacation far removed from the milling throngs and multiple entertainment choices aboard the big hulls.

The Itinerary

New England Island trips begin at the City Pier in **New London,** Connecticut, a busy waterfront scene shared with ferries to Block Island, Orient Point on Long Island, and Fishers Island. Frequent Amtrak trains operating between Washington, New York, and Boston stop at New London, and the station is within walking distance of the ship. On this trip, most of the enrichment lecturers come aboard at specific ports and give talks, usually after dinner in the lounge.

Leaving New London, the *American Eagle* sails out of the Thames River, past the New London Lighthouse and into **Long Island Sound.** Drawing only 6 feet, the ship can roll when there is a swell en route to **Martha's Vineyard.** If not taking the ship's tour, a day bus pass provides rides to upscale **Edgartown** harbor and back via **Oak Bluffs** with its pretty village green and gingerbread Victorian Methodist summer campground. Then it's on to **Nantucket**

Address/Phone: American Cruise Lines, One Marine Park, Haddam, CT 06428; (800) 814–6880; fax: (860) 345–4266; www.americancruiselines.com

The Ship: *American Eagle,* built in 2000, has a length of 165 feet and a shallow draft.

Passengers: 49, mostly Americans fifty and up

Dress: Casual

Officers/Crew: American

Cabins: 28 cabins, all outside with picture windows, 6 with balconies, and 7 are singles

Fare: $$$

What's included: Cruise fare, open bar before dinner and wine with dinner

What's not included: Airfare, port charges, tips

Highlights: Small-ship atmosphere with roomy cabins, excellent food

Other itineraries: Besides this seven-day New England Islands itinerary, which operates between June and the end of September, this ship and sister *American Glory* offer cruises from the coast of Maine to the west coast of Florida.

Island, where the town is a treasure trove of eighteenth- and nineteenth-century architecture, and an efficient local bus network allows independent touring to Siasconset or to the beach.

Returning across Nantucket Sound and through the Elizabeth Islands, the next call is at **New Bedford,** where a trolley bus makes stops at the outstanding whaling museum, a historic whaling captain's house, and Seamen's Bethel (Chapel), or just do the same on foot without much strain. Sail into Narragansett Bay and under the Mount Hope Bridge for a visit to the USS *Massachusetts* tied up at **Fall River.**

Newport is walkable for the Thames Street shops and adjacent historic district, or tour the Vanderbilt's Breakers or the equally impressive Marble House, so-called summer cottages lined up along Bellevue Avenue and Ocean Drive. A cliff walk of several miles runs between the mansions and the sea and makes a great hike and picnic outing. Then it's a couple hours' sail out to New Harbor, **Block Island.** Entering the protected anchorage, the ship threads among several hundred private yachts to reach the town wharf for an overnight stay. A minivan tour includes a look at Victorian Old Harbor and the majestic Southeast Lighthouse set atop 100-foot cliffs overlooking the Atlantic. Tying up on the busy **New London** waterfront, **Mystic Seaport,** a living museum of seafaring traditions, is a short drive.

The *American Eagle* and its slightly newer sister, *American Glory,* provide a low-key, uncrowded social cruising experience from New England to the Deep South and Florida via the Intracoastal Waterway.

CLIPPER CRUISE LINE'S
Nantucket Clipper
New York, the Hudson Valley, and Chesapeake Bay

 Clipper Cruise Line, based in St. Louis, got started in 1983, and its *Nantucket Clipper,* completed in 1984, is one of two similar shallow-draft cruisers. A young American crew gives friendly, professional service to mostly middle-age Americans from the West Coast and Sun Belt. In no time the ship takes on the atmosphere of an informal seagoing club.

The single lounge, decorated with bold colors and maple trim, faces forward with views ahead and to both sides. Ample seating makes this the social setting as well as the venue for local entertainers and enrichment programs about history and nature. The bar is to one side and the small library collection to the other. The dining room serves passengers and staff at one open sitting, with good table service and a few buffets. Chefs trained at the Culinary Institute of America use fresh ingredients to prepare an American menu that runs to excellent fish, grilled shrimp, veal, lots of different salads, and freshly baked desserts. The Clipper Chipper cookies are an afternoon staple. Hot and cold hors d'oeuvres are served before dinner in the lounge.

Cabins are all outside doubles with twin beds, radios, adequate stowage, and compact bathrooms with showers. Some passengers prefer a cabin that opens to a side deck, whereas others like the traditional door to a central corridor. A few lower-priced cabins have portholes instead of windows, and noise from the engines is minimal, though noticeable, in the cabins located aft. Deck space includes a narrow wraparound promenade, a partly covered Sun Deck, and an observation deck at the bow. The ship has no swimming pool, fitness facilities, or casino. Instead, the *Nantucket Clipper* excels in providing an intimate, social, American-style vehicle to view coastal waters and islands.

The Itinerary

The *Nantucket Clipper* undertakes a variety of seven-, ten-, and fourteen-day cruises along the Eastern Seaboard, and the ports will vary from cruise to cruise, so here are the highlights beginning in New York for a cruise that sails up the Hudson and south to the Chesapeake Bay. The ship's shallow draft permits close-in cruising, and while most of this cruise is on inland waterways, during the open sea stretch along the New Jersey coast, the unstabilized ship can roll.

Embarkation is the Chelsea Piers, a busy recreational waterfront sports complex located on **Manhattan**'s Lower West Side. After a brief sail into the Upper Bay proudly dominated by Lady Liberty, the ship turns north past the skyline and up the majestic **Hudson** paralleling the Palisades. The Hudson is navigable as well as tidal all the way past Albany to Troy, some 150 miles north of the city. In fall the autumn colors are outstanding, and stately homes with views straight out of the Hudson River School of painting face the river.

The stop at **Kingston,** more than halfway to Albany, gives access to Franklin D. Roosevelt's family home at **Hyde Park** with Eleanor Roosevelt's cottage retreat at Val Kill just a few miles away. Returning south, a stop is made at **West Point** for a visit to the U.S. Military Academy. The river here cuts through the Hudson Highlands, and the depth increases to more than 300 feet at the point where the Bear Mountain Bridge crosses.

Passing New York City, the *Nantucket Clipper* sails under the Verrazano-Narrows Bridge and out into the Atlantic for the voyage south along the New Jersey coast, then into the Delaware and through the **Chesapeake and Delaware Canal** into

---

Address/Phone: Clipper Cruise Line, 11969 Westline Industrial Drive, St. Louis, MO 63146; reservations: (800) 325–0010; brochures: (800) 282–7245; fax: (314) 655–6670; e-mail: clipper@ clippercruise.com; www.clippercruise. com

The Ship: *Nantucket Clipper*, built in 1984, has a tonnage of 95, a length of 207 feet, and a shallow draft of 8 feet.

Passengers: 100; mostly Americans fifty-five and up

Dress: Casual, with a jacket for the captain's reception

Officers/Crew: American

Cabins: 50 small doubles; all outside, most with windows, half opening onto a side deck

Fare: $$$

What's included: Cruise and port charges

What's not included: Airfare, shore excursions, drinks, tips

Highlights: Inshore, river, and island cruising, and an easy social life aboard

Other itineraries: In addition to these Eastern Seaboard cruises, which operate in the spring and fall, the *Nantucket Clipper* sails via the Maritime Provinces into the St. Lawrence River and the Great Lakes and along the Intracoastal Waterway to the Caribbean. The slightly larger *Yorktown Clipper* offers cruises between Panama, Baja California, the California Rivers, and Alaska's Inside Passage. The expedition-style *Clipper Adventurer* and *Clipper Odyssey* cover much of the world.

Chesapeake Bay, known for its abundant bird life, especially ducks and Canada geese, and of course, oysters, steamer clams, and the blue crab. Some cruises visit **Baltimore's** Inner Harbor, and all stop at **Annapolis,** boasting the oldest state capitol building, with a chance to tour the **U.S. Naval Academy.** On the Chesapeake's Eastern Shore, **St. Michael's** has a wonderful maritime museum featuring the specialized craft that "fished" for the bay's renowned shellfish and an example of a screw-pile (built on stilts) lighthouse.

Sailing into one of the world's largest natural harbors, Hampton Roads, the ship docks in **Norfolk** adjacent to its waterfront marketplace and city center. A ferry crosses the Elizabeth River to historic Portsmouth for a residential walking tour. The final leg is a sail northward through the bay to Old Town **Alexandria,** Virginia, near **Washington,** where the ship is your conveniently docked hotel for one last day and night.

From here the ship will embark a new lot of passengers for ports in the Deep South along the Intracoastal Waterway.

AMERICAN CANADIAN CARIBBEAN LINE'S
Grande Mariner
East Coast Inside Passage: New England to Florida

The *Grande Mariner* is the latest ship from Luther Blount's Rhode Island shipyard, and very similar to the earlier *Grande Caribe.* One hundred passengers, mainly well-traveled American retirees, are accommodated aboard, enjoying inland-waters cruising and one another's company rather than looking for the luxuries of a deep-sea cruise ship.

The lounge, located forward on the upper of two main accommodation decks, also serves as theater and lecture hall. One deck below, the dining room doubles as a card room and reading area after meals. The galley window opens into the dining room, where American fare is fresh, well prepared, and served family style at one open sitting. Lunch is usually soup, salad, pasta, or make-your-own sandwich. No alcohol is sold, so passengers bring their own stock and the ship provides storage and setups gratis. The long Sun Deck has a

protected viewing area, and the patented bow ramp lowers for dry beach landings. The fifty cabins, of which forty-four are outside with windows (some slide open) and portholes, have twin or double beds. Several cabins aft on the Sun Deck open out onto the deck; otherwise, they have access from a central corridor. Cabins have air-conditioning, limited stowage, and minuscule bathrooms with handheld showers. As on all three ACCL vessels, there is a stair lift between decks, and smoking is permitted only on the open decks.

The Itinerary
Although this coastal cruise may begin in either Florida or **Rhode Island,** the narrative here will start in the Yankee North at the company headquarters and shipyard. Embarking the tiny ship, the course aims south into Long Island Sound, passing **New York's** skyscrapers at dawn, then out through the Narrows along the New Jersey

coast for the only stretch of open ocean. Not far beyond Victorian Cape May, the *Grande Mariner* slices through the Delmarva Peninsula via the **Chesapeake and Delaware Canal** into the widening bay. There are stops at **Baltimore's Inner Harbor, Crisfield,** the capital for blue crabs, Norfolk's busy waterfront, and the U.S. naval base at **Newport News.** The waterway opens wide through **Abermarle** and **Pamlico Sounds,** then narrows again south of Cape Hatteras, where happily the ship remains inside the breakers away from the graveyard of the Atlantic. When you stop at **Beaufort,** N.C., and **Beaufort,** S.C., you quickly learn, but may not remember, that they are pronounced quite differently *(bow-* and *bew-*fort, respectively). **Georgetown,** S.C., was once the largest port in the South, but today there's little sign of that, while **Charleston** and **Savannah** certainly impress as you approach and explore ashore.

The waterway is rural again in Georgia, with a stop at **St. Simon's Island;** then crossing into Florida, **St. Augustine** qualifies as America's oldest permanent European settlement. The ship is almost part of a convoy of yachts heading south for the winter, and there are many drawbridges that open for the waterborne traffic. The **Intracoastal Waterway** is especially busy along the Florida coast, with the cruise ending at **Titusville** on the Indian River near the Kennedy Space Center, following two weeks of gradual climate change. Welcome to sunny Florida.

Address/Phone: American Canadian Caribbean Line, P.O. Box 368, Warren, RI 02885; (401) 247–0955 or (800) 556–7450; fax: (401) 247–2350; e-mail: info@accl-smallships.com; www.accl-smallships.com

The Ship: *Grande Mariner* was built in the company's shipyard in 1998, has a tonnage of 99, a length of 183 feet, and a shallow draft of just 6.5 feet.

Passengers: 100; age is fifty-five and up and mostly Americans

Dress: Casual at all times

Officers/Crew: American

Cabins: 50 cabins, all quite small with 6 inside

Fare: $$

What's included: Cruise and port charges, soft drinks, and setups for BYOB

What's not included: Airfare, shore excursions (very reasonably priced), tips

Highlights: An intracoastal route spanning the length of the East Coast offering a great variety of stops; a low-key social experience among like-minded passengers

Other itineraries: In addition to this fifteen-day inland waterways cruise, operating several times in spring and fall, ACCL offers summer options in New England, eastern Canada, Erie Canal, St. Lawrence Seaway, Great Lakes, and Mid-America, as well as winter cruises in Belize, Panama Canal, Caribbean, Orinoco River, and the Bahamas.

DELTA QUEEN STEAMBOAT'S
Delta Queen
Upper Mississippi River: St. Louis to St. Paul

 Delta Queen Steamboat Company dates back more than one hundred years to the Greene Line of Steamers. The steamboat *Delta Queen,* first built in Scotland then completed in California in 1926, was first designed for overnight service between San Francisco and Sacramento, running opposite her mate, *Delta King,* now a hotel and restaurant on the Sacramento waterfront. She is a quintessential piece of Americana, evident the moment one treads her wooden decks and eyes the white-painted wood superstructure. The *DQ* may not be the opulent wedding cake like her big sister *American Queen,* but she is the real thing.

The lower of two forward lounges, graced with fluted columns and potted plants, is suitable for reading, playing cards, and having tea. The wooden grand staircase with shiny brass steps rises to the Victorian-style Texas Lounge with a bar, daytime games, a singer-pianist, and a popcorn machine. Dinner is served at two sittings. Service is casual and friendly and the food thoroughly American, featuring some Cajun-style soups and stuffed catfish among the usual meat, fish, and shellfish entrees. Portions are relatively small, yet sensible for diners who sample all five courses, and preparation ranges from good to excellent. The desserts, such as Mississippi Mud and pecan pie, are almost sinful.

Evening entertainment is popular, and following dinner, the lower-level dining room becomes a well-attended, old-fashioned music hall featuring ragtime, Dixieland, jazz, and blues. The engine room, where passengers are most welcome, is a spotless, eye-popping feast of brass fittings, multiple dials, and heaving machinery, and I love to go down to watch the slowly undulating Pitman arms turn the thrashing red wooden sternwheel.

Most of the eighty-seven staterooms are plain, with pipe rack closets for hanging clothes, and functional baths. Many cabins open to covered or open decks with chairs on either side of the door. The better rooms feature stained-glass windows and are off the Betty Blake Lounge, a portrait and memorabilia gallery dotted with overstuffed chairs. The old-fashioned steam calliope over the bright red paddle wheel signals the steamboat's arrival at town landings, and the hearty toots to the shoreside warm even the most cynical hearts. People love to watch her pass, as she provides a glimpse of a bygone America. Some passengers are fiercely loyal to the *DQ* and would not consider sailing the other two "new boats."

The Itinerary

As the setting sun framed the **St. Louis** Gateway Arch one mid-August evening on my St. Paul–bound cruise, the *Delta Queen* eased away from the landing and headed upriver. In the week ahead we would sail 659 meandering miles and negotiate twenty-six locks en route to the headwaters of navigation. The average of 100 miles a day may take as many minutes in a car, but speed and distance become irrelevant after a full day on the river. Most travelers quickly find a favorite spot on deck for taking in the slowly passing scenery. Forested banks, marshy coves, and high bluffs are the main characteristics of the **Upper Mississippi.** The approach to each town becomes a major event, and the *Delta Queen's* throaty whistle and cheerful tunes from the century-old calliope announce the steamboat's arrival and draw people down to the river.

The Mississippi is a vibrant commercial waterway, and long strings of barges, pushed by towboats, move huge loads of grain, coal, scrap iron, and fuel. During locking operations people ashore share news, weather, and scenic highlights with passengers lining the rails. The passengers in turn answer questions about traveling aboard the *Delta Queen*. Daytime activities include kite flying and river lore and natural history talks at the bow and guided walks ashore. Stroll through Mark Twain's **Hanni-**

bal; visit historic riverfront sites such as Villa Louis at **Prairie du Chien,** first established as a French fur-trading post; and walk into the redbrick Victorian lead-mining town of **Galena,** where U. S. Grant had a home that is open to visitors. The highlight at poky **Wabasha** is a visit to the Anderson House, where guests may rent a feline bedmate with their room. The *Delta Queen* ties up at **St. Paul,** and many people choose to stay an extra night to visit the state capitol building, Fort Snelling, and railroad baron James J. Hill's house.

Address/Phone: Delta Queen Steamboat Company, Robin Street Wharf, 1380 Port of New Orleans Place, New Orleans, LA 70130-1890; (800) 543–1949; fax: (504) 585–0630; www.deltaqueen. com

The Ship: *Delta Queen* was completed in 1926 for the Sacramento River trade and has been cruising the Midwestern rivers since 1948. The gross tonnage is 3,360, the length 285 feet, and the draft shallow.

Passengers: 174; age range fifty-five and up; mostly Americans

Dress: Jacket and tie optional for special evenings

Officers/Crew: American

Cabins: 87 cabins, all outside and most opening onto the open side deck; 19 have upper and lower berths, with the rest offering twin or queen-size beds

Fare: $$$

What's included: Cruise fare and port charges

What's not included: Airfare, shore excursions, drinks, tips

Highlights: Lazy river cruising aboard a floating National Historic Landmark

Other itineraries: In addition to this cruise aboard the *Delta Queen,* which operates in the summer, the three steamboats together offer a huge range of itineraries on Midwest rivers, embarking in many different port cities and with cruises themed to big bands, great American performers, the Civil War, Kentucky Derby, fall foliage, old-fashioned holidays, and many more. See *American Queen* and *Mississippi Queen.*

AMERICAN CANADIAN CARIBBEAN LINE'S
Niagara Prince
An Intricate Maze of Waterways: Chicago to New Orleans

 American Canadian Caribbean Line, based on the Narragansett Bay at Warren, Rhode Island, is the creation of a Yankee entrepreneur named Luther Blount. In 1966 he initiated modern-day domestic coastal and inland cruises, and as the idea caught on, he designed purpose-built craft in his own shipyard.

The *Niagara Prince*, one of three nimble ships, can navigate the entire length of the Erie Canal because it reduces its height off the water to just 16.5 feet by lowering the pilothouse, dismantling the funnel, and folding the mast to slip under low, fixed bridges, built many years ago by the railroads in their efforts to kill off the competing barge canal business.

Unlike its running mates, the *Niagara Prince*'s dining room and lounge area adjoin each other rather than being located on separate decks. The dining tables and banquettes serve as additional lounge seating between meals for reading, cards, games, and puzzles. Video films and travel documentaries are shown at night on two screens. The roomy top deck has both covered and open portions. The food is good American cooking featuring excellent soups and salads, freshly baked breads and desserts, and entrees such as prime ribs, chicken stuffed with crabmeat, and yellowfin tuna. Lunch may be a build-your-own sandwich or salad and soup. For some diners the fixed-meal times of 8:00 A.M., noon, and 6:00 P.M. take getting used to. The ship is BYOB, and free setups and cold storage are provided.

All but two Main Deck cabins are outside, tiny doubles with two L-shaped lowers or upper and lower berths. The latter rooms may be used by single passengers. The higher grade Sun Deck cabins have sliding picture windows and twin or double beds, and six of the rooms open onto the narrow wraparound promenade. The curtained-off shower stall lies between the washbasin and toilet. Closet and drawer space are limited, but there is ample room beneath the bunks for storage, i.e., living out of a suitcase. Square footage is 72 to 96. First-timers will find no cabin keys, but soon they let the honor system prevail. Passengers are mostly well traveled, of retirement age, and looking for a social experience and new destinations. On my cruise out of Chicago, all but two passengers were ACCL repeaters. Normally, a 60 to 70 percent repeat level is not unusual.

The Itinerary

The *Niagara Prince* embarks at **Chicago's Navy Pier** and then crosses Illinois via the Calumet River, Calumet Sag Channel, Chicago Sanitary & Ship Canal, and the Des Plaines, Kankakee, and Illinois Rivers—interconnecting waterways used by rafts of barges transporting coal, scrap metal, salt, gravel, sand, and grain. On my cruise approaching the mighty Atchison, Topeka, & Santa Fe's Lemonte railroad bridge, the captain stood at the helm while his wife, the first mate, focused on the underside of the looming bridge and the eighty passengers lined the rails in hushed silence. When she gave her husband the signal to proceed, the boat slid beneath with but a few inches to spare. Seconds later, a locomotive whistle blew, and Amtrak's crack *Southwest Chief* en route to Los Angeles thundered across.

Once beyond the metropolitan region, the settings change to state forests, wooded bluffs, and open farmland. The controlled waterway is interrupted with 600-foot-long locks that lower the ship from 2 feet to as much as 35 feet. Occasionally, one looks over levees to see cattle peacefully grazing on the fields below. An enjoyable bus trip includes the log village of **New Salem,** Illinois, where Abraham Lincoln had failed at running a business and then launched a rather more successful political career. Docked in the shadow of the Great Arch at **St. Louis,** and at the confluence of the Mississippi and Ohio Rivers near **Cairo,** pronounced "cayrow," one sees how different the river waters can look. A walking tour visits the historic river

town of **Paducah,** Kentucky, and then in the Deep South, a call is made at **Waverly Plantation,** and two more calls offer Civil War buffs a look at the historic battle sites at **Demopolis** and **Shiloh.**

The *Niagara Prince* navigates the **Tennessee–Tombigbee Waterway,** which stirred up a lot of controversy as a pork barrel project when planned, then slips into **Mobile Bay** by the back door. The ship then turns west along the **Intracoastal Waterway** into **New Orleans.** When you look at a map, it is a wonder that any ship or boat could actually accomplish this circuitous route from Chicago to New Orleans.

Address/Phone: American Canadian Caribbean Line, P.O. Box 368, Warren, RI 02885; (401) 247–0955 or (800) 556–7450; fax: (401) 247–2350; e-mail: info@accl-smallships.com; www.accl-smallships.com

The Ship: *Niagara Prince* was built in the company's shipyard in 1994 and has a length of 175 feet and a shallow draft of just over 6 feet.

Passengers: 84; age fifty-five and up, mostly Americans

Dress: Casual at all times

Officers/Crew: American

Cabins: 42 cabins, all quite small and just two insides

Fare: $$

What's included: Cruise and port

charges, soft drinks, and setups for BYOB

What's not included: Airfare, shore excursions (very reasonably priced), tips

Highlights: An amazing route through Mid-America and the Deep South linking many waterways; a low-key social experience among like-minded passengers

Other itineraries: In addition to this fifteen-day inland waterways cruise, which operates several times a year, ACCL offers summer options in New England, eastern Canada, Erie Canal, the St. Lawrence Seaway, Great Lakes, Intracoastal Waterway, and winter cruises in Belize, Panama, Caribbean, Orinoco River, and the Bahamas.

DELTA QUEEN STEAMBOAT'S
American Queen
Cruising the Ohio River

 Delta Queen Steamboat Company traces its origins back to 1890, the oldest U.S. flag cruise line, and today, with its fleet of three steamboats, the company celebrates Americana in music, food, small-town life, big cities, plantation homes, history, and steamboat lore.

I would take the *American Queen* anywhere as long as I could also enjoy the steamboat's remarkable ambience and interiors. Mounting the Grand Staircase for the first time and entering the Cabin Deck Lobby, I was dazzled by a stunning suite of rooms that could easily be the stately home of a nineteenth-century steel magnate or robber baron. Mahogany, silver, stained glass, etched glass, brass, marble, lace, leather, iron, plaster molding, tin ceilings, patterned wallpaper, thick carpets, oil paintings, chandeliers, stuffed animals, and a plethora of knickknacks outfit two Victorian parlors and a richly decorated club lounge.

The Grand Saloon aboard the *American Queen* turns an evening of entertainment into a major event for the staging of American musicals, jazz concerts, Dixieland, and big-band sounds. Designed after a small-town opera house, the theater has upholstered armchairs in curved theater boxes and deep cushioned lounge chairs on the lower level. Two massive globes ringed by gas-style lamps hang from a plaster ceiling of twinkling stars.

The J. M. White Dining Room recalls the main cabin lounge aboard the late nineteenth-century namesake steamboat with a pair of soaring two-deck-high sections decorated with white filigree woodwork, colorful tapestries, and two huge, gilded antique mirrors. The food runs to American, Southern, and Cajun, with consistently satisfying prime ribs, roast duck, fried oysters, catfish stuffed with crab and wild rice, ravioli stuffed with shrimp, seafood gumbo, garlic and leek soup, Mississippi mud pie, and praline and pecan cheesecake.

On Cabin Deck above, the centrally positioned Mark Twain Gallery is a dark-paneled room that sparkles with display cases containing museum-quality collections of nineteenth-century maps, cameras, early radios, and showboat handbills and posters. River-related sheet music invites anyone to pluck the antique Steinway upright piano keys. In one corner a Victorian birdcage is home to a pair of chirpy tiger finches; and from an oversize armchair, there is a sneaky view down into the dining room.

To the right of the entrance foyer's Reed & Barton watercooler, the Gentlemen's Card Room welcomes both sexes to enjoy a game at cherry-wood tables encircled by a standing stuffed black bear, a working upright typewriter, a stereoscopic peep show, an iron fireplace, and Tiffany lamps ordered from an original nineteenth-century catalog. The Ladies' Parlor welcomes anyone to lounge on the swooning couch before a fireplace, its wooden mantle cluttered with black-and-white ancestral photographs and flanking vases. Floor lamps with linen shades, silver tea sets, a rosewood pump organ, and a floral wallpaper all add to the lovely room—a cozy spot for a read and for gazing out at the river through French doors or through a pretty curtained bay window.

The Front Porch of America, on Texas Deck, is aptly named for its sweeping views over the bow and furnishings of white wicker chairs and painted rockers. One deck above, the Chart Room is a hangout for the "riverlorian," who helps people get their bearings using flip charts and who spins tales every morning at eight.

Seven categories of cabins are beautifully decorated in elaborate Victorian style with patterned wallpaper and carpets, richly colored bedspreads, and wooden cabinets. Most cabins have cushioned wicker chairs and footstools and French doors that hook open to connect with the open deck. Twin beds are recessed into shallow arched niches, and bathrooms are tiled in black and white.

The *American Queen* is so much larger than her nineteenth-century predecessors that to slide under the numerous bridges on the Ohio and Upper Mississippi Rivers, the 109-foot-high twin feathered-topped stacks fold forward into cradles and the pilothouse cupola and rooster weather vane come off. Steam whistles are traditionally handed down from one boat to the next, and the *American Queen's* comes from the steamboat *Jason*, which accepted it from the *City of Memphis*, a boat that Mark Twain piloted.

The Itinerary

Pittsburgh, hemmed in by hills and sited where the confluence of the Allegheny and Monongahela Rivers form the Ohio, occupies the spot where steamboating originated in 1811. Embarkation takes place not far from the Golden Triangle, and once out of sight of the modern skyline, the Ohio becomes a feast of smokestack industry, towns that prospered because of the river location, soaring cliffs, and peaceful rural landscapes. The welcome mat is out at **Wellsburg,** West Virginia, a poky sort of place, whereas **Marietta,** Ohio, bustles by comparison along its tree-lined streets and at the Ohio River Museum's steamboat-era model and photo collection. The *W.P. Snyder, Jr.*, the last sternwheel steam-powered towboat, is open for a look into the crew's living quarters. At **Maysville,** on the Kentucky side, a coach tour visits three nearby covered bridges.

Cincinnati still exudes the importance of a river port as the skyline faces the mighty Ohio and waterfront parks link the landing with nearby Fountain Square. Tall Stacks, a huge civic celebration, draws thousands of spectators to see the gathering of steamboats, the most recent one being in the fall of 2003.

Address/Phone: Delta Queen Steamboat Company, Robin Street Wharf, 1380 Port of New Orleans Place, New Orleans, LA 70130-1890; (800) 543-1949; fax: (504) 585-0630; www.deltaqueen.com

The Ship: *American Queen* was completed in 1995 and has a gross tonnage of 3,707, a length of 418 feet, and a shallow draft.

Passengers: 436; age fifty-five and up, mostly Americans

Dress: Jacket with tie optional at special dinners

Officers/Crew: American

Cabins: 222 cabins, 168 outside; some opening onto the side deck as well as an inside corridor; some with verandas and some with bay windows

Fare: $$$

What's included: Cruise fare and port charges

What's not included: Airfare, shore excursions, drinks, tips

Highlights: Outstanding recreation of floating American Victoriana, terrific music

Other itineraries: In addition to this cruise aboard the *American Queen,* which operates in the summer, the three steamboats together offer a wide range of itineraries on Midwestern rivers, embarking in many different port cities and with cruises themed to big bands, great American performers, the Civil War, fall foliage, old-fashioned holidays, and many more. See the *Delta Queen* and *Mississippi Queen.*

DELTA QUEEN STEAMBOAT'S
Mississippi Queen
The Antebellum South

 Delta Queen Steamboat Company is the largest operator of inland river cruises in North America, and its stern-wheelers are American icons. The 414-passenger *Mississippi Queen,* built in 1976, is the second-largest stern-wheeler ever constructed after fleetmate *American Queen.* She seems more like a cruise ship than does the historic *Delta Queen.* This floating re-creation of nineteenth-century Americana has Victorian wall and fabric decor and furniture design alongside modern comfort and safety features.

The Paddlewheel Lounge rises two decks and overlooks the huge churning red wheel, and the Calliope Bar above also faces astern. The calliope is designed to impress the local town folks that a riverboat is coming, and the passengers take delight in feeling a tinge of importance at arriving in such a magnificent conveyance. The Grand Saloon, forward on the Observation Deck, serves well as the stylish brass-and-glass venue for a celebration of American music in the form of jazz groups, big bands, riverboat shows, Broadway revues, and cabarets. Port and starboard galleries house a card room-cum-lounge and a bar.

Dinner is at two sittings, and the best tables are by the large windows. The very good food is accented with regional flavors, particularly Cajun and Southern ones. Try the stuffed catfish, chilled blackened sirloin of beef, and crawfish en croute for something different.

All 208 cabins have Victorian-style bedspreads and curtains, phones, two-channel radios, and thermostats. Half of the cabins have private verandas, and seventy-three are inside, with the lowest priced having upper and lower berths. Two of the largest face forward and flank the pilot house, and two more face aft over the wheel. Sixteen suites on Promenade Deck and two on Cabin Deck have sitting areas, twin or king beds, baths, and balconies.

The Itinerary

This **Lower Mississippi** cruise has many variations in itinerary, but nearly all include the following calls once the steamboat gets beyond the industrial belt near **New Orleans.**

St. Francisville, built on high ground away from floods that destroyed the first settlement, may be seen on foot for its residential styles: antebellum, French colonial, Victorian, neoclassical, and dogtrot, a house divided by a breezeway. On upriver, **Natchez** has by far the largest collection of antebellum homes, numbering more than 200, and several house tours take in two or three of different styles. One, the largest octagonal house in the United States, remains unfinished, but it comes with an amazing tale of a mother bringing up the children in the basement after her husband was killed in the Civil War. Then **Vicksburg,** the site of a great battle during the War Between the States, offers a military-park tour, the Gray and Blue Naval Museum, and a Civil War–era gunboat that was dredged up from the muddy Mississippi. The first Coca-Cola was bottled here to be sent out into the country.

If it's spring, river fog may rise in the early evening, and the steamboat will make for the nearest stout tree to tie up for the night until visibility improves. The *Mississippi Queen* conveniently makes levee landings, and on the other side, there are classic antebellum homes to visit. **Houmas House** and **Oak Alley** both feature excellent costumed guides, good interior furnishings, and attractive gardens. They both provided settings for Bette Davis's horror film *Hush . . . Hush, Sweet Charlotte,* whereas Oak Alley also served Tom Cruise in *Interview with the Vampire.* Following a visit to the latter, I walked along the levee and wandered back through tiny church communities set among cane fields.

Baton Rouge, the state capital, invariably leads the guides to reciting colorful accounts of Louisiana's Governor Huey P. Long, none requiring embellishing. The highlight here is the Rural Life Museum, a collection of historic buildings that would have been out the back door of the plantation house, such as slave quarters, a barn, a small store, a one-room schoolhouse, an overseer's house, and a church. Another tour introduces Cajun music, language, customs, and food. The Lower Mississippi is not especially scenic, but this stretch provides an excellent glimpse into the antebellum and Civil War South.

Address/Phone: Delta Queen Steamboat Company, Robin Street Wharf, 1380 Port of New Orleans Place, New Orleans, LA 70130-1890; (800) 543–1949; fax: (504) 585–0630; www.deltaqueen.com

The Ship: *Mississippi Queen* was completed in 1976 and has a gross tonnage of 3,360, a length of 382 feet, and a shallow draft.

Passengers: 414; age fifty-five and up; mostly Americans

Dress: Jacket and tie optional for special evenings

Officers/Crew: American

Cabins: 208 in a variety of configurations, including 104 with verandas

Fare: $$$

What's included: Cruise fare and port charges

What's not included: Airfare, shore excursions, drinks, tips

Highlights: Musical entertainment aboard and the antebellum South ashore

Other itineraries: In addition to this Lower Mississippi cruise varying between four and seven days, the three steamboats offer a variety of river itineraries and embarkation cities such as New Orleans, Memphis, Chattanooga, St. Louis, Louisville, Cincinnati, Pittsburgh, and St. Paul. Theme cruises feature Dixieland music, the Old South, the annual "Great Steamboat Race," and a Kentucky Derby cruise, when she docks in Louisville. See the *American Queen* and the *Delta Queen.*

RIVERBARGE EXCURSION LINES'
River Explorer
Louisiana Bayou Cajun and Creole Cruising

 RiverBarge Excursion Lines is the creation of Eddie Conrad, a New Orleans towboat and barge owner. Building on his commercial experience, he constructed two three-deck hotel barges—one *(DeSoto)* for the cabin accommodations and the other *(LaSalle)* housing the public spaces—lashed them together, and had them propelled by a towboat *(Miss Nari)*. The complete rig is a sight to behold, having an ocean-liner length of 730 feet and a width of 54 feet, fitting snugly into the locks of the Intracoastal Waterway.

The interior design is spacious, modern in decor, and features huge view windows. My favorite spot is the Guest Pilot House, an observation lounge facing forward, where there are lots of charts and maps to study and communications between river pilots to listen to. The *River Explorer's* navigating pilot is one deck above, and he welcomes visitors when the barge is tied up.

The Lobby, aft of the Guest Pilot House, provides lounge and banquette seating, twenty-four-hour coffee, and a jumbo cookie jar. Pretty etched glass panels, which depict highway bridges crossing rivers, decorate the seat backs, and a giant steering wheel has been adapted as a centerpiece. The shop for regional and RiverBarge souvenirs is called the Louisiana Purchase, and the Governor Chavez is a midships lounge for borrowing books and videos and for playing board games and cards at three large octagonal tables. The Sprague, a bi-level room with mezzanine, provides the setting for local musicians, storytelling, and bingo during the day and after dinner.

All meals, apart from outdoor barbecues, are served in The Galley, a huge, light-filled space on the lowest passenger deck. Breakfast is buffet, with a cook to prepare omelets. Lunch (called dinner here) is also a buffet, with hot and cold selections, occasionally geared to the region, such as catfish and shrimp dishes on the southern excursions. Dinner (called supper) is wait-served and features an appetizer, a soup, a salad, a choice of two entrees, and freshly baked cakes and pies for dessert. Preparation is good to excellent, and the food reflects what most American passengers like when eating out at a proper restaurant. The helpful and upbeat staff serves coffee, tea, drinks, and wine.

Cabins, named after states and arranged in order of their entry into the Union, are larger than average, all with the same layout; those on the higher of the two decks have narrow verandas. Beds are twins or queens with wooden headboards and good individual reading lights. Cabins have windows that slide open, TV/VCR, fridge, desk, two chairs, and decent hanging and drawer space for what is a very casual cruise. Bathrooms have full tubs and showers.

Outdoor space, both covered and open, stretches for 500 feet along nearly the complete length of the top deck, with bar service, hot and cold hors d'oeuvres before dinner, and a popcorn machine.

The Itinerary

Most cruises last between six and eight days and travel the Mississippi, Missouri, Ohio, Cumberland, and Tennessee Rivers and the Intracoastal Waterway, running parallel to the Gulf of Mexico. My eight-night cruise, themed to Cajuns and Creoles, embarked in **New Orleans** and explored remote bayou country and the lower regions of the mighty Mississippi.

The first night docked at New Orleans allowed an afternoon and evening in the French Quarter. Two hours after setting off down river, the barge passed through the Algiers Lock into the **Intracoastal Waterway** that runs west and southwest across Louisiana and Texas to the Mexican border. The shipping channel, slicing through swamps and marshlands, was completed in 1949.

Following an overnight anchorage well out of sight of human habitation, we transferred to small launches for an exploratory trip into a cypress swamp to spot alligators, nutrias (a kind of rodent), great blue herons, great white egrets, cormorants, and even water moccasins. Then after a night docked at **Morgan City,** a full-day excursion went deep into **Cajun country,** settled by French-speaking Acadians.

The visits included the Joseph Jefferson House, built in 1870; the state's oldest rice company; the historic village of **St. Martinville** of the poem "Evangeline" fame; and Vermilionville, a collection of original and reconstructed Acadian buildings that represent how the Cajuns lived, worked, worshiped, and played. A very good seafood dinner took place at a lively Cajun dance hall.

Cruising north parallel to the Atchafalaya River, we enjoyed a barbecue lunch out on deck, which included Cajun spiced crayfish. By the afternoon of the fourth day, we left the bayous and entered the **Mississippi River** to tie up at **Baton Rouge,** the Louisiana state capital.

Most everything in Baton Rouge was within walking distance: the old state capitol building; the art deco capitol building; the USS *Kidd,* an authentically restored World War II destroyer; and two gambling boats. En route down the Mississippi, a final call at **Laura Plantation,** built in 1805, showed how a Creole family and their slaves lived.

Tying up at New Orleans in the afternoon of the final full day, we were allowed additional time to enjoy the city before disembarking the next morning.

Address/Phone: RiverBarge Excursion Lines, 201 Opelousas Avenue, New Orleans, LA 70114; (888) GO–BARGE or 456–2206; fax: (504) 365–0000; e-mail: reservation@riverbarge.com; www.riverbarge.com

The Ship: *River Explorer* was built in 1998 and has a gross tonnage of 8,864, a length, including both barges, of 590 feet, plus a 140-foot towboat, and a shallow draft.

Passengers: 198; Americans, fifty-five and up

Dress: Casual at all times

Officers/Crew: American

Cabins: 99; all similar in size; one deck with verandas and one deck without

Fare: $$

What's included: Cruise, port charges, shore excursions, tips

What's not included: Airfare, drinks

Highlights: Seeing America close up from its waterways, aboard a roomy floating home

Other itineraries: In addition to this eight-day Cajuns and Creoles cruise, there are four- to ten-day cruises of the Mississippi, Missouri, Ohio, Cumberland, and Tennessee Rivers and the Intracoastal Waterway along the Gulf Coast to the Mexican border.

CLIPPER CRUISE LINE'S
Yorktown Clipper
Exploring California by River

Clipper Cruise Line of St. Louis, in business since 1983, attracts a fairly homogeneous crowd of mostly well-traveled folks to its U.S. flag coastal ships *Nantucket Clipper* and *Yorktown Clipper* and its more newly acquired expeditions ships *Clipper Adventurer* and *Clipper Odyssey,* carrying between 102 and 138 passengers.

Aboard the *Yorktown Clipper,* the wraparound forward observation lounge provides a cozy, clubby experience before meals and during informal talks. The big-windowed dining room operates with one open sitting at tables of four to eight. The chefs, trained at the Culinary Institute of America in Hyde Park, New York, prepare excellent domestic fare using high-quality ingredients. There's an easy relationship between the passengers and the young American dining and cabin staff. Dinner's first course is served during cocktail hour, and the hot and cold appetizers include jumbo shrimp, steamed mussels, smoked salmon, and stuffed mushroom caps. In the restaurant the menu offers a soup, two kinds of salads, and a choice of four entrees, such as shrimp scampi, roast duckling, linguine with clam sauce, a pasta, and a vegetable pie, ending with a freshly prepared dessert, cheesecake, or a variety of ice creams. Wines are moderately priced. As an alternative, the observation lounge serves a continental breakfast and a light soup, sandwich, and salad lunch. Entertainment may be a jazz group one evening, a film on another, and talks by the naturalist and chef, but aboard it's mostly socializing among like-minded passengers.

The sixty-nine compact cabins, all outside, typically have parallel twin beds (some L-shaped beds) set before two picture windows, and thirty-eight open onto the promenade for access to the passing scene. There's a desk-cum-vanity, a chair, a half dozen small drawers, two closets, and a tiny bathroom with shower. Outside, fourteen times around the teak promenade equals a mile, and the sun deck above is partly covered and has a bar, but no swimming pool or whirlpool.

The Itinerary

Departure is from **Redwood City,** located south of San Francisco. The *Yorktown Clipper* then cruises northward, passing "the city by the bay" and Alcatraz to anchor off **Sausalito** for the night. A half-day tour to the awe-inspiring **Muir Woods** provides a walk among the giant redwood trees, or you can go ashore independently to explore Sausalito's several miles of waterfront, intriguing houseboat communities, and the Army Corps of Engineers working research model of San Francisco Bay. By passing into the narrow Carquinez Strait and entering Suisin Bay, you can view six decades of U.S. shipping—World War II Victory Ships, twin-funneled troopships, handsome conventional freighters, steam tankers, and naval vessels.

Urban and suburban landscapes turn to flat farmlands protected by parallel levees forming the deepwater ship channel inland to the California state capital. Tying up at a wharf just outside **Sacramento,** one group heads by road for an all-day tour to **Yosemite National Park** while another takes the free shuttle into **Old Sacramento,** a restored nineteenth-century riverfront commercial and tourist district. The main attraction is the California State Railroad Museum, where I love to walk through a gently rocking sleeping car, a traveling railway post office, and a 1938 Santa Fe Super Chief dining car set with two dozen examples of railroad china. Nearby, the seventy-year-old *Delta King,* the stern-wheeler *Delta Queen's* permanently tied-up sibling, serves as floating hotel, restaurant, and meeting facility. Within fifteen minutes' walk of Old Sacramento are a fine arts museum, a tour of the beautiful restored state capitol building, and a kind of archaeological dig of the soon-to-be restored Leland Stanford mansion.

A sail downriver to **Vallejo** connects to a mini-bus tour of several different **Napa Valley** wineries, including one using the champagne method. On the last full day, the *Yorktown Clipper* docks at Pier 35, **San Francisco's** cruise terminal, for easy access to Fisherman's Wharf, Ghirardelli Square, Coit Tower, Alcatraz by boat, and city highlights by coach. After dinner the captain may take his ship under the Golden Gate Bridge, then back along the twinkling skyline, and finally beneath the Oakland-Bay Bridge to tie up at Redwood City.

Address/Phone: Clipper Cruise Line, 11969 Westline Industrial Drive, St. Louis, MO 63146; reservations: (800) 325–0010; brochures: (800) 282–7245; fax: (314) 655–6670; e-mail: clipper@clippercruise.com; www.clippercruise.com

The Ship: *Yorktown Clipper,* built in 1988, has a gross tonnage of 97 tons, a special U.S. coastal measurement, a length of 257 feet, and a draft of 8 feet.

Passengers: 138; age fifty-five and up, nearly all Americans

Dress: Casual at all times, perhaps a jacket at the captain's welcome party

Officers/Crew: American

Cabins: 69; all outside, most with picture windows, none with verandas, but more than half with opening onto a side deck

Fare: $$$

What's included: Cruise only and port charges

What's not included: Airfare, shore excursions, tips, and drinks

Highlights: Destination-oriented itineraries; relaxed social atmosphere; great meals

Other itineraries: In addition to the above six-day California rivers cruise, offered in the fall, the *Yorktown Clipper* and *Nantucket Clipper,* between them, cruise to Alaska, British Columbia, Sea of Cortez (Mexico), Panama Canal, Caribbean, Orinoco River, East Coast via the Intracoastal Waterway, Chesapeake Bay, Hudson River, New England, Eastern Canada, and Great Lakes. Expedition ships *Clipper Adventurer* and *Clipper Odyssey* take in much of the world: Arctic, Antarctica, Amazon, northern Europe, the Mediterranean, the Far East, Southeast Asia, and Australasia.

LINDBLAD EXPEDITIONS'
Sea Lion and *Sea Bird*
Columbia and Snake Rivers in the Wake of Lewis and Clark

 Lindblad Expeditions, the brain-child of Sven Olof Lindblad, whose father, Lars Eric, pioneered expedition-style cruising, offers some of the most creative itineraries afloat, employs wonderful naturalists and historians, and attracts well-heeled passengers keen on seeing the world and sharing the experiences.

The seventy-passenger *Sea Lion* and fleetmate *Sea Bird* are not very fancy, but then luxurious accommodations and lounging by the pool are not why most people book. The 152-foot-long ships, really boats, have just four decks, and apart from a half dozen lower-deck cabins with a tiny porthole high in the cabin, rooms are outside doubles with large windows, parallel or angled twins or queen-size beds. All have tiny private bathrooms. Bridge and Upper Deck rooms open onto a covered side promenade, and those on Main Deck open into a central corridor linking the forward observation lounge and bar to the dining saloon. In the spirit of honesty that prevails onboard, there are no cabin keys, and on my cruise no one seemed to worry. Open seating prevails at all meals, and dinner may offer grilled salmon and roast duckling. Breakfast features freshly baked muffins and croissants and special hot dishes, and lunch consists of very good soups and tasty, overstuffed sandwiches. Wines include reds and whites from vineyards overlooking the river.

The Itinerary

The inland water route passes between forested slopes, apple orchards, and vineyards, cuts through deep gorges and wildlife refuges, and negotiates eight commercial locks. The upriver expedition is no sedentary deck-chair cruise. Instead, the inflatable Zodiac rafts, with professional naturalists at the helm, take passengers ashore for visits to tiny riverside villages and salmon fish ladders, and on hikes and exploratory trips along small streams. The Pacific Northwest's **Columbia** and **Snake Rivers** are the country's second-largest system, after the Mississippi and Missouri, in terms of length and area drained. At the beginning of the nineteenth century, Meriwether Lewis and William Clark descended the Columbia and Snake in canoes as part of their legendary Western expedition.

The *Sea Lion* embarks at **Portland,** Oregon, and the little ship eases away from its berth for an overnight sail downriver. At dawn in the half-light of a near full moon, I watched Pacific breakers pounding hard on the Columbia Bar, a sand spit that stretches partway across the river's misty mouth. Later the ship ties up at **Astoria**—a fur-trading post established by John Jacob Astor and now a lumber port dotted with Victorian houses—for visits to the Columbia River Maritime Museum and Fort Clatsop, the latter replicating the primitive conditions that Lewis and Clark faced during the very wet winter of 1805–1806.

During the night the *Sea Lion* sails upstream to the **Columbia Gorge,** narrows flanked by steep, forested cliffs, and then into a lock at the **Bonneville Dam,** a massive hydroelectric project completed during the Great Depression. A fish ladder allows the migrating steelhead trout and chinook, sockeye, and coho salmon to travel upriver to spawn and then die. Stop at the Columbia Gorge Discovery Center to learn about its cataclysmic geological origins and 10,000 years of history.

Farther upstream, the Columbia River completely alters its character. The well-watered landscape gives way to semiarid steppes, gracefully tapered buttes, and diminishing signs of habitation. From Zodiac landing craft the expedition leader points out great blue herons bobbing on the water, marsh hawks in trees, three soaring bald eagles, a white pelican with a 9-foot wingspan, and several mule deer on the shore. Entering the **Snake River,** the *Sea Lion* passes between the banks formed by the largest basaltic lava flow in the world and anchors at the mouth of the **Palouse River.** The ship's crew prepares an outdoor barbecue of salmon and steaks around a bonfire, and there's a chance to go kayaking.

One morning before sunrise, high-speed jetboats roar into Idaho's **Hells Canyon,** the deepest gorge in North America. The sluggish Snake River became increasingly turbulent on the way upstream, making it difficult to imagine the turn-of-the-twentieth-century stern-wheelers climbing through the white-water rapids, even with the aid of cables. The nimble jetboat noses up to 3,000-year-old Native American petroglyphs painted on the flat rocks, and we spot mountain bighorn sheep hundreds of feet up the cliff face. During the cruise downriver the ship may stop in midstream at an island set against a backdrop of orange and red rock cliffs. Underfoot, the ground cover exhibits the colors of yellow rabbit brush, pink and gray buckwheat, blue aster, and loose brown tumbleweed.

Address/Phone: Lindblad Expeditions, 720 Fifth Avenue, New York, NY 10019; (212) 765–7740 or (800) 397–3348; fax: (212) 265–3370; e-mail: explore@expeditions.com; www.expeditions.com

The Ship: *Sea Lion* (and *Sea Bird*) were built in 1981 and have a gross tonnage of 99.7, a special U.S. Coast Guard measurement, a length of 152 feet, and a draft of 8 feet.

Passengers: 70; ages fifty and up, almost exclusively Americans

Dress: Casual at all times

Officers/Crew: American

Cabins: 37 tiny outside cabins, 26 opening onto the promenade and 5 on the lower deck with a portlight high in the room

Fare: $$$

What's included: All shore excursions, entrance fees, tips to guides ashore, port charges

What's not included: Airfares, alcoholic beverages, tips to crew

Other itineraries: In addition to the above seven-night Columbia and Snake itinerary, offered in May, September, and October, the *Sea Lion* and *Sea Bird* cruise up to Alaska and south to the Sea of Cortez and Baja California. The *Polaris* is based in the Galápagos Islands, and the deep-sea expedition ship *Endeavour,* the former *Caledonian Star,* sails to Antarctica, South America, and Europe.

AMERICAN WEST STEAMBOAT COMPANY'S
Queen of the West
Stern-wheeler Cruise up the Columbia and Snake

 The American West Steamboat Company began trading in the Pacific Northwest in 1995, operating a diesel-driven stern-wheeler along three rivers that served as regular trading routes since the middle of the nineteenth century. Although considerably smaller than the Delta Queen Steamboat Company's three stern-wheelers, the ships' ambience and purpose are similar, a destination-oriented cruise with a strong onboard musical program designed for older Americans.

The 163-passenger *Queen of the West* and her new consort, the 235-passenger *Empress of the North*, ply the Columbia, Snake, and Willamette Rivers on seven-night voyages, some longer, nearly year-round, offering the longest cruise season and the most sailings of any operator. The itinerary and the shore programs differ from some seasonal cruise operators, and the boats are dedicated to this part of the world with the decor appropriately and attractively reflecting Indian and pioneering traditions of the Pacific Northwest.

Externally, the 230-foot *Queen of the West* has a simplified profile of a stern-wheel steamboat while the interiors echo a turn-of-the-twentieth-century style using modern materials. Good reproduction furnishings provide seating in the lounges and cabins, and elaborate metal moldings replicate tin and plaster-style ceilings. A splendid collection of full-color prints of Pacific Northwest Native Americans and early pioneers share corridor and stateroom walls with large framed black-and-white photographs of last century's western river steamboats.

The two principal public rooms, the Columbia Showroom and the Paddlewheel Lounge, are set up for watching the entertainment, a resident trio and pianist and engaging singing groups and guest bands that board for the evening. One night features big band dance music, another a barber shop quartet, and a third country and western. In addition, a historian gives talks from the deck.

The attractive chandeliered dining room seats all passengers at one open sitting, and half the tables are positioned next to windows. The food is consistently good American fare. Dinner begins with a salad, then includes soup and a choice of three entrees such as grilled salmon, lobster tail, a New York–cut steak, or half a roast duck, and freshly baked cakes and pies or a fruit plate. All breads and pastries are baked on board, and lunch offers a salad, sandwich, or hot entree such as pasta or lasagna. Light continental breakfast, hot dog lunches, and a twenty-four-hour beverage and popcorn service are available in the covered top deck Calliope Bar and Grill. Two decks have a wraparound promenade, and all four passenger decks are linked by a well-used elevator located amidships.

The seventy-three outside cabins, twenty-three with private verandas, are especially large for a vessel of this size. Full-height wooden armoires provide ample storage, and bedside tables have adequate drawer space. All cabins have large-view windows and TVs with a half-dozen cable channels, and a good selection of more recent films are available for use with the VCRs. Queen-size and twin beds are available, and all accommodations have showers.

The Itinerary

The Pacific Northwest's **Columbia** and **Snake Rivers** are America's second largest system, after the Mississippi and Missouri, in terms of length and area drained. At the beginning of the nineteenth century, Meriwether Lewis and William Clark descended the Columbia and Snake as part of their legendary Western expedition. This cruise retraces a portion of their history-making route.

The *Queen of the West* paddles away from its landing to first cruise the Willamette, passing through downtown Portland, continuing upstream a bit farther, then turning back to join the Columbia. By the next morning the boat enters the beautiful **Columbia River Gorge** and locks through a couple of impressive dams. The Bonneville Dam's lock and its 105-foot vertical lift is 20 feet greater than the Panama Canal's three Gatun Locks combined.

At The Dalles, visit the Columbia Gorge Discovery Center, providing palatable background to the geological origins of the region, Native American history, the Oregon Trail, and the now-controversial damming of the Columbia River. At **Bonneville Dam** see the turbine operations and the salmon fish ladder, and then drive parallel to the river to 620-foot-high **Multnomah Falls.** At the grain port of Umatilla, the route inland follows the Oregon Trail and pays a visit to **Pendleton**'s Rodeo Grounds to watch cowboy roundup activities, and also stops at a Native American Center for a dance program, oral history, and exhibits.

The landscape changes to semiarid steppes, gracefully tapered buttes, and diminishing signs of habitation bordering the Snake River en route upriver to **Lewiston, Idaho.** An excursion is first made to Nez Perce National Historic Park in Indian Territory, and then by jetboat into **Hells Canyon,** the deepest gorge in North America, where there's a good chance to see wildlife and ancient petroglyphs.

Cruising downriver with different stretches seen during daylight hours, a stop is made at **Maryhill,** a mansion turned European and Native American art museum located high on a cliff, and another stop for tasting the great wines of Oregon, Washington, and Idaho, some of which appear on the steamboat's wine list.

Passing through the Columbia River Gorge and landing at Longview, Washington, an excursion drives through the devastated countryside to a viewpoint overlooking the still-active volcano **Mount St.**

Address/Phone: American West Steamboat Company, 2101 Fourth Avenue, Suite 1150, Seattle, WA 98121; (800) 434–1232; fax: (206) 340–0975; www.columbiarivercruise.com

The Ship: *Queen of the West* was built in 1995 and is 230 feet in length with a shallow draft.

Passengers: 163 double occupancy, mostly Americans fifty-five and up

Dress: Casual

Officers/Crew: All American

Cabins: 73, all outside with some large suites and 23 with verandas

Fare: $$$

What's included: Cruise and shore excursions

What's not included: Airfare, port charges, drinks, and tips

Highlights: A great variety of scenery and activities, enjoyed aboard a gallery of Pacific Northwest history

Other itineraries: Besides these seven- and eleven-day Columbia–Snake cruises, which operate between mid-February and late December, the 2003-built *Empress of the North* makes eleven-day one-way Inside Passage cruises between Seattle and Juneau from late May to early September.

Helens, its peak lowered by 1,300 feet in a matter of minutes during a cataclysmic volcanic explosion in May 1980.

The *Queen of the West* ties up at **Astoria,** established as a fur trading post at the mouth of the Columbia River by John Jacob Astor, and today it's a lumber port dotted with seventy-one Victorian buildings listed on the National Register. The landing is adjacent to the Columbia River Maritime Museum, a well-laid-out repository of ship models, historic photographs, paintings, and steamboat relics. The excursion

includes reconstructed **Fort Clatsop,** where Lewis and Clark spent a miserable wet winter in 1805–1806, and an hour's stop at the popular wood-shingled resort of **Cannon Beach** fronting on the Pacific Ocean.

On the last afternoon, the boat sails overnight up the Columbia to the Portland landing for disembarkation. Consider staying a night before or after the cruise to visit the "City of Roses," its well-tended parks and gardens, and thriving nineteenth- and early-twentieth-century downtown.

ST. LAWRENCE CRUISE LINES'
Canadian Empress
Steamboating the St. Lawrence River

St. Lawrence Cruise Lines is a family operation based in Kingston, Ontario, that started in 1981 with the sixty-four-passenger *Canadian Empress*. Externally, the ship is odd-looking, whereas her interiors faithfully re-create the warm atmosphere of a turn-of-the-twentieth century Canadian steamboat. The Grand Saloon on Rideau Deck is a fine period combination dining room and lounge, from its pressed white tin ceiling to the red, orange, and yellow Axminster carpet.

Meals aboard may be one sitting or two, depending on the shore program. Main dishes at lunch and dinner include fresh fillet of perch, tender roast pork, and succulent roast beef. The soups are uniformly good, but the salads rather nondescript, and desserts are simple cakes, pastry, and puddings. The young waitresses, in keeping with the period decor, wear attractive long, formal, dark-blue skirts and white blouses at night and blue-and-white sailor suits during the day. Entertainment features a band

for dancing and sing-along, followed by a shore-side campfire weenie roast.

The thirty-two cabins are priced in four different categories, but twenty-eight are virtually identical, differing only in location. Most have parallel twin beds (four offer double beds) with the pillow-end set beneath the windows that open. The rooms are small, but during the day there is ample floor space, with one bed raised and the other becoming a sofa. Rosewood trim, red curtains and bedspreads, white walls, and white tin ceiling lend a pleasant air. All the cabins, apart from the four most expensive, have a pipe rack and hooks rather than a closet, and a curtain, rather than a separate stall, shields the shower from the toilet.

Observation decks placed fore and aft provide sheltered open-air viewing. The Sun Deck, running nearly the full length of the ship, offers yellow-and-white canvas directors chairs and yellow chaise longues, a relaxing setting to watch a game on the giant checkerboard, the pieces maneuvered with the help of hooked poles.

The Itinerary

The *Canadian Empress* sails from **Quebec City,** with its ramparts, city walls, and Old World charm, for a rural stretch of the St. Lawrence punctuated with village churches. Montreal's Market Basin is conveniently situated for visiting **Old Montreal,** and soon after sailing, the ship enters the **St. Lawrence Seaway**'s first set of seven locks that create a series of controlled channels and pools. In minutes the *Empress* rises from the gloomy depths of a dank chamber on a flood of gravity-flow water to reveal the broad countryside beyond. Shortly after completing the transit through St. Catherine's Lock, the *Canadian Empress* ties up, still within sight of the city lights atop Mont Royal. Great Lakes iron ore and grain carriers slide silently by during the night, gently rocking the little ship.

Upper Canada Village, highlight of the trips ashore, is a composite of houses, public and farm buildings, and churches spanning more than a hundred years of Canadian architecture. This working community came about in 1961, to save some-thing important from each of the eight towns that would soon be submerged by St. Lawrence Seaway construction. In the circa-1800 Ross-Baffin House, women explain how to make colorful quilts for the village beds and how to hook rugs for the floors.The Greek Revival Chrysler Hall offers a beautiful slide presentation showing Upper Canada Village at work and at play in all four seasons. Next door the bakery ovens produce fresh loaves of bread that will soon appear on *Canadian Empress* tables at lunchtime.

Fort Wellington served as a British garrison during the War of 1812 and later as a Royal Canadian Rifle Regiment to protect shipping. On the U.S. side the Frederic Remington Art Museum displays the master of Western American Art's paintings, watercolors, and bronzes depicting heroic and savage scenes of cowboys, soldiers, and Indians. The Antique Boat Museum houses the largest collection of inland water recreational boats in the world.

On the final day the *Canadian Empress* cruises among the fairyland of the rocky

---

Address/Phone: St. Lawrence Cruise Lines, 253 Ontario Street, Kingston, Ontario, Canada K7L 2Z4; (613) 549–8091 or (800) 267–7868; fax: (613) 549–8410; www.StLawrenceCruise Lines.com

The Ship: *Canadian Empress,* built in 1981, has a displacement tonnage of 321, a length of 108 feet, and a shallow draft of 4.9 feet.

Passengers: 66; age fifty-five and up, divided between Americans and Canadians

Dress: Casual; jacket and maybe a tie one night

Officers/Crew: Canadian

Cabins: 32; tiny but all outside with windows, a few forward with portholes

Fares: $$

What's included: Cruise, shore excursions

What's not included: Airfare and, if required, rail fare to embarkation port, drinks, tips

Highlights: Varied scenery, the Seaway, Upper Canada Village, friendly ambience on ship

Other itineraries: In addition to this six-night cruise from Quebec to Kingston, the ship also offers five-night cruises between Kingston and Ottawa. The season runs from early May to the end of October.

and wooded **Thousand Islands,** on which stand an enormous variety of simple and elaborate, shingled, clapboard, and stone summer houses. The American Narrows once attracted Helena Rubenstein, Mary Pickford, Irving Berlin, and John Jacob Astor. The granddaddy of all, **Boldt Castle**—a huge eclectic, medieval-style fortress—was never finished, and a trip ashore explores 120 rooms, formal gardens, and outbuildings. The cruise ends approaching **Kingston,** its well-proportioned skyline punctuated by the attractive limestone buildings of the Royal Military College, Old Port Henry, and City Hall.

ONTARIO WATERWAY CRUISES'
Kawartha Voyageur
Exploring the Trent-Severn Waterway

 In 1982 a farming family named Ackert went into the cruising business by offering overnight trips here and along the 125-mile Rideau Canal, the latter connecting Kingston and Ottawa, Canada's former and present capital. Between mid-May and mid-October, the forty-five-passenger *Kawartha Voyageur* offers three different five- and six-night itineraries.

At first sight docked at a downtown Peterborough marina, the trim blue-and-white vessel resembles an overgrown houseboat. As you step aboard, the main deck corridor leads to twenty-three outside cabins, minute by deep-sea cruise ship standards. Twenty-one doubles are fitted with twin beds, open shelves, pipe racks for hanging clothes, a curtained-off sink and toilet, and a large screened window that opens. Commodious showers with dressing rooms are located at the end of the passageway. Two additional cabins cater to the handicapped and single traveler. On the deck above, a cheerful observation lounge occupies the forward end with a one-sitting dining room amidships and a tiny library alcove off to the side. Aft is the galley and crew quarters for the captain, first mate, and an all-female crew. An open deck above runs the full length, and additional covered decks are located fore and aft on the main deck.

The family butcher provides the dinner meats, such as baked ham with candied yams, chicken breasts in melted Swiss cheese with brown and wild rice, and farm sausages with sauerkraut. The bran muffins, banana bread, lemon meringue pie, and English trifle are all baked onboard. Though there is no choice of menu, most passengers eat this kind of food at home, so the only "no thank you" would be for seconds. On average the mostly retired passengers are equally divided between Canadians and Americans who come to enjoy a slow-paced, scenic cruise with other genial folks. Many return to complete all three itineraries—Peterborough–Big Chute, Peterborough–Kingston, and Kingston–Ottawa.

The Itinerary
Embarking at **Peterborough,** Ontario, then not an hour into the cruise, the *Kawartha Voyageur* encounters a massive concrete structure and slides into an open chamber, and as the gates close behind, several small boats settle into a second parallel tub 65 feet above. Without getting too complicated, an extra foot of water in the upper chamber causes it to descend while raising its opposite, and soon passengers standing

at the stern are peering over a precipice to the channel far below.

Captain Marc Ackert, along with his brother John, constitute the second generation to own and operate the boat, while their wives, Robin and Joy, do the supplying and run the home office in **Orillia,** the largest town we visited. When the boat is tied up at a marina, they often show up, with one or more children in tow, to bring needed stores and to socialize. During the day intrepid Captain Marc Ackert takes us ashore to the nineteenth-century home of Stephen Leacock, Canada's Mark Twain, warns us to sit down when we are about to pass under a low bridge, points out an osprey nest, offers freshly baked cookies to lock masters to speed our way through twenty-two locks, and entertains us at the keyboard one night after dinner. He lets us loose on small canal towns to shop or search for historical curiosities and tells us when we might go for a walk between closely spaced locks. We tie up at night, usually adjacent to a quiet park, and get under way after breakfast, threading along wooded waterways dotted with summer camps and through areas devoid of human habitation. Then without warning, the boat comes to a vast expanse of water, makes the crossing, and enters yet another twisting channel.

On the final morning we dock adjacent to the **Big Chute Marine Railway,** an ingenious mechanism for lifting boats around a Severn River waterfall. Boats slide into a submerged transfer platform, and once they're tied down, the structure rises on rails out of the water, crosses a highway protected by gates and flashing lights, and then descends to settle back into the river below. What takes five days to cover by water is but two and a half hours by bus, returning passengers to their cars or to connecting transportation.

Address/Phone: Ontario Waterway Cruises, Box 6, Orillia, Ontario, L3V 6H9 Canada; reservations: (800) 561–5767; inquiries: (705) 327–5767; fax: (705) 327–5304; e-mail: info@ontariowaterwaycruises.com; www.ontariowaterwaycruises.com

The Ship: *Kawartha Voyageur* was built in 1983, enlarged in 1995, and has a length of 120 feet and a shallow draft.

Passengers: 45; mostly fifty-five and up, split between Americans and Canadians

Dress: Casual at all times

Officers/Crew: Canadian

Cabins: 23; 21 tiny twins, 1 handicapped-equipped, and 1 single

Fare: $$

What's included: Cruise, tips, port charges, excursions. and bus back to the starting point

What's not included: Airfare, drinks

Highlights: Scenic waterway cruising

Other itineraries: Besides this five-night cruise between Peterborough and Big Chute, operating between mid-May and mid-October in both directions, the *Kawartha Voyageur* makes five-night cruises between Kingston and Ottawa and Kingston and Peterborough.

ATLANTIC OCEAN

CELEBRITY CRUISES'
Zenith and *Horizon*
Bermuda Cruising

 Celebrity Cruises began as an upscale offshoot by the Greek Chandris family, and now the company is part of, but separate from, Royal Caribbean Cruises, Ltd. The *Zenith*'s and *Horizon*'s understated elegance comes through in the beautifully appointed, tastefully decorated, and immaculately maintained public spaces and cabins. Service is polished but not pretentious.

Celebrity ships all have a common layout that is apparent throughout the fleet, whether it is on the 47,000-ton *Zenith* or the larger 73,000-ton *Galaxy* and *Mercury* described in the Caribbean sections. Aboard the *Zenith*, the ship described here, Deck 12, atop the ship, offers sports facilities with a jogging track and very recently expanded Health Club facilities that look out over the ocean. Deck 11 has the pool amidships and a lido dining area aft, including an outdoor grill and twenty-four-hour pizza service with cabin delivery in a cardboard box. The Fleet Bar, located above the bridge, offers a magnificent 180-degree view, a quiet spot during the daytime and for dancing in the evenings. The room pays homage to older Chandris ships.

The two-tiered show lounge occupies the forward space on Decks 7 and 8 and has excellent sight lines no matter where you choose to sit. Amidships on Deck 8 is Harry's Tavern, a wonderful European-style piano bar. Michael's Club is Celebrity's answer to the old-fashioned smoking room, beautifully appointed with overstuffed chairs and a steward present who will hand roll cigars. Outside the dining room the Rendez-Vous Lounge and Tastings, a champagne and caviar bar, are gathering places for a drink before dinner.

Food on Celebrity ships rates among the best available at this moderate price level. The ingredients are fresh, and the presentation is terrific and sometimes fanciful. Delectable soups and wonderful seafood and beef entrees are overseen by Michel Roux, who has been Celebrity's head of catering since 1990 and runs his own three-star (Michelin) restaurants.

If you want nonstop excitement and constant action, do not pay for passage on a Celebrity vessel, where daytime activities tend to be subdued, and evening entertainment in the show lounge is limited by the Bermudian government's restriction against use of professional entertainers while the ship is in port. Instead a variety of musical events to listen or dance to takes place in each lounge every evening.

Most cabins on the *Zenith* are identical, with the exception of the two Royal Suites and twenty Deluxe Suites, and none have balconies. The cabins measure 172 square feet, and regardless of whether you select an inside or outside stateroom, they are tastefully decorated with color-coordinated bedspreads, curtains, and upholstery and have two lower twin-size beds, which can be pushed together into one large bed or arranged in an L configuration for more floor space. A dressing table with drawers doubles as a desk, and there's a television, telephone, radio, safe, minibar, and glass-top sitting table with two chairs. Bathrooms are larger than average, and hair dryers are provided.

The Itinerary
Cruises begin with a grand departure from **New York** or **Philadelphia** and offer two nights and a day at sea to settle into the ship's routine before docking in **Hamilton**

at Front Street. From this convenient location it's easy to explore **Bermuda** on a tour, by taxi, moped, scooter, bicycle, or by a well-organized bus and ferry network. Rental cars are not available in Bermuda. Duty-free shopping in Hamilton is good, with high-quality clothing, perfumes, bone china, and Irish linens available for sale in attractive settings.

The pastel-colored residences make a pretty picture on foot and when seen from afar by ferry to the **Royal Naval Dockyard,** which houses the maritime museum and is a center for crafts, shops, and nightclubs.

Nearby **Somerset** has lots of restaurants and more shops.

Understandably, the pink coral beaches are a major draw, as is the snorkeling amid well-developed, beautiful reefs that offer a great variety of sea life and fascinating shipwrecks, some at snorkeling depths. Windsurfing, fishing, golf, tennis, and horseback riding may all be arranged by calling around. You can also hike the **Bermuda Railway Trail** from just outside Hamilton in the direction of **St. George,** another port of call, and Somerset.

Address/Phone: Celebrity Cruises, 1050 Caribbean Way, Miami, FL 33132; (305) 539–6000 or (800) 437–3111; www.celebritycruises.com

The Ship: *Zenith* was built in 1992, has a gross tonnage of 47,255, a length of 681 feet, and a draft of 24 feet. *Horizon* was built in 1990, has a gross tonnage of 46,811, and the same length and draft.

Passengers: *Zenith* 1,374; *Horizon* 1,354; mostly American couples in their late thirties to sixties; some families, too

Dress: Suits or tuxes for formal nights; jackets for informal night; slacks and collared shirts for casual nights

Officers/Crew: Greek officers; international crew

Cabins: *Zenith* 687, of which 541 are outside; none have verandas; *Horizon* 677, of which 529 are outside; none have verandas.

Fare: $$

What's included: Cruise fare only

What's not included: Airfare, port charges, tips, drinks, shore excursions

Highlights: Stylish ship and great menus; Bermuda as a destination

Other itineraries: In addition to these seven-night Bermuda cruises from New York and Philadelphia, operating between April and October, the fleet also cruises the Caribbean, South America, Alaska, and Europe.

SEVEN SEAS'
Seven Seas Navigator
Bermuda-bound plus Norfolk—from Your Balcony

 The 33,000-ton *Seven Seas Navigator*, carrying just 490 passengers, is ultraspacious and an ideal size for a luxurious cruise, yet small enough to be intimate and large enough to offer plenty of places to roost. Furthermore, with one-and-a-half crew members for every guest, service is a high point, and so is the food in two open-seating restaurants. This ship will provide the most luxurious way to see the island of Bermuda.

The attractive decor is a marriage of classic and modern design, autumn hues, and deep blues, with contemporary wooden furniture, chairs upholstered in soft leather, draperies of silk brocade, walls covered in suede, dark-wood paneling, lighter burled veneer, and the use of decorative stainless steel. The ship's hull was originally built to become a Russian spy ship, but when bought, it was integrated into a passenger design and, with three additional decks added, developed a somewhat ungainly and top-heavy profile.

Most public rooms are found on Decks 6 and 7, just aft of the three-story atrium and main elevator bank. A well-stocked library and computer center with e-mail access is adjacent to a card room. Across the way, the cozy Navigator Lounge, paneled in mahogany and cherry wood, is a popular place for predinner cocktails. Next door is the Connoisseur Club cigar lounge, a masculine wood-paneled room with umber leather chairs. Down the hall is the roomier Stars Lounge, with a long, black-granite curved bar and clusters of oversize ocean-blue armchairs, where a live duo sings pop numbers nightly for listening and dancing. The two-story Seven Seas show lounge features sizable Vegas-style song and dance reviews.

High up and aft on Deck 12, Galileo's lounge, surrounded by windows on three sides, takes on a soft golden glow in the evening and becomes the venue for a pianist. On a balmy, starlit night, the doors open to the deck, creating a most romantic scene for dancing. By day, Galileo's sees use for continental breakfast, afternoon tea, and seminars. Another deck up, forward-facing Vista observation lounge is a great viewing spot, and one can step directly out to an open space over the bridge.

The spa vendor Judith Jackson provides seventeen first-rate treatments, including a relaxing twenty-minute hair and scalp oil massage and a one-hour four-hand massage, performed by a staff of five in six rooms. A pair of hot tubs share the midships pool area with a mezzanine of deck chairs above, and some afternoons a five-piece band plays oldies near the pool bar.

Elaborate and elegant meals in both the formal Compass Rose dining room and the more casual Portofino Grill restaurant are served by a mostly European staff. In both venues, red and white house wines are complimentary at dinner. Meals in the Compass Rose are served in a single open seating and start with appetizers like oven-roasted pheasant salad or avocado fritters in a spicy sauce, with main entrees including enticing zucchini-wrapped chicken breast stuffed with olives and tomatoes or herb-crusted roast leg of lamb.

The Portofino Grill serves a buffet-style breakfast and lunch and a sit-down, reservations-only dinner in an intimate setting with tables for two or four curtained off from the self-service section. In the evenings the grill is transformed into a cozy, dimly lit Northern Italian restaurant with antipasti choices of marinated salmon rings or bresaola carpaccio with parmesan cheese and mushrooms. The pasta course may feature a jumbo prawn risotto, and main courses include a grilled lobster or osso buco.

Elegant suites are cloaked in shades of deep gold, beige, and burnt-orange with caramel-toned wood furniture. Nearly 90 percent have private balconies, the highest for any ship until the 100-percent-suite *Seven Seas Mariner* arrived in 2001 followed by the *Seven Seas Voyager* in 2003.The standard suites are a roomy 301 square feet, plus a 55-square-foot balcony; and the eighteen top suites range from 448 square feet to 1,067 square feet, not including balconies. In addition to palatial marble-covered bathrooms, every abode has a wide walk-in closet, a tall built-in dresser, safe, terry robes, a TV/VCR, and minibar stocked with two complimentary bottles of wine or spirits. Twenty-four-hour room service includes a full-course dinner served in the sitting area or out on the private balcony facing the sea.

The Itinerary

Seven Seas Cruises is new to Bermuda, and the *Seven Seas Navigator* spent its first season, in 2003, providing by far the most high-end ship to serve the upscale Atlantic isle on a weekly summer-season basis. The ship also leaves **New York** midweek, offering its passengers an exclusive berth at Front Street, Hamilton, for a two-day stay. On Day Three, the ship moves around to **St. George,** the second oldest English city on the globe and a much quieter location.

It's the usual two-nights-and-one-day sail from New York to the island, ringed by the world's northernmost coral reefs. The ground coral and sand mix to produce the pink beaches. Island travel is by bus, taxi, ferry, bicycle, and moped as there are no rental cars available, a good thing as the roads are twisty and narrow.

Shore excursions include deep-sea fishing for yellowfin tuna, marlin, and wahoo; glass-bottom boat tours to see the fish life and colorful coral formations; a Bermuda National Trust tour to an eighteenth-century

---

Address/Phone: Seven Seas Cruises, 600 Corporate Drive, Suite 410, Ft. Lauderdale, FL 33334; (954) 776–6123; (800) 285–1835; brochures: (800) 477–7500; fax: (954) 772–3763; www.rssc.com

The Ship: *Seven Seas Navigator* was completed in 1999, has a gross tonnage of 33,000, a length of 560 feet, and a draft of 21 feet.

Passengers: 490, mostly Americans forty-five and up

Dress: Formal, informal, and casual nights

Officers/Crew: European officers and a largely European crew

Cabins: 245, all outside, and 196 with balconies

Fare: $$$$

What's included: Cruise fare, gratuities, wines with dinner, soft drinks and juices, stocked minibar

What's not included: Port charges, airfare, alcoholic drinks, shore excursions

Highlights: Spacious ship with nearly all balconies, top European service

Other itineraries: In addition to this seven-day Bermuda cruise, which operates on most weeks between May and September, the *Seven Seas Navigator* also undertakes some New England–Canada cruises during this period, and *Seven Seas Mariner, Seven Seas Voyager, Radisson Diamond, Paul Gauguin,* and seasonally chartered *Explorer II* together cover the entire world.

house and gardens and museum; and an art and architecture tour including the Anglican cathedral and, if desired, the 151-step climb up the bell tower for a rewarding island view and several art gallery visits to see contemporary Bermuda art. The ship can arrange a day with changing facilities at Elbow Beach. Although you can take a bike tour along the Railway Trail that runs almost continuously from one end of the island to the other, you can also do this yourself on foot. In many cases there is no need to backtrack, as the bus and ferry system will bring you directly back to Hamilton from roadside stops and several landings not far from the trail. Day travel passes covering all public transportation are available for sale,

a convenience and sometimes a saving.

Leaving Bermuda, the *Navigator* sails to **Norfolk,** passing over the Chesapeake Bay Tunnel into Hampton Roads, one of the world's largest harbors and the site of a U.S. naval base. From the pier, a ferry crosses the Elizabeth River to Portsmouth, a residential suburb for Norfolk with some beautiful eighteenth- and nineteenth-century houses all within easy walking distance of the landing.

Excursions fan out to **Colonial Williamsburg; Jamestown,** the first permanent European settlement in what became the thirteen colonies; and Revolutionary War–era **Yorktown.** Following a day here, the *Navigator* sails overnight back to New York City and disembarkation.

CUNARD LINE'S
Queen Mary 2
The Ultimate Crossing: New York to England on the Largest Ship in the World

 Will this be the ship we've been waiting for, to cross the Atlantic in the high-style manner enjoyed by previous generations? The most anticipated ship in decades, the *Queen Mary 2* is a ship of superlatives, including being the largest and most expensive passenger ship ever built. The first true ocean liner to appear in thirty-four years, the *QM2* crosses the Atlantic starting in 2004 with her own particular mix of historic Cunard tradition and modern cruise ship amenities.

For decades, we had accepted as a given that the *QE2* would be the last of the great transatlantic liners. So the ship many thought would never be built, the *Queen Mary 2,* is extraordinary by many measures. Her massive size—more than twice the gross tonnage of her famous fleet mate— seems almost impossible to grasp, and her

sharply raked prow recalls those storied ships of state such as the French liners *Normandie* and *France*. Built with a lean hull that has both the strength and the speed necessary to withstand the sometimes brutal Atlantic weather, the *Mary* is a true ocean liner and stands in stark contrast to the rest of the world's cruise ship fleet designed for placid seas.

While the *QE2* has developed a deserved and intensely loyal following, her advanced age and the absence of the latest trends and facilities have kept away travelers who felt this ship might be too old or, worse, too old-fashioned. Enter the *Queen Mary 2,* which builds on the traditions of the *QE2* and the liners before her while breaking new ground, offering passengers the cherished traditions of an Atlantic crossing but in a more updated and huge new version.

Cunard designed the *Queen Mary 2* to

wow the world and reign over the seven seas, and it appears that at the outset the line has succeeded. If building the world's largest, longest, and tallest ship in 2003 to be an Atlantic liner wasn't astonishing enough, Cunard has gone a step further in creating a ship that does more than just impress you—it stirs your emotions when first seen from shore. The *QM2* is a technical and stylish masterpiece, and seeing her charcoal gray hull crowned by the Cunard orange-red funnel sail past New York's skyline will be thrilling and, for some who recall the former Cunard giants, even timeless.

Inside, the *Queen Mary 2* borrows heavily from past classic ocean liners, with public rooms on a grand scale and ceiling heights 50 percent higher than those found on other ships. A traditional Winter Garden serves as the formal setting for the oh-so-English ritual of afternoon tea, and pampered pooches can travel in style in one of the few kennels left on the high seas.

With so many associating crossings with glamorous evenings, ballroom dancing, and delectable dining, the *Mary* fulfills these fantasies with a main dining room that soars three stories and features a grand staircase for those arrivals wishing to make their entry known to all. The domed Queen's Lounge, a dedicated ballroom, boasts the largest dance floor at sea, where ladies in long gowns and their tuxedoed gentlemen partners play Ginger and Fred to twirl the night away.

A roster of lectures and seminars will see interested passengers flooding into the theater all day long to take in topics such as the great liners that came before, finding the right actor for the lead part in a film, and ever-changing U.S.–Russian relations. Some speakers will be famous, such as John Cleese and David Bowie, and others less known but equally entertaining and enlightening.

A favorite activity on any crossing, communing with the restless ocean as it sweeps past, will get a big boost on the new

Queen. A traditional teak promenade, wide enough for constitutional walkers parading side by side past a row of wooden steamer chairs, wraps completely around the ship and is wind protected approaching the bow. The classic scene of rugged-up passengers gazing out to sea and walkers exchanging smiles will be alive and well for years to come.

So too the *Mary* answers the cry of those who want today's ship, with a virtually unlimited choice of activities to experience during the six-day Atlantic run. The Canyon Ranch Spa and its staff of fifty attendants qualify as the largest and most indulgent facility ever to put to sea. Families will discover the *QM2's* five swimming pools, a sheltered area for all manner of deck sports, and elaborate children's facilities, complete with an exclusive pool. The high-tech show lounge presents extravagant musical and stage productions, and a separate theater hosts lectures and first-run movies; it can then be magically transformed into the first seagoing planetarium for night sky extravaganzas.

In continuing with Cunard ocean liner tradition, your cabin category determines your restaurant. Most will dine at two seatings in the massive Britannia Restaurant, while those occupying higher category cabins and suites will have access to the more intimate Princess and Queens Grills. Additional dining venues will be found throughout the ship, including a Todd English Mediterranean restaurant on a poolside terrace overlooking the stern and a casual nest of eateries offering five different national menus.

Within the towering superstructure, public rooms come in all sizes and in many locations. Although the *QE2* lacks a proper observation lounge, the *Queen Mary 2's* Commodore Lounge has addressed that absence by providing a quiet piano bar setting with the dramatic sight of the ship's bow slicing the Atlantic swells. The professionally staffed library and an adjoining cafe occupy a similar high-up perch. To round out the public rooms, there's a two-level nightclub that stays open to the wee hours, a sprawling casino, a champagne bar, and an English pub with the best of Britain's most prized brews.

Despite her tremendous size, the passenger list numbers just 2,620 or fully a thousand souls fewer than on a mass-market ship, making the *Mary* one of the most spacious ships afloat with some of the largest standard cabins, not to mention huge suites. Seventy-three percent will feature private balconies, and as a safeguard against North Atlantic wave damage, three balconied decks are recessed into the steel hull. For those with unlimited budgets, grand suites include duplex apartments overlooking the stern and others stretching across the front of the ship a few decks below the bridge.

Life on the Atlantic run has changed continually since the first Cunarder, the *Britannia,* set out from Liverpool on July 4, 1840, propelled by primitive paddle wheels and carrying a live cow to provide milk. Founder Sir Samuel Cunard could never have envisioned such a ship as the *Queen Mary 2,* but it's doubtless he would be pleased with perhaps the ultimate company flagship, which blends the modern and high-tech with the storied history and romance of the North Atlantic.

The Itinerary

Providing approximately seventeen crossings a year between New York and Southampton, the *Queen Mary 2* will travel the world's most famous sea-lane in six nights. Unlike a cruise, this is a voyage from A to B, with the New World or the Old as the distant then rapidly approaching focus of the passage.

Veterans of North Atlantic sea travel prefer to sail westbound when clocks are retarded one hour on five of the six nights, creating a more genteel twenty-five-hour day. Sailing from **Southampton** at about 5:00 P.M., passengers line the railings to

Address/Phone: Cunard Line, 6100 Blue Lagoon Drive, Suite 400, Miami, FL 33126; (305) 463–3000 or (800) 7–CUNARD; fax: (305) 463–3010; www.cunard.com

The Ship: *Queen Mary 2*, completed in 2003, has a gross tonnage of 150,000, a length of 1,132 feet, and a draft of 33 feet.

Passengers: 2,620, Americans, British, Europeans, and other nationalities, all ages especially during the school holidays

Dress: Four formal nights and jacket and tie the first and last nights

Officers/Crew: British officers, international crew, British and American social staff

Cabins: 1,310 cabins, 1,017 outside, 879 with verandas, 12 with atrium view

Fare: $$–$$$$$

What's included: Cruise fare, port charges, one-way economy airfare between U.S. gateways and London

What's not included: Other airfares, excursions, tips

Highlights: Crossing aboard the world's largest and best-known ship

Other itineraries: Besides these regular transatlantic crossings between New York and Southampton, England, the *Queen Mary 2* cruises from New York, Fort Lauderdale, and Southampton. The *Queen Elizabeth 2* now cruises mainly from Southampton, making a couple of crossings a year to connect with the Christmas/New Year's and the annual world cruise, while the *Caronia* sails almost exclusively from Southampton until November 2004, when she leaves the fleet to sail for Saga Cruises.

watch their ship sail down Southampton Water, make the dogleg past **Isle of Wight,** and move into the Solent to disembark the pilot before heading west into the **English Channel.** With the *QM2* gathering speed, passengers begin heading below to dress for dinner, informal on the first night, and the focus inside shifts away from the land to the open **Atlantic** for the next five continuous days.

Time seems to slow without the frenzied pace of most cruises with a new port to face each morning, yet the days quickly melt together and disappear in a delightful blur of lively bar conversations, a steward pulling out your chair at the dinner table, so many choices on the menu, tinkling champagne glasses, entertaining stage productions, and fresh sea air at sunset. Passengers contentedly plan out their days only to have them slip away surprisingly quickly into the trailing wake. Racing alone across the Atlantic aboard an incomparable blend of power and speed, reality seems light-years away.

But it ends all too soon. On the last night, an air of nervous anticipation begins to rise as passengers prepare for the hassle of reentry into the real world. Before dawn the next morning, the decks are again thronged to partake in one of life's most thrilling experiences—a **New York** arrival by ocean liner. First-timers gathering on the afterdecks feel increasing concern that the funnel may not clear the **Verrazano-Narrows Bridge,** but it does with a scant 10 feet of clearance between span and ship. Soon, the lighted silhouette of the **Statue of Liberty** appears to port, followed by **Ellis Island,** the entry station for millions of previous arrivals.

Now in the **Hudson River,** the *QM2* slips past the skyscrapers of **Lower Manhattan,** providing a city tour from the water with views straight inland along cross-town streets, still relatively quiet and free of congestion so early in the morning. Gradually the ship slows and begins to angle between two finger piers to tie with bow pointed directly at **Midtown Manhattan** just steps away. Filing ashore, passengers turn to have one last look at what is now affectionately their ship before slumping into the backseat of a New York City yellow cab to take them to the next appointment. The *Mary* will rest but a few hours before setting off again for that classic dash across the North Atlantic.

CUNARD LINE'S
Queen Elizabeth 2
A Cult Crossing for Winter-Weather Aficionados

Although the *Queen Mary 2* has assumed most transatlantic sailings, the *Queen Elizabeth 2* still makes two crossings a year, in April on the last leg of the world cruise from Southampton to New York, and again in mid-December to operate the Christmas/New Year's cruise and to start the world cruise. It's the last that draws winter-weather aficionados, some like me who come every year.

December is a most unlikely month for choosing to sail across the North Atlantic, yet most years, Cunard's *Queen Elizabeth 2* is nearly fully booked. One couple I know makes their seasonal move from the cold of merry England to their warm winter abode in Florida via the port of Fort Lauderdale, the second call after New York. A dealer in ocean liner memorabilia returns by sea from an annual visit to Europe loaded with new treasures. Others have high hopes for stormy weather, and usually they are not disappointed.

One recent year, the QE2 had experienced the most continually rough passage in its thirty-five-year history. If there are low pressure systems en route upon sailing from Southampton, the Quarter Deck chart may show a rhumb line route running southwest from the English Channel to the Azores, then directly west to New York, avoiding the stormy northern track. With the ship's high speed, the extra 200 nautical miles will not affect an on-time arrival in New York. But the southerly route does not always result in a calm sailing, and waves exploding over the bow can be a most dramatic sight, followed by a rise and fall and wobble as the hull flexes to the uneven seas. Creaks within remind you that you are aboard a ship that knows these waters well.

Typically, the passengers are almost equally divided between British and North Americans, plus a goodly number of Germans and peripatetic Australians, who seem to be everywhere these days. The Brits like this preholiday crossing for shopping in New York before flying back to England.

With no ports of call, life at sea unfolds for five uninterrupted days, and how one spends the time varies as widely as the passenger makeup.

With her strong hull, variety of public spaces, and teak promenade decks, the QE2 is truly a liner well suited for the Atlantic run. The ship is more formal on a crossing, with four straight nights when tuxedos are in the majority. The focus is never the next day's port, but rather the New or Old World at either end, blissfully several days away.

As a holdover from the former class system, your cabin grade determines your restaurant. While the menus are basically the same throughout, there is a noticeable difference in service and ambience. The Mauretania restaurant is the largest and

---

Address/Phone: Cunard Line, 6100 Blue Lagoon Drive, Suite 400, Miami, FL 33126; (305) 463–3000 or (800) 7–CUNARD; fax: (305) 463–3010; www.cunardline.com

The Ship: Queen Elizabeth 2 was built in 1969. It has a gross tonnage of 70,327, a length of 963 feet, and a deep draft of 32 feet.

Passengers: 1,740; Americans, British, and Europeans of all ages

Dress: Formal on the middle four nights, with almost all passengers in the grills wearing tuxedos; informal the first and last night

Officers/Crew: British officers; international crew

Cabins: 925, in a wide variety of shapes and sizes, 150 singles, 30 with verandas. Cabin category determines your restaurant.

Fare: $$$ to $$$$$

What's included: Cruise fare, transfers, and return airfare

What's not included: Port charges, drinks, tips

Highlights: A true Atlantic crossing; social life and a wide variety of activities onboard

Other itineraries: In addition to this Atlantic crossing offered in April and December, the QE2 sails mostly from Southampton to cruise the Caribbean, Mediterranean, Canary Islands, or Europe. January to April, the ship undertakes her annual world cruise.

offers two traditional seatings. One category above is the single-sitting Caronia, resplendent in mahogany wood trim after a December 1999 makeover. The ship's smallest restaurants, the Britannia and Princess Grills, both seat just over one hundred people, and ordering off the menu is an added feature. At the very top is the Queens Grill, complete with its own private lounge. The three grills provide an unmistakable feeling of exclusivity, and each is reached by a private entrance. The Lido Restaurant provides three casual meals a day.

Over the years, the *QE2* has undergone many renovations and refits, transforming a product of the late 1960s into a celebration of the mid-1930s. The ship has never looked better. Of particular note is the Chart Room, a wonderful transatlantic setting adorned with the *Queen Mary's* original piano.

There is an amazing variety of spaces onboard, from elegant, large rooms to cozy corners in bars. The Queens Room, the ship's ballroom, boasts one of the two biggest dance floors at sea and is a cherished venue for a formal afternoon tea. An elaborate library and bookshop are supervised by professional librarians. The 550-seat, two-story theater screens films and hosts lectures by well-known experts on topics ranging from maritime history to America's influence on Russian culture. The two-story Grand Lounge is used for cabaret and play productions. The Golden Lion pub supplies beer aficionados contentment well into the night.

Outside shuffleboard, a driving range, deck tennis, and basketball keep the active happy, while a Nursery and Teens Club provides reassurance for harried parents. Since the *QE2* is used as relocation transportation, the ship offers a garage and pet kennels.

Cabins come in all shapes and sizes, and with the coupling of the restaurant to your cabin grade, this is a most important choice. The minimum-grade cabins, inside with upper and lower berths, are small and not what one expects on a luxury ship, but they allow the less well-heeled to travel. Cabins increase in size from there, and most have personality with odd shapes and quirky designs. Grill category cabins will have wood paneling, and the original One Deck suites are just gorgeous, complete with walk-in closets, satin-lined walls, and oval-shaped windows.

The Itinerary

Leaving Southampton, the ship sails down Southampton Water, passing the Isle of Wight, into the Solent and out to sea. The romance and appeal of being on the immense North Atlantic becomes unmistakable, and the *QE2* steaming at 26 knots exudes a sense of strength and power.

The North Atlantic in winter is not the sunny Caribbean, yet on a crisp day with the wind whipping off the tops of cresting waves, it is not unusual to see dozens out promenading on Boat Deck, bundling up in a steamer chair with a cup of hot bouillon, shooting baskets, and playing shuffleboard and paddle tennis. Sea air is invigorating, and the buffeting provides a good measure of exercise.

Occasionally, storm petrels are seen following the wake, and a tired bird may land on deck for a few hours' rest. And there's always a chance that a whale may breach, but only keen watchers are rewarded with this spectacle. After dark, it's a lonely figure that inhabits the decks, peering into the inky blackness or gazing up at the sky, which may be forbidding on one night and full of tiny lights the next.

No ship is dressier, and the middle four of six nights are formal, creating an atmosphere that goes against the common grain of dressing down. On the second evening at sea, men, women, and children arrive at the captain's cocktail party proudly wearing their finest, and it is perfectly acceptable to strike up a conversation with someone who looks interesting. That someone, and any of the others, just might reveal why crossing the North Atlantic in December provides a jolly good time.

The cycle of uninterrupted days holds much appeal for the solitary reader or the social being, and for many, the voyage ends too soon and usually very early, with first light just appearing behind the New York skyline. The QE2 slides under the Verrazano-Narrows Bridge, passes the Statue of Liberty, and angles into its West Side berth. Within eight hours, the QE2 will be cleaned, fueled, and victualled for a voyage south to warmer climes, and the rough seas quickly become a memory.

STAR CLIPPERS'
Royal Clipper
Mediterranean to the Caribbean under Sail

 As you approach by tender, five tall bare poles rise above everything else in the harbor, then the full length of a shapely steel hull appears, stretching from a rounded overhang at the stern forward to the angular raked bow. A thick black stripe runs the full length, and black gun-port squares below give the ship an extra sense of importance. If one did not have a passenger ticket in hand, this ship might pass for a man-of-war, or at least a commercial cargo carrier.

The 228-passenger *Royal Clipper*'s purposeful appearance contrasts sharply with its 168-passenger running mates, *Star Flyer* and *Star Clipper*, both resembling large, white-hull racing yachts. The *Royal Clipper* is a full-rigged ship, with square sails on all five masts, while the earlier four-masters are barkentine rigged. At 439 feet, the *Royal Clipper* is 79 feet longer and qualifies as the longest and largest sailing vessel ever built, besting the Russian training ship *Sedov* in length and the German Flying P Line *Preussen* (1902–10) in overall size at 5,000 gross tons. She carries 56,000 square feet of Dacron sail, compared to 36,000 for the *Star Clipper* and *Star Flyer*. The twenty-member deck crew uses electric winches to angle the twenty-six square sails, and electric motors to furl and unfurl the square sails stored in the yardarms and the eleven staysails, four jibs, and one gaff-rigged spanker.

On the Main Deck, an upward sloping observation lounge has a view of the forward deck and sees use for meetings, informal talks, and Internet connections. The main lounge, located amidships, is as comfortable as they come, with banquette, soft couch, and chair seating, a sit-up bar, and a central well that looks down into the dining room two decks below. Through the aft doors, the covered Tropical Bar recalls the earlier pair, as does the paneled Edwardian library with its electric fireplace, though on a much larger scale.

The handsome paneled dining room with brass wall lamps, reached via a freestanding staircase from the lounge, has a large upper level surrounding a central well with some tables and the buffet. Tables are rectangular, round, and banquette style. An omelet chef cooks to order at breakfast, and a carvery features roast beef, ham, and pork at lunch. Seating is open for all meals, and the lunch buffets are the biggest hit. The menu for the first day at sea includes jumbo shrimp, foie gras, artichoke hearts, herring, potato salad, lots of salad fixings, hot and cold salmon, meatballs, and sliced roast beef. The dining room is set low enough so that in any kind of sea, the water splashes washing machine–style over the portholes. For an actual underwater view, Captain Nemos, the gym, spa, tiled Turkish bath, and beauty salon, has lounge seating to the side where one can look for the creatures of the sea.

The deluxe suites are reached by walking along a central mahogany-paneled companionway, with a thick sloping mast penetrating the corridor at the forward end. The luxurious cabins, mahogany-paneled with rosewood framing and molding, contrast with an off-white ceiling and the upper portion of two walls. Pale gold-framed mirrors enlarge the space, and brass-framed windows bring in light to bathe the far corner sitting alcove. Brass wall lamps and sailing ship prints give the feel of a ship's cabin, upward sloping at that, not a hotel-style room on a hull.

A heavy wooden door leads to a private furnished teak veranda with shrouds passing upward from the ship's side. The huge marble bathroom comes with a Jacuzzi bath, which, like the TV and minibar, happily hidden from view, nods to an upscale cruise ship. There are fourteen of these 255-square-foot deluxe one-room suites, plus two even larger 320-square-foot owner's suites located at the stern and two 175-square-foot deluxe cabins that open onto the afterdeck. The most numerous standard cabins (eighty-eight) in categories 2 to 5 are 148 square feet and vary mostly by location. They have marble bathrooms with showers, TVs, satellite telephones, radio channels, private safes, and hair dryers. Six inside cabins round out the accommodations.

The real show is up on the Sun Deck. The full length of the Burma teak deck is cluttered with electric winches, halyards, belaying pins, lines, shackles, ventilators, lifeboats, and deck chairs arranged around three swimming pools. The center pool, 24 feet in length, has a glass bottom that drops into the piano lounge and serves as a skylight to the dining room three decks below.

A hydraulic platform stages the water sport activities, and the ship offers banana boats, water-skiing, diving, snorkeling, and swimming from the 16-foot inflatable raft. An interior stairway gives access to the marina. Two sixty-passenger tenders, resembling military landing craft, take passengers for beach landings. Two 150-

Address/Phone: Star Clippers, 4101 Salzebo Street, Coral Gables, FL 33146; (305) 442–0550 or (800) 442–0551; brochures: (800) 442–0556; fax: (305) 442–1611; www.starclippers.com

The Ship: *Royal Clipper* was built in 2000. It has a gross tonnage of 5,000, a length of 439 feet, and a draft of 18.5 feet.

Passengers: 228, all ages, Americans and European; English is the lingua franca

Dress: Casual at all times

Officers/Crew: European captain and officers; international crew

Cabins: 114; all but 6 outside, 14 with verandas

Fare: $$

What's included: Cruise only

What's not included: Airfare, port charges, tips, drinks

Highlights: The ultimate in a sailing ship experience; social bonding aboard

Other itineraries: Besides these two annual transatlantic crossings, which take place in the spring and fall, Star Clippers offers sailing ship cruises aboard the *Royal Clipper* and *Star Clipper* in the Caribbean, with all three ships in the Eastern or Western Mediterranean. In the fall the *Star Flyer* sails through Suez to cruise Malaysia and Thailand, returning via the Indian Ocean in April.

passenger fiberglass tenders ferry passengers between the anchored ship and pier.

The Itinerary

On the westbound ocean crossing, the *Royal Clipper* embarks in **Civitavecchia** (Rome) and makes calls in Spain, such as **Barcelona** and **Malaga,** the island of **Majorca,** then **Casablanca** in Morocco, and **Las Palmas** and **Tenerife** in the Canaries. The last landfall signals the start of why people really come, the eleven unbroken days at sea, under sail to Barbados.

In optimum wind conditions, the ship can attain 20 knots, but the schedule calls for half that. When there is no wind, the twin Caterpillar, 2,500-horsepower diesel engines can propel the ship at up to 14 knots. The exhaust leaves from the very top of the hollow mizzen and spanker masts, the highest being 197 feet above the waterline. However, the captains, being sailing ship enthusiasts, use the engines sparingly.

While passengers do not handle the sails as on the windjammers, they enjoy being part of the navigation by collecting on a raised platform with the helmsmen and one of the duty officers above the bridge and chart room. A lot of conversations ensue, and relationships develop over the periods of many days at sea. Crew members give lessons in sailing and rope tying. Passengers, wearing safety belts, may climb the steel masts to a crow's nest 60 feet above the deck, and they may also crawl out on the netting that cascades from the bow sprit. Suspended over the sea, they can watch the bow wave below and the masts swaying against the clouds and sky.

Every day at 10:00 A.M., the captain conducts story time, relating tales of the sea, defining nautical terms, and announcing special events. When the conditions are right, passengers can embark in one of the tenders to watch from a distance the ship proceeding under full sail. From a small boat at water level, the view of the *Royal Clipper* bearing down on you, fully dressed with all forty-two sails catching the wind and sun, is beyond words.

For those who have not crossed the Atlantic by sea, there is variation on the crossing-the-line ceremony, in which passengers and crew are initiated by King Neptune, his mermaid queen, and the ship's doctor.

CANADA MARITIME'S
Canmar Fleet
Freighter Travel Crossing for Europhiles

 The romantic notion of freighter travel is alive and well, and the world can be your oyster on voyages lasting from seven days up to four months. Life on a cargo ship can be solitary or social—your call—but it's all about enjoying the sea, being a member of a close-knit community, and watching freight handling in ports of call.

Cabin accommodations vary from plain to plush but are always comfortable, and fares are pegged at about $90 to $140 per day, less than for most cruise ships. But more to the point, your freighter travel budget will not be punctured by the lure of shipboard gambling, spa treatments, shopping, and extra tariff restaurants. With just a handful of fellow passengers, you take your chances, and the average freighter traveler is up there in age, with seventy to seventy-five typically the upper age limit because most freighters carry no doctor.

Flexibility is most important when considering cargo ship travel because it's the stacks of containers that provide the profits; hence a ship may leave earlier than scheduled or later. The container ships of Canada Maritime are usually not more than a day or two off schedule, and they generally hold to the itinerary. Be prepared for some rolling and pitching as the ships plow through all sorts of weather without the aid of stabilizers. Meals reflect the officers' nationality, so you will have lots of authentically spicy curries as Indians man the bridge, and preparation varies according to an individual chef's skill. The officers will speak good English, and mealtimes are shared, though passengers sit at separate tables except at deck barbecues when the weather permits.

The large comfortable lounges have TV, VCR, and music center, and you have access to a pantry for hot drinks, fruit, juices, and snacks. Wine, beer, and spirits are available at duty-free prices. Entertainment and activities include videos and tapes, board and card games, table tennis, small gym, walking the decks, and enjoying a good book in a deck chair located out of the wind. Most ships have an open bridge policy, and once you choose your favorite officer on watch, you may find yourself spending hours shooting the breeze and learning about container shipping, navigation, computers, radar, sea rescue, lifeboats, and the complex customs and cultures of India.

Canada Maritime operates four ships that hold down two routes to England and

Address/Phone: The Cruise People Ltd., 1252 Lawrence Avenue East, Suite 210, Don Mills, Ontario M3A 1C3 Canada; (416) 444–2410 or (800) 268–6523; fax: (416) 447–2628; e-mail: cruise@the cruisepeople.ca; www.thecruise people.ca. Canada Maritime has its own Web site for information only: www. canmar.com, then click on Passenger Services.

The Ships: *Canmar Pride* and *Canmar Honour* were built in 1998, have a gross tonnage of 39,174, and can carry 2,800 20-foot containers; *Canmar Fortune* and *Canmar Courage* were built in 1996, have a gross tonnage of 33,735, and can carry 2,200 20-foot containers.

Passengers: *Canmar Pride* and *Canmar Honour*: 4 passengers; *Canmar Fortune* and *Canmar Courage*: 5 passengers. Age limit is seventy-five; seventy in the winter months

Dress: Casual at all times

Officers/Crew: Largely Indian officers and crew

Cabins: *Canmar Pride* and *Canmar Honour*: one twin, two singles; *Canmar Fortune* and *Canmar Courage*: one twin, three singles

Fare: $$ one-way; $ round-trip

What's included: Ship fare, port charges

What's not included: Airfare, drinks, tips

Highlights: Being at sea and sharing the experience aboard a working ship

Other itineraries: For other freighter-passenger itineraries contact The Cruise People or TravLtips, P.O. Box 580188, Flushing, NY 11358; (800) 872–8584; fax: (718) 224–3247; e-mail: info@ travltips.com; www.travltips.com. This agency publishes a bimonthly publication listing options, plus special positioning type cruises, and has illustrated articles written by past passengers.

the Continent. The *Canmar Pride* and *Canmar Honour* carry four passengers in one roomy twin and two single cabins, while the *Canmar Fortune* and *Canmar Courage* take five in one twin and three singles. All are equipped with a small refrigerator and a shower bath. Forward-facing windows may have views blocked by containers, depending on how they are stacked.

This company is chosen to introduce freighter travel because voyages are relatively short with frequent departures, and the ships offer high standards as they are company-owned, not chartered, by Canadian Pacific. With England and the Continent as destinations, you may wish to stay over and sail or fly back. Sailings are offered year-round, but the crossing will be largely an indoor experience in winter. The other passengers, only four or five total, will be the luck of the draw, so singles may wish to travel with a friend.

The Itinerary

Both transatlantic routes sail from **Montreal** down the **St. Lawrence River** in protected waters for two days before reaching the open ocean. En route, the ships pass under several bridges, slide by the towering Citadel at Quebec City, then parallel the Ile d'Orleans, where at the far end the river begins to widen into what the Quebecois call *la mer* (the sea). The St. Lawrence narrows again as it flows into the open Atlantic, with one track to the north and the other to the south of Newfoundland.

One container service takes seven days to reach Thamesport, well down river from **London,** then crosses the Channel to dock at **Antwerp, Belgium** (nine days), and then to **Le Havre, France** (ten days), from where it's westbound direct to Montreal. The second route operates first to Antwerp (eight days) and on to **Hamburg** (nine days), where there is the bonus of a four-hour sail up the Elbe to the container berths. After unloading and reloading, the ship makes a return Atlantic crossing. Generally, the round-trips take eighteen days, but the useful nature of these services permits one-way passages in both direction from all ports. Port time ranges from about three to six hours, and in larger ports, the new sprawling container terminals may be well away from the city center. Passengers may elect to stay aboard during the cargo working or take an excursion by taxi.

Booking freighters requires considerable thought and planning to make sure it is the right choice, so be sure to consult an expert.

THE BAHAMAS AND
CARIBBEAN ISLANDS

DISNEY CRUISE LINE'S
Disney Wonder
Bahamas Cruising for All Ages

 Disney debuted its eagerly anticipated *Disney Magic* in 1998, promising creative innovations to family cruising. After some initial teething problems (including few activities for adults and poor food), the *Disney Magic* and *Disney Wonder* have settled down quite comfortably into a routine that pleases families, honeymooners, and Disney fans of all ages. While Disney's insistence on the ships being "just so" caused them to be delayed and over budget, the company also ended up with lavishly decorated ships with real pizzazz and style.

Inspired by classic ocean liner design, the 1999-built *Disney Wonder* looks very smart with her black hull, long bow, and twin funnels proudly adorned with Mickey's ears. Exploring further, you will find fanciful Disney touches everywhere, including an elaborate scrollwork of Steamboat Mickey on the bow, a larger-than-life Donald Duck hanging over the stern, painting the hull, and a bronze statue of Ariel from *The Little Mermaid* gracing the three-story atrium. However, these flourishes are fun and whimsical and do not overwhelm those with only a passing interest in cartoons.

In fact, much of the art nouveau decor is so stylish that it is hard to remember you are on a family-oriented cruise ship. Staircase railings are festooned with elaborate scrollwork, and the Promenade Lounge, with its wood veneer paneling, soothing dark colors, and chic furniture, is a delightful, elegant retreat from either the Caribbean sun or overactive kids.

In order to attract both families and those without kids, the ship has an "Adults Only" section with three types of entertainment. The Cadillac Lounge, a burgundy-colored piano bar with the fins of a 1958 DeVille on either end of the bar, is an atmospheric spot for predinner cocktails, while Wavebands, a large nightclub decorated with vintage radios and records, becomes popular late at night. Barrel of Laughs is a popular dueling pianos club you won't find on any other cruise line.

Of the three pools onboard, the most attractive one, nestled between the forward funnel and the mast, is off limits to kids. A modern health club and the ESPN Skybox (cleverly located inside the forward funnel) keep most adults happy. As part of Disney's fanaticism for family entertainment, there is no casino onboard. Surprisingly, the segregation of kids and adults works well and is rigidly enforced.

Of course, kids have plenty of room to frolic, with activities broken into six age groups including a dedicated nursery. A large computer and science lab entertains the eight- to twelve-year-olds, while a mock pirate ship is the scene for games of make-believe with the younger set. Teens find a hip coffeehouse all to themselves, filled with foosball tables, a big-screen TV, and large chairs for hanging out. With more than fifty youth counselors on some sailings, activities can be really creative, including kids-only shore excursions, animation classes, ship-wide treasure hunts, late-night supervised games on deck, and making commercials onboard. Two pools are also open to families, including one with Mickey's gloved hand supporting a slide. A movie theater shows Disney films throughout the day, while the Walt Disney Theatre performs well-received Broadway-style Disney favorites after dinner.

Cabins are large and designed for families, with some even accommodating five people. A unique feature is the one and a half bathrooms in every cabin (except categories 11 and 12).

Another Disney innovation is rotation dining, whereby you, your tablemates, and your waiters rotate each night through three dining rooms. One night you are in elegant Triton's, the next night you are transported to a tropical jungle in Parrot's Cay. Younger kids will probably like Animator's Palette the best (the walls, ceiling, and even the waiters' uniforms start off in only black and white but gradually change color through the meal). Food is standard cruise ship fare throughout, although the adults-only alternative restaurant, Palo, is well worth the moderate charge for both its stunning Italian design and far superior food.

The Itinerary

Most passengers take the cruise as part of a combined Disney resort package, and Dis-

ney has made the transition between ship and shore as seamless as possible. Not only does a fleet of custom Disney buses transport you from your hotel to the spectacular art deco cruise terminal in **Port Canaveral,** but the same key you used for your hotel will work in your cabin onboard as well. After a late afternoon sailing, you arrive the next morning in **Nassau** for shopping at the **Straw Market,** gambling, or a visit to the Atlantis resort. The ship stays until 1:30 A.M., and in the evening there is a party on deck that culminates with streamers and confetti. At **Castaway Cay,** Disney's private island, the ship actually docks. This is the only cruise line private island where anchoring offshore is not necessary. Certain areas of the island are sectioned off for kids or adults only. After a beach barbecue and last dip in the protected lagoon, it is time to head back to the ship and set sail for Port Canaveral.

Address/Phone: Disney Cruise Line, 210 Celebration Place, Suite 400, Celebration, FL 34747; (407) 566–7000 or (800) 951–3532; fax: (407) 566–7353; www.disney.com/disneycruise

The Ship: *Disney Wonder* was built in 1999 and has a gross tonnage of 83,000, a length of 964 feet, and a draft of 25 feet.

Passengers: 1,750; many more if all third, fourth, and fifth berths are occupied; mostly American families with kids and couples in their thirties to fifties who love the Disney concept

Dress: Jackets for men are expected in Triton's and Palo; collared shirts are fine in other restaurants. No shorts, jeans, or T-shirts in any restaurants.

Officers/Crew: International

Cabins: 875; 720 outside, 388 with verandas. Most cabins have one and a half baths and a sitting area with a convertible couch to sleep up to five.

Fare: $$$

What's included: Cruise fare, port charges

What's not included: Airfare, tips, drinks, and shore excursions; water sports, bicycles, and strollers on Castaway Cay

Highlights: Fantastic children's facilities and an attractive, creative, and fun ship for families; superb private island

Other itineraries: *Disney Wonder* does both a three- and four-night itinerary, with alternate four-night voyages substituting a day at sea with a port call in Freeport. The *Disney Magic* does a seven-night itinerary calling at St. Maarten, St. Thomas, St. John, and Castaway Cay, with alternate trips to the Western Caribbean ports of Key West, Grand Cayman, Cozumel, and Castaway Cay.

CUNARD LINE'S
Queen Mary 2
The World's Greatest Ship from New York to the Caribbean

 The ultimate transatlantic liner spends about half her year off the North Atlantic run, making cruises from New York and Florida to New England and Canada, the Caribbean, and South America and from Southampton, England, to European ports. Her high speed and sheer size give her advantages by offering additional ports, a more ambitious itinerary, and a smoother ride. The *QM2* is simply the largest, longest, tallest, and most expensive passenger ship ever built.

Cunard designed the *Queen Mary 2* to wow and impress at first sight at the pier or sailing past the New York skyline. Inside, the *Mary* borrows from the classic ocean liners of the past, with dramatic public rooms on a grand scale. A traditional Winter Garden is the turn-of-the-twentieth-century setting for the ritual of afternoon tea, and the domed Queen's Lounge is dedicated to ballroom dancing, with the largest dance floor at sea. Her main dining room soars three stories with a double staircase for that grand arrival.

During the day, lectures and classes will cover topics ranging from maritime history to U.S.–Russian relations, some given by celebrity authors, entertainment stars, and politicians. A traditional teak promenade deck, wrapping completely around the ship, is designed for communing with the restless sea and is wide enough for walkers and for those who like to wrap up in a steamer rug and spend the afternoon in a wooden deck chair.

For others who want a modern, up-to-the-minute ship, the Canyon Ranch Spa qualifies as the largest and most indulgent spa facility at sea, with a staff numbering more than fifty. A magnificent show lounge puts on extravagant productions, and the theater, used for lectures and films, doubles as the first seagoing planetarium when the ceiling opens to reveal a starlit sky.

Additional public rooms, scattered all over the ship and some tucked away up high, include the Commodore Lounge, a quiet piano bar that serves as an observation room, a forward-facing library and cafe, and an English pub, just a few of a grand total of fourteen bars and clubs.

Ten different restaurants cater to all tastes and pockets. As with the *QE2*, your cabin category will determine in which restaurant you eat. The vast majority of passengers will dine at one of two seatings in the Britannia Restaurant, while those occupying larger cabins dine in the more intimate Princess and Queens Grills. A Todd English restaurant, designed by the Boston restaurateur, serves a Mediterranean menu on a poolside terrace overlooking the stern, and the buffet offers five styles of food at night.

Cabins for 2,620 passengers are some of the largest standard cabins on any ship, and 73 percent feature balconies. To safeguard against possible North Atlantic wave damage, three decks of balconies are recessed into the steel hull. For those with money to splurge, grand suites range from duplex apartments overlooking the stern to a suite of rooms stretching across the front of the ship a few decks below the bridge.

The Itinerary

Queen Mary 2's cruise itineraries vary from short introductory trips to fourteen-day cruises to the deep Caribbean, so the one described here, sailing from New York to St. Maarten, Martinique, Barbados, Castries, and St. Thomas, is just a sampler.

Embarkation is on **New York**'s West Side, the location for Cunard departures for more than a century and a half. Sailing down the Hudson alongside Manhattan's unparalleled skyline, past the Statue of Liberty and with just feet to spare beneath the Verrazano-Narrows Bridge, the Sandy Hook pilot leaves at the Ambrose Channel entrance. The ship gathers speed for a three-night and two-day run into semitropical climes while the passengers get to know their remarkable conveyance.

The first landing is **Philipsburg,** the Dutch side of the island known as **St. Maarten,** where one finds no border formalities for a visit to French **St. Martin.** If Philipsburg is all about shopping and casinos, **Marigot** is for yachting, the arts, and the beach. Sailing overnight to Fort de France, **Martinique,** the flavor is definitely Caribbean French, immediately apparent from the smartly dressed women seen in the city's streets. The leafy city itself is worth a half day, enjoying the cafe life, the New Orleans–style wrought-iron balconies, the

Belle Epoque–style Schoelcher Library, dismantled at the 1899 Paris Exposition and moved here, and the late-nineteenth-century St. Louis Cathedral.

The island is hilly with deep valleys and lush rain forests, and is above all volcanic, the last feature providing the greatest moment in its history. On one day in 1902, **Mt. Pelée** blew its top and St. Pierre, the capital, lost 30,000 inhabitants in a matter of minutes. One ship excursion visits the ruins and the one-room museum and includes a ride through the rain forest and visits to a botanical garden and a butterfly farm.

Barbados is as far south as the Caribbean goes. The island is set up to please everyone, and most everything worth visiting is well beyond Bridgetown, where the ship ties up. You can get around by agreeing on a price and hiring a taxi, using the island's decent public buses and privately owned minibuses, or renting a car. Driving is on the left, and the signposting is only fair, so have a map in hand so as not to miss the boat at the end of the day. The

Address/Phone: Cunard Line, 6100 Blue Lagoon Drive, Suite 400, Miami, FL 33126; (305) 463–3000 or (800) 7–CUNARD; fax (305) 463–3010; www.cunard.com

The Ship: *Queen Mary 2*, completed in 2003, has a gross tonnage of 150,000, a length of 1,132 feet, and a draft of 33 feet.

Passengers: 2,620, Americans, British, Europeans, and other nationalities; all ages especially during the school holidays

Dress: Formal, informal, and casual nights

Officers/Crew: British officers, international crew, British and American social staff

Cabins: 1,310 cabins, 1,017 outside, 879 with verandas, 12 with atrium view

Fare: $$$

What's included: Cruise fare, port charges

What's not included: Airfare, excursions, tips

Highlights: Cruising aboard the world's largest and best-known ship

Other itineraries: Besides this ten-day Caribbean cruise from New York, operated on several occasions during the year, the *Queen Mary 2* makes regular transatlantic crossings between New York and Southampton, England, and cruises from Southampton and Fort Lauderdale. The *Queen Elizabeth 2* cruises mostly Southampton and makes an annual world cruise, and the *Caronia* sails almost exclusively from Southampton until November 2004, when Saga Cruises takes on the ship.

west coast beaches are best, while the Atlantic side is pounded by the surf and not suitable for swimming. The south coast beaches are the closest, and windsurfing is popular. Tourist destinations are Harrison's Cave for a view of the underground world, Francia Plantation house for an interior inspection, Gun Hill Signal Station for a sweeping island view, and it's all about rum at the Mount Gay rum site.

Moving onto the island of **St. Lucia,** the ship calls in at **Castries,** a busy modern town on the northwest coast that is worth a visit for its market, the Roman Catholic cathedral, and Victorian Government House. Out of town, there are planned excursions to the **Pitons,** a pair of dramatic coastal mountain peaks; La Soufriere, a volcano that can be driven into, and then a

walk past the steamy pools and sulfur springs; and a hike up to Fort Rodney at Pigeon Island National Landmark for a great view of the Pitons.

Then it's a last call at **St. Thomas,** where the active can take bike tours for what are mostly downhill rides and usually include a swim at the end, kayak through mangroves, and go on a nature walk at St. Peter Greathouse Estate and Gardens. Shoppers can do just that to their heart's content, and beachgoers have many choices, all reachable by taxi with an agreement in advance for a return pickup.

Following five ports of call in a row, most will look forward to returning to the ship and taking up life at sea on the three-night and two-day run back to New York for the completion of a ten-day cruise.

PRINCESS CRUISES'
Golden Princess
Eastern Caribbean Megaship Cruising

Princess Cruises, owned by the giant Carnival Corporation, is the largest and most innovative line in the cruise business. For the first eighteen months of its life, the 109,000-ton *Grand Princess* was the world's biggest and most expensive ($450 million) cruise ship; then came sister *Golden Princess*. With eighteen towering decks the ship is taller than the Statue of Liberty (from pedestal to torch) and too wide to fit through the Panama Canal.

The public areas range from the clubby, dimly lit Wheelhouse Bar, a repository of historic P&O paintings and maritime memorabilia, to Skywalkers, a spectacular observation lounge and nightclub suspended in a cylindrical pod 150 feet above the ocean at

the rear of the ship. Entertainment venues include a two-story show lounge for big-cast Broadway-style musicals, a smaller lounge to present hypnotists and singers, and a third for dancing to a live band. The dazzling Atlantis Casino is one of the largest at sea, and Snookers is a woody sports bar. Connecting the principal public areas is an elegant three-story atrium, where a resident string quartet entertains passersby with classical music, recalling a grander era of sea travel. The ship carries two full-time florists to create and care for impressive flower arrangements and a large variety of live plants.

The *Golden Princess* has lots of dining options, and overall the food is good—not great—but the variety is laudable. The casual Horizon Terrace feels much smaller than it actually is, and clusters of buffet stations feature stir-fry, a carvery for sides of beef, turkey, and pork, salad fixings galore, heaps of fruit, and cheeses from around the world. Buffet-style breakfast, lunch, and dinner, as well as between-meal specialties, make this a twenty-four-hour-a-day eatery. The three restaurants are named for Italian artists (Bernini, Canaletto, and Donatello), and the decor reflects their artworks. Choices run to five entrees including prime rib, king crab legs, halibut in a citrus-caper butter sauce, rack of lamb with Dijon sauce, and pan-roasted rabbit with rosemary and sage, plus vegetarian choices. Reservations are taken for the Southwestern and Italian specialty restaurants. For noshing during the day, there's always pizza and grill food on the main pool deck, and Häagen-Dazs by the scoop or in a sundae for a charge.

The *Golden Princess* has no fewer than 710 cabins with verandas, but as they are tiered, passengers above look down on those below. All have refrigerators, TVs that broadcast CNN and ESPN, and terry-cloth robes. The twenty-eight wheelchair-accessible cabins make for a wider choice than that offered by any other ship.

The shipboard activities more than fill the three sea days, and the list is a long one. For a start you can play a nine-hole miniature golf course, a golf simulator, basketball, volleyball, and paddle tennis, or disappear into a gigantic virtual-reality game room, where you can climb aboard for hang gliding, downhill skiing, flyfishing, or motorcycle riding. Punctuated around the 1.7 acres of open deck space, there are four great pools, nine hot tubs, and oodles of space for sunbathing. The Plantation Spa offers massages and has saunas, steam rooms, aerobics classes, and an oceanview gym and beauty parlor. Indoor activities include art auctions, bingo, cards, trivia games, port talks, beauty and spa demonstrations, and first-run movies. Kids enjoy a two-story, indoor-outdoor Fun Zone, with toys, tricycles, games, splash pool, hot tub, computers, and a ball bin. Teens who like privacy have a disco and their own patch of deck space with chaise longues. The captain performs legal marriages in an attractive wedding chapel on every cruise.

Address/Phone: Princess Cruises, 24305 Town Center Drive, Santa Clarita, CA 91355; (661) 753–0000 or (800) 774–6237; fax: (661) 259–3108; www.princesscruises.com

The Ship: *Golden Princess* was built in 2001 and has a gross tonnage of 109,000, a length of 951 feet, and a draft of 26 feet.

Passengers: 2,600; mostly Americans in their thirties to seventies

Dress: Suits or tuxedos for formal nights, jackets for semiformal nights, and slacks and collared shirts for casual nights

Officers/Crew: British and Italian offi-cers; international crew

Cabins: 1,300; 938 outside and 712 with private verandas

Fare: $$

What's included: Cruise fare and port charges

What's not included: Airfare, shore excursions, drinks, tips, lots of onboard extras

Highlights: Miniature golf course, golf simulator, virtual-reality game room, restaurants

Other itineraries: In addition to this seven-day Eastern Caribbean cruise, from May the *Golden Princess* makes alternating southern Caribbean cruises from San Juan.

The Itinerary

Embarkation is at **Fort Lauderdale** for what is a starter itinerary with three days, or fully half the trip, at sea to enjoy everything the ship has to offer, and the other half of the trip calling at two of the Caribbean's most visited ports and the company's private island. If you want more ports, or even a port a day, you might wish to choose another cruise. This one is more for shipboard lovers than for touring the Caribbean's hot spots by sea.

Following the first two sea days, the first call is **St. Maarten,** the Dutch side of the dual-nationality island, noted mainly for its shopping bazaar and gaming casinos, while the French side, **St. Martin,** has charming residential sections and the best beaches. For a single destination, take a taxi, agreeing first upon the price, and for independent touring, rent a car for the day with driving on the right on uncrowded roads once beyond **Philipsburg** and **Marigot.**

Sailing overnight, the ship then calls in at **St. Thomas** with Charlotte Amalie, the Caribbean's biggest shopping mecca with pockets of nineteenth-century houses, rising up from the center. Fort Christian, dating back to the Danes' arrival in the late seventeenth century; Seven Arches Museum, a 200-year-old furnished Danish house; St. Thomas Synagogue, built in 1833 by Sephardic Jews, are all within walking distance, but it's also an additional 1.5 mile busy-road hike into town. Consider springing for a shared open-air taxi.

Following another sea day, the third and final call is at **Princess Cays.** This palm-fringed Princess-owned private island is set up for a barbecue, lying in a hammock, beach walking, swimming, and water sports such as snorkeling, jet skiing, and banana boat rides for an extra charge. It's wind-down time before returning aboard the *Golden Princess* to pack for the next morning's arrival.

CARNIVAL CRUISE LINES'
Carnival Victory
Eastern and Western Caribbean Megaship Cruising

 Carnival Cruise Lines took a giant step in size with the building of the highly popular Carnival Destiny-class, and the third ship in this series, the *Carnival Victory,* boasts more than 500 veranda cabins and is extraordinarily popular. When the upper berths are filled, this ship's capacity climbs to 3,400, and when you add 1,000 crew members, you have 4,400 souls living on something less than 1,000 feet long. But they occupy a dozen passenger decks, more for the crew, and the ship is wide, in fact, too beamy to pass through the Panama Canal.

Four glass elevators soar through the ship's nine-deck atrium, which is more tasteful and less glitzy than the one aboard her predecessors. The three-deck Caribbean lounge can seat 1,500 for extravagant Las Vegas–style shows performed on a revolving stage and backed by an orchestra that rises out of the pit on a hydraulic lift. One club has a two-tiered dance floor surrounded by walls of video monitors, and the sports bar brings in the games on huge TV screens. The casino counts two dozen gaming tables and more than 300 slot machines, and for an intimate retreat, slip into the revolving piano bar.

The two bi-level dining rooms, the first for Carnival, have trios serenading during dinner, but the rooms are crowded, and the waiters work hard to keep up with the demand. The Mediterranean Buffet, designed as an international food court on two levels, seats more than 1,250 and serves everything the heart desires, including wok-prepared Chinese food, cooked-to-order pasta, and grilled hot dogs and hamburgers, and has a twenty-four-hour pizzeria.

Four outdoor pools, including one exclusively for children, a three-deck 214-foot spiral water slide, and seven whirlpools draw hundreds to the open decks, which can get crowded on the days at sea. The Lido Deck pool has the protection of a retractable dome and the novelty of a swim-up bar. The huge Nautica Spa features two more whirlpools, a large gym, aerobics, and massage, loofah, sauna, and steam rooms. Children are well looked after at Camp Carnival, a two-deck suite of play areas and activities.

The 1,379 cabins are among the most spacious and sophisticated in the Carnival fleet, with TVs that call up a selection of films for a charge, coffee tables, good closet space, hair dryers, and big showers. The ship has family cabins that sleep five and lots more that are interconnecting; more than half the outside cabins have balconies. No ship in the fleet is more popular than the *Carnival Victory*.

The Itinerary

Two alternating itineraries operate year-round and include two or three full days at sea. The ship's eastern Caribbean swing leaves **Miami,** spends a day at sea, and calls at **San Juan** for a flamenco-rumba show or city-sights tour, but you can easily do **Old San Juan** on your own, as it begins at the end of the pier. Sailing the short distance to **St. Maarten,** choose from a minibus tour of this Dutch-French island, snorkeling at an offshore island, 100 percent duty-free shopping, or on your own in a rental car. **St. Thomas** offers a party raft cruise with underwater viewing, snorkeling, and swimming, a trip up to Paradise Point for an island view, and shopping on a tour or on your own. The last two days are at sea, cruising slowly back to Miami.

On the ship's western Caribbean circuit, a full day is spent at sea before docking at **Cozumel,** where a ferry link to **Playa del**

Address/Phone: Carnival Cruise Lines, 3655 NW 87th Avenue, Miami, FL 33178; (305) 599–2600 or (800) 327–9501; fax: (305) 406–4740; www.carnival.com

The Ship: *Carnival Victory* was built in 2000 and has a gross tonnage of 102,000, a length of 893 feet, and a draft of 27 feet.

Passengers: 2,758; mostly Americans in their twenties to sixties

Dress: Suits or tuxes for two formal nights; slacks and collared shirts for casual nights

Officers/Crew: Italian officers; international crew

Cabins: 1,379; 853 outside and 508 with private verandas

Fare: $$

What's included: Cruise and port charges

What's not included: Airfare, shore excursions and water sports, drinks, tips

Highlights: Nonstop activities, entertainment, pool slide

Other itineraries: In addition to the *Carnival Victory*'s seven-day Caribbean cruises, Carnival has many other itineraries in the Caribbean, Bahamas, Mexican coast, Alaska, New England, Canada, and Bermuda.

Carmen provides access to snorkeling, scuba diving, horseback riding around a ranch, and a trip down the coast to the walled Mayan city of **Tulum.** A second sea day is spent sailing eastward for a day onto **Grand Cayman.** The shore program includes several tours to Stingray City, to which are added an island tour, a catamaran cruise, and scuba diving. It's an overnight sail to Jamaica, where the most popular tours in **Ocho Rios** are to Dunn's River Falls to scurry 600 feet up the slippery rocks, in the shape of a giant staircase; a peaceful, 3-mile river-tubing ride; and horseback riding along the beach and into the shallow waters. Then enjoy the ship for two final nights and a full day at sea, returning to Miami.

CARNIVAL CRUISE LINES'
Paradise
Smoke-free Caribbean Cruising

 Carnival Cruise Lines stays on top of industry trends—balconies, pizza, patisseries—and creates some new ones of its own, in this case a completely smoke-free ship. There is no lighting up anywhere for passengers or crew, not even on the open decks. The penalty for those who do is a $250 fine, disembarkation at the next port of call, forfeiture of the cruise fare, and a return home at one's own expense. Non-smokers love the idea, and those who don't have more than a dozen other Carnival ships from which to choose. The result is a more mellow atmosphere because the bars and discos on the *Paradise* are noticeably less bustling and wind down earlier in the evening. Still, the *Paradise* is full of fun and displays that fantasyland collage of color, texture, and flashing lights for which Carnival is so famous, if slightly more subtly.

Some of the public rooms are downright elegant and use quality materials—leathers and suede, marble, tile, and stained glass. The Normandie show lounge, for instance, has an attractive art deco motif with copper friezes and wall accents, cherry and rosewood details on seating and wall designs, and a massive chandelier, a feast for the eyes before the curtain is ever raised on the elaborate Vegas-style musicals. The ship's Blue Riband library is a graceful tribute to the great ocean liners of the past, featuring a full-size replica of the Blue Riband trophy (awarded to the fastest Atlantic liner), displays of ship memorabilia, and a ceiling mural of the great Atlantic shipping lanes. The Rex disco is cute, with faux animal-skin upholstery and carpeting, and the piano bar has an American flag and funnel motif. Like all eight Fantasy-class ships, the *Paradise* has a six-story atrium flanked by glass-sided elevators, but this one features a bar and live music trio on the ground floor.

In addition to two formal, well-planned dining rooms, there's a huge buffet-style lido restaurant serving breakfast, lunch, and dinner to casual diners who would rather skip the formality of the main restaurant. Here, yummy pizzas, Caesar salads, and garlic bread are served twenty-four hours a day, and self-serve frozen yogurt and soft-ice-cream machines are open most of the day. For passengers with an exotic palate, there's a bona fide, complimentary homemade sushi bar. Carnival's cuisine has really improved and is easily on par with the rest of the mainstream pack. Expect all-

American favorites like surf-and-turf, prime rib, and rib-eye steaks, as well as lots of pastas, grilled salmon, broiled halibut, Thai pork, and lamb dishes. There are also healthier "Nautica Spa" and vegetarian options on each menu.

Some passengers seem bent on dressing as casually as possible, even wearing jeans and T-shirts to dinner or rushing back to their cabins after the meal to change into tank tops and sandals. Some things the line does are tacky, too, such as using white plastic wine and ice buckets, plastic cups for beer on deck, and prepackaged creamers and butter pats.

The 12,000-square-foot Nautica Spa has everything—mirrored aerobics room, large windowed gym, men's and women's locker rooms, sauna and steam rooms, and whirlpools. There are three swimming pools and a water slide, and the Sun Deck offers jogging track covered with a rubberized surface. Standard cabins are a good size at 190 square feet, and all cabins, even the least expensive inside ones, have good storage, a safe, TV, desk and stool, chair, and reading lights for each bed, plus bathrooms with roomy showers and mirrored cabinets for toiletries.

The Itinerary

This eastern cruise is a balance between three days at sea and three port calls. After sailing from **Miami** in the afternoon, the *Paradise* aims eastward for a morning arrival at **Nassau** for the day. First-timers may wish to take a shore excursion, while the seasoned are more likely to tour independently, trying to find some new attraction under the Bahamian sun.

Then a day is spent at sea en route to **La Romana** in the **Dominican Republic,** where you might choose a jeep safari that heads into the sugar cane and fruit plantation region with sweet samples to taste, join an all-day trip into the New World's first capital at **Santo Domingo,** or climb aboard a catamaran for a beach-and-snorkeling outing. Arriving at **St. Thomas,** take the 150-foot Atlantis Submarine dive or ride an open-air taxi from the ship into town for shopping and a stroll upward into an attractive residential neighborhood with a view. Then partake of what many people enjoy—

Address/Phone: Carnival Cruise Lines, 3655 NW 87th Avenue, Miami, FL 33178; (305) 599–2600 or (800) 327–9501; fax (305) 406–4740; www.carnival.com

The Ship: *Paradise* was built in 1998 and has a gross tonnage of 70,367, a length of 855 feet, and a draft of 26 feet.

Passengers: 2,040; mostly Americans in their twenties to sixties

Dress: Suits or tuxes for two formal nights; slacks and collared shirts for the five casual nights

Officers/Crew: Italian officers; international crew

Cabins: 1,020; 618 outside and 26 with private veranda

Fare: $$

What's included: Cruise and port charges

What's not included: Airfare, shore excursions and water sports, drinks, tips

Highlights: Nonsmoking cruise, entertainment, sushi bar, pool slide

Other itineraries: In addition to these alternating seven-day *Paradise* cruises, Carnival has many other itineraries in the Caribbean, Bahamas, Mexican coast, Alaska, New England, Canada, and Bermuda.

the rhythm of three nights and two full sea days en route to Miami and disembarkation.

On the western loop, with just two sea days and four ports, **Belize,** the city and country, is first. One of the more unusual trips is out to a Mayan ceremonial center at Lamanai, reached by bus then boat along the New River. You pass through mangroves and Mennonite farms and spot crocodiles basking in the sun, unusual black orchids, and a variety of tropical birds. At the native site, you can climb one of the semi-buried structures to see the surrounding rain forest and life at treetop level. A completely different tour uses inner tubes as the conveyance to explore a continuous cave system that has you reemerging into daylight from time to time.

The call at **Roatan,** part of an island chain, offers kayaking through mangroves to look for moray eels and sea turtles, swimming with dolphins, snorkeling, certified diving, and visiting a botanical garden. Then comes **Grand Cayman,** which is well known for upscale shopping for black coral jewelry and perfumes, and for snorkeling, stingray feeding, and a day in the sun on gorgeous Seven Mile Beach. At the final call, the island of **Cozumel,** you can enjoy the beach and swimming or ferry across to the Yucatan mainland to swim in a lagoon at Xel-Ha and tour **Tulum,** the only significant Mayan ruins perched on a coastal bluff overlooking the sea. After four busy days ashore, unwind aboard the *Paradise* for two nights and a day on the return leg to Miami.

DISNEY CRUISE LINE'S
Disney Magic
A Full Week in the Caribbean

The *Disney Magic* was the Walt Disney Company's first foray into cruising, and naturally, it's a vehicle to tout Disney-style innovations in dining, entertainment, kids' facilities, and cabin design, which set the ship apart from its closest peers. In many ways the experience is more Disney than cruise—no casino or library—but first-timers and Disney fanatics, adults and children, will just have a ball. The seven-day cruises allow much more time to enjoy the ship and its activity schedule, while the sea time is punctuated by typical Caribbean ports. The shorter three- and four-day cruises aboard the *Disney Wonder* are more likely to be combined with a land-based Walt Disney World Resort package.

Disney Cruise Line got its cruising start in 1998 with the *Disney Magic* and took delivery of the *Disney Wonder* in 1999. Arriving at the pier, you will immediately notice Mickey's big-eared head on the pair of giant red funnels and fanciful golden curlicues on the pointy blue-black bow. But overall, the ship is engaging and elegant, and the Disney-isms are subtly sprinkled throughout the *Magic*'s mellow, art-deco–inspired interior. Framed story sketches from famous 1930s and '40s Disney animated movies blend tastefully against the caramel-colored wood paneling in the stairways and corridors.

One innovation, setting the *Magic* apart from the big-ship crowd, are three restaurants among which passengers and servers rotate over the course of the cruise. It's the ocean liner, 1930s-era Lumiere's one night, the tropical Parrot Cay another, and finally the signature Animator's Palate restaurant. This bustling, high-tech eatery starts out completely black and white, and then gradually becomes awash in reds, blues, and greens as the walls, ceiling, and even the servers' uniforms take on color. The food, however, is average cruise fare, tasty but nothing special—French onion soup, escargots, fish, steaks, pasta. For dessert, kids get scoops of ice cream served on a palate-shaped plate, and they can pretend to paint using chocolate and strawberry squeeze bottles.

The Topsider Café serves a buffet-style breakfast and lunch spread, and other options for noshing poolside include Pinocchio's Pizzeria, Pluto's Dog House for hamburgers, hot dogs, and fries, and Scoops ice-cream bar. There's twenty-four-hour room service from a limited menu, but no midnight buffet. For adults only, make early reservations for the romantic, away-from-the-fray Palo, a 138-seat, whimsically decorated Italian restaurant. It's well worth the small extra charge.

The *Magic's* fresh, family-oriented entertainment is a standout. In the nostalgic Walt Disney Theater, actors disappear into trapdoors, fly across the stage, and go through endless exciting costume changes. After-dinner performances include a sweet musical medley of Disney classics, taking the audience from *Peter Pan* and *The Lion King* to *Voyage of the Ghost Ship.*

Kids have as many as fifty dedicated counselors to supervise five age groups in two huge spaces. The Oceaneer Club, for

Address/Phone: Disney Cruise Line, 210 Celebration Place, Suite 400, Celebration, FL 34747; (407) 566–7000 or (800) 951–3532; fax: (407) 566–7353; www.disney.com/DisneyCruise

The Ship: *Disney Magic* was built in 1998, has a gross tonnage of 83,000, a length of 964 feet, and a draft of 25 feet.

Passengers: 1,750 double occupancy or 3,325 if all third, fourth, and fifth berths are occupied. Mostly American families with kids and couples in their thirties to fifties who love the Disney concept

Dress: Jackets for men are expected in Palo and Lumiere's restaurants; collared shirts are fine in other restaurants. No shorts, jeans, or T-shirts in any restaurant.

Officers/Crew: International

Cabins: 875, most with 1½ bathrooms and sitting area with convertible couch (and sometimes bunk) to comfortably sleep three or four; 625 outside and 378 with balconies

Fare: $$$

What's included: On the cruise: all meals, entertainment, and most activities

What's not included: Airfare, soft drinks, shore excursions, and water sports, bicycles, and strollers on Disney's private island, Castaway Cay

Highlights: Rotation-style dining in three restaurants; large family-friendly cabins with 1½ bathrooms; large play space and scope of children's programs; separate facilities for adults traveling without children; wonderful private island

Other itineraries: Besides these alternating one-week year-round Caribbean cruises, the *Disney Wonder* makes three- and four-day cruises to the Bahamas, and passengers often combine a cruise with a Walt Disney World Resort package, which offers a seamless transfer between land and sea.

ages three to seven, is a Captain Hook–themed playroom, where kids climb and crawl on a giant pirate-ship's bow and get dressed up from a trunkfull of costumes. For ages eight to twelve, the far-out Oceaneer Lab harbors all kinds of great activities, such as using microscopes, working on computers, and doing arts and crafts. And for teens, the cool Common Grounds coffee bar is the place to plop down into big comfy chairs, flip through magazines, or listen (through headphones) to a selection of more than seventy music CDs. Kids can eat dinner with counselors in the Topsiders Café; and if Mom and Dad want more time alone, Flounder's Reef Nursery takes kids, for a fee, from three months to three years between 6:00 P.M. and midnight and for a few hours during the day, dependent on the ship's schedule.

For gym enthusiasts, the fitness center is on the small side, although a pair of virtual-reality step machines is great fun, and the outdoor decks offer basketball and paddle tennis, a decent-size spa, and three pools (one for kids, one for adults, and one for all ages). The rules about who may use which are usually well enforced.

An adults-only entertainment enclave called Beat Street has three lounges: Sessions, an elegant piano bar; Offbeat, a 1970s-style whimsical comedy club; and Rockin' Bar D, a country-and-western-style disco, plus movies and enrichment lectures. The Promenade Lounge has a live jazz band, and the sports bar, ESPN Skybox, stays open until midnight.

The majority of the *Magic*'s cabins are thoughtfully equipped with two bathrooms—a sink and toilet in one, and a shower/tub combo and a sink in the other. Cabin size is a plus, too, with all of the 875 standard cabins having a sitting area with a sofa bed to sleep families of three. Some include a pull-down wall-bunk for a fourth, and nearly half have private verandas. Family suites sleep five. All come with hair dryers, safes, shower and short tub, mini-refrigerator, TV, and phone.

The Itinerary

Alternating year-round seven-day cruises sail on a Saturday from **Port Canaveral.** The Eastern Caribbean loop spends the first two days at sea en route to St. Maarten for the day, then St. Thomas and St. John, a day at sea, and finally Castaway Cay. At **St. Maarten,** the *Magic* docks at **Philipsburg** on the Dutch side, and apart from shopping near to where you leave the ship, the island boasts eight casinos, popular for those who miss one on the ship. There's horseback riding on a beach, biking and hiking tours in the hills and on the shore, and golf outings. A day later at **St. Thomas,** you can choose from a scuba diving trip, a bike tour, more golf, or head across to **St. John** to kayak, parasail, or windsurf.

Disney ships dock at **Castaway Cay,** the company's private island, allowing for a free flow between ship and shore during the day. The property has a section for adults a bit removed from the main area of activities, plus a section for teenage sports, and then of course specific areas set aside for children's activities and for the entire family to play. The barbecue dishes out hamburgers, hot dogs, fries, and corn on the cob with tables under shelter. The crescent beach faces a protected lagoon for boating activities and swimming. You might rent a sunfish and tack out to photograph your ship at rest.

The Western Caribbean circuit has only two days at sea, calling first at **Key West,** then a sea day, **Grand Cayman, Cozumel,** a sea day, **Castaway Cay,** and a return to Port Canaveral.

Adults traveling without children might wish to book outside the peak kids' summer and holiday seasons. For Disney fanatics and families not afraid of crowds, the *Magic* offers the classic Disney brand of wholesome fun in an elegant, seafaring setting.

ROYAL CARIBBEAN'S
Radiance of the Seas
A Western Caribbean Loop

 The *Radiance of the Seas* class, numbering four ships, represents a new direction for Royal Caribbean with much more attention being paid to a shippy look and the sense of sailing on a ship, from the more maritime-oriented decor, dark-wood paneling and deep-sea blues, to the walls of glass that let you see the sea while dining, imbibing, and conversing. The Centrum features a portside wall of glass soaring from Decks 5 through 10 and four sets of glass-enclosed elevators. Yes, there are still the Royal Caribbean trademark miniature golf and rock-climbing wall, now installed on all the ships.

Most of the public rooms—Crown & Anchor Lounge, Champagne Bar, Singapore Sling's piano bar, Windjammer Café, Sky Bar, and the topmost trademark Viking Crown Lounge—are sheathed in glass, great for viewing port arrivals.

Public spaces are fun to inhabit. One, the Colony Club, an interconnecting suite of five spaces, has a rich look with Oriental-patterned carpets, inlaid wood flooring, intimate seating arrangements, and subdued lighting. Another is Singapore Sling's piano bar, spanning the stern with great views over the wake through full-height windows. For an amazing scene, don't miss having a cocktail here on a moonlit night. Keeping the Asian theme but with a twist, the colonial-styled Bombay Billiard Club provides a patterned wood floor and redwood paneling setting for two high-tech pool tables cradled in gimbals and kept even by motorized gyroscopes to overcome any ship movement.

On the *Radiance*, the Solarium is a dose of Africa with stone elephants, a waterfall, watercolor scenes, and thatch umbrellas,

while on the *Brilliance*, it's an East Indian–themed Solarium with Indian elephants, bronze statues, and a ceramic-tiled peacock. Aboard the *Radiance*, the Aurora Theater has an Arctic theme decor with deep ocean greens and blues, and on the *Brilliance* it's gold, purple, and reds. For a direct association with the ship's Alaska cruise program, passengers can look up from the pool to see a 12-foot-high cedar totem pole carved by Native Alaskan artist Nathan Jackson.

More generally associated with Royal Caribbean are such places as the Casino Royale, with more than 200 slot machines and several score of gaming tables, a baseball-themed sports bar offering interactive games, the nautically decorated Schooner Bar, an always open Internet center, and the line's signature room, the Viking Crown Lounge, here a quiet retreat and a disco with rotating bar. Even the public bathrooms—bright, airy marbled spaces with mirrors shaped like portholes—will turn heads.

The two dining rooms are two stories high with an impressive double staircase joining the two levels and a cascading waterfall. More maritime inspiration is designed into the Windjammer Café with navy blue carpeting and fabrics, rich wood veneers, and scattered ship models. The number of food counters, eleven in all, spreads out the lines and reduces crowding, and food may be enjoyed indoors or out. Even more informal, the naturally lighted Seaview Café serves the usual fast foods during lunch and dinner hours at tables with rattan chairs.

For watching steaks being cooked in an open kitchen, the ninety-seat Chops Grill offers seats in high-backed booths and a great sea view. Next door, the larger 130-seat Portofino features an Italian menu, and both restaurants provide a sense of occasion that comes with an extra charge.

The ships have three pools, a Sports Deck that serves basketball, volleyball, and paddle-tennis court players, a nine-hole miniature golf course and golf simulators, jogging track, and a rock-climbing wall fixed to the funnel, now a feature on all RCI ships. For children, RCI's Adventure Ocean program offers four supervised age groups play stations with video games, a computer lab, splash pools, and a waterslide.

Historically, Royal Caribbean cabins have been on the small size, while more space has been allocated to public rooms, but on the *Radiance* class, they are respectable, some even more so, in size. Cabin decor has changed from Miami Beach pastels to rich navy blues and copper. All cabins have small fridges; cozy sitting areas; ample drawer and closet space; interactive televisions that tap into booking shore excursions, keep tabs on onboard spending, and check up on the ups and downs of the stock market;

desks-cum-vanities with a pullout shelf for personal laptop computers; and typically small RCI showers.

Suites receive butler service and have access to the Concierge Club for tour and travel information or the latest newspaper.

All Royal Caribbean ships are big and bustling, but this new *Radiance* class offers a higher standard of just about everything that makes a cruise vacation a happy experience at a moderate price level.

The Itinerary

This one-week starter itinerary leaves every other week from **Fort Lauderdale,** balancing two days at sea with calls at Key West, Cozumel, Costa Maya, and Grand Cayman.

The *Radiance of the Seas* is based in Fort Lauderdale during the winter months and makes two alternating Caribbean cruises, an eastern loop and a western one, the latter described here. Upon sailing from port, the ship turns south to sail overnight to anchor off **Key West** for the day. The town is compact and can be walked with visits to former President Truman's Winter White

Address/Phone: Royal Caribbean International, 1050 Caribbean Way, Miami, FL 33132; (305) 539–6000; brochures: (800) 327–6700; fax: (305) 374–7354; www.royalcaribbean.com

The Ship: *Radiance of the Seas* was completed in 2001, has a gross tonnage of 90,090, a length of 962 feet, and a draft of 27 feet.

Passengers: 2,100; mostly Americans with some Europeans and lots of families during the school holidays

Dress: Formal and casual nights

Officers/Crew: International officers and crew

Cabins: 1,050, with 813 outside and 577 with verandas

Fare: $$

What's included: Cruise fare, port charges

What's not included: Airfare, tips, drinks, shore excursions

Highlights: A stunningly decorated ship lacking none of the megaship amenities

Other itineraries: Besides this one-week cruise to the Western Caribbean, operating between November and April, the *Radiance of the Seas* makes an eastern loop, sails through the Panama Canal in the late spring to spend the summer cruising Alaska's Inside Passage, and returns south via a Pacific Ocean cruise to Hawaii. The huge RCI fleet covers most of North and South America and Europe.

House, Ernest Hemingway's first home, and John James Audubon's house. Those who prefer to ride can take the Conch Train on an old-town trolley tour. The more active can join a bike tour over the flat terrain or go "catch and release" fishing using light tackle to snare sailfish, tarpon, king mackerel, tuna, and grouper.

Then sail two nights and a day to the island of **Cozumel** located off the Yucatan Peninsula. Take a ferry across to Playa del Carmen and then a bus up to **Cancun,** the peninsula's premier resort for shopping, craft markets, swimming, and restaurants, or go south to **Xcaret** for swimming in a lagoon, in an underground river, and in the ocean. The site also has an aviary, botanical garden, and many places to eat.

Sail overnight down the coast to **Costa Maya,** a relatively new but rapidly building landing for the cruise ships. There are Mayan ruins to visit, such as recently rediscovered Chacchoba, and a combination biking and kayaking trip that passes

through the fishing village of **Majahual** in both directions. You can hop into a two-person motorized boat and go out to a snorkeling location or take an Unimog 4 x 4 all-terrain vehicle on an off-road adventure that travels through the forest en route to a secluded beach set up for swimming, volleyball, and kayaking.

Then the *Radiance* calls at its last port, **George Town** on **Grand Cayman,** where you can enjoy some upscale window shopping, head to Stingray City to swim among these gentle creatures, or board the luxury racing yacht *Safir* for a sail to an excellent snorkeling location. Then enjoy two nights and a full day aboard ship en route to Fort Lauderdale and disembarkation.

The Eastern Caribbean loop departs Fort Lauderdale, spends a day at sea, then calls at **San Juan, St. Maarten,** and **St. Thomas** on three successive days, then spends a day at sea again en route to Nassau, and finally, an overnight return to Fort Lauderdale.

CELEBRITY CRUISES'
Galaxy
Stylish and Affordable Caribbean Cruising

Celebrity Cruises began as an upscale brand for Chandris Lines, and soon the lower level Fantasy Cruises was phased out. In 1997 Royal Caribbean International bought Celebrity Cruises, but thus far the line is being operated as a separate brand.

The *Galaxy* is spacious and comfortable and exhibits a kind of glamorous, vaguely art deco style associated with classic ocean liners. The decor casts a chic and sophisticated mood, with lots of warm wood tones as well as rich, tactile textures and fabrics in

deep primaries, from faux zebra-skin to soft leathers. The ship attracts a wide range of ages and backgrounds.

Celebrity might be best known for its cuisine, which is indeed better than average. Dinners are served in high style in the ship's gorgeous two-deck main dining room, with a wall of glass facing astern to the ship's wakes and, if you're lucky, a moonlit night. The menu is likely to feature something along the lines of pan-fried salmon with parsleyed potatoes, Pad Thai (noodles and veggies in a peanut sauce), tournedos Rossini with foie gras and Madeira sauce, or prime rib with horseradish and baked potato.

Breakfast, lunch, and dinner (by reservation only) are served in the buffet-style lido restaurant. For snacking there's also ice cream, high tea, and pizza available, and pizza can be delivered in a cardboard box to your cabin. In place of traditional midnight buffets, the ship offers "Gourmet Bites," hors d'oeuvres served by waiters in the public lounges between midnight and 1:00 A.M. Waiters are poised and professional, and sommeliers circulate in the dining room and in the lido restaurant.

Activities during days at sea may include enrichment lectures on topics such as personal investing, body language, or handwriting analysis; wine tastings; bingo; art auctions; arts and crafts; spa and salon demonstrations; and dancing lessons. If you prefer solitude, some semblance of peace and quiet can be had on the far corners of the Sky Deck and on the aft Penthouse Deck. Inside there are many hideaways, including Michael's Club, the card room, or the edges of Rendez-Vous Square.

The ship has a well-stocked playroom, called the Fun Factory, and an attached outside deck area with wading pool. During summer and holidays supervised activities are offered all day long for four age groups between three and seventeen. The Aqua-Spas are among the best facilities at sea. The focal point is a 115,000-gallon thalassotherapy pool, huge hot tubs with warm jets of water. Although managed by Steiner, as on most other ships, there are more exotic treatments offered on this ship such as mud packs, herbal steam baths, and water-based treatments. In the good-sized, windowed gym, landscapes unfold on the color monitors of the ship's high-tech, virtual-reality stationary bikes. There are also aerobic classes in a separate room, an outdoor jogging track, a golf simulator, and a sports deck with basketball, paddle-tennis, and volleyball courts. There are three swimming pools; one is covered by an all-weather retractable roof.

In addition to the Broadway-style musicals performed on two stages, there are live dance bands and pianists performing in other lounges, as well as innovative enter-

---

Address/Phone: Celebrity Cruises, 1050 Caribbean Way, Miami, FL 33132; (305) 539–6000 or (800) 437–3111; www.celebritycruises.com

The Ships: *Galaxy* was built in 1996, has a gross tonnage of 77,713, a length of 866 feet, and a draft of 25 feet.

Passengers: 1,870; mostly American couples in their late thirties to sixties, some honeymooners and families, too

Dress: Suits or tuxes for the formal nights, jackets for semiformal nights, and slacks and collared shirts for casual nights; no shorts, jeans, or T-shirts in the restaurants

Officers/Crew: Greek officers; international crew

Cabins: 948; 639 outside and 220 with verandas

Fare: $$

What's included: Cruise fare only

What's not included: Airfare, port charges, excursions, water sports, drinks, tips

Highlights: AquaSpas are some of best at sea. Modern art collection is one of most interesting and provocative in the industry.

Other itineraries: In addition to this Caribbean itinerary, which operates between late November and March, Celebrity ships cruise to Alaska, Mexico, South America, Bermuda, and in Europe.

tainment like a strolling a cappella group and a strolling magician, who perform in various lounges and public areas.

With its crushed-velvet couches and leather wingback chairs, Michael's Club is a quiet, sophisticated spot for cigars, cordials, and conversation. The disco within the top-deck observation lounge is open until about 3:00 A.M. The cozy, dimly lit nightclub is the spot for cabaret, dancing, and karaoke. First-run movies are screened in the theater, and the ship has a spacious, sultry casino.

Pleasing cabin decor is based on monochromatic themes of muted bluish-purple, green, or red and light-colored furniture. Although inside cabins are about par for the industry standard, outside cabins are larger than usual, and four categories of suites are particularly spacious. Suite passengers are privy to a tuxedo-clad personal butler who serves afternoon tea and complimentary hors d'oeuvres from 6:00 to 8:00 P.M., handles laundry and shoe shining, and will serve you a full five-course dinner in your cabin. Cabin TVs are wired with an interactive system, from which you can order room service from on-screen menus, select the evening's wine, play casino-style games, or browse in "virtual" shops.

The Itinerary

The *Galaxy's* seven-night cruise departs **San Juan** and calls at Basseterre, St. Kitts; Bridgetown, Barbados; Margarita Island, Venezuela; and Orangestad, Aruba. Activities feature horseback riding, snorkeling, scuba diving, and windsurfing.

ROYAL CARIBBEAN'S
Voyager of the Seas
The Western Caribbean's Largest Cruise Ship

 Royal Caribbean clearly won the "who can build the biggest and best" competition with its new 137,000-ton *Voyager of the Seas,* a full 25 percent larger than the competing *Grand Princess* and *Carnival Destiny.* More importantly, however, the company started with a blank slate and came up with a ship that is more than just an oversized sistership—rather, she is a true trendsetter that leaves most passengers dazzled. Like her smaller fleet mate *Sovereign of the Seas,* the *Voyager* may well be remembered as a daring new ship that set a precedent for all ships to follow.

Unlike other megaships, which often try to hide their size through smaller public rooms, the *Voyager* makes no pretensions about being large—she is huge and she wants everyone to know it. From the Royal Promenade to the three-story dining room to the expansive upper deck space, the ship is full of grand sweeping vistas and cavernous spaces, constant reminders of how big she is. Of course, size does have its downsides as well, including less personal service and occasional waits for elevators or disembarkation.

The first thing that passengers notice upon boarding is the fascinating Royal Promenade, a 500-foot, four-story walkway running down the middle of the ship. Cafes and shops line the path, while three decks of "Promenade View" cabins look down onto the scene through large bay windows. The space is constantly brimming with passengers strolling by, stopping to listen to the piano player in the bar, or simply striking up a conversation at a sidewalk cafe. The space works well, and like any town center it takes on different moods throughout the day and into the evening, especially when street performers and buskers are about.

Just aft of the Royal Promenade is the ship's three-story dining room, easily one of the most spectacular rooms to put to sea within the last twenty years. Crowned by a striking chandelier and flanked by window walls on either side, the three levels are linked by a dramatic grand staircase. Unfortunately, despite attempts to improve the quality, the food does not live up to the decor in the main dining room, and it is hard to get a reservation for a better menu in the smaller alternative Portofino restaurant.

Much attention has been given to the ship's ice-skating rink, which is used for both shows and free skating for passengers. There is also a rock-climbing wall 200 feet above the keel on the after end of the funnel, and it is equally fun just to watch the passengers doing the actual climbing. For the active set, there is also a full-size basketball court, a miniature golf course, an in-line skating track, and a large spa. From the

elaborate children's facilities to the wedding chapel to the Johnny Rocket's 1950s-style diner, there really is something for everyone.

Traditionalists will delight in the ship's open deck space, including a wraparound promenade deck that actually cantilevers over the side, giving a unique perspective on the steel hull crashing through the seas. Even the bow is open to passengers, and it is fantastic to go all the way forward at night and gaze back at the darkened superstructure and spinning radar antennae.

Cabins are of good size and generally well laid out, and many have balconies with steel partitions on one side, offering true privacy from at least one of your neighbors. In addition to the standard inside and outside cabins, there are many "Promenade View" cabins (which are slightly more expensive than standard inside cabins) that offer bay windows looking down onto the Royal Promenade. For those who can't get enough of city life, these cabins are perfect—although other passengers can see in just as easily as you can see out unless the curtains are drawn.

Listing the additional spaces on board

Address/Phone: Royal Caribbean International, 1050 Caribbean Way, Miami, FL 33132; (305) 539–6000 or (800) 327–6700 for brochures; fax: (305) 374–7354; www.royalcaribbean.com

Ship: *Voyager of the Seas* was built in 1999. It has a gross tonnage of 137,000, a length of 1,020 feet, and a draft of 29 feet.

Passengers: 3,114 double occupancy; mostly Americans of all ages. As many as 3,608 passengers have been onboard at once, a peacetime record for any ship.

Dress: Suits or jacket and tie for the formal night and jackets for informal nights

Officers/Crew: International

Cabins: 1,557; 939 outside, 757 with balconies, and 138 "Promenade View"

cabins looking into the Royal Promenade

Fare: $$

What's included: Cruise fare only

What's not included: Airfare, port charges, tips, drinks, shore excursions

Highlights: An exciting, innovative ship with enough options to please everyone.

Other itineraries: In addition to these two October-to-May seven-day cruises, the *Voyager* sails from New York to Canada and to the Caribbean from May to October. The equally huge *Explorer of the Seas, Adventure of the Seas,* and *Serenade of the Seas* sail year-round on other Caribbean itineraries. Royal Caribbean cruises the Mexican Riviera, Alaska, Hawaii, and Europe.

will not do justice to the ship. This ship is visually fascinating, and the extensive use of glass permits some interesting people-watching vistas looking either within or out from the ship. This is not your standard cookie-cutter cruise ship, and the creativity shows.

The Itinerary

The *Voyager of the Seas* sails Sundays seasonally (October to May) from **Miami,** hits the larger Western Caribbean ports, and includes two sea days.

The first day is spent at sea, allowing passengers time to get acclimated and to find their way around. On Tuesday, the ship anchors off **Labadee,** which is Royal Caribbean's private "island," although it's actually a private, secluded stretch of the Haitian coastline. Passengers can enjoy the day sunning on the beach or renting a small sailboat. The next day is spent in **Ocho Rios,** Jamaica, where passengers can climb the famous Dunns River Falls or enjoy a guided bamboo raft journey down a tropical river.

Popular **Grand Cayman** offers some upscale shopping in **George Town** in addition to **Stingray City,** where tame stingrays surround swimmers offering them food. **Seven Mile Beach** and renowned diving on "The Wall" will satisfy those who yearn to spend all their time in the water or on the beach.

The last port is the resort island of **Cozumel,** Mexico. For those who are not into the excellent snorkeling and diving opportunities here, there are the Mayan coastal ruins at **Tulum** or a day trip to resorty **Cancun.** With a last day at sea, here's another chance to rediscover the ship all over again. On alternate weeks the port calls are Belize, Costa Maya, Cozumel, and Grand Cayman.

SEA CLOUD CRUISES'
Sea Cloud
Eastern Caribbean Island Hopping under Sail

After taking delivery of the new yacht in 1931, E. F. Hutton and his wife, Marjorie Post, spent most of the next four years aboard sailing the world, including to the Galápagos Islands, where they acquired a tortoise named Jumbo, who became a permanent resident of the ship. Several years later, following the couple's divorce, Mrs. Hutton rechristened the ship *Sea Cloud* and leased it to the U.S. government for $1.00 a year during World War II. After having several private owners, the *Sea Cloud* was abandoned in Panama by the late 1960s, then purchased in 1978 by some German businessmen, who brought her back to the Kiel shipyard and had cabins added for cruise service to take up to sixty-nine paying passengers.

Cabins number 1 to number 8 are original, looking more like suites at the Ritz Carlton or Waldorf Astoria than any found aboard even the most luxurious cruise ship. Marjorie's Suite (cabin number 1) displays an opulence reminiscent of Versailles: a blue-canopied bed in antique white with gold-leaf ornamentation, Louis Philippe chairs, a finely etched floor-to-ceiling dressing mirror, a marble fireplace with an elaborate mantel, chandeliers, plaster ceilings with intricate moldings, and a grand Carrara marble bathroom. Port-side, cabin number 2's dark paneling with deep-red furnishings, a large mahogany secretary, and highbacked chairs leaves no doubt that this was E. F. Hutton's domain. Distinctive furnishings help differentiate each original portholed cabin, all having a fireplace, a writing desk, a sitting area, and a marble bathroom.

Although the name *Sea Cloud* elicits images of grand living, most passengers occupy one of the twenty-six new cabins, added in 1979 and refitted in 1993. Nautically styled and roomy, they have wood paneling, brass fittings, fabrics in pastel colors, large windows, and marble bathrooms with shower.

One wouldn't normally think of an "open house" as a popular onboard cruise activity, but to most passengers aboard the *Sea Cloud*, it is the week's highlight sailing the Caribbean. On the penultimate evening, champagne and canapés are served on Main Deck, and the passengers dress for the occasion and tour the cabins. Whether one occupies the original or the added, it seems to have no impact on social life aboard.

Buffet breakfasts and formal dinners are served at open-seating tables for six to eight in the original dining room and saloon. Dark paneling, oil paintings, and fireplaces create an atmosphere of dining in a large private home. For dinner, formal table settings of navy blue, gold, and white china embossed with the ship's logo, silver napkin rings, candlelight, and fresh flowers add to the elegant scene. Local specialties, such as fresh Antigua spiny lobster, complement the delectable nouvelle cuisine fixed menu. Luncheon buffets are beautifully presented outside on the Promenade Deck, and helpful crew members carry the laden trays above to the Lido Lounge, protected from the midday sun under a blue awning. Entertainment before and after dinner is presented here by a popular piano player, and one evening crew members sing salty sea chanties.

Address/Phone: Sea Cloud Cruises, 32–40 North Dean Street, Englewood, NJ 07631; (201) 227–9404 or (888) 732–2568; fax: (201) 227–9424; e-mail: seacloud@att.net; www.seacloud.com. Agents are Abercrombie & Kent International, (800) 757–5884 for brochures or (800) 323–7308; and Elegant Cruises & Tours, Inc., (800) 683–6767.

The Ship: *Sea Cloud,* originally built as the *Hussar* in 1931, was rebuilt into a cruise ship in 1979. She has a gross tonnage of 2,532, a length of 360 feet, and a draft of 17 feet.

Passengers: 69 well-heeled Americans, often part of a group

Dress: Passengers smarten up for dinner and dress semiformally for the penultimate evening.

Officers/Crew: American or European captain; international crew

Cabins: 34; a wide range of choice, all outside with windows or portholes

Fare: $$$$

What's included: Unless part of a group, cruise only, some sight-seeing, soft drinks, plus wines at lunch and dinner

What's not included: Airfare, port charges, shore excursions, drinks, tips

Highlights: Experiencing the opulence of a former private yacht under sail and the company of like-minded passengers

Other itineraries: In addition to this seven-night cruise in the Caribbean, operating during the winter months, there is a second Caribbean loop, as well as one transatlantic voyage from the Mediterranean to the Caribbean in November. In 2001 the newly built *Sea Cloud II,* taking ninety-six passengers in more uniform accommodations, began Caribbean and Mediterranean cruising.

The Itinerary

Embarking in **Antigua,** the *Sea Cloud* motors out of the harbor, and then the call, "All hands on deck!" brings passengers above to watch the deck crew climb the masts to unfurl the sails. One by one, thirty billowing sails fill with wind, and the ship is under way. The time at sea is passed hanging about the wheelhouse, lying on cushioned benches either side of the bridge eyeing the progress, or sitting with a book in a shady spot. The Promenade Deck fantail is fitted with huge royal blue cushions, comfy for sunbathing and lying on one's back to gaze up at the brilliant stars at night.

The usual pattern sees passengers ashore most mornings, onboard for lunch, and under sail for the afternoon. The port of calls are usually Bequia, Grenada, Carriacou, Soufriere on St. Lucia, and Terre d'en Haut on Iles des Saintes. At **Bequia** you can visit the giant sea turtles in their natural, and protected, habitat or spend a day snorkeling and swimming on uncrowded beaches. St. George, on **Grenada,** is a pretty harbor town with a busy market square, and **Carriacou** offers a scenic mountain and garden drive. Soufriere, on beautiful **St. Lucia,** leads to a botanical garden, a waterfall, a volcano, and sulfur springs. A short, steep hike from **Terre d'en Haut,** on Iles des Saintes, brings you up to historic Fort Napoleon, for a spectacular view of the yachting harbor with the *Sea Cloud* as the centerpiece. The ports are fun, but life aboard the largest former private yacht is the real draw.

WINDSTAR CRUISES'
Wind Spirit
Motorsailing the Eastern Caribbean

Windstar Cruises, founded in 1986, operates three high-tech motor sail ships, the sails being a highly decorative feature that unfurl with the push of a button on the bridge and give an extra couple of knots when the winds are favorable.

With the distinctive profile of a large yacht and a maritime atmosphere within, the *Wind Spirit* immediately pleases the eye when boarding. The main lounge, located aft, has a sailing ship–style skylight over the dance floor that rises into an attractive centerpiece for the open deck above. It becomes the social venue before and after meals with light entertainment after dinner. An adjacent room offers a two-table casino and slot machines, but this is not a late-night ship. Many passengers enjoy selecting from several hundred videos or CDs and squirreling away in their cabins.

The wood-paneled dining room offers open-seating flexibility, and dress is always casual, with jackets and ties seen only at the captain's table. Entrees may feature linguine with frutti di mare, crisp duck breast, and grilled filet mignon. In good weather only dinner is served here, while the Veranda provides glass-enclosed protection for breakfast and lunch with sheltered tables out on deck and under parasols. Food is available from a menu or the buffet; at breakfast, a chef prepares omelets and pancakes and, at lunch, a pasta or a superb bouillabaisse. Bread pudding is a daily lunchtime staple.

Dinner takes place under the stars one evening, a romantic outdoor setting with tables arranged around the pool and with dancing on deck between courses. The spread includes jumbo shrimp, mussels, crab, lots of salad fixings, and freshly grilled tuna, lobster tails, steak, lamb chops, and chicken breasts.

The daytime gathering spot is the lido, partly a covered lounge with sit-up bar and partly an open area with a small pool for dipping, a whirlpool, deck chairs, and cushioned mats. The water-sports program is a big draw and includes diving instruction and snorkeling in several ports and complimentary use of sailboats, sailboards, banana boats, and kayaks that are launched from the marina deck. Gym equipment includes aerobic trainers, two treadmills, two bicycles, a rowing machine, weights, and a sauna.

The ship's seventy-four roomy outside cabins on two decks are similar, with beds, either twins or queen-size, set beneath twin portholes. Amenities include TVs—with news, features, and three movie channels—and a built-in combination of a CD player, VCR, minibar, and refrigerator. A dining table folds out for in-cabin dining from a full menu at mealtimes. The bathrooms have teakwood floors and circular, steel-gray shower and toilet stalls.

The Itinerary

The week's itinerary is planned around water sports, beach outings, and slow-paced sightseeing, a terrific combination for a week of unwinding.

At **St. Thomas,** the embarkation port, the harbor may be crowded with huge cruise liners, but once the *Wind Spirit* slips out of the harbor, another world is ahead. **St. John,** also in the U.S. Virgin Islands, is an overnight call where the ship gently swings at anchor. Spend the morning on a scenic island drive to the Virgin Islands National Park and the afternoon at the beach, one of the Caribbean's finest. Anchoring off **Marigot,** St. Martin, on the French/Dutch island's less commercial side, the most popular activity features a spirited sailing race aboard an America's Cup 12-meter boat with you acting as crew.

On nearby and upscale **St. Barts,** there's a chance to go horseback riding and snorkeling, and, for a change of venue, check

---

Address/Phone: Windstar Cruises, 300 Elliott Avenue West, Seattle, WA 98119; (206) 281–3535 or (800) 258–7245; brochures: (800) 626–9900; fax: (206) 286–3229; www.windstarcruises.com

The Ship: *Wind Spirit* was built in 1988 and has a gross tonnage of 5,350, a length of 440 feet, and a draft of 13 feet.

Passengers: 148; mostly American, forty and up

Dress: Casual

Officers/Crew: British officers; Filipino and Indonesian crew

Cabins: 74; all similar, roomy outside with portholes, apart from one owner's suite

Fare: $$$

What's included: Cruise fare and port charges, basic tips

What's not included: Airfare, drinks, shore excursions, extra tips

Highlights: A carefree and casual lifestyle in small Caribbean ports

Other itineraries: In addition to this seven-day Caribbean cruise aboard the *Wind Spirit,* which operates between December and April, the fleet includes sistership, *Wind Star,* and the 14,745-ton, 312-passenger *Wind Surf* (formerly *Club Med I*). Itineraries, mostly seven days, are offered in the Mediterranean and Caribbean, plus longer Signature Voyages, transatlantic crossings, and a renewed program in Tahiti.

out Gustavia's restaurants lining the small harbor. They all have menus out front, and once you have made a choice, go inside to make a reservation for dinner, as the ship does not sail until 11:00 P.M. Tortola and Jost Van Dyke, both in the British Virgin Islands, are serenely peaceful places. Cruising to **Tortola,** take a taxi to Mount Sage National Park for a hike along the Rain For-est Trail or the Mahogany Forest Trail. **Jost Van Dyke** is an ideal destination for a morning on the beach. The ship anchors overnight at **Virgin Gorda,** and from the stern marina, you can go for a sail or take out a kayak. The most popular excursion is to the Baths, an area of massive boulders by the sea, where there are narrow rock cuts and caves to explore.

STAR CLIPPERS'
Star Clipper
Caribbean Cruising under Sail

The *Star Clipper* and sistership *Star Flyer* were conceived by Swedish yachting enthusiast Mikael Krafft as near replicas of mid-nineteenth-century fast clipper ships. Built in Ghent, Belgium, in the early 1990s, the pair qualify as two of the largest and tallest sailing ships ever built and, in summer 2000, were joined by the brand-new, five-masted *Royal Clipper.*

In price and accommodations the *Star Clipper* falls between the simpler Windjammer Barefoot fleet and the upscale four Windstar Cruise vessels. At sea the ship is generally under sail from late evening to early or mid-morning the next day. Passengers may help with the lines, but there is no pressure to do so. When the wind dies, the 1,370-horsepower Caterpillar diesel engine kicks in.

The Tropical Bar provides the *Star Clipper*'s social center, located amidships on a sheltered deck under a protective canvas awning. One of the two public rooms is an Edwardian-style library, with a wall of mahogany-fronted bookcases flanking a fireplace and comfy seating for reading and cards on a rainy day. The other, with light wood-paneled walls and recessed seating,

serves as a piano lounge, with a pianist seated beneath circular skylights cut into the bottom of the suspended swimming pool.

In good weather the lounge and library see little use during the day, and most passengers gather around the wheelhouse and the two sun-deck swimming pools or at the midships bar. In the morning the captain holds forth at story time, when he recites sailing-ship traditions and rules of navigation and discusses the day's program.

Meals are served to both officers and passengers at one open sitting in a wood- and brass-accented dining room. Breakfast and lunch are buffet style, with a good choice of hot and cold items, while dinner is served by a waiter with the menu offering a fish, meat, and vegetarian entree. The food is of good quality and well prepared but by no means gourmet. Dress is casual but never ragged.

Cabins, nearly all outside and some shaped by the ship's hull, are of moderate size and have a sailing-ship feel, using wood trim, electric lamps mounted in gimbals, and decorative brass counter railings. Amenities include phones and televisions and tiny bathrooms with water-saving push-button showers.

The Itinerary

The Treasure Islands week embarks and disembarks at **St. Maarten,** the Dutch and shopping half of the island shared with St. Martin, the more peaceful French side. The first call is at the upscale resort island of **Anguilla,** then the beaches at **Sandy Cay** and **Soper's Hole** provide opportunities for swimming, snorkeling, and windsurfing. Norman Island is where Robert Louis Stevenson wrote *Treasure Island,* and **Virgin Gorda,** an overnight stay, is noted for its **Baths,** an area of massive boulders by the sea, with narrow rock cuts and caves to explore.

Jost Van Dyke is an offbeat stop for cruise ships, and the *Star Clipper* is likely to be the largest vessel in the Great Harbour. Wander over to Foxy's, a classic beach bar for locals and the yachting set.

At **St. Kitts** there is an island tour to old plantation sites, great views from Brimstone Hill, golfing, and a chance to shop at **Bas-**seterre. Off **St. Barts,** always a favorite stop, the little harbor island at **Gustavia** provides an appropriate setting for the *Star Clipper.* It being the biggest sailing ship to call, you can expect a lot of curious onlookers. There are moderately priced and expensive restaurants within walking distance of the landing, and the shopping here is good and less frenetic than on **St. Maarten,** where the cruise ends.

When the weather permits, a very special treat is offered, a Zodiac ride to observe just how splendid the *Star Clipper* looks slicing majestically through the water, with all sixteen sails catching the wind. From a water-level position ahead of the bow, passengers watch the ship bear down on them; and viewed from the stern, the ship appears to be leaving you behind. The *Star Clipper* is a democratic experience—it's not easy to tell the difference between passengers with money and those who have saved up for this easygoing cruise with visits to small ports.

Address/Phone: Star Clippers, 4101 Salzebo Street, Coral Gables, FL 33146; (305) 442–0550 or reservations: (800) 442–0551; brochures: (800) 442–0556; fax: (305) 442–1611; www.starclippers.com

The Ship: *Star Clipper* was built in 1992 and has a gross tonnage of 2,298, a length of 360 feet, and a draft of 18.5 feet.

Passengers: 168; all ages; some Europeans, but English is the lingua franca

Dress: Casual at all times

Officers/Crew: European officers; international crew

Cabins: 84; 78 outside, most relatively compact; no verandas

Fare: $$

What's included: Usually cruise only, although cruise tour rates will include air, hotels, some meals, some sightseeing, and transfers

What's not included: For cruise only, airfare, port charges, tips, drinks

Highlights: A terrific outdoor sailing experience; small yachting ports; thoroughly relaxed, social atmosphere

Other itineraries: Besides this and an alternative seven-night Caribbean cruise, which operates between November and April, the *Star Clipper* offers two Western Mediterranean itineraries and spring and fall transatlantic positioning voyages. The sistership *Star Flyer* operates in the Greek islands and along the Turkish coast from May to October, then travels via the Suez Canal to cruise the coasts of Malaysia and Thailand, returning through the Indian Ocean in April. The five-masted *Royal Clipper,* completed in 2000 and the largest sailing vessel ever built, also cruises the Caribbean, Mediterranean, and Atlantic.

WINDJAMMER BAREFOOT CRUISES'
Legacy
Eastern Caribbean Sailing Fancy-Free

 The famous Captain Mike Burke, now retired, founded the company in 1947. He purchased a slew of ships with interesting histories, transformed them into one-of-a-kind sailing vessels, and for years hosted party cruises popular with singles. Burke's children run the company now and, over the past few years, have been making a conscious effort to shake off the vestiges of the old self and create a more mainstream experience. Windjammer has recently hired its first hotel manager to improve the overall quality of the dining and cabin service, has added a kids' program (arts and crafts, snorkeling trips) on the *Legacy* during the summer months, and has plans to build additional new sailing ships.

Launched in 1997, the *Legacy* is the line's newest acquisition, its biggest and most modern. Built in France in 1959 as a research vessel called the *France II,* the ship was acquired by Windjammer in 1989 and converted into a traditional tall ship. The brightest and most spacious in the fleet, the *Legacy* is a departure from Windjammer's fleet of old-timers. It has comfortable cabins with bunk-style beds and good-sized private bathrooms, a cheerful dining saloon with large, round booths, and a roomy expanse of outdoor deck space. There's space to move around and then some.

Dining is informal family-style and ranges from unmemorable to really tasty. All breads and pastries are homemade, and at dinner, after soup and salad are served, passengers can choose from two main entrees, such as curried shrimp and roast pork with garlic sauce. Unlimited carafes of red and white wine are complimentary. Tasty breakfast, like eggs Benedict as well as the normal fare, and lunch, such as lobster pizza and apple salad, are served buffet style. At Jost Van Dyke the crew lugs ashore a picnic lunch for an afternoon beach party.

The Itinerary
The *Legacy* makes its way to off-the-beaten-track Caribbean ports of call like **Buck Island, Jost Van Dyke, Norman Island,** and **St. John** (as well as touristy ones like **St. Thomas**), anchoring offshore a mile or two and shuttling passengers back and forth by tender. Landings may require wading through knee-deep water to get ashore. Several excursions, like island tours and snorkeling, are offered in each port. The ship is usually the biggest vessel in port, and you'll feel like a quiet visitor, not an interloper.

With a palpable pirate-ship feel, the four-masted barquentine (powered by both sails and engines) and its yards of sails, chunky portholes, and generous use of wood lures passengers into a fantasy world of fairytale adventure. Guests are invited to help pull in the sails, crawl into the bow net, which juts out over the water, and sleep out on deck whenever they please (mats are provided). There are few rules and lots of freedom. The *Legacy* delivers an ultrainformal seafaring adventure rich in eccentricities. For example, there are no keys for the cabins (you can only lock cabins from the inside), rum punch is served in paper cups, daily announcements are written in magic marker on a bulletin board, and the purser doubles as the nurse and gift-shop manager.

Corny yet cute rituals make the trip feel like summer camp for adults: for instance, the doubloon system at the bar (a debit card of sorts that is punched with holes each time you buy a drink), the hymn

"Amazing Grace" loudly broadcast over the PA system each time the ship's sails are hoisted, and morning "story time," when the captain regales guests with the day's schedule and some funny tall tale he's concocted on the fly.

Besides this morning dose of down-home entertainment, you're on your own until happy hour. Just about every day is spent in port somewhere, and the occasional day at sea might feature a knot-tying demonstration and a bridge tour. The entertainment is the ship itself and the camaraderie among passengers. At 5:00 P.M. every day gallons of complimentary rum swizzles are generously offered with hors d'oeuvres like spicy meatballs, chicken fingers, and cheese and crackers. Guests gather on deck, often still in their sarongs and shorts, mingling in the fresh sea air, with taped music playing in the background. Sometimes an impromptu song or skit takes shape from a couple of fun-loving, down-to-earth guests. After dinner head up to the bar for drinks—you won't spend more than $3.00 a pop—or grab a chaise longue or mat and hit the deck. One or two nights a week a local pop band is brought on board for a few hours of dancing and there's a weekly barbecue buffet dinner and a costume party. Generally the ship stays late in one or two ports so that passengers can head ashore to one of the island watering holes. From honeymooning couples in their twenties to grandparents in their seventies, Windjammer attracts a broad range of adventurers, who return again and again.

Address/Phone: Windjammer Barefoot Cruises, 1759 Bay Road, Miami Beach, FL 33119; (305) 672–6453 or (800) 327–2601; fax: (305) 674–1219; www.windjammer.com

The Ship: *Legacy* was built in 1959 as the research vessel *France II* and was converted in 1997 to a windjammer. It has a gross tonnage of 1,165, a length of 294 feet, and a draft of 23 feet.

Passengers: 122; all ages and mostly Americans

Dress: Casual at all times

Officers/Crew: American and British officers; West Indian crew

Cabins: 62 cabins, outside with either a window or porthole and relatively compact

Fare: $$

What's included: Cruise only, rum punch at happy hour, and wine at dinner

What's not included: Airfare, port charges, shore excursions, tips, bar drinks

Highlights: Carefree, very casual onboard atmosphere; unstructured; few rules

Other itineraries: In addition to the Legacy's seven-night Caribbean cruises in winter and spring, round-trip from Fajardo, Puerto Rico, visiting the British and U.S. Virgin Islands, the fleet includes four other windjammers (*Flying Cloud, Mandalay, Polynesia,* and *Yankee Clipper*) plus the passenger supply vessel *Amazing Grace,* which sails year-round in the Bahamas and Caribbean.

LATIN AMERICA

CRUISE WEST'S
Spirit of Endeavour
Small-Ship Adventure Cruising in the Sea of Cortez

 Cruise West, an American firm in business since 1973, may be the best known of the Alaska-to-Mexico small-ship operating companies, offering intimate encounters along the West Coast of North America with a casual, folksy atmosphere aboard seven ships. One of the company's most sophisticated vessels is the 102-passenger *Spirit of Endeavour,* once belonging to Clipper Cruise and a near sister to the *Nantucket Clipper.* From its decks, you are able to get ever so close to nature and the sea and all that inhabits therein, and even on occasion practically reach out and touch friendly whales. That's the beauty of exploring by small ship, foraging for adventure in a remote northwest corner of Mexico.

Oak and teak are used throughout this light and airy ship. There's an all-purpose lounge bathed in windows where guests congregate, socialize, and listen to presentations by the expedition leaders on the landscape, geology, and local culture. In keeping with the informal atmosphere, the speakers mingle with passengers to answer questions and share experiences.

The dining room serves up well-prepared American fare and Mexican specialties in one open-seating arrangement. Young crew members earn an A in enthusiasm and a B on the finer points of dining room service, contributing to Cruise West's laid-back, summer-camp feel. Before dinner each evening, there will be an informal talk about the next day's attractions and a question-and-answer session. Videos and books are available for borrowing.

All cabins are outside, most with picture windows for superb views, and Upper Deck cabins open to the side promenade. The TVs are closed circuit for viewing the ship's video collection.

Outside decks are ample fore, aft, and topside for relaxing and viewing. It's commonplace for the captain to speed up, slow down, backtrack, or do whatever it takes to spot the wildlife, such as gray whales, sea lions, and bottle-nose dolphins, that inhabits the Pacific lagoons.

The Itinerary

The *Spirit of Endeavour* sticks mainly to the uninhabited or sparsely populated islands along the Sea of Cortez's Baja California coast, anchoring at dinner time and then often moving in the middle of the night to allow passengers a day of hiking, kayaking, and snorkeling at a new location. It is unusual to see another ship, and if so, it is only another small expedition vessel.

Cruise West carries an expedition leader and assistant, both Americans, and a Mexican park ranger. Passengers have access to two-person kayaks, and they may go paddling in groups with a naturalist or on their own within sight of the ship.

The week's cruise begins and ends at **La Paz, Baja California,** a busy place with a long seafront promenade lined with souvenir and craft shops, hawkers, a strip lined with bars, and teenagers cruising in cars. But once away, it's another world for nearly a full week, mostly nature oriented but also including visits to small towns and a Mexican mission.

Passengers go ashore in the *Endeavour*'s inflatable boats at Bonanza Beach, where the desert is a lively tropical world with water-based plants and animal life with all manner of bugs living underneath. The terrain here is treated with great care like in the Galápagos, and no one is allowed to stray from a recognized path.

Isla San Jose and **Isla San Francisco** are pristine volcanic islands, and the energetic can climb one of the peaks and gaze down on kayakers dotted about the mangrove-backed lagoon below. Others go swimming, snorkeling, and beachcombing.

The **Loreto Mission,** founded at the end of the seventeenth century, hosts a wine and cheese reception accompanied by a singer and guitarist. Loreto also offers a small museum and an optional four-hour fishing tour, where it's catch and then throw back yellowfin tuna, grouper, sea bass, and trigger fish.

During the ship's winter season, the best whale sightings are in the Pacific, so passengers transfer across the Baja peninsula to **Bahia Magdalena** to board eight-person motorized pangas. There is a good chance, but no certainty, of seeing gray whales and their calves stopping in lagoons during their annual migration. Sometimes a 40-foot whale might swim right up to the side of the boat and allow you to pat it. When they dive, the water is so clear, you can see the entire whale and calf swimming below the boat.

The captain cruises slowly by a seamount called Los Isotes to see a colony of blue-footed boobies, one of the unusual species that is also found in the Galápagos. The location is a favorite spot for sea lions, and often there is a chance to swim among them. On a clear night, the ship may shut off the deck lights, and a crew member, an amateur astronomer, will point out the stars and constellations.

Bottle-nose dolphins abound in these waters, and it is fun to watch them jumping over the bow waves and playing in the wake. Birds are not quite as numerous, but there should be sightings of turkey vultures, brown pelicans, and diving cormorants.

After a stop at Ensenada Grande on **Isla Partida** for a beach and nature walk, the captain hosts a farewell dinner back on board. Returning to La Paz in the morning, there's time to wander before attending a private fiesta with Mexican musicians and dancers on the terrace of the Governor's mansion.

Following the cruise, consider taking the four-night extension, which includes a train ride into the roadless interior and deep into the **Copper Canyon,** which is four times larger and 1,000 feet deeper than the Grand Canyon, with a night spent at a rustic hotel perched on the rim.

Address/Phone: Cruise West, 2401 Fourth Avenue, Suite 700, Seattle, WA 98121; (800) 888–9378; fax: (206) 441–4757; www.cruisewest.com

The Ship: *Spirit of Endeavour* was built in 1983 as the *Newport Clipper* and has a length of 217 feet and a shallow draft.

Passengers: 102 double occupancy; mostly Americans in their forties to seventies, but also families during the school holidays

Dress: Casual morning, noon, and night

Officers/Crew: American

Cabins: 51, all outside, most with windows, and most have twin beds, some at right angles

Fare: $$$

What's included: Cruise fare, port charges, shore excursions

What's not included: Airfare, drinks, tips, some optional shore excursions

Highlights: A fantastic opportunity to get close to nature while also having a warm, comfortable ship to come home to at day's end

Other itineraries: In addition to this seven-day cruise in the Sea of Cortez, which operates between December and April, there are many additional Cruise West expedition-style cruises throughout Alaska, including overland extensions, in the Pacific Northwest, along the Columbia and Snake Rivers, and in California Wine Country.

CARNIVAL CRUISE LINES'
Carnival Pride
Mexico and the Hotel *Queen Mary*

 This winning combination of a pre- or post-cruise stay aboard the grand old former ocean liner *Queen Mary*, moored at Long Beach, California, and a week's Mexican Riviera itinerary aboard a newish, high standard Carnival ship more than justifies inclusion.

The *Carnival Pride* is the second in the Spirit class and is miles ahead of the Fantasy class in the proliferation of balcony cabins and innovative features, plus the addition of a supper club. This class, at 88,500 gross tons, is smaller than but similar to the larger 101,000-ton *Destiny* class but full of the now-expected Carnival glitz.

The public rooms range fore and aft of a spectacular nine-deck atrium, the ship's main point of orientation. Music and entertainment venues include a piano bar, jazz nightclub with karaoke hours, two-deck-high disco with video wall, sports bar, three-deck-high show lounge, library and Internet center, and a video arcade for kids.

Dining is traditional, a two-deck formal restaurant with early and late seatings dishing out lots of good food. For informal eating, the sprawling buffet offers numerous stations that feature Caesar salads, New York–style deli sandwiches, and pizza twenty-four hours a day. But for a real treat that achieves a new high benchmark for Carnival, pay the freight (extra charge) to have at least one dinner in the Supper Club. Its location is at the top level of the atrium away from all the bustle, and beneath a glass skylight that dramatically reveals the ship's funnel looming above. Tables are mostly for two and four, and service is excellent. The specialty menu, carefully explained at your table, presents a choice of excellent porterhouse and New York strip steaks, prime rib, grilled lamb chops, stone crabs, and Chilean sea bass.

Deck space is generous and a big draw on sea days. Passengers gravitate to the three pools, four hot tubs, the two-level gym and spa, jogging deck, basketball and volleyball court, and the water slide.

On this class, the cabins are less plain and have more attractive design features. They are roomy with good storage space, and 65 percent come with balconies, though very small and sparsely furnished with a deck chair, single chair, and a small table.

In spring 2003, Carnival opened a new cruise terminal at Long Beach, adjacent to the *Queen Mary*, the record-breaking Cunard liner that set sail in 1936 and after 1,001 Atlantic crossings, retired to Southern California to become a major attraction, hotel, and dining destination. Carnival's one- to three-night pre- and post-cruise land packages include overnight accommodations aboard the *Queen Mary*, a self-guided tour of the ship, and a rental car.

Listed on the National Register of Historic Places, the 81,237-ton *Queen Mary* is longer than the *Carnival Pride* but not quite so large. Recalling the grand era of ocean liner travel, she offers 365 wood-paneled staterooms, a splendid art deco–style observation lounge with musical entertainment, and a range of dining options that include Sir Winston's, featuring excellent California and continental cuisine and Chelsea, a seafood restaurant. The Sunday brunch in the former first-class restaurant has a large following as does the guided and self-guided ship tours. Both the *Queen Mary* and the *Carnival Pride* have onboard wedding chapels.

The Itinerary

The *Carnival Pride* sails from **Long Beach** every Sunday, after the *Queen Mary* brunch, for Puerto Vallarta, Mazatlan, and Cabo San Lucas, a Mexican Riviera itinerary that offers white-sand beaches, water sports, trips into the interior, and three sea days aboard the ship.

After two nights and a day sailing south along the coast of Baja California, the *Carnival Pride* sails into **Puerto Vallarta,** where the active can go off-road biking using 21-speed mountain bikes or join an ecohiking trip into the surrounding hills with a swim in a mineral spring. For the more sedentary, a bus heads inland through fields of bananas, coconuts, mangos, and papaya to a market farm village. Then, sailing overnight to **Mazatlan,** you can go sport fishing for marlin, with the largest catch at 750 pounds, or drive up into the Sierra Madre Mountains to a former gold mining town and visit a factory making roof tiles, jars, flower posts, and dishes and another making Mexican-style furniture. A day at a guest ranch includes swimming and horseback riding.

At **Cabo San Lucas,** a popular resort destination on Baja's southern tip, a sailing tour visits a sea lion colony, and from December to March, there's a very good chance of seeing whales close up. But if you want to play independently, then enjoy the white-sand beaches and some of the world's best snorkeling and scuba diving.

After three successive port calls in three days, the ship provides two nights and a day on your northward return to Long Beach.

Address/Phone: Carnival Cruise Lines, 3655 NW 87th Avenue, Miami, FL 33178; (305) 599–2600 or (800) 327–9501; fax: (305) 406–4740; www.carnival.com. Information on the *Queen Mary* can be obtained by calling (562) 435–3511 or at www.queen mary.com.

The Ship: *Carnival Pride*, built in 2002, has a gross tonnage of 88,500, a length of 960 feet, and a draft of 25.5 feet.

Passengers: 2,124; mostly Americans, all ages

Dress: Formal and casual (collared shirts and slacks)

Officers/Crew: Italian and international officers and international crew

Cabins: 1,062; 849 outside and 682 with balconies

Fare: $$

What's included: Cruise fare

What's not included: Airfare, port charges, excursions, drinks, tips

Highlights: Nonstop activities and entertainment; pre/post-cruise stays on the *Queen Mary*

Other itineraries: Besides this one-week Mexican Riviera cruise, operating year-round, Carnival operates shorter cruises to Mexico and cruises in Alaska, Hawaii, the Caribbean, New England, Canada, and Bermuda.

ROYAL CARIBBEAN'S
Vision of the Seas
Megaship Mexican Riviera

Counting the world's biggest cruise ships, such as the 137,000-ton, 3,100-passenger *Voyager of the Seas* and *Explorer of the Seas,* Royal Caribbean has fourteen ships in its mostly-mega fleet, and more are in the works. The 78,491-ton, 2,000-passenger *Vision of the Seas* is the newest and last member of the line's Vision Class, all built between 1995 and 1998.

The *Vision of the Seas,* like its sisters, is bathed in glass (especially good in Alaska), with glass canopies and windbreaks, skylights, and floor-to-ceiling windows with sweeping views. The focal point is a soaring, seven-story atrium with a huge, dramatic sculpture within and lots of shops around it. Overall, the ship is designed with warm woods and brass, fountains and foliage, crystal, soft leathers, and eye-catching artwork. The *Vision* is easy to navigate, despite its size. Glass elevators take passengers up through the Centrum atrium into the stunning Viking Crown Lounge, the line's signature, glass-sheathed observation-lounge-cum-disco, perched high above the rest of the ship. The Schooner Bar is a casual piano bar with lots of wood and rope, befitting its nautical name, and ditto the Champagne Bar, at the foot of the atrium, where you can listen and dance to a trio while sipping wine or a glass of bubbly. Full musical revues are staged in the two-story show lounge, which has an orchestra pit that can be hydraulically raised and lowered. Likewise, the sprawling casino is dressed in Vegas-style flash and splash and assures gambling folk of an atmosphere conducive to at least having fun trying to beat the odds.

The ship's vast open areas include the Sun Deck's two swimming pools (one covered by a retractable glass roof), six whirlpools, and the Windjammer buffet-style restaurant. Poolside, you'll find loud, live music serenading the party along with silly contests that most passengers seem to just love. The soothing ShipShape spa is truly one of the most attractive around, and adjacent is a spacious solarium with a pool, chaise longues, floor-to-ceiling windows, and a retractable glass ceiling. Surprisingly, the gym is small for the ship's size. Families will like the extensive, supervised kids' activities for four age groups, including a children's playroom, a teen center and disco, and a video arcade.

The large dining room spans two decks that are interconnected with a very grand staircase and flanked with walls of glass nearly 20 feet high. Each has contemporary and tasteful decor, replete with stainless steel, mirrors, dramatic chandeliers, and a massive grand piano for dinnertime serenading. The food is generally tasty enough for a ship of this size, featuring choices like oven-roasted crispy duck served with rhubarb sauce or grilled pork tenderloin on a bed of stewed tomatoes and eggplant. A light and healthy vegetarian dish and pasta are offered at each meal.

Standard cabins are compact, although larger than the cramped cubicles featured aboard the company's older ships. Nearly one-fourth of the cabins have private verandas, and all have TVs (offering some twenty channels of video, four music channels, three for movies, and three with satellite programming), preprogrammed radios, and safes. Bathrooms are small.

The Itinerary
Exploring the **Mexican Riviera** on this floating resort couldn't be more enjoyable.

Sailing seven-night cruises round-trip from **Los Angeles** and sometimes **San Diego,** you can savor the spice of Mexico's culture, its dramatic rocky shoreline, and great beaches at a string of Pacific coast ports.

Cruising south, two nights and a day at sea bring the ship within sight of the dramatic rock formations of **Cabo San Lucas** peninsula. During the port call snorkel, take a seat in a glass-bottom boat or semisubmersible to view the reefs and sea life and spend the day at a beach resort for sunbathing and swimming. While waiting for the tender back to the ship, browse the open-air craft market. Sailing overnight to **Mazatlan,** a city that's worth exploring on foot or a tour for its main square, historic district, huge produce market, and lots of handicrafts and practical clothing for these hot climes for sale. Take a drive inland to picturesque colonial villages and mission churches set among the **Sierre Madre Mountains,** go deep-sea fishing for marlin and sailfish, and take in a folkloric show.

Just down the coast beautiful **Puerto Vallarta** is often the favorite call for its setting, winding cobblestone streets, tropical gardens, and now-distant connections to Elizabeth Taylor and Richard Burton and *Night of the Iguana.* Enjoy two full sea days back north to San Diego.

Address/Phone: Royal Caribbean International, 1050 Caribbean Way, Miami, FL 33132; (305) 539–6000 or (800) 327–6700 for brochures; fax: (305) 374–7354; www.royalcaribbean.com

The Ship: *Vision of the Seas* was built in 1998, has a gross tonnage of 78,491, a length of 915 feet, and a draft of 25 feet.

Passengers: 2,000; mostly American, all ages, especially during school holidays

Dress: Suits or tuxes for the formal nights, jackets for informal nights, and slacks and collared shirts for casual nights

Officers/Crew: International

Cabins: 1,000 average size, 593 outside, 25 percent with verandas

Fare: $$

What's included: Cruise and port charges

What's not included: Airfare, shore excursions, drinks, tips

Highlights: Spa and solarium, overall design, lots of outdoor activities aboard and ashore

Other itineraries: In addition to these seven-night *Vision of the Seas* Mexican Riviera cruises, operating from September to May, the ship cruises Alaska in summer and occasionally the Panama Canal and Hawaii. Other Royal Caribbean ships cruise the Caribbean, New England/Canada, and Europe.

CRUISE WEST'S
Pacific Explorer
Costa Rica's Pacific Coast

Cruise West's *Pacific Explorer* focuses on protecting the natural environment while enabling tourists to visit unusual sites in Costa Rica, Belize, Guatemala, and Panama. Originally built as a U.S. supply ship, the *Pacific Explorer* was converted into a passenger ship in 1995 and sails exclusively along Costa Rica's Pacific coast and on to Panama. The ship takes up to ninety-nine passengers in a friendly atmosphere on an all-inclusive program of shore excursions. The passengers are likely to include families, couples of all ages, and singles.

The forward observation lounge has comfortable chairs and couches for quiet reading, watching the sights, or browsing the corner library's local reference books and donated paperbacks. Socializing takes place at the Tortuga Bar on Upper Deck, where drinks are complimentary. Entertainment may be local musicians or dancing under the stars.

Open-sitting meals are served in a pleasant dining room at tables and at banquettes next to large panoramic windows. Continental breakfast is available on deck, but most passengers choose the dining-room buffet for fresh fruit, croissants, pastries, cold cereals, and hot dishes to order such as huevos rancheros or French toast. Lunch is served buffet style on the Upper Deck or on the beach at tables with red-checkered tablecloths. The choices may be cold cuts and salads and entrees such as sea bass, roast turkey, chicken, and pizza. For dinner passengers sign up for one of three flavorful entrees such as tenderloin steak with mushroom sauce, mahimahi with tartar sauce, and fettuccine with tomato sauce.

The attractive cabins are simply furnished with either twin or queen beds, matching night tables, a double closet and storage drawers below, a five-shelved unit, and a demilune table beneath a mirror. Rich Costa Rican woods are used in the furniture highlighted by the maroon red, dark green, and navy blue–striped bedspreads. Cabin windows open to bring in the sounds of the birds and the sea. The bathroom is functional and has a shower. At day's end a briefing session, held in the Toucan Lounge, lays out the upcoming shore activities, which invariably means an early wake-up knock.

The Itinerary

Experienced and highly competent local naturalists lead groups of fourteen to sixteen on hikes rated as easy, medium, and difficult, depending on length and terrain. Shore excursions begin at the swim platform, the launching spot for the Zodiacs and for taking a kayak or banana boat or water-skiing.

The *Pacific Explorer* sails from **Los Seuños,** Herradura Bay, to the Nicoya Peninsula and the privately owned **Curu Wildlife Refuge.** The dry, tropical-forest vegetation allows relatively easy spotting of howler monkeys and native birds such as trogons, blue-tailed manakins, and motmots. On **Isla Tortuga** passengers swim or snorkel from the white sandy beach, or they can try the Canopy Ride, where people "fall" from a platform in the treetops with the aid of a harness attached to a cable-and-pulley system.

In the evening the ship sails south overnight to **Corcovado National Park,** one of the most remote parks in Costa Rica. Located 75 miles north of the Panamanian border, it covers 108,000 acres and is one of the richest, most diverse tropical regions in the world. Although biologists have identified 285 species of birds, 500 species of trees, 139 species of mammals, and 116 of amphibians and reptiles, we were content with spotting howler monkeys, scarlet macaws, morpho butterflies, and pizotes (raccoonlike animals).

Sailing to the large Panamanian Isla de Coiba, snorkel among white-tipped reef sharks, manta rays, and puffer fish. Offshore, **Isla Cano,** an ancient burial site, is excellent for snorkeling. Deep-sea-fishing and scuba diving enthusiasts spent the morning on a chartered boat.

Midweek we anchored in **Golfo Dulce** off **Golfito,** once an important port for the United Fruit Company. We visited two privately owned preserves, the lush rain forests and beautiful gardens at **Cana Blanca,** a peaceful, family-owned resort complete with its own resident scarlet macaw; and **Casa Orquideas,** a landscaped botanical garden.

On the last day we visited **Manuel Antonio National Park** to finally spot the elusive two-toed sloth high on the branches of a ceiba tree, iguanas, whitefaced or capuchin monkeys, and agoutis (native rodents). During a final afternoon swim and snorkel beneath Cathedral Point came the sound of howler monkeys in the distance.

Address/Phone: Cruise West, 2401 Fourth Avenue, Suite 700, Seattle, WA 98121; (800) 426–7702; fax: (206) 441–4757; e-mail: info@cruisewest.com; www.cruisewest.com

The Ship: *Pacific Explorer* was first built in 1970 and completely rebuilt in 1995 and has a length of 185 feet and a draft of 12.5 feet.

Passengers: 100; average age fifty; families welcome; 95 percent American

Dress: Very casual

Officers/Crew: Costa Rican, American expedition leader

Cabins: 46 double cabins and 4 suites; all with large picture windows

Fare: $$$

What's included: Cruise, port charges, drinks, excursions, water sports, laundry service

What's not included: Airfare, tips

Highlights: Exploring remote areas of Costa Rica's Pacific coast and Panama; seeing lots of wildlife

Other itineraries: In addition to this seven-day cruise, which operates in March, April, November, and December, plus a slightly altered route in June, July, and August, there are other Central American itineraries in January and February that sail farther south to Panama, including a canal transit. Cruise West also operates cruises from Baja California north to Alaska and around the Pacific Rim.

LINDBLAD EXPEDITIONS'
Sea Voyager
From Costa Rica to the Panama Canal

 For anyone with the experience of ocean travel, the immediate impression on first seeing the *Sea Voyager* is one of astonishment and delight—how tiny this ship is! Advantages are soon apparent. The vessel is compact and cozy and rides low in the water, so that one feels a part of the ocean and not the more usual remote observer aloft. The *Sea Voyager* is an ideal conveyance to the remote Pacific coastal and island side of Central America.

The passenger cabins are sited on all three decks, and they are outside with windows. Twin beds in some standard cabins convert to a double while in the deluxe category they form a queen-size bed. The Bridge Deck (highest) cabins open onto the side promenade. The lounge is aft on this same deck and opens onto the partly covered sun deck. A small fitness center and a reference library face forward, and the latter opens onto the forward observation deck.

The dining room on Main Deck has large-view windows facing to port and starboard. Varied and delicious meals are served at one open seating, and the Honduran serving staff is friendly and helpful. Breakfast is a buffet in the dining room; lunch is buffet in the dining room or on deck; and dinner is a served meal in the restaurant with a choice of entrees that always includes meat, fish, and vegetarian dishes. The *Sea Voyager* is a most comfortable conveyance for this creative expedition-style itinerary.

The Itinerary
Each day there is a tempting choice of activities, all involving Zodiacs (stable motorized rubber dinghies), for trips ashore to a secluded beach, to a national park, and to observe birds and wildlife. Apart from the Panama Canal transit, it is rare to even see another ship, as this trip is "far from the maddening crowd." The trip starts with a transfer from San Jose Airport to the Pacific coastal port at **Herradura.**

Lindblad trips include an expedition leader and naturalist staff who take passengers ashore and host briefings in the lounge each evening before dinner. At the end of the cruise, passengers receive a trip diary including a complete list of animals and birds seen.

Landing at **Manuel Antonio National Park,** the naturalists will seek out the very lethargic three-toed tree sloth and spot the difficult-to-see tropical birds blended into the thick vegetation.

An early-morning landing at San Pedrillo involves a hike through the **Corcovado National Park** with likely sightings of howler, capuchin, and white-faced monkeys. You can also swim in waterfall pools and ride a horse on the beach. In the **Golfo Dulce,** go kayaking and visit the Casa Orquideas gardens, an unexpected surprise, a veritable botanical garden with a fine collection of plants, shrubs, and trees—and visiting exotic birds—that is in no way artificial but a controlled extension of the natural wild.

Off the coast of Panama the **Isla Coiba** is a relatively new national park with hiking along lush forest trails, snorkeling to see tropical fish, and swimming. The ship's underwater specialist will photograph the fish life and present a film that evening before dinner.

Then **Las Perlas Islands,** sited in the Gulf of Panama, provide a lingering Zodiac visit among hundreds of seabirds—brown pelicans, brown and blue-footed boobies, and the magnificent frigate birds.

The grand finale is the **Panama Canal** transit from the Pacific to the Atlantic, and a very different experience aboard a tiny ship rising and descending in the huge lock chambers. Two sets of locks, then a single set, raise the ship to the level of the **Gatun Lake,** where the vessel anchors for the night and includes a visit by special arrangement to **Barro Colorado Island,** accompanied by scientists from the Smithsonian Research Station to look for marmosets, sloths, tapirs, and peccaries.

The *Sea Voyager* then leaves Gatun Lake via the three lock chambers down to the level of the Caribbean and docks at **Colon** for a coach transfer to Panama City for the flight back to the United States.

Address/Phone: Lindblad Expeditions, 720 Fifth Avenue, New York, NY 10019; (212) 765–7740 or (800) 397–3348; fax: (212) 265–3370; e-mail: explore@ expeditions.com; www.expeditions.com

The Ship: *Sea Voyager*, built in 1982 as the *America* later becoming the *Temptress Voyager*, has a gross tonnage of 1,195, is 175 feet long and has a draft of eight feet.

Passengers: 62, mostly Americans, fifty and older

Dress: Casual at all times

Officers/Crew: Honduran officers, crew, and staff; American expedition leader

Cabins: 31 cabins, all outside with sliding windows

Fare: $$$

What's included: Cruise fare, port charges, all shore excursions, transfer between group flights and the ship, tips to local guides/drivers, soft drinks, services of ship's doctor

What's not included: Airfare, tips to ship's crew, alcoholic drinks

Highlights: An expedition cruise to remote Central America and numerous wildlife sightings

Other itineraries: Besides this seven-day expedition cruise from Costa Rica to Panama, operating in both directions between November and April, the *Sea Voyager* also cruises from Panama to Guatemala, Honduras, and Belize. Other Lindblad ships offer expedition trips in the Galápagos, Baja California and the Sea of Cortez, Columbia–Snake Rivers, Alaska, Antarctica, Canada, Greenland, Iceland, northern Europe, and the Mediterranean.

CRYSTAL CRUISES'
Crystal Harmony
The Panama Canal and Caribbean -

 Established in 1990, Crystal Cruises' ships are among the largest in the luxury sector, and the three-ship fleet provides a refined cruise for passengers who appreciate superb service and top-notch cuisine. Overall, the decor is breezy, light, and cheerful, with lots of white and beige as well as dabs of pinks, mints, and blues.

Crystal is owned by Nippon Yusen Kaisha (NYK), Japan's largest container-shipping enterprise, and yet most passengers will not be aware of this fact. More than anything, Crystal is international, with a strong emphasis on European service. The Japanese flavor comes through subtly in the excellent Asian alternative restaurant, in the theme buffets, and the handful of Japanese passengers.

The *Crystal Harmony* is a social, active ship with four restaurants, a half dozen bars and entertainment lounges, a sizable gym and spa, two pools (one covered by a retractable glass roof), an uninterrupted jogging circuit, a paddle-tennis court, Ping-Pong, shuffleboard, golf driving nets, and a putting green.

The *Harmony*'s two reservations-only alternative restaurants—Kyoto, a Japanese restaurant, and Prego, an Italian one—are two of the best at sea. Kyoto, completely authentic, offers miso soup, beef teriyaki, and pork dishes, served with chopsticks and little rests; sake, in tiny sake cups; and sushi, presented on thick, blocky glass platters.

The main dining room, with its stylish, white Doric columns and roomy table arrangements, serves dinner in two seatings, whereas breakfast and lunch are one. Dishes may be a roasted duck with apricot-sage stuffing served with a Grand Marnier orange sauce, or broiled Black Angus sirloin steak, or seared sea scallops and jumbo shrimp served with a light lobster beurre blanc over a bed of pumpkin risotto. A low-fat selection is broiled fillet of Chilean sea bass served with steamed vegetables. Crystal inventories one of the most sophisticated selections of fairly priced California wines on the high seas. Service by the team of ultraprofessional, gracious European male waiters is excellent.

Themed luncheon buffets—Asian, Mediterranean, or a western barbecue—are excellent and generously spread out by the pool. For a casual lunch you can order beef, chicken, and salmon burgers, pizza, tuna melts, chicken wraps, Caesar salad, and fruit from the pool-side Trident Grill. For afternoon tea the revenue is the ultrachic Palm Court, a sprawling space on a high deck bathed in floor-to-ceiling windows and with pale blue and white furniture in leather and rattan as well as a harpist in residence.

Count on several enrichment lectures such as those given by a Panama Canal historian, a movie critic, or a celebrity guest speaker. Learn to swing or do the rumba and merengue, play bridge and trivia games, partake of arts-and-crafts sessions like glass etching, or take golf lessons. The computer lab has twenty work stations, and classes are offered on basic introduction, understanding the Internet, how to buy a computer, and using e-mail, with access readily available.

Shows encompass classical concerts, comedy acts, dancers, and lead singers performing Cole Porter or Rodgers and Hammerstein. Other venues host ballroom dancing, a pianist in the paneled and very romantic Avenue Saloon, and first-run movies.

Despite their high price tag, the large

majority of Crystal's cabins are smaller than these aboard the small luxury competitors. About half the accommodations have small verandas, measuring about 6 by 8 feet. Drawer space is adequate, hanging closets are tight, bathrooms compact, and sound-proofing is fair. All cabins have a sitting area, a bathtub (a compact one on the lower category cabins) and shower, TVs broadcasting CNN, ESPN, and other channels, a VCR, a minibar, a hair dryer, and a safe.

The Itinerary

The *Crystal Harmony* is a fine, roomy, well-laid-out ship to take you through the Canal and to spend five or six days at sea. Recline on your private balcony, head to one of the quiet, concave slices of the aft tiered decks, or get cozy in one of the ocean-facing ban-quettes in the Palm Court/Vista Lounge observation lounge.

Sailings of mostly eleven nights between **New Orleans** or **Fort Lauderdale** and **Los Angeles** call variously at **Playa del Carmen/Cozumel,** for the Mayan ruins at **Tulum** and **Chichen Itza; Aruba,** for the beach; **Grand Cayman,** for shopping and the beach; and **Puerto Caldera,** Costa Rica, for a rain-forest tour. The highlight, of course, is the daylong **Panama Canal** transit with three sets of one-, two-, and three-chamber locks, the peace and serenity of the Gatun Lake, and the narrow passage through the Gaillard Cut in the Continental Divide. A Panama Canal company narrator will provide lots of interesting material during the passage between the seas. Then, in the **Pacific,** the successive, rhythmic days at sea show how Crystal shines.

Address/Phone: Crystal Cruises, 2049 Century Park East, Suite 1400, Los Angeles, CA 90067; (310) 785–9300 or (800) 446–6620 for information; (800) 820–6663 for brochures; fax: (310) 785–3891; www.crystalcruises.com

The Ship: *Crystal Harmony* was built in 1990, has a gross tonnage of 49,400, a length of 790 feet, and a draft of 25 feet.

Passengers: 960; mostly North Americans, age fifty-five plus

Dress: Fit to kill on formal nights, jackets and ties on informal nights

Officers/Crew: Norwegian and Japanese officers; European and Filipino crew

Cabins: 480; 461 outside, 260 with private verandas

Fare: $$$$

What's included: Cruise fare, port charges, soft drinks, and specialty coffees

What's not included: Airfare, alcoholic drinks, shore excursions, tips

Highlights: Japanese and Italian restaurants, waiter/bar service, lots of onboard amenities

Other itineraries: In addition to these eleven-day Panama Canal cruises, which operate in January and October–November, the trio including the *Crystal Symphony* cruises most of the world, including northern Europe and the Mediterranean.

HOLLAND AMERICA LINE'S
Veendam
The Panama Canal and More

Holland America Line, one of the world's oldest shipping companies, has long had a solid reputation of friendly service and well-run ships. The 55,451-ton *Veendam,* built in 1996, is the fourth ship in the Statendam series.

Two levels of public rooms, punctuated by a glass sculpture rising dramatically through the three-deck atrium, run the length of the ship along Promenade and Upper Promenade decks, creating a rhythmic flow as passengers seek out their favorite spots and pass to and from the two-story dining room. An impressive double staircase links the two, and a Filipino orchestra serenades diners from an upper-level platform, with the sound quality well distributed. Holland America perpetuates its tradition of good, uncomplicated food, and service by the Filipino and Indonesian staff is attentive. For informal dining the spacious lido restaurant has picture windows and seating under cover near the pool.

The bi-level show lounge, well designed with good views (except from the rear balcony), presents elaborate Broadway-style entertainment. A band plays for listening and dancing in the attractive Ocean Bar, the ship's social center. The Crow's Nest provides the indoor perch for the canal transit, and it doubles as a daytime lounge for tea and as a nighttime disco. The piano bar is a cozy hideaway, whereas the Explorer's Lounge is open to passersby.

The roof of the central pool retracts in good weather, and sandwiches and satay are served informally at lunch. A gym, massage and steam rooms, saunas, and a juice bar look over the stubby bow. A jogging track encircles the mezzanine above the

lido, and a much longer walk can be made on the Lower Promenade Deck.

Cabins are arranged over five decks, and those on the topmost two have verandas. To provide as many outside cabins as possible, the result is a long, narrow room with small sitting areas, TVs, VCRs, and minibars.

The Itinerary
Most passengers booking the canal cruise for the first time focus on that one day, but every line brackets the experience with the Caribbean and Pacific coast of Central American ports. In the *Veendam*'s case the ship sails from **Fort Lauderdale** and first calls (last call in the reverse direction) at Holland America's private Bahamian island, **Half Moon Cay,** for a barbecue, snorkeling, swimming, hiking nature trails, or relaxing on the beach.

St. Thomas, in the U.S. Virgin Islands, is well set up for the tourist shopper, but you can also take a boat over to nearby **St. John** for the beautiful beaches at Trunk Bay or Hawksnest Bay. Sailing due south to **Oranjestad,** the island of Aruba provides another outdoor day at a hotel beach or at the shopping plaza next to the ship, but all this is a prelude to the big event—the **Panama Canal** transit.

Two pilots from the canal company come aboard early in the morning to guide the ship into the first set of three Gatun Locks, with electric engines called mules taking the lines to ease the ship forward. The side-by-side chambers provide a two-way transit whereby your ship is raised 85 feet while another, heading to the Caribbean, is lowered. Once clear of the third dock, the ship proceeds through Gatun Lake, a giant reservoir for the

Address/Phone: Holland America Line, 300 Elliott Avenue West, Seattle, WA 98119; (800) 426–0327; fax: (206) 281–7110; www.hollandamerica.com

The Ship: *Veendam* was built in 1996 and has a gross tonnage of 55,451, a length of 719 feet, and a draft of 25 feet.

Passengers: 1,266; mostly Americans, age fifty-five and up

Dress: Formal, informal, and casual nights

Officers/Crew: Dutch officers; Indonesian and Filipino crew

Cabins: 633; 502 outside and 150 with verandas

Fare: $$$

What's included: Cruise only, unless a fly-cruise package is purchased, basic tips

What's not included: Airfare, port charges, shore excursions, drinks, extra tips

Highlights: The Panama Canal transit on a most attractive ship with lots to do

Other itineraries: In addition to these nine-day Panama Canal cruises, which operate January to March, the *Veendam* cruises to Europe. Holland America's large fleet covers the globe: Alaska, Hawaii, around the world.

---

gravity-flow system. The channel narrows at Gamboa, the canal headquarters, to slice through the Continental Divide; then the ship enters the single Pedro Miguel and finally the double Miraflores Locks. About eight to ten hours after leaving the Caribbean, the pilots disembark off Balboa, and the ship sails freely into the broad Pacific, turning north along the Central American coast.

San Juan del Sur, Nicaragua, a new port of call, leads to Masaya National Park for a visit to the rim of the Santiago Crater, the colonial city of Granada on the shore of Lago de Nicaragua, and an island cruise on this huge freshwater lake. Disembarkation is at **Puerto Caldera,** a tiny, deep-water port in Costa Rica, for transfer up to San Jose. If you prefer, you can linger in this natural paradise on a post-cruise package.

PRINCESS CRUISES'
Coral Princess
The Western Caribbean and Panama Canal

this is not the cruise we are taking but, is the same ship.

French-built *Coral Princess* and her same-year (2003) sister, *Island Princess,* represent advances in cruise ship design over both the *Grand Princess* and *Sun Princess* classes. From the exterior, the pair looks less like slab-sided structures on a hull and veer more toward a sleek cruise liner

profile. Twenty percent larger than the *Sun Princess* class, the *Coral Princess* boards just about the same number of passengers, so there's more space for everyone. At more than 91,000 tons, the ship is hardly small, but Princess has been successful in creating a smaller ship feel with the downsized scale and greater number of public rooms. Some shared spaces, such as the Wheelhouse Bar, are wood-paneled, traditional, and clubby, while others are cruise-ship-slick bars.

Most public rooms range over two decks, and one of the largest is the Princess Theater, located forward on one gradually sloping level with very good sightlines. Another entertainment venue is the Explorer's Lounge for cabaret-style revues, game shows, and before-dinner dancing. All the way aft, the innovative Universe Lounge sees lots of varied uses such as cooking demonstrations from an onstage kitchen, computer instruction with fifty computers, straight lectures on finance and photography, and ambitious stage productions on a multilevel stage.

Always a favorite for me on Princess ships is the Wheelhouse Bar, a paneled space with leather couches and chairs set in private recesses and groupings. The maritime theme touts P&O's 169-year history with displays from the company's collection, here a brass bell from the 1950s Orient liner Oronsay and a collection of postcards from the recently departed and much loved SS Canberra. Classical music is performed by a quartet in the afternoon and a dancing band plays in the evenings.

A four-deck atrium is rimmed by shops,

a big-windowed yet very cozy cigar lounge, a trendy piano bar with solo pianist, and the Internet center with a news ticker. On the next deck down, the large ship's library and card room suffer from being walk-through spaces.

Children's facilities are well thought out with a Fun Zone, Pelican's Playhouse, and an outdoor play area with a pool for kids and parents. Off Limits for teenagers is equipped with computers, music for dancing, or just lounging about. In the same area, adults gravitate to a pottery studio for hands-on lessons in design and hand-painting ceramics.

Princess's Personal Choice concept features two similar restaurants with both fixed-seating dining and dine-when-you-wish. There are two specialty restaurants, with service charges: Sabatini's Trattoria, a traditional-looking Italian eatery with an open kitchen that provides a set menu with dish after dish brought to one's table, plus a choice of entree and the adjacent Bayou Café, with a New Orleans decor and a jazz trio, serving appetizers such as exotic barbecued alligator ribs, fried catfish, seafood gumbo, and chicken-and-chorizo jambalaya.

The Horizon Court buffet, open twenty-

Address/Phone: Princess Cruises, 24305 Town Center Drive, Santa Clarita, CA 91355; (661) 753–0000 or (800) 774–6237; fax: (661) 259–3108; www.princesscruises.com

The Ship: *Coral Princess,* completed in 2003, has a gross tonnage of 91,627, a length of 964.5 feet, and a draft of 26 feet.

Passengers: 1,970; mostly Americans; all ages and some families, especially during the school holidays

Dress: Formal and casual

Officers/Crew: British and Italian officers and international crew

Cabins: 987; 879 outside and 727 with verandas

Fare: $$

What's included: Cruise fare and port charges

What's not included: Airfare, shore excursions, tips, drinks

Highlights: Spanking new ship and varied itinerary

Other itineraries: Besides these ten-night Panama Canal cruises, which operate between late September and April, the *Coral Princess* and other Princess ships cruise to Alaska, the Caribbean, and Europe.

brings the *cruise* changes as we continue... where our *cruise* changes as we continue... this is

four hours, may be the only space that ever gets crowded, but picking one's arrival time can cut down on waiting. Above the main pool a grill serves hot dogs and hamburgers and next to the pool is a pizzeria. Those using the main swimming pool, three large hot tubs, and sunning areas with white plastic chairs are serenaded during the day by a steel-drum duo, while the Lotus Pool, protected by a sliding glass roof, is quieter, with a Balinese theme and handsome wooden deck chairs. Additional chairs line the wraparound promenade deck. Exercise activities take place in the gym and aerobics room, Lotus Spa; on the basketball cum volleyball court; at the computerized golf simulator; and on a nine-hole miniature golf course.

The cabin accommodations boast 74 percent with tiered private balconies, a very high figure for a popularly priced ship. The balcony size is more generous than the *Sun Princess* class but otherwise even with most of the competition. Most cabins are similar in design with nonflashy decor and vary by location such as high up or low down, forward, amidships, or aft. Standard features are good storage space, TVs broadcasting CNN, CNBC, ESPN, and lots of entertainment channels and films, hair dryers, and safes. Minisuites come with much more space for the sitting area, larger verandas, two TVs, and bathrooms with tub baths and good storage space. Sixteen proper two-room suites have curtain-divided sitting and sleeping areas, walk-in closets, spacious balconies, a wet bar, whirlpool tub baths, and separate showers.

The Itinerary

This ten-day itinerary combines a trip into, but not entirely through, the Panama Canal, popular Western Caribbean ports, and three days at sea to explore this new ship. Embarkation and disembarkation are at **Fort Lauderdale.**

Sailing from the South Florida port, you have three nights and two full days on a route that rounds the state's southernmost

tip and aims west-southwest toward the port of **Cartagena** on Colombia's north coast. The city's seventeenth century Felipe Fortress, an engineering and architectural feat that took twenty-seven years to build, was designed, along with the narrow streets, to foil pirates who came to steal gold bound for the Spanish crown. Visit the 130-foot-high fort or another, Fort Bocachica, on a cool boat ride out to the harbor entrance.

Then it's an overnight sail to the entrance to the **Panama Canal.** The *Coral Princess* is lifted 80 feet through a set of three locks into the **Gatun Lake,** the reservoir for the canal's gravity-flow operation. Anchoring here, passengers have numerous choices of excursions: to an observation point to view the ships passing through the lock system, to an Indian tribe living deep in the rain forest, or a dome car train ride along the Panama Railroad, the world's shortest true transcontinental route, which runs mostly parallel to the canal's 50-mile length.

Exiting the canal, the ship turns north to **Puerto Limon, Costa Rica**'s principal outlet on its Atlantic side. Trips are made inland to the misty cloud forests, home to more than 800 species of birds, including the colorful quetzal, for an aerial tram ride over the treetops of **Brauillo Carillo National Park.** Another trip boards a boat to explore the **Tortuguero Canal** and its tributaries to look for howler monkeys, crocodiles, sloths, and toucans. The narrow-gauge railway, built to carry bananas from inland plantations to the coast, is again open for tourist train travel, providing a two-hour ride through the rain forest and over bridges spanning numerous streams.

Sailing east to **Grand Cayman,** a British colony and a tax haven for the rich, you can rent a bike and travel around this relatively flat island, stopping at Seven Mile Beach for swimming and lunch. Stingray City is perhaps the most popular attraction, where hundreds of people descend on the shallow waters that are home to from thirty to one hundred tame stingrays that, when you don snorkeling gear, you can feed and gently stroke. Another excursion is a ride in a submersible down 100 feet alongside a portion of the 500 foot drop of the Cayman Wall sloping away to a depth of 6,000 feet. Another, very expensive, venture for just two at a time drops 800 feet past the "sponge belt" to view the deeper coral and the giant limestone pinnacles.

The last call at the Mexican island of Cozumel gives access to great beaches, horseback riding, snorkeling, shopping, and sport fishing—a catch-and-release outing for dolphins, barracuda, sierra, wahoo, and tuna. The short trip across to the Yucatan Peninsula is the jumping-off landing for the Mayan coastal ruins at **Tulum** and some very fine beaches.

The final two nights and a day are spent returning through the Caribbean to Fort Lauderdale for disembarkation.

AMAZON TOURS & CRUISES'
Arca and *Rio Amazonas*
Upper Amazon Expedition-Style Cruising

 Amazon Tours & Cruises, in business for more than a quarter century, is run by an American living in Iquitos, Peru. Although the firm's riverboat fleet numbers a half dozen, only the two largest, making the full six-night cruises to and from Iquitos, Peru, are described here.

The twenty-nine-passenger *Arca*, the smaller of the two, is a three-deck riverboat that was most recently upgraded in 1995. Public areas include a non-air-conditioned covered and uncovered top deck. The dining room and lounge are air-conditioned, as are the sixteen cedar- and mahogany-paneled cabins, ten with upper and lower berths, and three triples with lower berths; all cabins have private showers.

The *Rio Amazonas*, the largest in the fleet, is a true veteran of the Amazon with a battered white steel hull to prove it. First built in 1896 as a passenger-cargo boat, then rebuilt into a river cruise vessel in 1981, it was last refitted in 1994. The public spaces include an air-conditioned dining room and a small library, a lounge and bar, and a Sun Deck with open and covered seating, hammocks, and a hot tub. The air-conditioned cabins, all outside with showers and baths, have two lower beds; three are triples.

Both vessels have buffet-style dining. The food includes fresh fish, vegetables, and fruit, but some food is preserved to avoid spoilage in this tropical climate.

The Itineraries
Cruises operate downstream and upstream, with some different landings for each three-night segment between Iquitos and the small Peruvian port of Santa Rosa opposite Leticia (Colombia) and Tabatinga (Brazil). Either or both riverboats may be used. The days are always warm, with rain likely once a day from December through March. Jungle walks are invariably hot and sticky, but when cruising and at night, the temperatures are surprisingly moderate. Air-conditioning during meals and while asleep provides additional relief.

Downstream: Iquitos, located east of the Andes, may qualify as the world's largest city with no road access to the outside world. Navigable rivers provide local transportation. This sprawling city experienced a very brief rubber boom, and there is some evidence of past wealth but not much, so it is a relief to begin the downriver cruise. There are no channel markers, so the pilots simply memorize the river. The water level can change 30 to 40 feet between the dry and rainy seasons, and any buoys would simply be carried away by the high and fast-flowing waters.

The first full day is spent visiting **Indian villages,** isolated communities that depend on the river for transportation, water, and fishing. There is a tour of the stilted compounds and a blowgun demonstration. At the larger town of **Pevas,** built mostly on high ground, there is a chance to visit an artist's house. The landscape paintings draw on the colors of the bromeliads in the forest.

The second full day begins with a rain-forest walk to see the giant water lilies and perhaps howler monkeys. While they are easily heard, without a good guide or binoculars they are often hard to spot. Piranha fishing is not as frightening as it may sound, but the setting, a dark backwater pond beneath a thick canopy of tree branches, can be an eerie experience. If the catch, including catfish, is large enough, the cook onboard will prepare it for dinner. The afternoon is spent visiting a missionary village, and after sunset, small boats take passengers into a reedy swamp for Amazon caiman spotting, using flashlights to set the eyes aglow.

Passengers on the three-night cruise transfer across the Amazon to **Leticia,** Colombia, for onward flights; a new group boards here, joining those making the round-trip voyage.

Upstream: The boundaries of Brazil, Colombia, and Peru come together at the turnaround location, and the river traffic is busy. The first afternoon may include a rainforest walk or a river tributary exploration.

The first full day provides a fishing trip, using hand lines, deep into the forest canopy for catfish or piranha. In the afternoon there is a visit to a leper colony at **San Pablo** and time to buy wood carvings, dolls, and artwork. After dark the launches follow a tributary, and there will be red-eyed caiman to spot with the aid of flashlights.

Address/Phone: Amazon Tours & Cruises, 275 Fontainebleau Boulevard, Suite 173, Miami, FL 33172; (305) 227–2266 or (800) 423–2791; fax: (305) 227–1880; e-mail: info@amazon tours.net; www.amazontours.net

The Ships: Arca was built in 1980, has a gross tonnage of 95, a length of 99 feet, and a shallow draft. Rio Amazonas was first built in 1896, then rebuilt in 1981, and has a gross tonnage of 350, a length of 146 feet, and a shallow draft.

Passengers: Arca, 29; Rio Amazonas, 44 (maximum capacity); age thirty and up, Americans and Europeans

Dress: Casual

Officers/Crew: Peruvian

Cabins: Arca, 13; Rio Amazonas, 21; twin beds, upper/lower berths, some with a third upper berth; all air-conditioned, outside, and with shower and toilet

Fare: $$

What's included: Cruise fare, port charges, excursions

What's not included: Airfare, drinks, tips

Highlights: Remote and roadless Upper Amazon; exotic bird life, Indian villages

Other itineraries: In addition to these year-round three- and six-night cruises, the company runs four smaller vessels, some for charter, on other parts of the Upper Amazon, its tributaries, and the Rio Negro. Lodge and jungle camp stays can be added.

The second day revisits **Pevas** and a last chance to trade items for local handicrafts of handmade masks and bark paintings. As the current can be strong, the upriver cruise provides less time ashore.

If you are taking only one segment, it is highly recommended to add a stay at one of the lodges or campsites. Whatever stretch is chosen, the line is a highly experienced Amazonian operator, and its river vessels offer comfortable accommodations and a very good value.

CANODROS'
Galapagos Explorer II
The Galápagos Archipelago

 Canodros, S.A. bought the *Renaissance III* in 1997 and renamed her *Galapagos Explorer II* to replace an older ship of the same name for three-, four-, and seven-night itineraries.

The Main Lounge on Deck 3 serves as the lecture hall for briefings before shore excursions and for dancing to local bands or one made up from the crew. The piano bar aft on Deck 4 is popular, as all drinks are complimentary, except wines and champagne.

The attractive dining room on Deck 2 is partitioned into three distinct areas, with tables set for two, four, six, or eight. Open seating is the rule at breakfast and lunch, but passengers are asked to sit at the same table for dinner. Breakfast is buffet, catering to American and European tastes, plus South American delicacies such as fried plantains with cheese. At dinnertime the fixed menu might include melon and prosciutto, soup, salad, entrees such as Galápagos lobster with curry sauce, filet mignon with mushroom sauce, or fresh local fish and a dessert. Food is tasty but not gourmet; the staff is friendly and willing, but the standard of English is often low. Lunch is usually served on Deck 5 with buffet, bar, and tables around the pool. Selections include salads, soup, a local Ecuadorian dish, and spaghetti or sweet and sour pork. Next to the pool the Jacuzzi is popular after shore expeditions.

The fifty cabins are spacious suites lined with dark paneling and decorated in pastels. Three picture windows provide ample daylight, and a sitting area, with a sofa, chair, and small glass-topped table, encourages passengers to read and relax. Additional amenities include two drawers that lock, two full-length closets, a hair dryer, a telephone, a minibar, and a TV/VCR.

The Itinerary

On a typical seven-day cruise, you visit ten of the thirteen islands in the archipelago, and you will see species uniquely adapted to these islands as described by Charles Darwin in *The Origin of Species* (1859).

A few hours after landing on the tiny airstrip at **San Cristobal,** you may be crouching on a dark sand beach staring eye to eye at sea lions while, above, brown pelicans swoop down to the clear blue water looking for their evening meal. Blue-footed boobies perch on nearby cliffs, and frigate birds soar above the pangas (dinghies) as the sun sets between the twin peaks of Kicker Rock. Wildlife seems completely oblivious to human visitors, a surprise and perhaps the highlight of a Galápagos trip.

The rhythm of life onboard begins with an early-morning wake-up call and buffet breakfast. Then it's all aboard the pangas by 8:00 A.M., dressed accordingly for dry or wet landings. During briefings by the Ecuadorian expedition leader, you get an idea of what wildlife is likely to be seen, while the environments vary from beaches of different colors—red, olive green, white—to flat lava rocks, steep cliffs, and rocky coastlines.

Wooden stairs lead to superb views on **Bartolomé** out to surrounding islands and the many lava spatter cones, remnants of volcanic activity. Down on the beach you have a chance to slip into the water to enjoy swimming among sea lions and watching a variety of brightly colored fish darting in and out of the rocks, with curious Galápagos penguins rushing by at speeds up to 40 miles per hour.

The beautiful white-sand beach at Gardner Bay on the island of **Española** proves to be a challenging wet landing. The reward is a pristine setting shared with sea lions, endemic scavenger hawks, oystercatchers, and finches. At Devil's Crown, off **Floreana,** some of the party on my trip were lucky to spot a white shark.

At **Point Espinoza** on the northern end of **Fernandina,** the terrain is dominated by scaly marine iguanas, a modern miniature version of the ancient dinosaur and the

world's only true marine lizard. These creatures, which look prehistoric, huddle in groups and move slowly in and out of the shallow water, spitting saltwater to aid the digestion of seaweed. The spiny ridges down their backs determine the sex, with males having higher and more predominant features, and their bodies blend so well with the land that it is difficult to avoid stepping on them. A strong stench is present, due to the many iguana carcasses. The scene includes flightless cormorants perched on algae-covered rocks and sea lions and Sally Lightfoot crabs moving about rock pools and on the beach.

Civilization appears when landing at **Puerto Ayora,** the main town on **Santa Cruz Island.** At the Charles Darwin Research Station, you get the chance to observe tortoises (the Spanish word is *galápagos*) from different islands, separated into environments that replicate their natural ones. They are now studied and bred in captivity, where once they almost became extinct by sailors using them for fresh meat during long Pacific Ocean voyages. When the offspring are strong enough, they are

Address/Phone: Galapagos Inc., 7800 Red Road, Suite 112, South Miami, FL 33142; (305) 665–0841 or (800) 327–9854; www.canodros.com. Elegant Cruise & Tours: (800) 683–6767

The Ship: *Galapagos Explorer II,* built in 1990 as the *Renaissance III,* came under new ownership in 1997. Gross tonnage is 4,077, length 290 feet, and draft 12 feet.

Passengers: 100; all ages; mostly Americans and some Europeans and South Americans

Dress: Casual at all times

Officers/Crew: Ecuadorian

Cabins: 50 luxury outside suites with sitting areas

Fare: $$$

What's included: Cruise fare, port charges, flights between Ecuador mainland and the Galápagos, shore excursions, drinks (except wines)

What's not included: Airfare to Ecuador, overnight accommodations between flights, wines, tips to guides and ship's staff

Highlights: Seeing unique wildlife species in native habitats, most without fear of humans

Other itineraries: In addition to year-round cruises, Canodros, S.A. operates Kapawi, an ecological reserve in the Amazon Basin of southeastern Ecuador. Tours of three or seven nights can be arranged in conjunction with itineraries of the *Galapagos Explorer II.*

returned to their natural habitats; as a result, their numbers are increasing significantly.

On a trip into the highlands, the sights are banana and papaya plantations, cattle and horse farms, and scalesia trees covered in Spanish moss, a habitat far removed from the sea. A visit to Steve's Farm gives the opportunity to observe giant tortoises in their natural environment, where they come to drink from the water holes as they have done for hundreds of years.

LINDBLAD EXPEDITIONS'
Polaris
The Galápagos Islands

 Lindblad Expeditions was founded by Sven-Olof Lindblad, the son of Lars Eric Lindblad, the pioneer of expedition-style cruising. The eighty-passenger *Polaris* has cruised worldwide and now spends most of the year in the Galápagos.

The Vega Lounge and well-stocked bar can seat all passengers at once for lectures and briefings, the latter taking place before dinner, when cocktails and hot hors d'oeuvres are served. Several TVs positioned around the room show videos after dinner. Adjacent, the Polaris Room is the ship's reference and reading library, with a good selection of books and games. The partially

Address/Phone: Lindblad Expeditions, 720 Fifth Avenue, New York, NY 10019; (212) 765–7740 or (800) 397–3348 or (800) GALAPAGOS; fax: (212) 265–3370; e-mail: travel@expeditions. com; www.expeditions.com

The Ship: *Polaris*, originally built in 1960 as the day ferry *Öresund*, was rebuilt into the cruise ship *Lindblad Polaris* in 1982, then simply *Polaris* after 1986. The ship has a gross tonnage of 2,138, a length of 238 feet, and a draft of 14 feet.

Passengers: 80; age fifty and up, mostly Americans

Dress: Casual at all times

Officers/Crew: Ecuadorian

Cabins: 41; mostly small, all outside with windows, portholes on A Deck

Fare: $$$$

What's included: Cruise fare and port charges, transfers on group flights, two hotel nights at Guayaquil, all shore excursions, entrance fees, tips to local guides

What's not included: Airfare, drinks, tips to crew and naturalists, pooled at the end of the trip

Highlights: One of the finest natural history cruises; species unique to the Galápagos

Other itineraries: In addition to the above seven-night cruise aboard the *Polaris*, which is offered weekly except in September, the *Sea Lion* and *Sea Bird* cruise the Columbia and Snake Rivers, the British Columbia coast up to Alaska, and in the Sea of Cortez and Baja California, Mexico. The deep-sea expedition ship *Endeavour*, the former *Caledonian Star*, sails in Antarctica, South America, and Europe.

covered aft deck has old-fashioned, heavy wooden deck furniture. Above the Sky Deck is an open space over the bridge with wood benches and deck chairs. On a clear night the expedition leader will point out the stars and constellations.

The dining room is a delight, located forward with large wraparound windows with a captain's table for ten to twelve persons and others for two to seven. Meals, served at one open seating, are buffet style at breakfast and lunch and from a menu at dinner. Food is good but not necessarily memorable. The shop carries clothing and souvenirs related to the destination, and there is a sauna with separate times for men and women, as well as unisex hours. Passengers go ashore in pangas, with a naturalist for every sixteen passengers. The expedition leader and naturalists travel with the ship and mingle onboard and at meals. Family cruises operate during summer holidays with staff experienced in youth activities and adventure travel.

The Itinerary

The itinerary for this chapter is shared with the *Galapagos Explorer II*.

SEABOURN CRUISE LINE'S
Seabourn Pride
Down South America Way

Seabourn Cruise Line, now part of Cunard Line and both owned by the Carnival Corporation, operates a similar trio of all-suite ships, the *Seabourn Pride, Seabourn Legend,* and *Seabourn Spirit*. Although a Seabourn cruise is about as sophisticated an experience as one will find at sea, the atmosphere is less stuffy and more friendly and relaxed than in the past.

The principal public spaces revolve around The Club, a trio of glass-partitioned rooms, offering an intimate lounge setting, a cozy bar, and a small casino for blackjack, poker, and roulette. The location is popular before dinner, with hot hors d'oeuvres served and live music; after dinner a small group performs cabaret acts, and a band plays for dancing. The tiered main lounge is used for the captain's parties, films, special-interest lectures, and piano concerts. A quiet spot is the observation lounge for an unimpeded view forward and for checking the ship's position. A tiny library stocks books and videos to take out.

Outside, the attractive lido deck has sun-protected areas for chairs, two heated whirlpools, and a little-used swimming pool awkwardly sited in a shadowy pit. Constitutional walks and jogging take place on the circular deck above.

Dining aboard a Seabourn ship may be as private or as social as one would like, an option that extends to all times of the day. On two formal nights a week, the top officers host tables, and, on informal evenings, there may be invitations from the cruise staff or the enrichment lecturers. The main restaurant meals are uniformly excellent, with memorable dishes being the fresh fish, veal dishes, and beef tenderloin. For an Italian dinner, with reservations required, the Veranda Café has a set menu that might include antipasto, minestrone, linguine al Don Alfredo, tender osso buco, and tiramisù. Complimentary wines are served at lunch and dinner. The indoor-outdoor Veranda Café never repeats its lunch menu and is equally a lovely spot for breakfast, especially at a table under the awning-covered afterdeck poised over the stern. Once during the cruise, an outdoor barbecue will feature a cold buffet of jumbo shrimp, smoked mussels, smoked salmon, oysters, caviar, and salad fixings galore, while the hot carvery will offer sliced roast beef, duck, and ham.

The Seabourn suites are most inviting, with blond wood grain outlining the furnishings and cabinetry and natural light pouring through the 5-foot-wide picture window. Thirty-six suites now have French balconies in place of the window. The refrigerator is stocked and replenished daily with sodas, beer, and, as ordered prior to the cruise, one complimentary bottle of red and white wine or spirits. The walk-in closet has ample hanging space and a safe, but drawer space is limited and shallow. The bed is queen-size (or two twin-size) with good, focused reading lights, and the lounge has a sofa, two chairs, two stools, and a coffee table that could be raised for in-suite entertaining and dining.

The Itinerary

The northbound direction of the four-week cruise outlined here may in some years operate in reverse, southbound from Fort Lauderdale. Passengers may elect to take the shorter segments from Rio to Manaus or Manaus to Fort Lauderdale.

Embarking in **Rio de Janeiro,** the sail out past Sugar Loaf is a breathtaking spectacle. Reaching the Atlantic, the *Seabourn Pride* turns northward along the Brazilian coast with leisurely days at sea en route to **Salvador de Bahia.** The high-rises of the new city envelop the old, the latter best visited on a walking tour. The architecture of the 400-year-old colonial upper city reflects the former Portuguese capital's opulence and has been designated a UNESCO world heritage site. The next call is **Natal,** a seaport for exporting cotton, coffee, hides, and sugar, located on the extreme east of Brazil's bulge. During World War II, Natal served as the base for the shortest flying route across

Address/Phone: Seabourn Cruise Line, 610 Blue Lagoon Drive, Suite 400, Miami, FL 33126; (305) 463–3000 or (800) 929–9391; fax: (305) 463–3010; www.seabourn.com

The Ship: *Seabourn Pride* was built in 1988 and has a gross tonnage of 9,975, a length of 440 feet, and a draft of 17 feet.

Passengers: 204; mostly Americans in their fifties, some Europeans and South Americans in the mix

Dress: Formal, informal, and casual nights

Officers/Crew: Norwegian officers; mostly European crew, plus some Filipinos

Cabins: 102; all outside suites, the majority identical except for location.

Thirty-six French balconies (window-type double doors set before a railing) have been added to some suites in place of sealed windows.

Fare: $$$$$

What's included: Cruise fare, port charges, wine and drinks, gratuities

What's not included: Airfare, transfers, shore excursions

Highlights: Exotic ports and a most luxurious ship to come home to at day's end

Other itineraries: In addition to this twenty-eight-day cruise from Rio de Janeiro via the Amazon to Fort Lauderdale operating during the northern winter, the Seabourn trio offers itineraries that cover the globe, including Vietnam.

the Atlantic to West Africa. Farther north, **Forteleza** is known for its lace, beaches, and beachfront fish restaurants.

The waters begin to turn muddy more than 100 miles from the mouth of the **Amazon.** Although the Nile is slightly longer, the Amazon discharges sixty times more freshwater, fully one-third of the world's supply, much of its content laden with silt. The river mouths are a confusing complex of navigable waterways leading inland from the open Atlantic.

Upstream, a stop is made at **Alter do Chao,** where the blue waters of the Rio Tapajos join the Amazon and provide a sandy beach worry-free of piranhas. The Lower Amazon officially ends 1,000 miles upstream at **Manaus,** a deepwater port near to where the waters of the **Rio Negro** merge into the main stream. Once a rubber-boom city that boasts an opera house and a market pavilion built by Gustav Eiffel, the sprawling urban center is by far the largest

in the Amazon basin, and the river traffic is intense. Some passengers will leave the *Pride* here and others will join.

Sailing back down the heavily forested Amazon highway, calls are made at **Parintins,** a town known for its folkloric samba dancing, and **Santarem,** a sizeable city where you should see some gray and pink freshwater dolphins in the vicinity.

Exiting the Amazon, the ship crosses the equator at Macapa, then heads out to **Devil's Island,** where a picnic takes place in honor of the notorious former French penal colony's most famous prisoner, Papillon. Depending on the specific cruise chosen, the Caribbean ports will vary, but one recent one included **Bridgetown** on the island of **Barbados** with its British heritage; **Gustavia** on the upscale French island of **St. Barts;** and American **St. Thomas** for shopping and sight-seeing, before a relaxing last stint at sea en route to **Fort Lauderdale** and disembarkation.

ORIENT LINES'
Marco Polo
Passages from the East to West Coast of South America

Orient Lines, originally a British-owned company, is now a separate brand for Star Cruises, also owners of Norwegian Cruise Line. The 840-passenger *Marco Polo* was designed for worldwide cruising. First built in 1965 for the Soviet Black Sea Shipping Company as a rugged ice-strengthened transatlantic liner, the ship was completely rebuilt in 1993 as the *Marco Polo,* happily retaining her handsome ocean liner profile.

Public rooms, with an understated decor, and the outdoor swimming pool and lido bar occupy one deck and include the forward Ambassador Lounge, the venue for enrichment lectures on such topics as Indian

and European influences and South American politics, plus entertainment. Further aft is the Polo Lounge, a piano bar; the Palm Court, furnished with cane chairs for afternoon tea; Le Bar, a cozy watering hole; a card room; a well-stocked library; and a small casino.

Raffles offers varied high-quality buffet selections for breakfast and lunch and gets magically transformed at night for an Oriental dinner (extra charge for tip and wine). The outdoor grill prepares steaks, sausages, and hamburgers by the pool. On the decks above are the Charleston Club's dance band and disco and the well-equipped Health Club and Beauty Center. The Sky Deck

Jacuzzis, overlooking the stern, become a popular gathering spot when the ship is leaving port. Deck space is attractively tiered, and wooden steamer chairs line the wide teak Promenade Deck. The circular Boat Deck above, while narrow, is for serious walkers.

The Seven Seas Restaurant provides two sittings at dinner and a tasty selection of salads and soups such as curried pumpkin and lentil. Entrees include grilled sea shrimp, Alaska salmon with almonds and ginger crust, and seared prime beef with tempura vegetables.

The 425 cabins have mostly twin beds, some convertible to queen-size, with lightwood trim, TVs with VCRs, three-channel radios, phones, good storage, and hair dryers. Large staterooms and suites have tub baths. The cabin dividers are thin and leak noise from the neighbors.

The Itinerary

Argentina to Chile: Happily, there are still frontiers that offer travelers an unusual and uncrowded cruising experience, and Argentina's **Patagonia** and the **Chilean fjords** are just such places. Together they possess great scenic beauty, unusual wildlife, a thinly scattered population, and limited access. This South American itinerary may operate in the reverse direction and add or subtract ports.

The cruise tour begins with two full days in the stylish European city of **Buenos Aires.** Argentina's capital is a feast of flamboyant Victorian and beaux arts buildings. The outdoor cafes and restaurants, handsome limestone apartment buildings, and smart shopping arcades seem even more French than those in Paris. The rich hire dog walkers; smartly dressed ladies lunch with friends; schoolboys wear blue blazers, ties, and white shirts; and no one likes to eat before ten o'clock. In Recoleta, a smart residential neighborhood, Eva Peron is buried in a cemetery of elaborate mausoleums.

The cruise begins in earnest by sailing across the muddy Rio de la Plata to **Monte-**

video, Uruguay's capital. The nearby resort of **Punta del Este** attracts jetsetting South Americans.

Sailing into the South Atlantic, the *Marco Polo* calls at **Port Stanley** and **West Point** in the **Falkland Islands,** a British colony with the look of a northern Scottish isle. Sheep raising and fishing are the main occupations, and the islands are home to cute rockhopper penguins and southern elephant seals.

Sailing westward around **Cape Horn,** the land to starboard is **Tierra del Fuego,** shared by Argentina and Chile. At **Ushuaia,** a catamaran cruise into the Beagle Channel visits an island covered with seals. The next call, **Punta Arenas,** is Chile's southernmost city, the center for the sheep farming industry and gateway to **Patagonia.** Climb La Cruz Hill for great views of the surrounding forests, lakes, sand cliffs, **Strait of Magellan,** and **Tierra del Fuego.**

Glaciers come down to calve into the sea, and when the channel widens, the *Marco Polo* leaves the sheltered waters and aims westward and northward to the Pacific and the Chilean fjords. There are more than 5,000 islands in the Chilean archipelago, and most channels have had no soundings. Navigation is made even trickier by unexpected mountain downdrafts that strike ships broadside. A call is made at the fishing village **Puerto Chacabuco,** set along a coast of soaring fjords and Andean peaks, then you'll sail north to **Puerto Montt,** located at the northern end of the Chilean fjords in the lake district. **Lake Llanquihue,** the country's largest lake, is overlooked by the conical 8,000-foot **Osorno** volcano, one of more than two thousand in Chile alone.

Cruising back into the Pacific, this leg of the cruise ends at **Valparaiso,** Chile's main port and now the location for the country's parliament. The lower and upper sections of Valparaiso are connected by more than one dozen hundred-year-old elevators or funicular railways, a diversion for those so inclined. Five miles distant is **Vina del Mar,** one of the continent's foremost resorts with an elegant seafront, a presidential summer palace, and a splendid casino, maintaining a strict dress code, set among formal gardens.

Santiago, the capital, is 75 miles inland, a modern city at the foot of the snow-capped **Andes,** with enough attractions to warrant the additional nights tacked onto the cruise. You can travel by a good subway system to visit the cultural center housed in a now-disused railway station, arcaded Plaza de Armas, the 1805 Palacio de la Moneda, now a museum for paintings and sculpture. In the evening the arty Bellavista District is the place for street life, shops selling lapis lazuli, art galleries, theaters, cafes, and restaurants.

Chile via Panama to Barbados: Santiago, Chile's sprawling capital, is nestled in the Andes Mountains east of the main seaport of **Valparaiso,** where the *Marco Polo* is waiting to sail. This northbound itinerary is nicely spaced, with a day at sea between most ports. At Coquimbo, Gustav Eiffel (of Eiffel Tower fame) built one of the churches, while nearby **La Serena** is a beach resort with no less than twenty-six churches.

The coastline changes dramatically as the ship reaches **Arica,** Chile's northern-most city, rising among the foothills of the Andes. To the east the **Atacama Desert** qualifies as the driest place on earth, while beyond are the **High Andes.** The archaeological museum displays mummies that are reputed to be older than those in Egypt, and the desert hills have pre-Columbian petroglyphs. There's a terrific city and sea view from the Morro, a fort, and in Arica be sure to visit iron San Marcos Cathedral and the equally splendid custom house.

After cruising up the coast to **Callao,** the commercial port for **Lima,** it's a short drive to Peru's colonial capital quarter. Lima now counts roughly seven million inhabitants, and tours are highly recommended

---

Address/Phone: Orient Lines, 7600 Corporate Drive Center, Miami, FL 33126; (305) 436–4000 or (800) 333–7300; fax: (305) 436–4124; e-mail: info@orientlines.com; www.orientlines.com

The Ship: *Marco Polo* was originally built in 1965 as the Soviet-flag *Alexandr Pushkin,* then completely rebuilt from the hull up in 1993. She has a gross tonnage of 22,080, a length of 578 feet, and a deep draft of 27 feet.

Passengers: 840 double occupancy; age range is fifty and up, mostly English speaking

Dress: Some formal nights, otherwise jacket and tie, with casual nights in port

Officers/Crew: Scandinavian captain; mostly European officers and Filipino crew

Cabins: 425, most average size; 294 are outsides, none with verandas

Fare: $$$

What's included: Cruise, hotel nights, sight-seeing, transfers

What's not included: Low airfare add-ons from U.S. gateways, port charges, shore excursions, tips, drinks

Highlights: Exotic itinerary to some remote coastal locations at an affordable package price. Great ambience on board.

Other itineraries: In addition to the twenty-day cruise tour from Buenos Aires to Santiago and the twenty-one-day cruise tour from Santiago to Barbados, combinable into one thirty-four-day trip, which operate from February into April, the *Marco Polo* spends the summer in Northern Europe and the Mediterranean and winter in Antarctica.

here and at all the ports along the coast. In Lima, the cathedral on the Plaza de Armas has a splendid interior with finely carved seventeenth-century stalls, silver-covered altars, and beautiful wall mosaics. **Miraflores,** a trendy, expensive suburb and Lima's social center, is worth a visit for beaches and the upscale shops built around a handsome park.

Salinas is a popular Ecuadorian beach resort, and to the north are **Machalilla National Park,** a dry tropical forest, and **Isla de la Plata,** home to a colony of blue-footed boobies. There is also a flying excursion inland to Quito, the capital.

Before sailing though the Panama Canal, the ship docks in **Balboa,** the port for **Panama City.** Its San Felipe district is a United Nation's World Heritage Site featuring a mixture of Spanish, French, and early American architecture. A tour visited a village on stilts in the rainforest.

Taking on the pilots early the next morning, the ship begins the **Panama Canal** transit with the 85-foot climb through the two Miraflores Locks and a half hour later moves into the single Pedro Miguel Lock.

The ship then begins a peaceful sail amid lovely tropical surroundings to the Gaillard Cut through the Continental Divide and past the canal headquarters at Gamboa and into **Gatun Lake.** At the eastward end, the three-step, 85-foot drop through the Gatun Locks lowers the ship to sea level again. By mid-afternoon the pilots disembark at **Cristobal-Colon** and the ship sails into the Caribbean.

After an overnight sail, **Puerto Limon,** Costa Rica's Caribbean port, is the gateway to the inland cloud forests, home to more than 800 species of birds including the flamboyant quetzal. Two nights and a day at sea bring the ship to the north coast of South America and Colombia's main port of **Cartagena.** The city's 1533-built San Felipe Fortress and twisting streets were designed to foil the pirates who came to steal the gold bound for the Spanish crown. There's one last call at **Oranjestad** on the island of **Aruba,** whose attractions range from beaches and desert plants species to Dutch-style architecture and a last chance for some shopping before the ship sails east to **Barbados,** the cruise disembarkation port.

SILVERSEA CRUISES'
Silver Wind
Around the Bottom of South America

The newest line in the ultraluxury cruise market, Silversea Cruises made a splash in 1994 when it introduced the brand-new, 296-passenger *Silver Cloud* and *Silver Wind* followed by the 388-passenger *Silver Shadow* and *Silver Whisper.* The ships combine the spaciousness and entertainment options of a larger ship with the best of intimate, yachtlike cruising.

Following a refit in 2003, the *Silver Wind*'s public areas, inside and out, are

again stylish and open. Dusty blues, teal greens, and deep burgundies and violet are blended with lots of Italian marble and the odd tile mosaic tabletop. Entertainment is low-key, but there are decent options, considering the small size of the ship. Afternoon tea is served in the windowed Panorama Lounge and evenings a pianist plays there. Broadway-style production numbers with a four-dancer cast are performed in the two-story Venetian show lounge, and most nights a dance band plays oldies or a DJ spins rock and roll in the intimate, softly lit Bar. Organized activities include trivia contests, port talks, movies, and wine tasting. Mostly people socialize, read in the library, surf in the new Computer Center, or roam around the roomy decks.

The outdoor deck space is sweeping, and there's never overcrowding in and around the pool, two hot tubs, and new ocean-view gym.

The formal, open-seating dining venue is delicately decorated in pale pink and gold, and elegant candlelit tables are set with heavy crystal glasses, chunky Christofle silverware, and doily-covered silver show plates. Rivaling the best restaurants in New York City or Paris, delectable dishes like grilled tournedos of beef with foie gras and truffles and marinated crab with leek salad and star anise are prepared in conjunction with Le Cordon Bleu Culinary School. Several nights a week, the Terrace Café, where buffet-style breakfast and lunch are served, is transformed into a cozy, reservations-only alternative-dining venue, featuring mostly regional Italian cuisine. Here the ambience is darker and more intimate, and there are a good number of tables for two. The wine bar, Le Champagne, offers intimate dinners for thirty.

All 148 suites have sitting areas, roomy walk-in closets, bathtubs, vanities, TVs and VCRs, and stocked minibars. Natural light pours in through the glass veranda doors, casting a warm glow on the creamy-beige fabrics and the abundant golden-brown-colored wood. Swirled peachy-gray marble covers the bathroom from head to toe.

The Itinerary

Embarking in **Valparaiso,** 75 miles from Chile's capital at Santiago, the *Silver Wind* sets sail for **Puerto Montt,** located in the lake district at the northern end of the Chilean fjords. Just to the east, **Lake Llanquihue,** the country's largest lake, is overlooked by the conical, 8,000-foot Osorno volcano.

Sailing south in protected waters, the

Address/Phone: Silversea Cruises, 110 East Broward Boulevard, Fort Lauderdale, FL 33301; (954) 522–4477 or (800) 774–9996; fax: (954) 522–4499; www.silversea.com

The Ship: The *Silver Wind* was built in 1995 and has a gross tonnage of 16,800, a length of 514 feet, and a draft of 17 feet.

Passengers: 296; mostly North American couples in their late fifties to seventies

Dress: Formal nights; informal jacket evenings; jackets and slacks for casual nights

Officers/Crew: Italian officers; European and Filipino crew

Cabins: 148; all outside and all but 38 with verandas

Fare: $$$$$

What's included: Cruise fare, port charges, one shore excursion, unlimited wines and liquors, tips, and sometimes airfare

What's not included: Most excursions and airfare when not part of a package

Highlights: The outstanding beauty of Chile and Argentina; veranda suites, cuisine, service, ship's interiors

Other itineraries: In addition to this sixteen-day *Silver Wind* itinerary between Valparaiso and Buenos Aires, which operates in both directions in December and January, there are South American cruises on other stretches of both coasts. With two new larger ships now in service, Silversea truly covers the world in great style, including the Indian Ocean, South Africa, and Australia/New Zealand.

ship comes to the weathered **Chiloe Island** town of Castro, where unpainted wooden houses perch on stilts. Leaving the *Silver Wind* in the ship's launches, a complimentary excursion enters **Laguna San Rafael,** a saltwater lake connected to the sea by a narrow tidal channel. Cruising amid broken ice, the launch eases toward 25-mile-long San Valentine glacier. The pack ice reveals a wonderful kaleidoscope of colors and shapes.

Two more days are spent cruising the fjords and the **Beagle Channel,** often within sight of glacial remnants of the Ice Age, to **Ushuaia,** Argentina, on Tierra del Fuego, where a catamaran heads out to island rookeries for a close-up view of lounging, smelly sea lions and the protected nests of black-and-white cormorants. After a cruise past **Cape Horn,** the ship returns to protected waters and calls at **Punta Arenas,** Chile, for a two-day stay.

The excursion to **Torres del Paine National Park** is an absolute must, where you will encounter herds of guanaco (an American relative of the camel that resem-bles the llama), Darwin's flightless rhea, Chilean flamingos, black-necked swans, buff-necked ibis, and the soaring Andean condor, with a 10-foot wingspan. Gauchos with their horses sit by the roadside brewing tea. A footpath leads to a rolling, tufted green-and-yellow alpine meadow that recedes toward a deep chasm, behind which rise jagged granite peaks, each topped with a layer of brown lava. The higher, snow-covered mountains are draped with hanging glaciers.

From Punta Arenas the ship sails along the **Strait of Magellan** and out into the Atlantic Ocean to **Puerto Madryn,** a town settled by Welsh in the mid-nineteenth century. To the south **Punta Tombo** is a refuge for up to one million Magellanic penguins, who swim ashore to lay their eggs in dusty, shallow burrows. The last day is spent negotiating the muddy River Plate while en route to the European-style city of **Buenos Aires,** a civilized and sophisticated cap to the sixteen-day cruise. Plan to stay on to take in this most European of cities.

PACIFIC OCEAN

CAPTAIN COOK CRUISES'
Reef Endeavour
Australia's Great Barrier Reef

 Captain Cook Cruises operates small cruise ships in several Australian locations and in the Fiji Islands. The closest North American equivalent in size and layout would be the *Nantucket Clipper* or the *Yorktown Clipper,* but the passenger list is an international one of all ages from North America, Europe, Australia, and New Zealand.

Public rooms include a forward-facing observation lounge, and, high up on the Sun Deck, a second, smaller observation lounge; aft are two spa pools, a sauna, a gym, and an outdoor bar. The main lounge, furnished with cane seating, has a bar and a grand piano; mouthwatering hors d'oeuvres are served here before dinner, and the room opens back onto the outdoor pool and lido area. In addition, there's a small library, a gift shop, and a self-service laundry.

The amidships dining room on D Deck runs the width of the ship, with buffet-style, open-seating breakfasts and lunches and with waiter-served, one-seating dinners. During my barrier-reef cruise, I enjoyed a seafood terrine, grilled barramundi (a local fish), and roast beef with Yorkshire pudding, accompanied by good Australian wines. Breakfast offers honeydew, rock melon, passion fruit, kiwi, mango, pawpaw (papaya), papino (pear and melon), juices, cereals, eggs to order, American and English styles of bacon, as well as sausage, toast, danish, and freshly baked croissants. One hot-and-cold lunch buffet displayed more seafood than I have ever encountered—cold whole salmon, smoked salmon, red emperor, prawns, raw oysters, curried mussels, scallops, whitebait fritters, mud crabs with huge claws, and Moreton Bay bugs (a saltwater crayfish). It

would be sinful not to overeat. An outdoor deck barbecue featured steak, sausage, spareribs, chicken, and prawns.

The seventy-five similar outside cabins, arranged on four decks, fall into three categories, varying more in location than size. Most have a door opening onto the side promenade. The D-Deck cabins have portholes and open onto an inside passageway. Wooden furniture consists of a desk, a low table, a chair, two night-tables, a good-size closet, and limited drawer space. All bathrooms have showers.

The Itinerary

The *Reef Endeavour* leaves from **Cairns,** northern Queensland, twice a week on three- and four-day cruises that can be combined into a full week. The reef, located at an average distance of 40 miles from the coast, is not one continuous coral wall, but comprises 1,500 major and 1,000 minor separate living reefs ranging in age from two to twenty million years old and is home for more than 1,500 species of fish.

On the three-day cruise the *Reef Endeavour* sails south to **Fitzroy Island** for a rainforest walk, followed by a full day anchored off **Hedley Reef** for scuba diving, snorkeling with gear provided by the ship, and viewing the undersea world from a glass-bottom boat. With the ribbon reef protection from the pounding Pacific Ocean, I saw fish as colorful as their names—clownfish, yellowtail fusilier, blue angelfish, moorish idol, surgeonfish, butterfly fish, sergeant major, sweet lip, fox-faced rabbit fish, feather starfish, blue starfish, sea cucumber, and giant clams with openings 2 or 3 feet across—in a setting of blue-tip and golden staghorn, and brain, honeycomb, boulder, and lettuce-leaf coral.

As the ship enters the beautiful **Hinchinbrook Channel,** flanked by an island and the very mountainous Queensland coast, the marine biologist talks about the nearby saltwater mangrove swamp that provides home for mud crabs, saltwater crocodiles, hammerhead and whale sharks, dugongs (similar to a manatee or sea cow), box jellyfish, and lots of fishes. In the skies above are ibis, reef herons, shags, and spoonbills. Later in the day, anchored off **Dunk Island,** a national park, a rainforest walk might reveal bush turkeys and birdwing, tiger, and Ulysses butterflies, and a rewarding climb affords a sweeping panorama of islands, forested coastline, and seascape stretching to the far horizon.

The four-day cruise heads north to **Cooktown,** a former gold-rush site with a colorful history and architectural relics, then out to **Two Isles,** an uninhabited, except for bird life, coral cay. **Lizard Island,** location for the poshest resort on the Barrier Reef, offers a morning hike to the highest hill and a day of snorkeling and diving, and, as a finale, the best variety of sea creatures inhabit **Ribbon Reef No. 5,** at the edge of the continental shelf.

Address/Phone: Captain Cook Cruises, No. 6 Jetty, Circular Quay, Sydney NSW 2000 Australia; (011) 61–2–92–06–1122 or (888) 292–2775 for information and brochures only; fax: (011) 61–2–92–51–4725; e-mail: cruise@captcookcrus.com.au; www.captcookcrus.com.au

The Ship: *Reef Endeavour* was built in 1995, has a gross tonnage of 3,125, a length of 243 feet, and a shallow draft.

Passengers: 150; all ages; Australian, European, and American, with English the lingua franca

Dress: Casual at all times

Officers/Crew: Australian

Cabins: 75; all outside, most with windows and doors that open onto a promenade

Fare: $$

What's included: Cruise fare, port charges, most excursions

What's not included: Airfare, drinks, optional shore excursions such as diving

Highlights: Spending time along the Great Barrier Reef, one of the world's natural wonders; Australian hospitality

Other itineraries: The above cruise may be segmented into three or four days. Captain Cook Cruises operates other small ships from Sydney, along the Murray River in South Australia, and in the Fiji Islands (both cruise ship and sail cruise).

SILVERSEA CRUISES'
Silver Shadow
New Zealand and Australia

 Silversea Cruises operates a fleet of four ships, and the *Silver Shadow* is the first of the larger 388-passenger pair, completed in 2000. The quartet covers the globe, and from year to year the exact ship that will assume a certain itinerary will change. Designed for the upper end of the market, Silversea ships are larger than the Seabourn trio and smaller than the newest in the Seven Seas fleet. Registered in the Bahamas, the beautiful *Silver Shadow* measures 28,258 tons, and her passenger–space ratio is among the highest afloat.

The design layout sees cabins placed forward on six decks away from the public rooms and stacked aft on seven decks, so the efficient elevators see quite a lot of use. As with the smaller pair, the show lounge faces aft and is entered from both sides at stage level via a shipwide bar and lounge. Passengers gather here before lunch and before and after dinner for drinks and dancing to a small band. Silversea attracts many nationalities who are drawn to the sophisticated European-style service; the majority, however, are American.

For viewing the coastal scenery and harbor arrivals, the Panorama Lounge affords sweeping views on three sides. For intimate places to linger and talk, the Humidor draws the cigar smokers and brandy sippers to an English club setting, and the paneled wine bar caters to the grape aficionados.

Dining is open seating, and you can ask for a table for two or join others in the large but thoughtfully laid-out main restaurant located on the lowest and most stable deck. The Terrace Café serves breakfast and lunch with a delightful covered afterdeck usually protected against the wind. Theme din-ners—Italian, French, or a menu reflecting the cruising region—are by reservation but at no extra charge. Complimentary table wines are served in both restaurants at lunch and dinner. A poolside grill serves those who prefer to stay out on deck.

The small casino is located off the main lobby, and the fitness center and spa, operated by Mandara, assumes the highest position on the ship. Internet access is available in the computer center and in the suites.

Deck chairs surround the pool and whirlpools out in the open and under cover, and additional chairs ring the perimeter of the deck above.

The ship's suite accommodations put Silversea right at the top, and the smallest, called Vista suites, measure 287 square feet. The next and most numerous category, the Veranda suites, have the same interior area and add a balcony. The top accommodations fall into four more categories and range from 701 feet to 1,435 feet.

Accommodations come with sofas, cocktail tables that rise to become suitable for in-suite dining, TVs and VCRs, refrigerators, cocktail cabinets, arched curtain dividers, walk-in closets with good storage, and two-basin marble bathrooms with tubs and stall showers, hair dryers, robes, and slippers.

Silversea provides top service, food, and accommodations on a calendar of cruises that span the world.

The Itinerary

Silversea Cruises operates several cruises a year, usually during the summer season in the Southern Hemisphere, that include Australian and New Zealand ports. Because of the distance to reach the lands down under, it is wise to take advantage of a pre- and post-cruise stay to see some more beyond the two terminal ports.

Auckland, the embarkation port for this cruise, is also New Zealand's largest city. Its lively inner-city neighborhoods and the Maori Collection at Auckland Museum lie a short distance from the ship and the busy waterfront. The ferry terminal is adjacent to the cruise ship pier, and boats fan out to Devonport, a nineteenth-century suburb, and to Waiheke Island with its bed-and-breakfasts, beaches, farms, and vineyards.

Sailing out of Auckland, the ship passes the city's eastern side and volcanic Rangitoto Island to spend two nights and a day en route to the port of Lyttelton, which gives access to **Christchurch,** located a few miles inland. This Victorian English-garden city was laid out by Anglican immigrants and offers punting on the River Avon, which flows serenely through town, superb botanical gardens, art and natural history museums, and on weekends, a bustling arts and crafts show, a flea market, and buskers (street entertainers).

Dunedin, just an overnight sail to the south, was settled by Scottish Presbyterians. Visit Larnach Castle, a Scottish-style hilltop estate, or take a nature cruise below the coastal cliffs to view seals, seabirds, and a royal albatross nesting ground.

Then enjoy a long and leisurely, and sometimes rough, sail around the bottom of the South Island, then across the **Tasman Sea** to **Hobart,** the capital of **Tasmania,** an Australian island state. The countryside is England with a soft rural landscape, rough stone houses, and pretty parish churches. Near Hobart, **Port Arthur** at one time had the reputation of being Australia's toughest penal colony. The first prisoners, incarcerated for major crimes, established the timber industry, and eventually some 10,000 arrived. Nearby **Bonorong Wildlife Park** lets you observe such creatures peculiar to Australia as the Tasmanian devil, kangaroos, wallabies, wombats, and cuddly koalas.

Sailing around Tasmania's coast, the *Silver Shadow* crosses the Bass Strait, noted for its choppy waters, to dock at **Melbourne**'s Station Pier for two days. Located in the state of Victoria, Melbourne has an older and softer feel than fast-paced Sydney, perhaps a parallel to Boston and New York. Here you might think about buying a day transit pass and riding the famous green-and-yellow trams that glide along

---

Address/Phone: Silversea Cruises, 110 East Broward Boulevard, Fort Lauderdale, FL 33301; (954) 522–4477 or (800) 722–9995; fax: (954) 522–4499

The Ship: The *Silver Shadow* was completed in 2000, has a gross tonnage of 28,258, a length of 610 feet, and a draft of 19.6 feet.

Passengers: 388; many Americans, some Europeans; forty-five and up

Dress: Formal, informal, and casual nights

Officers/Crew: Italian officers and a European and Filipino crew

Cabins: 194 spacious one-room suites, all outside, and 157 with balconies

Fare: $$$$$

What's included: Cruise fare, port charges, often a hotel stay, drinks and wines at lunch and dinner, gratuities, and usually a special shore side event

What's not included: Airfare, shore excursions

Highlights: Stylish atmosphere, unusual itinerary

Other itineraries: Besides this *Silver Shadow* warm-weather cruise in Australia and New Zealand, the Silversea four-ship fleet, including the *Silver Cloud, Silver Whisper,* and *Silver Wind,* cover virtually the entire world.

Collins Street, the principal center-city shopping precinct, with routes fanning out to the Victorian Arts Center, botanical gardens, smart suburbs, and seaside **St. Kilda.** An excursion includes lunch on the Colonial Tramcar Restaurant, a 1927 trolley that glides along the city streets while you dine in style.

Sailing east, it's two nights and a day to **Eden,** a port on the extreme south coast of New South Wales where there are spectacular drives to enjoy along the ocean highway.

Finally, the *Silver Shadow* sails between **Sydney**'s North and South Heads into one of the world's most magnificent harbors, cruising past the shoreline's national park, Taronga Zoo, beaches, and suburbs. The most breathtaking feature is the unfurled white sails design of the Sydney Opera House, and the ship may dock just opposite at Circular Quay or pass under the Sydney Harbor Bridge to tie up at Darling Harbor.

Whichever the berth, there is still one more night aboard with the city at your doorstep. One of the most popular outings is a harbor bridge climb, suitable even for those with mild, but certainly not severe, vertigo. Linger a few days to take in the city's energy, its cultural attractions, neighborhoods such as The Rocks, the first settlement, and **Paddington** for its display of Victorian wrought-iron bungalows and terraced houses. An excursion heads west into the Blue Mountains, the blue created by mist from the eucalyptus forests, for some spectacular scenery, waterfalls, and a steep funicular ride.

HOLLAND AMERICA LINE'S
Statendam
Southern California to Hawaii

 Holland America Line dates back to 1873, operating transatlantic passenger service for the first one hundred years, and now has one of the largest and most attractive fleets in the industry. Purchased by Carnival Corporation in 1988, an infusion of money resulted in a spate of new ship orders, the first being the 55,451-ton *Statendam* in 1992.

This ten-deck ship accommodates 1,266 passengers, and the public rooms are located on Sports, Lido, Upper Promenade, and Promenade Decks. These include the Crows Nest forward on the Sports Deck, a delightful observation lounge during the day and an intimate nightclub in the evening. The Lido Deck offers health and fitness facilities, a large pool area (covered during cool weather by a retractable roof) amidships, and the spacious Lido Restaurant aft. Upper Promenade is anchored forward by the Van Gogh show lounge's balcony seating and the *Rotterdam* dining room's upper level aft. In between are shops, the Casino, the Ocean Bar for a drink and dancing, a card room, a library, and the Explorer's Lounge, also with a dance floor. On the Promenade Deck the orchestra level of the show room and the dining room's main level bracket the front desk, Java Café, and the Wajang Theater, which serves freshly popped popcorn at show time.

Carnival's influence is most apparent in the high quality of the shows performed nightly while at sea. These "Las Vegas–style" productions are full of energy, bright lights, and good staging. The show room is also the venue for popular local Hawaiian entertainment that boards in at least two ports. In the two-level dining room, the traditions of Holland America shine. The dignified Indonesian waiter service is the perfect complement to the culinary delights presented at each meal, and a Filipino band serenades at dinner.

The 633 cabins and suites, spread along five decks, range from 187-square-foot inside cabins to four-room penthouse suites measuring 1,126 square feet. Most cabins are outside, and two decks feature private verandas. Avoid cabins located above the theater if you retire early.

The Itinerary

By law only U.S.-registered ships may carry passengers between Hawaiian ports; hence, the Dutch-registered *Statendam* embarks at **San Diego** for the four-day ocean voyage to then call at five Hawaiian ports before sailing back to San Diego, a nifty combination cruise and double crossing. The days at sea are filled with traditional shipboard activities and by Holland America's lecture series, which includes such topics as finance, world politics, self-improvement,

Polynesian life, Hawaiian royalty, and Hawaiian culture. One elegant evening hosts the superbly orchestrated "Black and White Ball," when all the ship's officers appear in formal white waistcoats. The crossing is a prelude to the beauty and spectacular experience of Hawaii, where, at each port, there is a wide range of shore excursions, some including lunch and a luau with traditional Hawaiian dancing.

From **Hilo** on the "Big Island" of **Hawaii,** take in the Queen Lili'uokalani Gardens or drive through the tropical forest to gaze into the Kilauea crater from Volcano House, perched right on the rim of the world's largest volcano. For a nonorganized tour rent a car or take one of the free shuttle buses to a shopping mall and the beach. Especially dramatic is the after-dark view, from the deck, of hot lava flowing down the slopes into the sea.

Sailing past Diamond Head to dock at the Aloha Tower in **Honolulu,** tour Lolani Palace, the only royal palace in the United States; drive out to Diamond Head, and shop on Kalakaua Avenue. At Pearl Harbor see the film that recalls the Japanese attack on December 7, 1941, then board a boat out to the USS *Arizona* Memorial and visit

Address/Phone: Holland America Line, 300 Elliott Avenue West, Seattle, WA 98119; (800) 426–0327; fax: (800) 628–4855; www.hollandamerica.com

The Ship: *Statendam* was built in 1992, has a gross tonnage of 55,451, a length of 719 feet, and a draft of 25 feet.

Passengers: 1,266; mostly Americans, fifty-five and up

Dress: Formal, informal, and casual nights

Officers/Crew: Dutch officers; Indonesian and Filipino crew

Cabins: 633; 502 outside and 150 with verandas

Fare: $$$

What's included: Cruise only

What's not included: Airfare, port charges, shore excursions, drinks, tips

Highlights: Attractive ship on which to spend many sea days; lots to do ashore in Hawaii

Other itineraries: In addition to these fifteen-day Hawaii cruises from San Diego, which operate January to April and October to December, the *Statendam* cruises to Alaska. Other Holland America ships cruise the Caribbean, the Panama Canal, and South America, and the *Prinsendam* cruises around the world. Holland America's large fleet covers the globe.

the recently opened USS *Missouri*, the battleship on which the Japanese surrendered.

At **Nawiliwili** on the garden island of **Kaui**, take a jeep safari to the rim of Waimea Canyon, the Grand Canyon of the Pacific, and a helicopter flight over the breathtaking Na Pali Coast; then enjoy a water-level view as the *Statendam* sails past. On **Maui** in April there is a good chance to see humpback whales up close, or ascend nearly 10,000 feet to visit Haleakala, Maui's largest volcano. At **Kona**

on the far side of the "Big Island" of **Hawaii,** visit the 250,000-acre Parker Ranch, the largest single-owner cattle ranch in the United States; see Kealakekua Bay—even snorkel here—where Captain James Cook lost his life in 1779; and explore Pu'uhonua o Honaunau, a sacred Hawaiian "City of Refuge," with its sanctuary for defeated warriors, wooden carvings, and ancient temples. Following the intensive sight-seeing, relax and enjoy the ship's social life on the way back to the mainland.

COMPAGNIE POLYNESIENNE DE TRANSPORT MARITIME'S
Aranui III
Freighter Travel to Paradise

The world has shrunk to the point that most places on Earth are reached by air, but thankfully there are a few exceptions where the sea route is still paramount and the destinations remote and unspoiled. The island of St. Helena in the South Atlantic is one, and the Marquesas and Tuomotu Islands in the South Pacific are another.

The South Pacific islands have been accessible by passenger freighters named *Aranui* ("great highway" in Maori) since 1959. In 2003 a brand-new one, purpose-built, larger, and much better appointed, arrived from a Romanian shipyard located hundreds of miles up the Danube. The 200-passenger *Aranui III* then took over the sixteen-day round-trip voyages from the *Aranui II*, a general cargo ship that had been rebuilt to carry 100 passengers. The new ship carries all manner of cargo to the remote archipelago and up to 130 20-foot containers, and, because of her far greater berth capacity, she is classified as a passenger ship.

The passenger accommodations are of a high standard and include a main lounge, a library, a gym, hairdresser, small shop, laundry, and outdoor bar and lounge area by the swimming pool. A video room has a TV and a video player. An aft platform can be lowered for swimming, fishing, snorkeling, and scuba diving. On some sailings the ship carries an enrichment lecturer, and when one is not on board, a member of the crew steps in. The crew is mostly Marquesan, friendly and burly men whose bodies are colorfully decorated with tattoos.

The dining room seats up to 168, and there are normally two seatings. The food may vaguely be described as a Westernized version of Polynesian fare, using local pork, poultry, fish, fruits and vegetables, and New Zealand beef. French wines are included with lunch and dinner. Breakfast is buffet style, and lunch and dinner are served family style. Many of the passengers are French as Polynesia is still part of France, and some American passengers complain of cultural differences that cause annoyances, often a result of the size of the group.

Cabins range from sixty-three standard moderate-size twins with portholes, shower and toilet to twelve windowed deluxe cabins with queen-size bed, refrigerator, and bathtub, to ten suites, eight with private balcony, highly unusual for a freighter.

The Itinerary

Most days are spent docked or at anchor off an island loading and unloading cargo, but three days are at sea. Time in port varies from a few hours to a full day, sometimes a bit more. Where the *Aranui III* does not dock, passengers need to be reasonably fit to clamber down ladders into the ship's tenders and to get out of them on shore which might well be through the surf. But there are always strong, willing hands to assist. March through August is the dry season, though it may shower then, too, while September through February is the rainy season. Temperatures are generally in the 80s (Fahrenheit) during the day and drop to the 60s and 70s at night.

Departures from **Papeete,** the main port on the island of **Tahiti,** take place about every three to four weeks for the sixteen-day voyage that calls at two **Tuomotu Islands** and many more **Marquesas.**

At the first island call, Takapoto, the activities are watching how black pearls are harvested, swimming, and snorkeling. As you approach Ua Pou, sharp volcanic peaks pierce the clouds, with one soaring more than 4,000 feet. A delectable lunch ashore includes breadfruit, barbecued rock lobster, and something called *poisson cru,* raw fish marinated in lime juice and coconut milk.

Herman Melville fled his whaling ship and sought refuge in the Taipivai Valley on Nuku Hiva, where you board vehicles for a mountain ride to see a collection of stone tiki gods, human-like religious sculptures, and boulders strewn about carved with images of birds, fish, and turtles. The island has the only airstrip in the Marquesas, otherwise access is entirely by sea. Tahuata is simply a tiny village visit, and Fatu Hiva, a lush island formed by two extinct volcanoes, is known for its beautiful bay.

On Hiva Oa, a jeep safari takes you to see an even more important collection of tikis that recall the much larger ancient pieces on Easter Island. Paul Gauguin lived

Address/Phone: For information: Compagnie Polynesienne de Transport Maritime, 2028 El Camino Real South, Suite B, San Mateo, CA 94403; (650) 574–2575 or (800) 972–7268; e-mail cptm@aranui.com; www.aranui.com; for bookings: TravLtips, P.O. Box 580188, Flushing, NY 11358-0188; (800) 872–8584; fax: (718) 224–3247; e-mail: info@travltips.com; www.travltips.com

The Ship: *Aranui III*, completed in 2003, has a deadweight tonnage of 3,800, a length of 386 feet, and a draft of 8.8 feet.

Passengers: 200, French about 50 percent, Americans 30 percent, also Australians, British, and others; wide age range but few children

Dress: Casual at all times

Officers/Crew: Polynesian, mostly Marquesans

Cabins: 85 cabins; all outside, 8 with balconies, plus two 12-berth dormitories (male and female)

Fare: $$$

What's included: Cruise fare, all shore excursions, including meals ashore, wine with lunch and dinner

What's not included: Airfare, VAT, tourism tax and port charges, tips, drinks

Highlights: A most comfortable working ship to a beautiful remote part of the world

Other itineraries: All cruises are sixteen-day voyages year-round from Papeete, Tahiti.

here in the village of Atuona until his death in 1903, and you can visit his gravesite, sited next to that of Jacques Brel, the Belgian songwriter who also resided here.

Ua Hika and other islands display Marquesan handicafts, and this one is also known for its 2,000-strong horse population that roams freely. For visitors, they are saddled up for a ride into the mountains.

Fakarava, the last stop, is the world's largest atoll, and the day is spent on the beach (lunch provided) snorkeling among the coral with tropical fish and parasailing.

Many of the ports visited have no other regular access, so the arrival of the *Aranui III* becomes a major event. The Marquesans are warm and friendly, a contrast to the more sullen people encountered at Papeete.

SEVEN SEAS CRUISES'
Paul Gauguin
Cruising in Paradise

 The 320-passenger *Paul Gauguin* flies the French flag and is sold through Seven Seas Cruises. Overall, the ship is more French modern than South Pacific in decor, but the corridors are a gallery of intriguing photographs of turn-of-the-century Tahiti, and a small Fare Tahiti museum displays a few Paul Gauguin drawings and carved ceremonial canoe paddles, wooden flyswatters, and a trio of ironwood shark hooks. The pool is a generous size for a small ship, and deck chairs abound, but with little protection from the intense sun. For the active types the ship's marina opens up for waterskiing, windsurfing, kayaking, scuba diving, and snorkeling, but the latter two sports must be done away from the ship.

Most public rooms, including the two restaurants, are stacked aft and have wraparound windows. On the two highest decks, two pretty observation lounges offer venues for a quiet read during the day, a formal afternoon tea with piano music, drinks before meals, private parties, a cabaret, and a late-night disco.

L'Étoile, the principal restaurant, has a high ceiling and spacious open seating for the continental dinner menu. Above, the cheery 130-seat La Veranda offers a menu and a buffet for breakfast and lunch, while dinner, by reservation, alternates between two French menus. On one night the cold starter was a dollop of Sevruga caviar set atop a charlotte of potatoes, followed by lobster ravioli in dim sum, grilled sea bass, and grilled tenderloin of beef, with crème brûlée and a Tahitian vanilla sauce for dessert. Complimentary wine accompanies both lunch and dinner. Le Grill, located outside and under cover near the midships pool, serves all three meals.

The tiered show lounge offers a wonderfully inventive multi-instrumental singing Filipino quintet and three great shows of dancing and singing islanders, from a two-year-old making her debut to teenagers and grandmothers.

Every cabin is outside, with generous-size bathrooms and tubs, and 50 percent have private verandas for enjoying breakfast and the cool early-evening breezes before dinner.

The TV comes with a VCR, and the minibar is stocked with beer, soda, tonic, and water (except for the beer, these are replenished daily without charge), as well as complimentary bottles of gin, vodka, and scotch.

The Itinerary

For ten months of the year, the 513-foot ship sails Saturdays from **Papeete,** Tahiti, on a seven-day subequatorial loop that takes in the four **Society Islands** of Raiatea, Taha'a, Bora Bora, and Moorea, with much of the week spent lazily at anchor in one gorgeous aqua-blue-water bay after another and just two nights under way. Most passengers, completely seduced by the islands' incredible beauty, seem to like it that way, and while riding at anchor, the ship gently swings about 120 degrees, revealing continually changing views of jagged mountain peaks, palm-fringed reefs, and the pounding surf just beyond.

The shore program offers a lot of variety, and because French Polynesia is an expensive region, the organized excursions are on the pricey side. At **Raiatea** a motorized outrigger canoe speeds along the coast to the Society Island chain's only river, from where it is said that the Polynesians set out to populate Hawaii, Easter Island, and New Zealand. Nearby, the seventeenth-century temple **Marae Taputapuatea** served as the center of religion and sacrifice until the Christian missionaries arrived and largely destroyed it. The ruins are being gradually pieced back to better demonstrate the island's heritage.

The adjacent island of **Taha'a** offers a jeep safari deep into the hills over a rutted road fringed by pink and red ginger, white gardenia, red hibiscus, and tiare, the fragrant flower the Polynesians wear over their ear. There's a stop to watch coconuts sliced open for sampling the sweet water, milk, dried coconut, and the mushy young meat. Another taste, a bit bland, is breadfruit, the crop that Captain Bligh and the *Bounty* had come to collect for replanting as a food crop for the West Indian slaves.

Address/Phone: Seven Seas Cruises, 600 Corporate Drive, Suite 410, Fort Lauderdale, FL 33334; (954) 776–6123 or (800) 285–1835; brochures: (800) 477–7500; fax: (954) 722–6763; www.rssc.com

The Ship: *Paul Gauguin* was completed in late 1997, has a gross tonnage of 18,800, a length of 513 feet, and a draft of 17 feet.

Passengers: 320; age forty and up, mostly Americans

Dress: Casual at all times

Officers/Crew: French officers; European and Filipino crew

Cabins: 160; all outside, 80 with verandas

Fare: $$$

What's included: Cruise, wine at meals, stocked minibar, tips

What's not included: Airfare, port charges, shore excursions, drinks at the bars

Highlights: Cruising among some of the most beautiful islands in the world; sophisticated yet relaxed onboard ambience

Other itineraries: In addition to the above seven-night cruise aboard the *Paul Gauguin,* which operates ten months of the year, the ship makes an occasional fourteen-night cruise to the Marquesas Islands in December. Seven Seas' 350-passenger catamaran *Radisson Diamond* cruises in Europe. The line also operates the 490-passenger *Seven Seas Navigator,* the 720-passenger *Seven Seas Mariner,* and *Seven Seas Voyager.*

Taha'a, a typical volcanic island, is surrounded by a protective reef, and palm-bedecked sandy islands called *motus* offer swimming, snorkeling, and a barbecue lunch ashore.

Anchoring off **Bora Bora,** with its fantastic pointy mountain spires, outrigger canoes head out to the fringing reef, where the guides feed the black-tipped reef sharks and stingrays ranging close by (in shallow waters stingrays, if fed, do not mind being stroked). A jeep ride leads to terrific island views and locations where World War II American cannon point to sea. Author James Michener was stationed here in 1942, and his *Tales of the South Pacific* refer to Bora Bora as "the most beautiful island in the world."

Moorea may be the favorite island of most visitors, but it's a close call. Snorkeling brings the sight of picasso triggerfish and butterfly, angel, surgeon, and parrot fish. On land, plantation agriculture shows fields of pineapples, mangos, papaya, guava, bananas, taro, vanilla, melons, and avocados. Days can be hot and humid, but the water is always nearby, and on clear nights the sky reveals the Southern Cross, False Cross, Orion's Belt, and Castor and Pollux.

At the end of the cruise, visit Tahiti's fine museum, with its displays of sailing craft, tiki sculpture, and maps of Polynesian immigration and European exploration. Another museum is dedicated to Paul Gauguin's life rather than his artistic works. Even after a short visit, it is easy to see how one might be taken over by the islands' incredible lure and the genuine friendliness of the local Polynesians.

EUROPE

CRYSTAL CRUISES'
Crystal Symphony
Northern European Capital Cities

 Crystal Cruises, owned by Japan's NYK Line, offers European service to a largely American clientele. The newer *Crystal Symphony,* built in Finland rather than Japan as with the *Harmony,* is designed for worldwide cruising and spending delightful days at sea.

The primarily European hotel and restaurant staff provides impeccable service throughout the ship in the restaurants, lounges, and on deck. The most popular lounge is the Palm Court, on this ship, one large wraparound room that serves as the venue for sightseeing in cool northern climes, reading, enjoying formal afternoon tea, and drinks before and after dinner during the long summer evenings. On this same Lido Deck, there's an outdoor lap pool, a second indoor-outdoor pool and adjoining Jacuzzis, lots of deck chairs in a wide variety of groupings, a snack and ice-cream bar, and an indoor-outdoor buffet. The deck above has one of the largest ocean-view spas at sea, with an elaborate fitness center, saunas, steam rooms, aerobics, and body treatments, plus a paddle-tennis court, a golf driving range, and a putting green. The jogging/walking deck at the promenade level runs the full length of the superstructure.

Dining is a delight, and the two special dinner options by reservation are Prego, a smartly decorated Italian restaurant, and the Jade Garden, Chinese on this ship rather than Japanese as aboard the *Harmony.* The main dining room has two seatings, unusual for a ship of this caliber, but the food is excellent, and the wine list, emphasizing California, is fairly priced.

All cabins are outside, and well over half have private verandas. Amenities include a sitting area, queen or twin beds, a desk, a TV and VCR, a refrigerator, a safe, and bathrooms with stall showers and tubs. Room service from an extensive menu is available twenty-four hours.

The Itinerary
In summer the *Crystal Symphony's* Baltic Sea cruises, with some variations, call at Scandinavian capitals and St. Petersburg, embarking at Dover, England, and Stockholm, Sweden.

Departing **Stockholm,** one of Europe's best preserved low-rise capitals, the ship gingerly threads through a vast wooded archipelago into the Baltic with a sea day en route to **St. Petersburg** for a two-day stay. Highlights are the artworks in the Hermitage Museum, the Winter Palace, St. Isaac's Cathedral, Peter and Paul Fortress, and an evening at the ballet.

Docking next to the center of **Helsinki,** you can visit the Finnish capital on foot, beginning with the Kauppatoru (Market Square) for its fruits, vegetables, flowers, and handicrafts; and just around the harbor, the old market hall sells meat and fish. One of Finland's great architects, Eliel Saarinen, built the massive stone railway terminal, adorned with great red-granite figures, where trains depart for the lake district, Moscow, and St. Petersburg.

Sailing west through the Baltic, Warnemunde is the port for the long day trip to Europe's largest construction site, **Berlin,** the new German capital. Walk the Unter den Linden, the city's grand boulevard, to the Brandenburg Gate, where, just beyond, the Reichstag, after a long hiatus, is once again the seat of government. Several of the world's most powerful corporations have taken over Potsdamer Platz, reviving one of the city's great crossroads.

Good walkers can enjoy the promenade from **Copenhagen**'s cruise terminal into the city center for the classy Stroget (pedestrian streets), Amalienborg Palace, the royal residence for 200 years, the tightly packed line of outdoor cafes and restaurants along the Nyhavn, and Tivoli, the 160-year-old amusement park, restaurant, and entertainment center in a garden setting that inspired Walt Disney to create his stateside equivalents.

About two hours after leaving Copenhagen, sail past Hamlet's Castle at **Helsingor.** Then you continue overnight and a 60-mile cruise up the Oslofjord to **Oslo,** Norway's capital, where again you dock conveniently within walking distance of the center. Take the ferry for an outing among Norway's maritime heritage centers to see the expedition raft *Kon Tiki,* the polar exploration ship *Fram*, traditional Viking ships, and cruise-liner models. Following a leisurely two-night sail, the cruise ends at **Dover,** nestled beneath the famous white cliffs, just ninety minutes from London.

Address/Phone: Crystal Cruises, 2049 Century Park East, Suite 1400, Los Angeles, CA 90067; (310) 785–9300 or (800) 446–6620; (800) 820–6663 for brochures; fax: (310) 785–3891; www.crystalcruises.com

The Ship: *Crystal Symphony* was built in 1995, has a gross tonnage of 51,044, a length of 781 feet, and a draft of 25 feet.

Passengers: 940; mostly North Americans age fifty-five plus

Dress: Fit to kill; formal nights, jackets and ties on informal nights

Officers/Crew: Norwegian and Japanese officers; European and Filipino crew

Cabins: 470; all outside and more than half with private verandas

Fare: $$$$

What's included: Cruise fare, port charges, all soft drinks and specialty coffees

What's not included: Airfare, alcoholic drinks, shore excursions, tips

Highlights: Alternative Chinese and Italian restaurants, excellent waiter/bar service, lots of onboard amenities

Other itineraries: In addition to these eleven- and twelve-day Scandinavian/Baltic cruises, which operate in June and July, the *Crystal Symphony, Crystal Harmony,* and *Crystal Serenity* cruise most of the world.

CUNARD LINE'S
Queen Elizabeth 2
Norway, the North Cape, and Amsterdam

 Cunard Line is virtually synonymous with cruising and transatlantic travel, with ships that have plied the world's oceans since 1840. Today, the company continues to steep itself in its history and British formality, happily keeping the classic era very much alive. In early 2004 a new Cunard liner, the *Queen Mary 2,* debuts, ensuring an almost uninterrupted seventy-year continuum of North Atlantic *Queens.* The *QE2* now spends much of the year based in England for cruises from Southampton.

As a holdover from the former class system, your cabin grade determines the restaurant in which you will dine. Although the menus are basically the same throughout, there is a noticeable difference in preparation and service, not to mention ambience. The Mauretania restaurant is the largest and offers two traditional seatings. One category above is the single-sitting Caronia, resplendent in mahogany wood trim after a December 1999 makeover. The ship's smallest restaurants, the Britannia Grill and Princess Grill, both seat slightly more than 100 people, and here, ordering off the menu is an added feature.

At the very top of the ship is the Queens Grill, complete with its own private lounge. The three grills provide an unmistakable feeling of exclusivity, and each is reached by a private entrance. In addition, the Lido Restaurant provides three casual meals a day.

Over the years, the *QE2* has undergone many renovations and refits, transforming a product of the late 1960s into a somewhat successful celebration of the mid-1930s. The ship has never looked better. Of particular note is the Chart Room, a wonderful transatlantic setting adorned with the *Queen Mary*'s original piano.

There is an amazing variety of spaces onboard, from elegant, large rooms to cozy corners in bars. The Queens Room, the ship's ballroom, boasts the biggest dance floor at sea and is the cherished venue for a formal afternoon tea. An elaborate library and book shop are supervised by the only seagoing professional librarians. The remodeled spa and gymnasium are deep down in the ship, offering thalossotherapy and a saltwater indoor pool. The 550-seat, two-story theater screens films and hosts lectures by well-known experts on topics ranging from maritime history to America's influence on Russian culture. The two-story Grand Lounge is used for cabaret and play productions, and the Golden Lion Pub supplies beer aficionados with contentment well into the night.

Outside shuffleboard, golf driving, deck tennis, and basketball keep the active happy, while a nursery and teens club provide reassurance for harried parents.

Cabins come in all shapes and sizes, and with the coupling of the restaurant to your cabin grade, this is a most important choice. The minimum-grade cabins, inside with upper and lower berths, are small and not what one expects on a luxury ship, but they allow the less well-heeled to travel, ensuring that the passenger load includes most income levels. Cabins increase in size from there, and most have personality, with odd shapes and quirky designs. Grill category cabins have wood paneling, and the original One Deck rooms are just gorgeous, complete with walk-in closet, satin-lined walls, and oval-shaped windows.

The *QE2* has developed one of the most loyal followings afloat, and past passengers return time and time again. For anyone wishing to experience a trip in the grand style of the past, a cruise on one of the most famous ships in the world is absolutely not to be missed.

The Itinerary

The *Queen Elizabeth 2,* now mostly based in Southampton, England, undertakes a variety of nonrepeating cruises to Northern Europe, the Atlantic Islands, and into the Mediterranean. One attractive North Cape cruise featured here cruises the Norwegian coast and its fjords, and makes an overnight call in Amsterdam. Other cruises operate somewhat similar northern itineraries between May and August that may add German and Danish ports to the mix.

The North Cape cruise to the Land of the Midnight Sun is the longest-running show at sea, dating back 150 years to the early steamship era. Passengers then as now were mainly British, German, and North American. This cruise begins with a late-afternoon departure from the Queen Elizabeth II Terminal in **Southampton** and an overnight sail to the entrance to the **North Sea Canal** leading inland to **Amsterdam,** where the ship ties up for the night. Passengers can have the evening out without fear of missing the boat, and during the day take a canal cruise and visit the Rijksmuseum, Van Gogh Museum, and the Anne Frank House.

Leaving via the North Sea Canal, the *QE2* aims northward through the North Sea on a two-night and one-day passage to the mouth of the **Sognefjord** and a sail well inland to the tiny town of **Flaam.** The port, located at the head of a narrow fjord, is the terminus for the world's steepest adhesion railway with a spectacular climb up past waterfalls to the town of Myrdal, a junction on the main Oslo-Bergen rail line. Leaving the Sognefjord, the ship sails on north to **Aalesund,** a town destroyed by fire in 1904

Address/Phone: Cunard Line, 6100 Blue Lagoon Drive, Suite 400, Miami, FL 33126; (305) 463–3000 or (800) 7–CUNARD; fax: (305) 463–3020; www.cunardline.com

The Ship: The *Queen Elizabeth 2* was built in 1969, has a gross tonnage of 70,327 tons, a length of 963 feet, and a deep draft of 32 feet.

Passengers: 1,740; mostly British, some Americans, and Europeans of all ages, especially during the summer vacation months

Dress: Formal, informal, and casual nights

Officers/Crew: British officers and international crew

Cabins: 925 in a wide variety of shapes and sizes; 30 with verandas. Cabin category determines your restaurant. There are more than 100 single cabins available.

Fare: $$ to $$$$$

What's included: Cruise fare, transfers, and return airfare

What's not included: Port charges, drinks, tips

Highlights: Cruising on a true liner to the magnificence of Norway; social life and a wide variety of activities onboard

Other itineraries: In addition to this summer cruise to Norway and Amsterdam, the *QE2* makes other northern European cruises and sails to the Canary Islands and Mediterranean, with the occasional crossing between Southampton and New York to connect to the Christmas/New Year's Caribbean cruise and the annual January to April world cruise. Fleetmate *Queen Mary 2* makes crossings between New York and Southampton and cruises from both ports and from Florida, and the *Caronia* is based in Southampton until the end of 2004.

and rebuilt into a handsome Norwegian style of art nouveau. The fit can easily make the twenty-minute climb to an observation point overlooking Aalesund and the *QE2* docked below. On north to **Trondheim,** the much older town center features an eleventh-century medieval cathedral and a colorful wooden Hanseatic League–style waterfront. Visit the Bishop's Palace alongside the Nidaros Cathedral, the Musical Museum, and open-air Folk Museum.

Crossing the Arctic Circle, where a ladle of ice-cold water down one's back is the typical initiation, the ship arrives at the **North Cape.** In June on a clear day the sun should remain visible above the horizon for the complete twenty-four-hour cycle, and even on a cloudy night, the sky should be light enough to read and take photographs. The North Cape Center is heavily visited during the midnight sun period, so the best sense of how far north you are may come from the deck of the ship looking up at the North Cape.

After a call at the northernmost fishing port of **Skarsvag,** sail on south for two nights and a day to enter the **Geirange-**

fjord, Norway's most famous, passing pencil-thin Seven Sisters and Bridal Veil Falls to disembark passengers at **Hellesylt** for a mountain drive to the famous fjord overlook at Geiranger.

Sailing out into the Norwegian Sea, the ship turns south to visit **Bergen,** Norway's second-largest city and major west coast port. Much of the city is walkable from the ship, and be sure to take in the fish market at the end of the inner harbor; the Bergen Art Museum featuring Norwegian artists plus Braque, Picasso, and Paul Klee; Bryggen with its row of timbered Hanseatic League buildings, once merchant houses and now shops and cafes; and if the weather cooperates, take the Floibanen Funicular up the mountain for a superb view of the city and seascape.

A last call is made at **Stavanger,** with its twelfth-century medieval cathedral and wooden old city representing the past, and the base for the North Sea oil business the present. As a finale, the *QE2* takes two nights and a day to cross the North Sea and then into the English Channel for disembarkation at Southampton.

CUNARD LINE'S
Caronia
Classic Liner to the Baltic Capitals

Cunard's British-flagged *Caronia* draws legions of loyal passengers, who come to enjoy one of the few remaining classic cruise experiences afloat today. In spite of her relatively small size by today's standards, the 24,292-ton *Caronia* is indeed imposing, aided by her long, upwardly raked bow, majestic superstructure amidships, and the large single funnel sporting the orange-red Cunard colors. Her handsome profile turns heads when she pulls into port, and she is the third Cunarder to

bear the name *Caronia*, assuming it in December 1999 at Southampton following a major refit. And she is a most worthy successor.

First built at Newcastle-upon-Tyne in 1973 as the *Vistafjord*, she became the final ship delivered to Norwegian America Line, a venerable company that once transported Scandinavian migrants to Canada and America and later provided one of the most luxurious cruise experiences to the mon-eyed upper class.

The ship cuts the smart appearance of a

latter-day ocean liner, but after her initial maiden departure from Oslo to New York on May 22, 1973, she went into full-time worldwide cruising for between 550 and 620 one-class passengers.

In 1980 she and the marginally smaller 1965-built *Sagafjord* were sold to Norwegian America Cruises, and both ships received additional cabins and public spaces. Then in 1983 the Cunard Line bought the pair, and in December 1997 the *Sagafjord* was sold. Two years later the *Vistafjord* was renamed *Caronia,* reflagged and commanded by a British captain. However, she remains much the same classic ship, the choice for world travelers who like European-style service, low-key stage entertainment, ballroom dancing, classic concerts, proper afternoon tea, and a certain formality that is now almost lost on the increasingly casual high seas.

My wife and I first sailed in her as the *Vistafjord* on a trans–Panama Canal cruise over New Year's, and what a fine time we had dressing up, being pampered at our window table for two, and ringing in the new year with champagne and heaps of caviar and smoked salmon. For us, the real beauty of the cruise was little interruption of life aboard, with just two throwaway Caribbean ports in nine days. More recently in the Baltic, once the ship had been renamed *Caronia,* we enjoyed scattered days at sea and wonderful ports between Southampton, England, and St. Petersburg, Russia.

She now cruises exclusively from Southampton to ports close to home, the northern isles, Norway, the Baltic, Iberia, the Canaries, the Mediterranean, and to and from the Caribbean.

Walking aboard, one enters a European-style boutique hotel with large floral arrangements set against handsome woodwork. But apart from the White Star Bar, with dark paneling and formal steamship posters, the *Caronia* is much lighter in decor than her former running mate, the *Sagafjord.*

The most attractive space is unquestionably the semicircular Garden Lounge, where windows arc 180 degrees and the dominant colors are soft grays and blue-greens. The room sweeps upward toward the bow, and the perimeter seating is slightly raised above the center section, which is occupied by additional seating, a dance floor, and bandstand.

Passengers enjoy a read in this light, airy space early in the day, and in the afternoon one of the best formal teas at sea takes place. Stewards wheel carts laden with crustless sandwiches, pastries, and creamy scones while a pianist plays in the background. After dinner the room takes on a restful glow from bands of recessed ceiling lights, and the formally dressed gather for a classical concert and liqueur. More informally, a buffet-style tea takes place in the ballroom, also extremely well attended.

The high-ceiling ballroom is just that, a throwback to the days when the main event was, and on this ship still is, dancing to a good band. Of course, today's passengers expect to be entertained, so the room hosts vocalists, instrumentalists, small acts, and local groups who come aboard in port. On the final evening, it's "Last Night at the *Caronia* Proms," with old favorites such as "Rule Britannia" and "Land of Hope and Glory."

A traditional cinema screens first-run films and provides the venue for special-interest lectures, and not far away is a casino, appropriately downsized for passengers for whom gaming is not an important activity.

The library, while offering a well-chosen hardcover and reference collection, is tiny with just a couple of chairs and a sofa, so most people make their selections and leave to read elsewhere. The expanded retail shops have replaced the card room, and the bridge tables have been relocated to the Piccadilly Club.

Once a two-deck-high nightclub, the Piccadilly Club space serves multiple functions—a quiet lounge and late-night club on the lower level and a place for bridge instruction and the Tivoli Restaurant upstairs. Dinner by reservation is offered here every evening for just thirty-five diners. Tables for two to eight face aft through big windows over the stern, a magical setting that has none of the gimmicks or over-the-top decoration found on some ships' Italian restaurants. With its generous menu, many people enjoy returning for another meal.

The 700-seat Franconia Restaurant appears larger in scale than the rest of the ship, but it can take the full complement of passengers and top officers at one open sitting. Apart from a slightly raised center section, the ceiling is low and the room spreads far and wide. Brass art nouveau wall decorations and sconces brighten up the space. There are many tables for two, including by the windows, and when the ship is not heavily booked, tables for four become twos.

Because most passengers are now British, with just a scattering of Americans and the occasional German, the menu has added a daily English roast, variety of fish, lunchtime curries, and cheese board, and at breakfast, kippers and black pudding. Menus do not repeat, even on very long cruises. The dining staff is largely European and the bar staff British, well trained to serve passengers for whom dining is one of the major reasons to cruise. On a twelve-day cruise, typically three or four nights will be black tie and an equal number informal jacket and tie, while in-port evenings are casual.

The Lido buffet, with its varnished teak floor, faces onto the afterdeck. The breakfast and lunch selections vary from day to day, and as a treat, locally purchased fresh fish or shellfish might appear at the noonday meal. As built, the ship never had a proper buffet facility, and the seating is limited, requiring some passengers to take their meals into the ballroom or, if the weather is conducive, outside near the pool.

Because it is a classic ship, the cabins vary greatly even within the same category, so have a careful look at the deck plans and ask a travel agent who knows the ship. One of the best features are the seventy-three single cabins: small, yes, but specifically designed for the person traveling alone.

The 375 cabins comprise 321 outside, 54 inside, 10 suites, and 2 penthouse suites, and 34 offer verandas. All staterooms have twenty-four-hour full-menu room service, fruit baskets, thermostat-controlled air-conditioning, minibar, color television, VCR, radio, telephone, in-room safes, terry robes, private bathroom with shower or tub, and 110/220-volt outlets.

Most of the largest cabins and suites are high up on the Promenade, Sun, and Bridge Decks. Some of the largest face down onto the side promenade, and my favorites look ahead over the bow. Cabin 151, which I occupied in the Baltic, had three windows facing forward, set high enough not to be ogled by those making constitutional rounds. During the Scandinavian summer, the daylight view is nearly twenty-four hours, and curiously, it is just one of two C-category cabins that has shower only and no tub bath.

Outdoor deck space is more than adequate, and the Promenade Deck has shady recesses for reading and dozing. It's the small after-facing tiered decks that are the most sought-after locations for a read or conversation and the view down to the outdoor pool and out to the ship's wake. Counterclockwise walkers appear in force after breakfast, and two narrow doorways cut into the steel wind protectors briefly interrupt what is an otherwise smooth flow.

As the Caronia was built to cruise in cool as well as warm waters, the ship has one of the few remaining indoor pools and saunas deep down on C Deck, two decks below the lowest passenger cabin level. The spa is small and constricted by the limited space, but the variety of treatments available is quite generous. There are separate-sex saunas, three treatment rooms, massage, and a gymnasium with four treadmills, four bikes, two stepping machines, and weights. High up by the Cunard-red funnel there is miniature golf and a driving net.

Additional amenities and services are a computer learning center with ten stations for e-mail, a medical center staffed by a doctor and a nurse, laundry and dry cleaning services, passenger launderette, twenty-four-hour purser's desk, concierge service, and an excursion office.

The *Caronia's* consort is the *Queen Elizabeth 2*, also cruising from Southampton and making an occasional transatlantic crossing to New York. These two fine ships make a classic cruise combination. The *Caronia* will leave the Cunard fleet at the end of 2004 and join Saga, a British operator that plans to run her in much the same style, so if you miss her at Cunard, you still have plenty of time to sample this liner-style ship.

The Itinerary

The *Caronia* makes two summer cruises to the Baltic capitals from England that vary only slightly in itinerary. After you leave **Southampton** in the late afternoon with the sun, if shining, still high in the sky, the first day is spent sailing eastward through the southern **North Sea.** On the second day, the ship takes the shortcut to the **Baltic** via the **Kiel Canal,** a busy north German waterway with both rural and industrial scenes to enjoy. At the far end, a day's steaming northeastward through the Baltic brings the ship to **Stockholm** via a three-hour transit through the Swedish archipelago, islands dotted with weekend retreats and homes within commuting distance of the capital.

Stockholm, a city built around a pretty harbor and facing a lake, has maintained its traditional skyline by sensible zoning, and it is relatively compact and easily walkable. The most prominent buildings are the

Address/Phone: Cunard Line, 6100 Blue Lagoon Drive, Suite 400, Miami, FL 33126; (800) 7–CUNARD or (305) 563–3000; fax: (305) 463–3010; www.cunardline.com

The Ship: *Caronia* was completed in 1973 as the *Vistafjord* and has a gross tonnage of 24,492, a length of 627 feet, and a draft of 27 feet.

Passengers: 668; single and double occupancy; ages forty-five and up; mostly British, some German, and a few Americans and Europeans

Dress: Formal, informal, and casual nights

Officers/Crew: British officers; European and Filipino crew

Cabins: 376; 324 outside, 73 singles, and 25 with verandas

Fare: $$$$

What's included: Cruise fare and port charges

What's not included: Airfare, shore excursions, drinks, and tips

Highlights: One of the few remaining traditional ocean liners with excellent food and service; varied European itineraries

Other itineraries: In addition to these fourteen-day Baltic Capitals cruises, which take place in the summer months, the *Caronia* cruises to islands and other ports in northern Europe, to the Iberian Peninsula, the Mediterranean, and to and from the Caribbean. Note that the *Caronia* sails for Cunard through November 2004, when she will be transferred to Saga Cruises and is expected to continue operating with much the same style but under a new name.

palace, the Grand Hotel, and the Wasa Museum.

If you missed the early-morning sail through the archipelago, you get another chance outbound for the overnight sail through the Baltic, gingerly negotiating narrow channels to reach **Helsinki.** Docking adjacent to the city center and an outdoor craft and produce market, Finland's capital is a treasure trove of art nouveau architecture and perhaps best visited independently using the Loop Tram. The tracks make a figure eight starting out from near the port to run into residential neighborhoods and to Eliel Sarineen's magnificent 1912-built railway station and the Rock Church, set in a stone quarry and a site for summer concerts.

Next, the *Caronia* plies the long complex route past the old naval fortress at Kronstadt to **St. Petersburg,** usually docking for two days within sight of the St. Peter and Paul Fortress and the **Winter Palace.** Shore excursions are the best route here, easing the way to negotiate the crowds and hassles at the Hermitage to take in the Italian, Flemish, Dutch, and French art and eighteenth- and nineteenth-century czarist opulence, St. Isaacs Cathedral, and an evening ballet performance. Usually, there is a bit of time to wander the nearby streets and squares to soak up the atmosphere of Peter the Great's Window on Europe.

The daylong call at **Tallinn, Estonia**'s capital, reveals during a walking tour, then on one's own, a lively medieval Hanseatic League city speaking a language that has Finnish connections, hence the huge numbers of Finns who visit by ship. After a day at sea, the ship calls at **Warnemunde,** a north German port with access, though via a very long bus ride, to **Berlin,** the country's recently reestablished capital. The fast overview reveals one of Europe's great revived cities, burgeoning with new construction around Potsdam Square and maintaining its handsome prewar scale along Unter den Linden, the principal cultural and architectural artery.

On one Baltic cruise, the ship makes a second Kiel Canal passage to enter the North Sea Canal en route to **Amsterdam,** docking at the cruise terminal relatively near the city center. The city's sights—the Rijksmusum, Van Gogh Museum, Anne Frank House, and canal boats rides—are well-known outings, but lesser known are the Rembrandt Huis, where he lived and painted, and the wonderful museum dedicated to Dutch maritime exploits. Most destinations are reachable by Loop Tram #20 from Central Station making a wide circle in both directions. This final stop is just an overnight sail from disembarkation in Southampton.

On the alternate itinerary, the last call is adjacent to **Copenhagen**'s landscaped waterfront promenade, which leads past the Little Mermaid and the royal palace to Nyhavn's canal-side outdoor restaurants and to the busy Stroget, a pedestrian shopping street. From the Danish capital, the ship passes Hamlet's Castle and skirts the northern tip of Denmark on a run of two nights and a day back to Southampton.

SWAN HELLENIC'S
Minerva II
Highlands and Islands

 Swan Hellenic, owned by one of the world's largest and oldest shipping lines, P&O of London, operates in a distinctly different world from a U.S.-based line or even British-based P&O Cruises. Prospective passengers must feel comfortable with the very English onboard style, including the mostly British fellow passengers, and considerable mind stimulation from the strong lecture program that leads to well-orchestrated visits ashore.

Swan's *Minerva II* is twice as large as the *Minerva* it replaced and offers more public rooms, a greater variety of restaurant dining, and lots of cabins with balconies. The cabin TV brings in both the BBC and Euronews, and with the British being news-hounds, the ship provides wire-service-generated news sheets and, when available, daily newspapers attached to long wooden sticks hung up on hooks in the library. The comfy library is easily twice the size of that aboard the *QE2* and the kind of place to which I gravitate to spend a rainy day, always a distinct possibility on a cruise around the British Isles.

The English, clubby atmosphere continues in the Wheeler Bar, a gracious lounge with a resident pianist playing before and after dinner. In the evenings the forward lounge is the setting for classical and jazz concerts, dancers, and drama; during the day it's the venue for the lectures integral to the Swan experience. On this cruise, eyes are opened to understanding some pretty amazing sights ashore, such as tropical gardens thriving in a cold climate and Scotland's prehistoric rings of standing stones and Bronze Age archaeological sites. The British learn, somewhat unhappily, that they are really as mongrel as most Americans, with ancestors who were Angles, Celts,

Normans, Picts, Saxons, Scots, and Vikings.

Five decks higher up, the Orpheus Bar, which paid homage to the dowdy but much loved Greek ship that Swan chartered for twenty-one years, is a bright and airy observation lounge.

The main restaurant is open for all three meals, and the Swan policy is a variation on open seating whereby passengers are shown to a table as they arrive. That way, fellow passengers meet and share experiences throughout the cruise. One can also request a table for two, and at breakfast a quiet corner is reserved for those who like to eat in silence. The alternatives are the Mediterranean-style Swan restaurant, an adjacent grill room, and, one deck below the Bridge Cafe, a buffet dining room that serves breakfast, lunch, and dinner with additional tables outside under cover.

The Itinerary

This annual Swan cruise circumnavigates the British Isles, and as no place in Britain is more than 60 miles from the sea, the British passengers are traveling not very far from home. Embarkation is at **Dover,** with a backdrop of its medieval castle atop the famous white cliffs. The *Minerva II* first turns eastward through the misty waters of the English Channel, then north toward Scotland and **Leith,** the port for **Edinburgh.** Docking at right angles to the former Royal Yacht *Britannia*, you can walk a few hundred yards and go aboard to see how the royals lived when they toured the British Empire. Edinburgh, its Royal Mile from the Castle down to the Palace of Holyroodhouse, the Old Town, New Town, and Princes Street are just a few miles inland.

Then up the coast at **Invergordon,** visit Urquart Castle on the shores of **Loch Ness** or Cawdor Castle, reputedly the home of

Macbeth. Well out to sea to the north of Scotland, the **Shetland** and the **Orkney** Islands provide a look at early Viking settlements and much further back to the Bronze Age. On Shetland, the village of Jarlshof overlooks the sea at Sumburgh Head, and at the Neolithic community at Skara Brae on Orkney, sophisticated houses boast beds in recessed alcoves. The Bishop of Cornwall, one of the lecturers, accompanied us into St. Magnus Cathedral at **Kirkwall** on Orkney, a magnificent red and yellow sandstone structure, to aid us in unraveling the Romanesque, transitional Norman, and Gothic styles.

Sailing north into **Loch Ewe,** an impressive stand of trees rises from otherwise denuded hillsides, and the wind-protected **Inverewe Gardens** are creatively laid out in arcing walled closures, among heaps of rocks, and on tiny glacial ponds. South African wildflowers and Australian eucalyptus trees are thriving in the far north of Scotland, and on a map it's the same latitude as Labrador, where the offshore cold currents escorted an iceberg south to sink the *Titanic.*

The *Minerva II* sails over the sea to **Skye** for a visit to Dunvegan Castle, ancestral home of the Macleods, then cruises up Loch Fyne to anchor off **Inveraray,** a magical setting for the Gothic-revival turreted and towered castle where the twenty-sixth Duke of Argyll resides. After delighting in the Beauvais tapestries and the 100-foot-high armorial hall featuring some of the most vicious-looking weapons seen since the film *Braveheart,* we spied a stone tower atop a nearby hill and climbed an hour up through the woods for a spectacular view down the length of the loch.

Sailing into the **Firth of Clyde,** the *Minerva II* moors off the nineteenth-century Scottish resort town of **Rothesay.** From the landing, it's a short drive out to Mount Stuart, a Victorian Gothic fantasy, built with red sandstone and multicolored marble and decorated with stained-glass windows depicting astrological and mythological figures.

The daylong call at **Dublin** allows time

Address/Phone: Swan Hellenic Cruises, 631 Commack Road, Suite 1A, Commack, NY 11725; (877) 219–4239; fax: (631) 858–1279; e-mail: swanhellenic@kainyc.com; www.swanhellenic.com

The Ship: *Minerva II* was built in 2001 as the *R8* and has a gross tonnage of 30,277, a length of 594 feet, and a draft of 20 feet.

Passengers: 684; mostly British, fifty and up

Dress: Jacket and tie is expected on evenings at sea in the three main restaurants.

Officers/Crew: British and European officers; Filipino and Ukrainian crew

Cabins: 342; 317 outside and 242 with balconies

Fare: $$$$

What's included: Cruise and port charges, program of shore excursions for every port, all tips aboard and for guides ashore, flights between London and the ship

What's not included: Airfare between the United States and London, optional shore excursions, drinks

Highlights: Excellent enrichment program, terrific organization aboard and ashore

Other itineraries: In addition to the above cruise around the British Isles, which is offered in late summer, the *Minerva II* makes year-round, nonrepeating four-to-fifteen-day cruises in the Mediterranean, around Britain, to Scandinavia, and across the Atlantic to South and North America.

for visits to Dublin Castle, Trinity College, and the illuminated Book of Kells, and free time to enjoy the lively street life and those justly famous row houses noted for brightly painted doors and elaborate fan transoms. Just outside the capital is Powerscourt and Helen Dillon's famous city garden.

At the town of **Cobh** on the southeast Irish coast, ferret out the myriad of ocean liner connections in a town that has seen more than three million Irish embark for new lives in Australia and America, from the potato famine days of the mid-1840s to the end of emigration by sea in 1970. Adjacent to the landing, the Heritage Center, housed in the Victorian railway station, tells this story and those of two major shipping events in the port's history. In April 1912, Cobh (then Queenstown) was the last port of call for the White Star liner *Titanic,* and the Cunard liner *Lusitania* was torpedoed

off here in May 1915. Many of those lost and recovered are buried in a cemetery just out of town.

Sailing south, we hear from the garden expert that there are more garden plants— 240,000 variations—in Britain than anywhere else in the world, and at **Tresco** in the **Isles of Scilly,** we see the results of a marvelous microclimate created by California Monterey pines as wind protection, the absence of killing frosts, humidity from the sea, adequate rainfall, and abundant sunshine. The terraced gardens at Tresco Abby do not disappoint, nor did the sun, which beamed down during our visit, led by a resident student guide who obviously loved the place.

The last call is at **St. Peter Port** on the island of **Guernsey,** one of the Channel Islands off the coast of France, and then it's an overnight sail back to Dover for disembarkation.

HEBRIDEAN ISLAND CRUISES'
Hebridean Princess
Scotland's Western Isles

Hebridean Island Cruises, a well-kept secret in North America, got its start in 1989, when a 600-passenger Scottish ferry was transformed into a posh, floating country house for a maximum of fifty mostly British guests. She came under new ownership in 1997, and the public rooms have been completely redecorated, making her even more attractive.

The cozy public rooms evoke the feel of an old-fashioned country inn, nowhere more so than in the forward observation lounge, with its comfy upholstered armchairs and settees and rustic brick-and-timber fireplace. A small bar is off to one side. The library has leather and tartan-upholstered seating. Two other lounges feature afternoon tea and

cigar smoking amid wicker furniture. Some evenings are formal, and in warm weather, passengers gather aft on deck for champagne receptions with hot hors d'oeuvres. Topdeck spaces also include comfy, wind-protected chairs for reading.

The restaurant operates like a hotel dining room. Passengers sit with friends or at tables for two, but singles are seated with fellow singles and usually an officer. Presentation and service are top-notch. The menu is typically British, featuring a Sunday roast with Yorkshire pudding at lunch, sliced duckling at dinner, black pudding and kippers at breakfast, and fresh strawberries on meringue for dessert. Other dinner choices include Scottish highland game and mushroom pie, sautéed and smoked salmon, and raw oysters. Unfamiliar Scottish delicacies that may startle the palate are haggis, a mixture of calf or lamb hearts, lungs, and liver with onion, suet, and seasonings, and kedgeree, a rice and smoked-fish combination.

The twenty-nine individually designed and furnished cabins, carrying the names of Scottish isles, lochs, sounds, and castles, vary widely, but all show fabric frills above headboards and around windows that open. TVs, refrigerated bars, coffee- and tea makers, irons and ironing boards, trouser presses, hair dryers, dressing tables, and ample stowage are standard throughout. Two cabins on the lowest deck share baths, and there are eleven dedicated inside and outside singles. The ship is not air-conditioned, but this is seldom a problem in these northerly waters. Although the fares are as high as they get, the *Hebridean Princess* is a one-of-a-kind treasure appeal-ing to the well-heeled, many of whom come back year after year.

The Itinerary

A guide accompanies all cruises, and excursions include visits to stately homes, country gardens, fishing villages, and remote, rugged islands. Passengers should come prepared for Scottish mists and uncertain weather, and the ship anchors or ties up at night except on an occasional overnight sail to the outer islands and across the North Sea to Norway's fjords. The *Hebridean Princess* most often boards in **Oban,** a popular Scottish seaside resort about two hours by train northwest of Glasgow. Port descriptions here are meant to be typical examples, as itineraries vary from cruise to cruise. A two-hour sail takes you to **Tobermory Bay** on the **Isle of Mull** for a guided tour of the neat, white-washed town, founded by the British Fisheries Society. Underway, the ship cruises into

Address/Phone: Hebridean Island Cruises, Griffin House, Broughton Hall, Skipton, North Yorkshire, BD23 3AN England; (011) 44–1756–704704 or (800) 659–2648 (9:00 A.M.–5:15 P.M. U.K. time); fax: (011) 44–1756–701455; e-mail: reservations@hebridean.co.uk; www.hebridean.co.uk

The Ship: *Hebridean Princess* was rebuilt in 1989 from the Scottish ferry *Columba* and has a gross tonnage of 2,115, a length of 235 feet, and a shallow draft of 10 feet.

Passengers: 50; age fifty and up, largely British with perhaps a handful of Americans

Dress: Formal some nights, jacket and tie on others

Officers/Crew: British

Cabins: 29; wide range of shapes and sizes but all prettily furnished

Fare: $$$$$

What's included: Cruise and port charges, excursions, tips, drinks on special nights

What's not included: Airfare, drinks

Highlights: Sailing aboard a most genteel, floating, country-house hotel to a beautiful part of the world, weather cooperating

Other itineraries: In addition to the one-week cruise among the Inner Hebrides, the *Hebridean Princess* offers many different six- to nine-night Scottish itineraries, plus trips to Norway, Northern Ireland, and the Isle of Man from March through November. The seventy-eight passenger, 4,200-ton *Hebridean Spirit* joined the fleet in mid-2001, offering wider-ranging cruises to Norway, the Baltic, the Mediterranean, and through Suez into the Red Sea and Indian Ocean.

Loch Stuart, overlooked by the rugged and scenic beauty of **Ardnamurchan Peninsula,** where its point is the most westerly mainland in the British Isles, beating out much-better-known Land's End by 20 miles.

The **Sound of Sleat,** separating the mainland from the **Isle of Skye,** leads to the pastel-fronted island capital of **Portree** for a bit of a wander. In **Upper Loch Torridin** the surrounding peaks create a dramatic setting for an overnight anchorage. The village of **Plonkton** offers the unusual sight, in these northerly parts, of an arc of palm trees, and later in the day from the dock at the **Kyle of Lochalsh,** a drive explores **Cuillin Hills** across the sea on Skye.

Cruising past Rhum and Eigg, the ship anchors off **Muck** for a beach landing and a walk across the island to have a proper afternoon tea with local residents. A cruise up **Loch Linnhe** may offer a glimpse of Scotland's highest peak, **Ben Nevis,** snow-capped for much of the year. Northwest Scotland's remarkable climate has encouraged the creation of some beautiful gardens, including those at **Torosay Castle,** which exhibit, depending on the time of one's visit, glorious spring flowers or colorful autumnal leaves. The *Hebridean Princess* spends one more night at anchor, then slips into Oban in the morning.

NORTHLINK FERRIES'
Hjaltland and *Hrossey*
To the Isles North of Scotland

For well over a century, a fleet of "North Boats" has linked Scotland's Orkney and Shetland Islands with the mainland. The ships are designed to sail in some of the world's roughest seas, but when the weather cooperates, the island scenery is absolutely gorgeous. With frequent schedules, it is quite easy to plan the sea trip and then stop over a couple of days on each island chain. The ship names *Hjaltland* and *Hrossey* (old Norse for Shetland and Orkney) are the only aspects of this service that are not brand-new. Taking over the concession from P&O Scottish Ferries in 2002, Northlink, a joint venture between Scottish west coast ferry operator Caledonian MacBrayne and the Royal Bank of Scotland, had a fleet of fast, 24-knot, high-standard ships built in Finland. To match this investment, the Scottish Execu-

tive built new terminals at all the ports.

Every day in the late afternoon, a ship leaves Aberdeen for the 200-mile overnight journey north to Lerwick (Shetland), calling en route on alternate sailings at Kirkwall (Orkney) about midnight. Aberdeen boarding takes place up to two hours before sailing, allowing passengers to settle into their comfortable, tastefully furnished outside two-bed cabins or more economically in an inside four-berth cabin. Private facilities and hair dryers are included in all cabins.

The forward bar, the live entertainment center of the ship, overlooks the bow and is a particularly pleasant spot for a drink before dinner. The small à la carte restaurant (booking essential) offers high-quality ingredients, including lamb, steaks, fish, and scallops, sourced mainly from the islands and carefully prepared and beautifully presented in elegant surroundings. The fine food is complemented by a fairly extensive wine list, and coffee may be taken after dinner in the adjacent lounge. Other facilities include a large self-service restaurant for dinner and breakfast, a cinema, a childrens' playroom, and a small shop carrying necessities, souvenirs, and local knitwear. The public spaces throughout are furnished with wood-effect paneling, and outside there are small semi-sheltered areas amidships and a large open deck aft. Although the arrival comes early, at 7:00 A.M., breakfast is served until 9:30 A.M., and final disembarkation is at 10:00 A.M. For a small fee, including breakfast, the ship's staff will unload those traveling with a car and put it on the quayside, allowing a more leisurely disembarkation.

The Itinerary

As these ships operate mostly overnight, sight-seeing en route is limited, though lengthened summertime daylight extends viewing hours.

Aberdeen's harbor, packed with oil rig supply vessels and numerous fishing boats, is a tight squeeze for the *Hjaltland* and *Hrossey* on their way out to the North Sea. The ships turn north to parallel the Aberdeenshire coast for about two hours,

then in the morning the ship docks at **Lerwick,** the principal town of the 100-island chain.

The Shetlands are much wilder than Orkney, with crofting (small farm holdings) and fishing the main industries. At anchor may be Russian and Polish fish factory ships known locally as klondykers, which arrive every summer to buy and process herring and mackerel.

If you have not arrived with a car, you can rent one or hire a taxi for the short ride to numerous bed and breakfasts or a small hotel. The Lerwick Hotel, located on the south side of town, has good views across the water to the Island of Brassay, but it is quite expensive.

Directly accessible from the pier is a headland walk leading to the ruins of **Clickimin Broch,** a first-century fortified stone tower built in a shallow loch by the Picts. Then in the afternoon, tour the countryside dotted with stacks of freshly cut peat and ruins of old stone crofts. There are sweeping views to both sides out to the North Sea and to the Atlantic Ocean. Stop at **Jarlshoff,** Sir Walter Scott's early-nineteenth-century name for an ancient site that saw 3,000 years of habitation, from the Stone Age to the seventeenth century.

Address/Phone: Northlink Orkney and Shetland Ferries Limited, Ferry Terminal, Stromness, Orkney, KW16 3BH Scotland; +44 1856 851144; fax: +44 1856 851155; e-mail: info@northlink ferries.co.uk; www.northlinkferries. co.uk (the site has helpful tourist information)

The Ships: The *Hjaltland* and *Hrossey* were both purpose-built in Finland in 2002, have a gross tonnage of 11,486, a length of 409 feet, and a draft of 17 feet.

Passengers: 600 total occupancy; the majority of passengers are British

Dress: Casual at all times

Officers/Crew: British (many from the previous P&O operation)

Cabins: 300 berths in 50 outside twins and 50 inside fours, all with private facilities. Two recliner lounges.

Fare: $ to $$

What's included: Fare, with cabin if purchased, port charges

What's not included: Connecting transportation, meals, drinks

Highlights: High standard on board and beautiful island destinations

In the distance Sumburgh Head, the Shetlands' most southerly point, beckons walkers for a few hours' hike.

The crossing from Lerwick to **Kirkwall** on Orkney takes about six and a half hours, and the new terminal, also serving cruise ships, is about 2 to 3 miles by road from the center of town. A taxi transfer is the best option. The arrival, whether from Aberdeen or Lerwick, is usually just before midnight, but the hotel operators are used to latecomers.

One recommended place to stay is the Orkney Hotel (formerly the Royal Hotel) on Victoria Street, Kirkwall. The rooms are attractive, and the restaurant food is excellent with the Scottish breakfasts especially good. The hotel is located about 100 yards from **St. Magnus** cathedral, built in Norman times of weathered red sandstone. The town itself and the stone harbor are interesting places to explore on foot, and local ferries sail from here to the northern islands for additional exploring ashore.

Not far from town, the Italian chapel, crafted from scrap metal by Italian prisoners of World War II and overlooking the historic naval anchorage at Scapa Flow, is well worth a visit, as is **Maes Howe,** a neolithic burial chamber built before 2700 B.C. Most of the island is gently rolling farmland and grazing fields for cattle and sheep, but the shoreline has sharp edges. Driving is a joy and roads are uncrowded.

Sailings return from Kirkwall overnight to Aberdeen, or alternatively from the Orcadian port of **Stromness** on a ninety-minute crossing to the very northern tip of Scotland at **Scrabster.** By road from Kirkwall to Stromness, the journey takes about twenty-five minutes, and buses travel the route and meet the ferries. Orkney's second city is an intriguing rabbit warren of quiet lanes and is another good place to spend the night. The largest hotel is the Stromness, overlooking the harbor, and the local maritime museum at the edge of town crams a lot of history into a small space.

On the very-early-morning ferry departure for the mainland, passengers may board about 10:00 P.M. the night before and occupy a cabin until the morning's arrival at Scrabster. The Scrabster ferry *Hamnavoe* has a self-service restaurant, two large bars, a shop, and small play area. Decor is similar to the larger ships. She measures 8,780 gross tons, is 366 feet long, and carries the Old Norse name for safe haven (a name associated with Stromness).

The route passes some of Europe's highest vertical cliffs and a 450-foot-high pinnacle of rock known as the **Old Man of Hoy** about twenty-five minutes out of Stromness. It serves as the nesting grounds for thousands of noisy gannets, kittiwakes, puffins, razorbills, and oystercatchers.

At the port of Scrabster, a bus operates to the railway station at **Thurso,** the end of the rail line that links the far north of Scotland with **Inverness** and points south. Three trains a day take about three and a half hours over a highly scenic line to reach Inverness.

NORWEGIAN COASTAL VOYAGE'S
Nordkapp
Norwegian Coastal Voyage

 The locals refer to their domestic passenger and cargo service as the _Hurtigruten_—fast route. For more than one hundred years, a fleet of ships owned by several different companies has operated a water highway linking three dozen towns along the rugged Norwegian coast between Bergen in the south and the North Cape and beyond. Norwegian Coastal Voyage markets them all in North America. The ships' role as the primary means of access has diminished, and while many Norwegians still travel this way and expedite their cargo, the _Hurtigruten_'s future lies with local and overseas tourism.

The eleven ships fall into three categories, the newest being the Millennium class ships of 15,000 gross tons with 674 berths, some with balconies. In the next few years, this class will grow to five and replace two of a trio of Mid-Generation ships, built and then enlarged in the 1980s to 4,200 tons with 325 passenger berths. The Contemporary class numbers six 11,300-ton, 490-berth ships built between 1993 and the end of the decade. As this class is the most numerous, one of these, the _Nordkapp_, will be used as the example.

At 11,300 tons, the 1996-built _Nordkapp_ can take up to 490 cabin passengers. Most cabins are of a uniform design, with large windows, two lower beds, a vanity, decent storage space, and private facilities. The _Nordkapp_ is beautifully decorated in attractive bold colors and with distinctive Norwegian paintings of landscapes, seascapes, and historic steamers, plus lots of glass and mirrors, creating a most cheerful atmosphere. The large, 110-seat panorama lounge, done in blues and greens, has sweeping views in three directions, and aft a spacious lounge/bar looks out to port and starboard. A second deck of public rooms includes a lounge with musical entertainment offered during the high season, conference rooms, a quiet reading room, a twenty-four-hour cafeteria, a souvenir shop, a children's playroom, and a long gallery lounge leading aft to a big, windowed dining room that seats 240.

The size of the ship and the presence of tour groups often make meeting other passengers more difficult than on the more intimate ships. There is limited outdoor seating on three afterdecks and a wrap-around deck for walking. Cargo is wheeled through doors in the ship's side, and watching the handling is less a pastime than on the older crane-loading ships.

The food is Norwegian, which means, besides standard continental-breakfast items, eggs and bacon (on some mornings), cold meats, cheeses, and a variety of herring. Lunch, also a buffet, is the most elaborate meal, with a choice of several hot and cold entrees such as salmon, halibut, lamb chops, and veal, as well as soup, salads, cheeses, and desserts. Dinner is a set three-course menu, but a certain sameness sets in after a week aboard. Alcohol is heavily taxed. A bottle of beer costs about $6.00, and wine starts at $25.00 per bottle. If you like a drink before dinner, bring your own.

The Itinerary
Tourists are attracted to Norway's scenery, which does not disappoint in good weather. The route is a coastal one, and the ships do not penetrate the deepest fjords, except for summertime visits to the Geiranger Fjord, but there are some quite spectacular narrow passages that the big cruise ships cannot negotiate.

The thirty-five ports, called at different hours northbound and southbound, range from small villages and good-size fishing ports to major market centers, most rebuilt after World War II. Time in port ranges from fifteen minutes to several hours, but a quick walk is nearly always possible.

The cities vary considerably in their offerings. **Aalesund,** destroyed by fire in 1904, was rebuilt into a handsome Norwegian style of art nouveau. **Trondheim** has a much older center, a magnificent eleventh-century medieval cathedral, and a wooden waterfront. An excursion is offered both northbound and southbound, including the Museum of Music History on the latter.

Crossing the **Arctic Circle** is marked with a globe set on an island, and the ship celebrates the event with proclamations and an ice-water "ceremony."

The **Lofoten Islands,** a popular subject for maritime artists, rise dramatically out of the sea as the coastal express approaches from **Bodo.** Depending on the weather the ship is likely to sail into the narrow **Troll Fjord** and turn 180 degrees in a very tight basin surrounded by steep cliffs oozing water that become cascading waterfalls in the wetter seasons.

One of my favorite excursions leaves the southbound ship at **Harstad,** stops at a thirteenth-century stone church, continues into interior farming regions, crosses a fjord by ferry, and rejoins the ship at **Sortland. Tromso** is a delightful university city. The Arctic Cathedral, built in a layered A-frame style, possesses Europe's largest glass mosaic.

The landscape becomes more rugged and less populated, and, at **Honnigsvåg,** if snow isn't blocking the road (normally open by mid-May), there is an excursion to the **North Cape** that passes reindeer and an

---

Address/Phone: Norwegian Coastal Voyage, Inc., 405 Park Avenue, New York, NY 10022; (800) 323–7436 or (212) 319–1300; brochures: (800) 666–2374; fax: (212) 319–1390; www.coastalvoyage.com

The Ship: *Nordkapp* was built in 1996 and has a gross tonnage of 11,200 and a length of 414 feet.

Passengers: 490; all ages; mostly forty and up, traveling as individuals or groups (aboard the newer ships); largely Norwegian, German, and British, with some Americans and other Europeans

Dress: Casual

Officers/Crew: Norwegian

Cabins: 217, all outside, plain but decent size

Fare: $$

What's included: Varies, from cruise only, including port charges, to a complete package, airfare, hotel, tips, transfers, and a prepaid shore-excursions package

What's not included: Drinks, and airfares when not part of a package

Highlights: Norway's spectacular coast; cargo handling, especially aboard the older ships; maritime atmosphere; Norwegian art aboard the newer ships

Other itineraries: The coastal voyage may be taken as an eleven-day round-trip, calling at thirty-five ports each way, leaving Bergen almost every night at 10:30 P.M. throughout the year. One-way five- and six-day sea-air trips are available between Bergen and Kirkenes and can be combined with hotel stays and the highly recommended Bergen-Oslo train ride. The northbound itinerary has better port timings for Aalesund, Trondhiem, Tromso, and the North Cape. The midnight sun is visible in clear weather above the Arctic Circle between mid-May and late July, whereas the Northern Lights are most often seen in winter. The summer months see many deck passengers, but by early September they are mostly gone.

encampment of the indigenous Sami people and then culminates in a glorious view
northward over the sea.

Rounding the top of Norway, the ship
skirts some of Europe's highest sea cliffs,
populated with nesting gannets. Again the
coastal steamer is exposed to the open sea,

so be prepared for hours of pitching before
reaching **Kirkenes.** This is where most one-
way passengers leave to fly south or come
north to join the trip. Roundtrippers will
stop at the same ports but at different times
of the day, so those missed at night come
during the day.

DFDS SEAWAYS'
Crown of Scandinavia
Ferry Cruising between Copenhagen and Oslo

DFDS (Det Forende Dampskibs
Selskab—The United Steamship
Company), Denmark's largest
and oldest passenger
shipowner, began sailing the Capital Cities
Route in 1866. The company now operates
a fleet of seven overnight cruise ferries on
routes between Denmark, England, Sweden, Norway, Germany, and Holland.
Advertising proudly proclaims DFDS as
"Masters of the Northern Seas," and there
is no disagreement here.

In recent years this route annually carried
about 750,000 passengers, of which Norwegians and Danes accounted for about 75
percent. Many British and American passengers also use this service, and language
presents no problems, as English is generally spoken throughout Scandinavia. Sailings are geared to the business traveler and
tourist, with daily departures at 5:00 P.M.
from terminals close to both city centers
and arrivals at 9:00 A.M. next day.

Crown of Scandinavia is the newest passenger ferry in the fleet, the last in a series
of four ships built at Split in Croatia for various Scandinavian owners. Delivered in July
1994, she runs alongside the slightly larger
Pearl of Scandinavia, dating from 1989.
Boarding by car or on foot, the passenger
arrives at the spacious reception area to be
directed to the cabin. *Crown of*

Scandinavia's 662 cabins include, unusual
for a ferry, twenty-two with verandas, and a
further forty-six larger cabins feature extra
facilities and limited room service, designated as Commodore Class. Every cabin has
a shower and a toilet.

Dining options cater to all price ranges.
The most popular is the Seven Seas restaurant, with its panoramic forward view, serving buffet dinners and traditional
Scandinavian smorgasbord. Dinner with
wine costs about $65 for two. The window
seats at breakfast are quickly taken during
the transit up the Oslofjord. My preferred
dining option is the elegant, Chinese-style
setting of Sailors Corner, with its dark cherry
furniture and paneling. Grilled meats, fish,
and shellfish are specialties here, and a drink,
wine, and coffee are included in the three-
course price ($105 for two). Always book a
table in either restaurant on embarkation. As
an alternative, the Scandia Café provides
light meals and snacks.

The well-patronized Admiral Pub, adjacent to the Sailors Corner, is modeled on a
dark wood–furnished English bar, a style
featured on a number of Scandinavian ferries. The main lounge is the Columbus
Club, with three bars, a dance floor, and a
nearby casino. Entertainment includes a
singing group, bingo, and shipboard horse
racing. In the afternoon this lounge

provides a good position to view the passing scenery, and outside the extensive sundecks provide more viewing platforms. Other facilities aboard include cinemas, a disco, a Jacuzzi, a sauna, an indoor pool, a children's playroom, and teen activities.

The Itinerary

As the ship sails from **Copenhagen,** the cruise-ship quay can be seen on the starboard side. Shortly after entering the **Öresund,** Middleground Fort is rounded and a course set for **Helsingborg** in Sweden, where the ship arrives at about 6:45 P.M.; this is a brief call to pick up passengers and vehicles for Oslo. Helsingborg is a busy ferry port annually handling more than thirteen million passengers, most traveling to **Helsingor** in Denmark.

Ten minutes after sailing from Helsingborg, the *Crown of Scandinavia* passes to port **Kronborg Castle** at Helsingor, famous as the setting for *Hamlet.* Soon the ship enters the **Kattegat,** following the Swedish coastline northward for about another hour. During the night the **Skaggerak** is crossed, and arrival at the mouth of **Oslofjord** is at about 5:00 A.M.

The 60-mile passage to **Oslo** takes about four hours, and at 7:30 the ship enters the narrowest part after passing **Oscarsborg Fortress.** At 9:00 A.M. the *Crown of Scandinavia* docks adjacent to the thirteenth-century **Akershus Castle,** a short walk from the city center. On arrival all passengers (including the roundtrippers) must disembark, but returning passengers can leave luggage aboard. The nightly departures permit flexible planning.

Address/Phone: DFDS Seaways, Sea Europe Holidays, Inc., 6801 Lake Worth Road, Suite 103, Lake Worth, FL 33467; (800) 533–3755; e-mail: admin@sea europe.com; www.seaeurope.com

The Ship: *Crown of Scandinavia* was built in 1994 and has a gross tonnage of 35,498 and a length of 559 feet.

Passengers: 2,400 full capacity; mostly Danish and Norwegian, but English spoken

Dress: Casual

Officers/Crew: Mostly Danish, some Filipinos

Cabins: 662, inside and out, with a total of 2,126 beds

Fare: $ to $$

What's included: Cruise only; Commodore class includes breakfast

What's not included: Meals, drinks, tips

Highlights: Lots to do and eat aboard; scenic approaches to and from both capitals

Other itineraries: In addition to this overnight ferry cruise between Copenhagen and Oslo, which operates every day of the year except Christmas Eve and Christmas Day, DFDS operates popular overnight sailings between Denmark, Germany, the Netherlands, and England with coordinated bus connections at both sea terminals.

SILJA LINE'S
Silja Serenade and *Silja Symphony*
Cruise Ferries in the Baltic

 The Silja Line, headquartered in Helsinki, has been trading in ships for larger new ones as often as Americans trade in their cars. Among the world's largest cruise ferries, the *Silja Europa* has a gross tonnage of 59,914 and passenger capacity of 3,013; near sisters *Silja Symphony* and *Silja Serenade* are slightly smaller at 58,400 tons and take up to 2,852.

On the *Serenade* and *Symphony*, Decks 2 to 12 are fitted with cabins, restaurants, cafes, bars, nightclubs, a cinema, lots of shopping, a casino, a children's playroom, a video arcade, saunas, small pools, whirlpools, and several levels for vehicles of all shapes and sizes.

Dining options include no less than three à la carte restaurants: Maxim à la Carte, with a large menu; Casa Bonita for steaks; and Happy Lobster, a fish and seafood eatery. The latter features smoked, slightly salted, grilled, and poached fish, mustard herring, Baltic herring, fish roe and shrimp, and if desired, Finlandia vodka. Buffet Serenade and Buffet Symphony (smorgasbord) have an incredible range of food for one set price, with reserved timed entry to avoid queues. Snack bars and cafes for light meals and hot hors d'oeuvres are scattered about the ship.

Most spectacular is the Promenade, a shopping and restaurant arcade running fore and aft for 475 feet, five decks and 60 feet high, decorated with mobiles and topped with skylights. Glass-enclosed bridges run across the horizontal atrium.

Entertainment and drinking venues are Atlantis Palace, a tiered cocktail lounge and nightclub with dance music; a casino for roulette, blackjack, and slots; Stardust, for karaoke and disco, located under the fun-

nel; a British-style pub; and a panorama bar and pastry café overlooking the stern. High up, the Sunflower Oasis is the spa with small pools and whirlpools, and low down is a bank of saunas. Siljaland is a play area for children, and the electric bazaar features the latest video games. Seminars and corporate meetings are big business, and the Conference Center can be adapted to large or small gatherings.

Nine hundred eighty-five cabins with 2,980 berths fall into eight categories, the top being Commodore class, set high up and forward; others include standard outsides with windows, insides, promenade-view cabins, and budget accommodations below vehicle decks. Deck 12 is open for viewing in all directions, and the enclosed central portion looks down into the Promenade Arcade. Deck 7 permits a walk under lifeboats completely around the ship.

The onboard atmosphere is that of an urban entertainment center, with everything geared to encouraging passengers to spend money and have a good time doing it. It's one late-night party, but with cabins located on separate decks, passengers wishing to sleep can do so.

The Itinerary
The Silja Line and its arch competitor, the Viking Line (sporting bright-red hulls), offer daily year-round overnight service between Stockholm and Helsinki, and both overnight and daylight sailings between Stockholm and Turku, some departures calling at the scenic **Åland Islands.** The most popular trip leaves Stockholm at 5:00 P.M., sails overnight to Helsinki, arriving at 9:30 A.M. for a day in the Finnish capital, and then returns overnight to Stockholm.

Departing **Stockholm,** the ship threads

for three hours through an amazing wooded archipelago— some islands residences for daily commuters into the city, others summer and weekend camps, and many uninhabited. The outdoor experience is best enjoyed in the late spring and summer, when the lingering daylight stretches almost to midnight. The approach to **Helsinki**'s inner harbor the next morning is among rocky islands.

If making the return sailing, you keep your cabin and spend the day ashore sightseeing the Finnish capital, its waterfront markets, neighborhoods, and individual styles of architecture. If staying longer, consider the daylight, all-island route from **Turku,** Finland's second port, 125 miles and two hours by train from Helsinki. The sophistication and size of these cruise ferries exist almost nowhere else in the world.

Address/Phone: SeaEurope Holiday, Inc., 6801 Lake Worth Road, Suite 103, Lake Worth, FL 33467; (800) 533–3755; e-mail: admin@seaeurope.com; www.seaeurope.com

The Ships: Sisters *Silja Serenade* and *Silja Symphony,* built in 1990 and 1991, have a gross tonnage of 58,400, a length of 656 feet, and a draft of 23 feet.

Passengers: 2,852 maximum capacity; all ages, mostly Swedes and Finns but also Germans, other Europeans, and some Americans (language not a problem)

Dress: Casual

Officers/Crew: Finnish officers; Scandinavian crew

Cabins: 985; modern and simply furnished, outsides and insides

Fare: $ to $$

What's included: Cruise fare only

What's not included: Everything is extra unless part of a package.

Highlights: A floating restaurant, cafe, and nightlife center; island scenery in summer

Other itineraries: Besides the above overnight cruise, SeaEurope, Inc. represents DFDS Seaways with Scandinavian and North Sea routes.

SWAN HELLENIC'S
Minerva II
Iberian Cultural Cruise: British Style

 Swan Hellenic, a long-established British firm based in London, has traditionally drawn its clientele from the upper end of the British market, plus a modest percentage of North Americans to its cultural-enrichment cruises in Europe, the Americas, and the Nile Valley.

The 30,277-ton *Minerva II* was built as the *R8* for Renaissance Cruises and is now chartered by P&O Princess Cruises for its subsidiary Swan Hellenic. The newly acquired ship, replacing the much smaller 12,500-ton *Minerva*, made its debut in April 2003. The *Minerva II*'s more elaborate surroundings are meant to woo a slightly younger clientele (age forty and up) and more Americans. Cruising with Swan Hellenic does not come cheaply, but the advertised rates are virtually all-inclusive.

The ship's hotel decor is traditional Britain afloat from stem to stern, and original paintings, prints, antique maps, and passenger-donated photographs line the public room and corridor walls.

In a high-up location on its own, the large library, stocked with about 4,000 volumes, offers travel guides, references, and novels for all destinations, tables for opening an atlas, and lots of comfy chairs. Guest speakers, integral to any Swan Hellenic voyage, include noted historians, archaeologists, diplomats, writers, broadcasters, clergy, and chefs who give forty-five-minute talks in the main lounge. In the evening, the lounge hosts concerts, drama or comedy performances, and local artists.

The Orpheus Room, recalling the name of a long-serving Swan Hellenic ship, serves as a forward observation lounge, while the pre- and post-dinner cocktail set gravitate to the traditional Wheeler Bar, with a nightly pianist in attendance, and the Gallery Bar adjacent to the main restaurant.

Four open-sitting dining venues help break down the barriers between the reserved British and more open American passengers. Besides the large main restaurant, the Swan Restaurant features Mediterranean fare, while next door the Grill is the place for steaks and chops. For informality, the Bridge Cafe offers buffet meals indoors and out on deck.

A sheltered lido deck pool, flanked by a pair of Jacuzzis, jogging track, a couple of shops, beauty salon, fitness center, card room, and Internet room round out the comprehensive facilities.

Cabins are roomy and well equipped, most are outside, and many have private balconies. TVs bring in the lecture program, but attending the talks in person is highly recommended.

Address/Phone: Swan Hellenic Cruises, 631 Commack Road, Suite 1A, Commack, NY 11725; (877) 219–4239; fax: (631) 858–1279; e-mail: swanhellenic@ kainyc.com; www.swanhellenic.com

The Ship: *Minerva II* was built in 2001 as the *R8* and has a gross tonnage of 30,277, a length of 594 feet, and a draft of 20 feet.

Passengers: 684; mostly British, fifty and up

Dress: Jacket and tie is expected on evenings at sea in the three main restaurants.

Officers/Crew: British and European officers; Filipino and Ukrainian crew

Cabins: 342, with 317 outside and 242 with balconies

Fare: $$$$

What's included: Cruise and port charges, program of shore excursions for every port, all tips aboard and for guides ashore, flights between London and the ship

What's not included: Airfare between the United States and London, optional shore excursions, drinks

Highlights: Excellent enrichment program, terrific organization aboard and ashore

Other itineraries: In addition to the above cruise between England and the Iberian Peninsula, which is offered in the early and late summer, the *Minerva II* makes year-round, nonrepeating four-to-fifteen-day cruises in the Mediterranean, around Britain, to Scandinavia, and across the Atlantic to South and North America.

The Itinerary

Swan Hellenic cruises offer onboard seminars. Names and short biographies of the historians, archaeologists, anthropologists, geologists, and clergy appear in the brochure. Most hail from British universities. For this Iberian cruise, topics range from historic connections between Britain and Iberia to the wine trade. The program forms an integral part of the cruise experience, and lecturers join passengers at meals and accompany them ashore. The ports of call vary every year but include calls in France and Iberian ports on the Atlantic and Mediterranean coasts. All cruises start or end in England, paired with a one-way charter flight between the ship and London.

Sailing up the **Loire,** the ship stops at **Nantes,** which has a fine cathedral, a good museum housed in a medieval castle, and beautifully maintained botanical gardens; an excursion is offered out to the Muscadet vineyards. Docking adjacent to the handsome city of **Bordeaux** allows for walking tours to see the neoclassical architecture, wide boulevards, and narrow streets of Old Town. During the transit along the **Gironde,** the wine expert points out the south bank's Médoc vineyards.

Sailing westward through the Bay of Biscay to **Vigo,** northwest Spain, you make the historic pilgrimage to **Santiago de Compostela,** where, at the magnificent Roman Catholic cathedral, Swan arranges for the giant incense burner, requiring eight men on the ropes, to perform its dramatic swings over head, soaring to the rafters.

The Douro River city of **Oporto** is famous for its port-wine production, narrow, cobbled streets, and outstanding Baroque architecture. The old-fashioned capital city of **Lisbon** spreads over hills above the **Tagus River.** The residential neighborhoods are best enjoyed with a bus-and-tram day pass. Great museums and waterfront monuments demonstrate Portugal's pioneering maritime feats of exploration.

The attractive port of **Cadiz** leads inland to **Seville** for its great Gothic cathedral, Moorish Alcazar Palace, and quiet residential squares. From coastal **Malaga** the excursion visits **Granada**'s Alhambra Palace and magnificent Arab-style formal gardens. Disembarking at **Barcelona,** you'll have time to enjoy cafes and restaurants lining the medieval streets, a Gothic district, and the Picasso Museum.

VIKING RIVER CRUISES'
Viking Neptune and *Viking Pride*
Cruising the Danube from Budapest to Nuremberg

 Viking River Cruises got its start in 1997, and when the company bought KD River Cruises, a venerable German company dating back to 1827, it instantly counted up the largest riverboat fleet in Europe. Ten of Viking's two dozen ships cater exclusively to Americans, which sets them apart from

Peter Deilmann's vessels, which draw an international clientele. The seven-day cruise described here, operating between Budapest and Nuremberg, is just one of more than a dozen European river itineraries.

The 150-passenger *Viking Neptune* and *Viking Pride* are sleek three-deckers built in

2001 and designed to slip under low bridges, including a hydraulically lowered wheelhouse. On the Upper Deck boarding level, the forward observation lounge affords terrific views of the river and has a bar, music for dancing, and coffee, tea, and snacks in the morning and afternoon. A small library is adjacent and the bi-level lobby serves as a second lounge. The ships are completely nonsmoking within.

The restaurant, located aft, offers open seating and good views to port and starboard. Breakfast and lunch are either buffet or from a menu, while the five-course dinner is served. European regional entrees include braised venison, Viennese schnitzel, and Hungarian goulash while North American–style favorites include roast beef and poached salmon. All soups are made on board.

Seventy-five cabins are arranged on three decks, and the sixty-three deluxe rooms on the two highest decks have windows that slide open, showers, telephones, TVs, safes, and hair dryers.

Most of the top deck is available for passenger viewing, and portions are sheltered from the sun and rain. A viewing promenade envelops the observation lounge.

The Itinerary

For this seven-day itinerary embarking from Budapest, the cruise manager will advise passengers, when it's recommended, to take an organized tour and, when it's convenient, to take independent walks. While cruising in daylight, English and German commentary picks out the castles, bridges, monuments, and natural sights; most nights are spent tied up.

The call at **Vienna** allows an afternoon, overnight, and morning to visit the tree-lined Ringstrasse, St. Stephen's Cathedral, and eighteenth-century French-style Schönbrunn Palace, at one time the summer home of the Austrian monarchs, set in a large park with shaped trees and flower beds. From Krems to Melk the boat passes through the narrow and steep **Wachau Valley,** with woods clinging to the slopes on the left and vineyards on the sunny right side. Among the castles and picturesque villages, **Durnstein,** one of the latter, offers a walking tour and wine tasting, and **Melk** is

Address/Phone: Viking River Cruises, 21810 Burbank Boulevard, Woodland Hills, CA 91367; (818) 227–1227 or (877) 668–4546; fax: (818) 227–1237; www.vikingrivercruises.com

The Ships: *Viking Neptune* and *Viking Pride,* built in 2001, have a length of 375 feet and a shallow draft.

Passengers: 150; mostly Americans fifty and up

Dress: Two dress-up evenings; otherwise casual

Officers/Crew: European

Cabins: 75; all outside, and 63 have windows that slide open

Fare: $$$

What's included: Cruise fare, port charges, local transfers, and shore excursions. Airfares are included in some cruise tours.

What's not included: Airfare, drinks, tips

Highlights: Scenic Danube River cruising and lots to see ashore in towns and cities

Other itineraries: In addition to this seven-day Danube cruise, which operates between mid-May and mid-November, there are five- to seventeen-day cruises along the Rhine, Main, Moselle, the full length of the Danube, Elbe, Seine, Rhone, Soane, and Russian Rivers. Extend your stay with cruise tour packages.

marked by a yellow baroque abbey sitting high on a rock.

Crossing into **Bavaria, Passau** is located at the junction of three rivers. Here you can take a walking tour and visit Feste Oberhaus, a castle atop a steep hill. **Regensburg**'s city center contains thirteenth- and fourteenth-century houses, a fourteenth-century city hall, and baroque and Gothic churches; Walhalla, the German Hall of Fame built in the nineteenth-century, honors German heroes. Near the end of the upstream cruise, the *Viking Neptune* or *Viking Pride* enter the 106-mile **Main-Danube Canal** and the first few of sixteen locks, which raise the riverboat 30 to 50 feet each time. Completed in 1992, the canal connects the Danube's 1,498 navigable miles to the Main River and the Rhine. The cruise ends with a bus transfer to **Nuremberg.**

PETER DEILMANN'S
Mozart
Cruising the Danube in Style

 This Danube River cruise, like the middle Rhine, is a traditional favorite for first-time river cruisers as the itinerary includes well-known cities such as Vienna and Budapest, romantic small towns, and some delightful rural river scenery. Unlike stretches of the Rhine, the Danube is not paralleled by major highways, and often there is not a road nor railway in sight. The peaceful, strong-flowing river is punctuated by numerous locks and low bridges requiring the pilot house and wind screens to be lowered.

Boarding the *Mozart* at the Danube River port of Passau, one senses spaciousness throughout the vessel, in the rosewood paneled foyers, public rooms, main restaurant, and in the cabins. In fact, the 96 outside cabins (three are inside) measure a uniform and roomy 203 square feet. Upper deck cabins have a large picture window while one deck below it's two smaller divided panes. The water laps at the side of the boat about a foot below the glass, and from time to time the window gets a wash from the passing river traffic. Two beds can be pushed together to form a generous queen.

The lounge area is furnished with a two-seat couch, coffee table, and desk-cum-vanity. Triple-slatted wood doors open to hanging closets and generous shelf space. The TV broadcasts both CNN and CNBC, and the radio airs music channels. A stocked minibar's contents are available for a moderate charge. The adjoining bath has a circular shower stall, sink surrounded by generous counter surface, a hair dryer, and terry cloth robes. The light, airy room is attractive for enjoying a few hours' read after the sun goes down and it gets too chilly topside for outdoor sight-seeing.

The observation lounge provides seating for all passengers and sees use mostly for after-dinner entertainment, which runs from classical concerts and operetta to a pianist and a joyful crew show, put on by a mostly Hungarian staff. Most live in or near Budapest, so they get to see their families once a week, a regular rhythm that results in a very happy atmosphere.

A small lounge cafe hosts afternoon tea with pastries and evening dessert treats. A bar with sit-up stools and window tables runs fore and aft between the main lounge and the central foyer. A paneled library offers deep leather chairs, glass-fronted bookshelves with a small English-language collection, and a large-screen TV.

As one of the most elaborate European river vessels, the *Mozart* boasts a fitness center facing forward though big glass windows and is equipped with an indoor swimming pool, whirlpool, massage and sauna, plus a gift shop and beauty salon.

Less formal and lighter in decor is the main restaurant, where tables seat from two to eight people, many located by the large-view windows. Meals are a sheer delight and feature both a menu and an elaborate buffet for breakfast and lunch. The midday meal is my favorite, and while I may order hot carrot cream soup with oranges or the cold tipsy peach soup, I invariably find the buffet so appetizing that I save menu ordering for dinner. Choices include avocado and shrimp with choice of dressings, roll mops, smoked salmon, several types of salad beans and cole slaw, cabbage, cold lobster tails, artichoke hearts, a pasta station, leg of duck in orange sauce, and roasted fillet of plaice.

Dinner on three occasions offers a sampler menu of eight to nine delicious courses that lists several appetizers, two soups, two salads, two hot entrees, sherbet, two main courses, several desserts, and a selection of cheeses and biscuits. My favorite entrees were roasted piglet with braised cabbage and dumplings and roasted knuckle of veal with jus and sour cream and wine sauerkraut.

Service by two Hungarian waiters and a wine steward is most attentive, friendly, and knowledgeable, especially important when larking off into unfamiliar Middle European cuisine. We dined in true European style, enhancing the travel experience, rather than being offered menus that pander to American tastes. Apart from Americans, fellow passengers are largely German. Going beyond a nodding relationship with table neighbors requires some effort, and initial conversations usually occur more successfully on deck.

The Itinerary

Before setting off, there is time to explore **Passau,** a German town wedged on a narrow peninsula between two rivers with a third emptying into the Danube at the town's pointy end. Happily, few cars roam the angled stone-paved streets, so one can enjoy the pastel-colored architecture and pretty plantings without keeping a constant eye out for traffic.

As you cruise down the **Danube** on a Monday afternoon, Austria's **Wachau Valley** is bathed in a patchwork of sunlight and shadow. To the left, sloping vineyards produce some excellent dry white wines that are sampled aboard, while to the right the land is forested and stands of bushy trees rise from the river during the high-water period. Small towns appear around nearly every bend, tightly clustered around a church or situated beneath a castle poised on a rocky promontory. Standing next to me were a couple of passengers who live near the Danube in Germany, on board to see what their river looks like in Austria and Hungary.

After an overnight sail, the first landing at **Durnstein** in the Wachau Valley provides a forty-five-minute climb to a ruined twelfth-century castle for a rewarding valley view. A bus tour is also available.

Vienna's docking location is some distance from the city center, so many passengers take a coach tour, but for those familiar with urban living, it's a ten-minute walk to the Metro, then a fifteen-minute ride into Stefanplatz to tour the area of the Sacher Hotel and opera house, Gothic city hall, some handsome residential neighborhoods, and very pretty parks.

Esztergom, once the capital of Hungary and still titular capital of Catholic Church, now exudes a small-town atmosphere with leafy residential squares and a lively street market, overlooked by a huge Renaissance basilica fortress. The riverine scenery then turns rural and wooded, and we pass a medieval wall that connects the river to a fortress high on the hill.

Approaching **Budapest,** the outlying districts are pretty bland, but soon the *Mozart* is sailing right through the heart of the city past the English-derivative Gothic Parliament Buildings and under a half dozen bridges between **Buda** rising to the right and **Pest** laid out on the left. The overnight landing is located just above the bridge leading over to the Gellert Hotel and Spa.

On the first afternoon, walk the streets that parallel the river and enjoy looking into the stylish stores and up at the handsome art nouveau and art deco architecture. Apart from some shabby facades near the *Mozart's* landing, the city sparkles and offers a livelier atmosphere than Vienna.

The next morning, a ship's tour visits both the Pest and Buda sides with the latter pro-

viding a visit to the thirteenth- to fifteenth-century Gothic-style Matthias or Coronation Church and the adjoining conical bastion towers of the fishermen's market. If there is time, spend an hour at the grand tiled market hall (1897) inspecting the fresh produce on the ground floor and souvenirs, handicrafts, embroidery, and food stalls on the upper level.

At departure, afternoon tea is served up on deck, and the *Mozart* sails upstream through the city center for an overnight cruise to **Bratislava,** the capital of **Slovak Republic.** The heart of the city is a lovely, tranquil pedestrian precinct with squares, churches, theater, opera, cafes, stores, and a large castle looming over all. From the ramparts, look across the Danube to the largest Soviet-inspired housing complex in the world, row after row of monotonously identical white concrete and brick apartment blocks.

Melk, a smallish city, offers a tour to an outstanding eleventh-century mustard-

Address/Phone: Peter Deilmann Cruises, 1800 Diagonal Road, Suit 170, Alexandria, VA 22314; (703) 549–1741 or (800) 348–8287; fax: (703) 549–7924; www.deilmann-cruises.com

The Ship: *Mozart,* built in 1987, has a length of 396 feet and a draft of 5 feet.

Passengers: 200; age fifty-five and up, mostly Germans and Americans

Dress: Informal is the norm, with jacket and tie the standard dress

Officers/Crew: Hungarian and a few Germans

Cabins: 200, roomy, and 97 are outside with windows

Fare: $$$

What's included: Cruise and port charges

What's not included: Airfare, excursions, tips, and drinks

Highlights: Views while sailing of beautiful scenery, castles, and villages; easy access for independent touring at most landings; wonderful onboard restaurant

Other itineraries: In addition to the above seven-day Danube, which operates from Passau between late March and early October, the *Mozart* occasionally extends the Danube cruise all the way to the Black Sea. Deilmann's riverboat fleet cruises the Rhine, Moselle, Main, Elbe, Oder, Danube, Po, Rhone, Soane, and the Belgian and Dutch waterways.

colored Benedictine monastery located high above town, later rebuilt in a high baroque style and now part monastic, part grammar school, part museum. Down in the town center, it is a Saturday morning and several wedding parties are gathered outside the town hall.

The small river town of **Grein,** the last stop, is essentially closed on Saturday after-noon, but one can climb to a castle over-looking the small town square and the river highway leading back to Passau and disem-barkation. The *Mozart's* seven-day cruise through Austria to the Slovak Republic and Hungary has a distinctly international flavor shared with German-speaking passengers cruising not far from home.

PETER DEILMANN'S
Frederic Chopin
The River Elbe from Berlin to Prague

Glancing at a map of Europe, the Continent is laced with canals and waterways, built for commerce and increasingly fre-quented by creative cruising itineraries that stretch from Amsterdam to the Black Sea and from the south of France deep into Poland. Riverboat vacations mean unpack-ing just once, then settling in for delightful doses of sight-seeing from the top deck and daily excursions ashore to market towns and cathedral cities, riverfront palaces and hilltop castles. Many landings are within walking distance or a short drive to the sights, and separate guides are provided for each group.

Operated by German ship owner Peter Deilmann, the 2002-built, two-deck-high *Frederic Chopin* was designed to slip under the very low bridges that span Central Europe's waterways. When clearances per-mit remaining on the Sun Deck, the ship's surgeon keeps a watchful eye, and if the gap narrows to mere inches, it's time to clear off. The railings and chairs collapse to deck level, and in turn, the captain low-ers his pilothouse and pops up now and again to keep the boat on the straight and narrow.

The passenger capacity is seventy-nine, split between English-speaking and Ger-man-speaking passengers. Most of the lat-ter and the German staff speak good English, and for the majority, it is often a first visit to eastern Germany since unifica-tion.

All cabins have the same dimensions (140 square feet), shower baths, and TVs with CNN broadcasts. The preferred upper deck units come with French doors that open inward, while lower deck rooms have large picture windows with the sill barely above river level. A forward observation lounge, decorated in art nouveau style, offers 180-degree viewing, conversational seating, bar, morning bouillon and after-noon coffee, tea, cakes and pastries, a pianist, and occasional evening cabaret.

In the similarly styled restaurant, tables are assigned and located next to large pic-ture windows. Breakfast and lunch provide elaborate menu and buffet selections, and the very long dinner hours run to five courses and up to nine on special occasions. We enjoyed excellent evening meals such as sliced duck with kumquat sauce, sweet-breads on a bed of lentils, and fresh grilled salmon. Cheese selections vary daily, but there are no biscuits, only breads. Wines and beers are fairly priced.

The Itinerary

As this week's cruise on the **Elbe** begins either in Berlin (embarking in nearby Potsdam) or Prague, it would be wise to consider staying a couple of nights in one or both capital cities. All cruises include one night docked on the Vltava River near Prague's Charles Bridge, and some port calls vary depending on the direction of travel, though all include Magdeburg, Wittenburg, Meissen, and Dresden.

Berlin reveals a boomtown atmosphere and the most amazing transformation of neighborhoods from empty lots left over from WWII bombing to thriving office, hotel, residential, cultural, and entertainment complexes. For me, who knew Berlin before the wall and during its construction in August 1961, many sections have become unrecognizable, especially the new corporate and entertainment complex at Potsdamer Platz and the city's most famous avenue, Unter den Linden.

Before boarding at **Potsdam,** visit **Sanssouci,** one of the great palaces and tiered gardens of Europe, and the Tudor-style **Cecilienhof,** a manor house that served as the site for the last World War II conference, involving Truman, Stalin, Churchill, and Attlee, that partitioned Germany.

Joining the River Elbe, the *Frederic Chopin* sails along fast-flowing portions and slack water sections between locks. Some bridges are low enough to make us duck if standing up on the top deck and high enough, in most cases, to pass under while sitting down. The ship's doctor keeps an eye on everyone, happily allowing passengers to remain outside to enjoy the passing scene of tidy farms, small-town life, people fishing and swimming, and the busy river traffic. Barges laden with coal, stone, sand, grain, lumber, and fuels glide past, outfitted with all the comforts of home, including a patch back aft to park the family car.

Madgeburg, largely destroyed in 1945, has monumental Middle Age and Baroque buildings set among monotonous rows of

---

Address/Phone: Peter Deilmann Cruises, 1800 Diagonal Road, Suite 170, Alexandria, VA 22324; (703) 549–1741 or (800) 348–8287; fax: (703) 549–7924; www.deilmann-cruises.com

The Ship: *Frederic Chopin*, built in 2002, has a length of 272 feet and a very shallow draft of 3.5 feet.

Passengers: 79; fifty-five and up, mostly split between German and Americans

Dress: Informal is the norm, with jacket and tie the standard dress

Officers/Crew: Czechs and Germans

Cabins: 41 cabins; all outside, with the upper deck units having French doors

Fare: $$$

What's included: Cruise fare and port charges

What's not included: Airfare, excursions, tips, and drinks

Highlights: Views while sailing of beautiful scenery, castles, and villages; easy access for independent touring at most landings

Other itineraries: In addition to the above seven-day Elbe itinerary, which operates between Berlin and Prague from early May to early November, the *Frederic Chopin* also operates along the Oder River from Germany into Poland. Deilmann's riverboat fleet cruises the Rhine, Moselle, Main, Elbe, Oder, Danube, Po, Rhone, Soane, and the Belgian and Dutch waterways.

Communist-era apartment blocks, while **Wittenberg** most attractively trades on Martin Luther's life and activity during the start of the Protestant Reformation. According to the guide, the town facades, now sparkling with colorful restorations, were mostly gray and dilapidated during the German Democratic Republic days.

The stop at **Meissen** includes the china factory tour to see how the prized porcelain is sculpted and hand-painted, followed by a scenic drive along the Elbe to **Dresden,** perhaps the most amazing twentieth-century example of a city rebuilt after total destruction during one awful night in 1945. The Semper Opera House, **Zwinger Palace,** churches, royal residences, museums, offices, and many apartments have been reconstructed in the original styles, an ongoing fifty-year project that has brought back grandeur to one of Europe's most beautiful cities. Over time, the sandstone has weathered, and someone who knew nothing of the wartime bombing might not realize that the city center is now quite young. At night, from the deck of our ship, the floodlighting provides a wondrous spectacle and a draw to partake of the smart cafe life.

The countryside now becomes hilly in what is known as **Saxon Switzerland,** and a trip to **Pillnitz Palace** shows a delicate eighteenth-century royal retreat with Italian and Oriental influences and an English-style botanical garden. After a short drive along the Elbe, the bus climbs along a twisting drive to **Konigstein,** a castle fortress perched on a promontory overlooking a horseshoe bend in the Elbe, where one can watch the boats approach and tie up alongside the town far below.

On the final leg, the *Frederic Chopin* passes out of Germany and the Elbe into the **Czech Republic** and the **Vltava,** stopping at **Leitmeritz,** a riverside market town, followed by a scenic river transit into the heart of **Prague** to dock near the center and within the shadow of **Prague Castle.** Architecturally, the Czech capital is one of Europe's most spectacular, with displays of Romanesque, Gothic, Renaissance, baroque, rococo, art nouveau, and turn-of-the-twentieth-century Paris, contrasting yet neighborly styles often lined up side by side.

Walk the city's embankments, cross the tower-gated **Charles Bridge,** the city's gathering place all day and into the night, and climb up to the Prague Castle complex. Visit the Old Market Square and its 500-year-old astronomical clock and the Mucha Museum (Alphonse Mucha created the art nouveau style in poster art and architectural design). At night the city is beautifully floodlit and the top deck of *Frederic Chopin* provides an orchestra seat, one very hard to vacate at the end of the cruise.

ABERCROMBIE & KENT'S
L'Abercrombie
Barge Canal Cruising in Burgundy

 The fleet that A&K charters was established by a Francophile Englishman in 1966 and now numbers twenty hotel and charter barges and riverboats. *L'Abercrombie* takes up to twenty-two passengers and a young French and English crew of eight. The barge has two decks, one with a forward plant-filled sun deck, a salon with bar, and a dining room. There are two twin cabins aft, and the rest of the accommodations are on the deck below.

A dinner bell summons passengers at 8:00 P.M. from the foredeck and lounge bar to the adjoining oak-paneled dining room, where one chooses places at four candlelit tables. Both lunch and dinner begin with brief descriptions of the white and red wines and the cheese course. On the first evening on my cruise, the appetizer was whiting in a phyllo pastry with sorrel sauce, followed by grilled lamb with thyme, cheese, and a peach tart. On another occasion we started with a mild gazpacho and continued with tender pork cutlets, ending with a rich chocolate mousse. Lunch is a lighter meal that might include sausage in puff pastry, cold roast beef or pasta, and a variety of salads. Breakfast consists of fresh juices, cereals, bread, croissants, and pastries fetched by the deckhand, who, before you rise, peddles off to the nearest village bakery.

Air-conditioned accommodations are five twin and four double-bed cabins on the lower deck, with opening portholes, and two windowed twins on the upper deck. There's adequate floor space for two to move about, reasonable drawer and closet stowage, and a tiny bathroom with shower. Insulation from outside noise is excellent.

The Itinerary

The Burgundy itinerary described here is just one example of this type of cruising, and under the A&K umbrella there are numerous variations within this region and elsewhere in France. A&K exclusively handles all *L'Abercombie* and sister *Lafayete* departures while also selling cabins on more than two dozen additional hotel and charter barges.

Ten minutes out of **Paris,** the rakish high-speed TGV hits 168 miles an hour, streaking southeast to Dijon, and just over two hours later, the pace drops to the speed of a slow walk aboard the 128-foot hotel barge negotiating the **Burgundy Canal.** Boarding at **Vandenesse-en-Auxois,** the deep-blue hulled *L'Abercrombie* travels the short distance to the village of **La Repe** to moor before dinner and for the night. In warm weather it's drinks out on the foredeck while on a chilly night the cozy bar welcomes the newly embarked.

An A&K coach parallels the route and takes passengers on a half day trip to the

---

Address/Phone: Abercrombie & Kent International, 1520 Kensington Road, Oak Brook, IL 60523; (630) 954–2944 or (800) 323–7308; brochures only: (800) 757–5884; fax: (630) 954–3324; e-mail: info@abercrombiekent.com; www. abercrombiekent.com

The Ship: *L'Abercrombie* was first built in 1982 as a commercial barge and has a gross tonnage of 250, a length of 128 feet, and a shallow draft.

Passengers: 22; all ages, mostly Americans; families welcome

Dress: Casual at all times

Officers/Crew: French and British

Cabins: 11; 4 doubles and 7 twins

Fare: $$$$

What's included: Cruise, port charges, excursions (except ballooning), drinks, and wines, TGV first class to/from Paris, transfers

What's not included: Airfare, tips

Highlights: Food, wines, and the lovely Burgundy countryside at a relaxing pace

Other itineraries: Besides this six-night cruise through Burgundy aboard the *L'Abercrombie,* which operates from April into November, there are many other itineraries along the French waterways, the Danube and Po Rivers, and in Holland, Belgium, Ireland, and England, some with themes such as walking, wine, antiques, châteaux, gardens, golf, and tulip time.

Chateau at Commarin and the medieval village of Chateauneuf-en-Auxois. Moving along the canal to Pont d'Ouche, there's time to borrow one of the bicycles for a ride along the smooth towpath or peddle off into the countryside. Noncyclists can walk the towpath and stroll into the village. The canals once handled commercial traffic in coal, locally manufactured tiles, and farm product, but the waterway now sees pleasure boats and barges. Cruising through the Ouche Valley, time seems to have stood still on the rolling farmlands and fields, either side populated by the attractive white Charolais cattle.

Visits to châteaux and wineries are planned at the medieval cellars in the village of Meursault in the Cote de Beaune and two days later at Beaune itself. Beaune is Burgundy's wine capital and the site of one of the finest examples of medieval architecture, the Hotel Dieu, built in the fifteenth century as a charity hospital. Here at Beaune, or at one of the other wineries, the crew may take back a case of wine for dinner on board that night.

Dijon is Burgundy's regional capital and an important market town. The excursion takes in the Ducal Palace, the stronghold of the Dukes of Burgundy, and the historic city center with time at the end to wander the open market. On the last day, the visit is to Clos de Vougeot, a center for making wine since the twelfth century, where the process is described and antique presses are on display. The final afternoon is spent cruising onto Dijon, where the barge ties up for a farewell dinner and the night. After breakfast, passengers transfer back to Gare de Lyon Paris by TGV. Barging is a terrific way to sample the culinary, potable, historical, and scenic delights of La Belle France and rivers and canals throughout Europe.

ROYAL CARIBBEAN'S
Brilliance of the Seas
The Mediterranean Eastward from Barcelona

The *Radiance of the Seas* class, numbering four ships, represents a new direction for Royal Caribbean with much more attention being paid to a shippy look and the sense of sailing on a ship, from the more maritime-oriented decor, dark-wood paneling and deep sea blues, to the walls of glass to let you see the sea while dining, imbibing, and conversing. The Centrum features a portside glass wall soaring from Decks 5 through 10 and four sets of glass-enclosed elevators. Yes, there is still the Royal Caribbean trademark rock-climbing wall and miniature golf.

Most of the public rooms—Crown & Anchor Lounge, Champagne Bar, Singapore Sling's piano bar, Windjammer Café, Sky Bar, and the trademark Viking Crown Lounge—are sheathed in glass, great for viewing arrivals in the world's ports.

Public spaces are fun to inhabit. One, the Colony Club, an interconnecting suite of five spaces, has a rich look with Oriental-patterned carpets, inlaid wood flooring, intimate seating arrangements, and subdued lighting. One room is Singapore Sling's piano bar, spanning the stern with great views over the wake through full-height windows. For amazing views, don't miss having a cocktail here on a moonlit night. Keeping the Asian theme but with a twist, the colonial-styled Bombay Billiard Club provides a patterned wood floor and redwood paneling setting for two high-tech pool tables cradled in gimbals and kept even by motorized gyroscopes to overcome any ship movement.

On the *Brilliance,* the Solarium is East Indian–themed with Indian elephants, bronze statues and a ceramic-tiled peacock, and in the Aurora Theater the colors are gold, purple, and reds. More generally associated with Royal Caribbean are such places as the Casino Royale, with more than 200 slot machines and several score of gaming tables; a baseball-themed sports bar offering interactive games; the nautically decorated Schooner Bar; an always-open Internet center; and the line's signature room, the Viking Crown Lounge, here a quiet retreat and a disco with rotating bar. Even the public bathrooms will turn heads, bright, airy, marbled spaces with mirrors shaped like portholes.

The two dining rooms are two stories high with an impressive double staircase joining the two levels and a cascading waterfall. More maritime inspiration is designed into the Windjammer Café with navy blue carpeting and fabrics, rich wood veneers, and scattered ship models. The number of food counters, eleven in all, spreads out the lines and reduces crowding, and food may be enjoyed indoors or out. Even more informal, the naturally lighted Seaview Café serves the usual fast foods during lunch and dinner hours at tables with rattan chairs.

For watching steaks being cooked in an open kitchen, the ninety-seat Chops Grill offers seats in high-backed booths and a great sea view. Next door, the larger 130-seat Portofino features an Italian menu, and both restaurants provide a sense of occasion that comes with an extra charge.

The ships have three pools, a Sports Deck that serves basketball, volleyball, and paddle-tennis players, a nine-hole miniature golf course and golf simulators, jogging track, and a rock-climbing wall fixed to the funnel, now a feature on all RCI ships. For children, RCI's Adventure Ocean program offers four supervised age groups play stations with video games, a computer lab, splash pools, and a waterslide.

Historically, Royal Caribbean cabins have been on the small size while more space has been allocated to public rooms, but on the *Radiance* class, they are respectable, some even more than respectable, in size. Cabin decor has changed from Miami Beach pastels to rich navy blues and copper.

All cabins have small fridges; cozy sitting areas; ample drawer and closet space; interactive televisions that tap into booking shore excursions, keep tabs on onboard spending, and check up on the ups and downs of the stock market; desks-cum-vanities with a pullout shelf for personal laptop computers; and typically small RCI showers. Suites receive butler service and have access to the Concierge Club for tour and travel information or the latest newspaper.

All Royal Caribbean ships are big and bustling, but this new *Radiance* class offers a higher standard of just about everything that makes a cruise vacation a happy experience at a moderate price level.

The Itinerary

In spring the *Brilliance of the Sea,* with its speedy 25-knot service speed, sails transatlantic to the **Mediterranean** to take up residence at Barcelona for the summer. Alternate sailings head eastward to the Adriatic or to Greece and Turkey, while both itineraries share the ports of Villefranche for Nice, Livorno for Pisa and Florence, Naples for Capri, Pompeii, and the Amalfi Drive, and Civitavecchia for Rome. In this instance we will feature the one that sails into the Adriatic.

Barcelona is much more than an embarkation port, and you would be wise to spend a couple of nights to take in the city's cafe life, medieval streets, the Gothic Quarter, Picasso Museum, and Antonio Gaudi's art nouveau architectural masterpieces.

Then embark in the *Brilliance* and sail to the **French Riviera,** anchoring off **Villefranche** to visit the elegant casino and palace in the Principality of **Monaco,** the classy urban resort of **Nice** with a seafront walk on the Promenade des Anglais, or the pretty medieval hill town of **Eze,** perched above the azure sea.

Sailing overnight along the Italian coast to **Livorno,** excursions head inland to the Leaning Tower of **Pisa** and to **Florence** for the Duomo, Ponte Vecchio spanning the Arno, and the works of Michelangelo. On down the coast, the ship enters the **Bay of Naples** and docks at the city's elegant old maritime station, where, in decades past, millions of Italian immigrants left for new lives in North and South America and Australia.

Mount Vesuvius is clearly visible across the bay, and during the boat ride to the **Isle of Capri** or on the road to the ruins at **Pompeii** and to **Sorrento,** where you join the famous cliffside Amalfi Drive to **Positano,** one of Europe's most charming seaside resorts.

Leaving Naples, you have two nights and a day to enjoy the ship as she passes through the Strait of Messina, under the shadow of still-active Mt. Etna then around Italy's boot and a turn northward into the Adriatic. Enter **Venice** via its lagoon, dock at the edge of the island city, and spend the day getting lost, if only briefly, in the pedestrian streets and alleyways. A day pass will allow you to hop on and off the vaporettos, the Venetian canal buses plying the Grand Canal, heading across to the Lido and stopping at the glass factory island of **Murano.**

It's an overnight sail south through the Adriatic to **Dubrovnik,** the medieval city that survived the nasty Balkan War and is again receiving visitors to explore the streets and enjoy the seaside setting during a walk of the walls, which completely enclose the old town. The next call is at **Corfu,** an island favored by European tourists for its climate, the beaches, and Corfu Town's arcaded cafe life. Linger over a cup of espresso and let the world go by.

Enjoy a full sea day en route to **Civitavecchia,** the port for **Rome,** and the ninety-minute drive into the Eternal City. First-time visitors will want to take a tour to get an overview of the city, and then perhaps concentrate on Vatican City, its art collection, and St. Peter's Cathedral or ancient Rome, represented by the Coliseum, the Forum, Arch of Constantine, and the Palatine Hill.

Address/Phone: Royal Caribbean International, 1050 Caribbean Way, Miami, FL 33132; (305) 539–6000; brochures: (800) 327–6700; fax: (305) 374–7354; www.royalcaribbean.com

The Ship: *Brilliance of the Seas* was completed in 2002, has a gross tonnage of 90,090, a length of 962 feet, and a draft of 27 feet.

Passengers: 2,100; mostly Americans with some Europeans and lots of families during the school holidays

Dress: Formal and casual nights

Officers/Crew: International officers and crew

Cabins: 1,050; with 813 outside and 577 with verandas

Fare: $$

What's included: Cruise fare, port charges

What's not included: Airfare, tips, drinks, shore excursions

Highlights: A stunningly decorated ship lacking none of the megaship amenities

Other itineraries: Besides this Mediterranean cruise, operating in late spring, summer, and early fall, Royal Caribbean ships cover itineraries in North and South America and Hawaii.

After the hectic pace of trying to see one of the world's foremost capitals in one day, the *Brilliance* puts to sea again and takes two leisurely nights and a day westward en route to Barcelona and disembarkation.

On alternate weeks, the Eastern Mediterranean ports include the islands of **Mykonos** and **Santorini,** Piraeus, the port for **Athens,** and Kusadasi on the Turkish coast for the outstanding ruins at **Ephesus.** Shared ports with the first itinerary are Villefranche (Nice), Livorno (Pisa and Florence), Civitavecchia (Rome), and Naples (Capri, Pompeii, Sorrento, and the Amalfi Drive).

SEVEN SEAS CRUISES'
Radisson Diamond
Two One-Week Port Hoppers

Seven Seas Cruises owns the *Radisson Diamond* and markets the *Paul Gauguin* (320 passengers), *Seven Seas Navigator* (490 passengers), *Seven Seas Mariner* (720 passengers), and *Seven Seas Voyager* (700 passengers), a fleet of top cruisers that cover the globe.

Upon boarding the *Radisson Diamond*, one enters the foyer and atrium of a sophisticated European hotel furnished with demilune tables set with large floral bouquets against mirrored walls. Two glass-enclosed elevators rise five decks next to an arcing staircase.

The public rooms are an odd lot, and they see less use than on most ships. The tri-level observation lounge looks forward through two decks of glass; however, sight lines are poor for the entertainment, which consists of a small band for dancing, a singing duo, a pianist, and perhaps a comedian. Just aft, a central corridor divides the casino's fifty slot machines from the blackjack and stud-poker tables. On the deck above, the Club piano bar, although stylishly furnished, suffers from no windows and is lightly patronized. The big-windowed fitness room looks over the stern, and outdoor deck space is terrific, with a variety of open, covered, sheltered, and divided deck-

chair seating areas shared with a whirlpool, a splash pool, and a sit-up bar.

The two-deck-high aft dining room is one of the most attractive afloat, with 270-degree large window views and a center portion fringed with colorful mythological friezes on three sides. The room seats 330 at an open sitting, and I never failed to get a well-placed table for two. The menu includes appetizers such as escargots, jumbo shrimp, and seafood pancakes, a different salad every night, and entrees that included beef tenderloin in a creamy peppercorn sauce, grilled lobster tails, and pork chops in a wonderful sage sauce. Memorable desserts included a warm cheese strudel, strawberry cream cake, and the parfaits. Poured wines are complimentary. The grill's alternate buffet at breakfast and lunch rates high in terms of quality and variety. Lunch features a daily theme—Chinese, Japanese sushi, Indonesian sate, Mexican—plus freshly grilled swordfish, tuna, steaks, and sausages. At night the grill section becomes a reservations-only Italian bistro with a set menu and singing waiters.

All 177 cabins are outside with the same 220-square-foot dimensions, and 123 have verandas. The tan wood trim is matched with shades of green, medium blue, and cream in the patterned curtains, upholstery, bedspreads, and carpets. A queen-size bed (or twins) shares floor space with a two-seat sofa, a chair, a table for dining, and a desk-cum-vanity. For storage the room has two shallow closets, two cabinets, and nine drawers. The minibar includes complimentary bottles of liquor, beer, soft drinks, and mineral water. Videos for the VCR are available in the open-shelf library, and the TV brings in CNN, Sky News, and local programs. The blue-gray tiled bathroom has a half-tub and shower. The supremely designed private balcony has solid bulkhead dividers, slatted wooden wainscoting, and teak decking. Two padded lounge chairs and a round white table provide a relaxing setting.

The Itinerary

The *Radisson Diamond* spends late spring to early autumn cruising from the Western Mediterranean through the Eastern Mediterranean and into the Black Sea. Two seven-day itineraries are featured that would also make a splendid fourteen-day cruise.

Embarkation is at **Monte Carlo;** the *Diamond* then heads westward for **Barcelona,** one of Europe's great walking cities. Stroll the medieval streets, the Gothic district, and visit the Picasso Museum and Antonio Gaudi's contribution to art nouveau architecture as seen in his churches, office buildings, and apartments. Then it's northeast along the Spanish and French coasts to **Marseille,** one of the liveliest of Europe's reborn cities. Most of the action takes place in the area surrounding the Vieux Port, and be sure to stop at a cafe for a bowl of bouillabaisse, a fish and shellfish stew originating here and a meal in itself. Tours go inland to **Nimes,**

Address/Phone: Seven Seas Cruises, 600 Corporate Drive, Suite 410, Fort Lauderdale, FL 33334; (954) 776–6123 or (800) 285–1835; brochures: (800) 477–7500; fax: (954) 722–6763; www.rssc.com

The Ship: *Radisson Diamond,* built in 1992, has a gross tonnage of 20,295, a length of 423 feet, and a draft of 26 feet.

Passengers: 354; age forty and up, largely American, many repeaters

Dress: Suit or tuxedo on a few nights, otherwise jacket and tie, and casual

Officers/Crew: Scandinavian officers; European stewardesses; some Filipino staff in the dining room and deck department

Cabins: 177; all outside and 123 with verandas

Fare: $$$$

What's included: Cruise; airfare from East Coast, wines at dinner, stocked minibar, tips

What's not included: Port charges, shore excursions, and drinks at the bar

Highlights: Great food at buffets and in beautiful restaurant; the spacious veranda cabins and well-designed outdoor deck space; culturally interesting itinerary

Other itineraries: In addition to the European port-hopping cruise, which operates in spring and fall, *Radisson Diamond* spends May through October in North Europe and the Mediterranean, mid-November through mid-April in the Caribbean and on Panama Canal transits, plus spring and fall transatlantic crossings. The 320-passenger *Paul Gauguin* cruises from Tahiti. The 490-passenger *Seven Seas Navigator,* the 720-passenger *Seven Seas Mariner,* and the 700-passenger *Seven Seas Voyager* are new and range worldwide.

Arles, and **Avignon.** Then eastward along the Riviera, the ship calls in at **Cannes,** one of the French Riviera's largest and classiest resorts, for a walk along the seafront promenade and into the back streets.

The next two ports are Italian, first **Livorno** for a trip to **Pisa** and its Leaning Tower or to museum-rich **Florence** located on the banks of the Arno, and then to **Portofino,** where there is no need to take a tour. Just tender ashore and enjoy the tiny town sandwiched into a valley, and take a walk up to the Hotel Splendido, one of the great hotels of Europe.

The *Diamond* then sails south to **Civitavecchia,** the port for **Rome,** about ninety minutes away by road. The next seven-day segment embarks here, and the ship sails overnight to anchor off the **Isle of Capri.** The main town ranges up the cliff from the port, and it's a steep walk up, or take the funicular, to the main square, where it can be very busy in the summer, but the numbers of sightseers drop markedly when exploring the side streets and lanes. Moving across the Bay of Naples to **Sorrento,** another old-style European resort, most of the attractions are a bus or taxi ride away, such as the well-known ruins at **Pompeii** or the less visited ones at **Herculaneum,** both destroyed by the explosion of Mt. Vesuvius in A.D. 79, and the famous narrow, twisting **Amalfi Drive** to absolutely charming little Positano.

The *Diamond* then sails on south, passing through the Strait of Messina to call in at the little port of Naxos for the transfer up to the mountain resort town at **Taormina,** located in the shadow of the still-active **Mount Etna.** Drop down from the main street to get the best of Taormina's residential flavor and perhaps stop at an outdoor cafe for a drink, snack, or lunch.

With Mount Etna dropping astern, the twin-hulled *Diamond* sails around the bottom of the boot of Italy and turns north into the Adriatic Sea with two nights and a day en route to **Dubrovnik.** The medieval walled city was very badly damaged during the Balkan War but now has been almost entirely rebuilt to its former charm. A walking tour takes you to most of the important sites within the walls, and if there is time, you can walk the walls for an overview of the city and the sea. Finally, the *Diamond* sails northward through the Adriatic to enter the lagoon at **Venice,** passing the Lido and cruising by St. Marks Square to berth at the edge of the island city.

STAR CLIPPERS'
Star Clipper
French and Italian Rivieras under Sail

 Designed after the mid-nineteenth-century fast clipper ships, the *Star Clipper* and *Star Flyer* are the brainchildren of Swedish yachting enthusiast Mikael Krafft. Completed in Ghent, Belgium, in 1991 and 1992, respectively, they are among the largest and tallest sailing ships ever built, with mainmasts topping 226 feet. In price and accommodations they fall somewhere between the Windjammer Barefoot experience and the upscale three Windstar Cruise vessels, skewed to Windstar. As a sailing experience, they are not unlike the historic, former private yacht *Sea Cloud*.

The *Star Clipper* is generally under sail from late evening to early or mid-morning the next day. Passengers are invited to help with the lines, and some do, while most are content to sit back and look on. The 1,370-horsepower Caterpillar diesel engine kicks in when the wind dies down and is used for maneuvering in tight harbors. The social center is a sheltered deck amidships under a canvas awning, with a sit-up bar and stools around tables. The forward end opens into a lounge, where a grand piano, played by the resident pianist, is tucked under circular skylights cut into the bottom of the suspended swimming pool. Aft of the bar the Edwardian-style library has a clubby atmosphere, with a fireplace and a wall of mahogany-fronted bookcases containing a good selection of popular fiction, travel,

and coffee-table books. The furniture, arranged around card tables and in conversational groupings, includes comfy chairs and sofas for a delightful retreat on a damp day.

The open sitting for all meals encourages mixing among the passengers and officers. Breakfast and lunch are served buffet style, with a generous selection of hot and cold items. Dinner, with fish, meat, and vegetarian entrees, is served by waiters. The food is of good quality and well prepared, and at dinner, passengers dress casually but not sloppily.

The moderately sized cabins, some shaped by the ship's hull, have twin beds or a queen and touches that include wood trim, electric lamps mounted in gimbals, and decorative brass counter railings to prevent items from sliding onto the floor. But the *Star Clipper* hardly lists at all; water tanks see to that. Cabins have phones and

Address/Phone: Star Clippers, 4101 Salzebo Street, Coral Gables, FL 33146; (305) 442–0550; reservations: (800) 442–0551; brochures: (800) 442–0550; fax: (305) 442–1611; www.starclippers.com

The Ship: *Star Clipper* was built in 1992, has a gross tonnage of 2,298, a length of 360 feet, and a draft of 18.5 feet.

Passengers: 168; all ages, including some Europeans; English is the lingua franca

Dress: Casual at all times

Officers/Crew: European officers; international crew

Cabins: 84; 78 outside and most relatively compact; no verandas

Fare: $$

What's included: Usually cruise only, although cruise-tour rates will include airfare, hotels, some meals, some sightseeing, and transfers

What's not included: For cruise only, airfare, port charges, tips, drinks

Highlights: A terrific outdoor sailing experience; charming ports; relaxed atmosphere

Other itineraries: Besides this seven-night Western Mediterranean cruise, which operates between May and September, the *Star Clipper* offers an alternative Western Mediterranean cruise, spring and fall transatlantic positioning voyages, and two winter Caribbean itineraries. Sistership *Star Flyer* operates in the Greek islands and along the Turkish coast from May to October, then travels via the Suez Canal to cruise Malaysia and Thailand, returning through the Indian Ocean in April. The 226-passenger *Royal Clipper* also operates in the Western Mediterranean and the Caribbean and undertakes spring and fall transatlantic crossings.

televisions that screen films, bathrooms are tiny, and there is no room service. In good weather this cruise is a shared, outdoor experience, with conversation, navigation, and sail handling providing the entertainment. At sea most passengers congregate around the wheelhouse and the two sun-deck swimming pools.

The Itinerary

Leaving **Cannes** and the French Riviera behind, the helmsman sets a course for the island of **Corsica.** The first night at sea under full sail is magic, and it's difficult to leave the deck for the cabin below. In the morning the *Star Clipper* lowers its sails and motors in the yacht harbor at **St. Florent.** Some may wish to hang around and look at all the gathered boats, while others take an excursion up to Cape Corse, where medieval towers rim the cliffs.

Approaching the island of **Elba,** the captain demonstrates his considerable skill reversing into the tiny basin at **Portoferraio.** From the castle wall, you can look down onto the ship, anchored in an idyllic setting and towering over the quayside of red-tiled and pastel-colored houses. Napoleon lived in exile here for about ten months before escaping to France, and his two houses are worth visiting.

If the weather permits, the *Star Clipper* will drop anchor for a beach visit and then call at **Bastia,** a Corsican port city known for its Italianate architecture. The massive stone citadel houses the Ethnographic Museum, which tells the story of Corsican

independence from Genoa, just in time for Napoleon to be born French.

Then it's overnight to the Italian coast at **Portonevere,** where it's a drive inland to see the Leaning Tower at **Pisa** or a bit farther to **Florence,** the city of art on the Arno. Sailing up the Italian coast, **Portofino** is always a favorite stop, a miniature seaside village wedged into a narrow valley, overlooked by handsome Italianate villas and the stylish Hotel Splendido. Most passengers go no farther than the town's main square for a leisurely lunch and a bit of shopping. The more energetic might take my tip and walk up to a network of paths that hug the hillside with great views down to the sea. You can continue for two hours to **Santa Margarita,** a larger old-fashioned Italian Riviera resort. For the return, the choice is a quick bus or boat ride back to Portofino.

The last call is **Monte Carlo** in the principality of **Monaco,** the domain of the rich and famous with its opulent international casino and one of Europe's finest yachting centers. On the last night, the ship sails along the French Riviera for disembarkation at **Cannes.**

The *Star Clipper* is a great leveler. There are couples aboard who could buy and sell the ship and others who are working people, and it's not easy to tell one from the other. The ships cater to passengers who have done the big ships and who enjoy a working sailing ship, small ports, informality, and making friends in a relaxed setting.

SEADREAM YACHT CLUB'S
SeaDream I and *SeaDream II*
Mediterranean Living on a Yacht

 SeaDream I and *SeaDream II* began life as the 116-passenger *Sea Goddess I* and *II*, two identical pioneering ships catering to the very top end of the cruise market. After a short time operating for an independent company, Cunard bought the pair, then in 2001 the two passed to Atle Brynestad, a Norwegian shipowner, to sail under the SeaDream Yacht Club banner.

If private yacht can be applied to any cruise ship, this pair deserves the term because of their size, amenities, and the pampering. The atmosphere is highly sophisticated yet casual, more relaxed than when Cunard operated them. A younger crowd, wearing good clothes but not dressing up, is drawn to the one-week itineraries in the Caribbean and the Mediterranean. Rather than days at sea, the ship is more often found at anchor with its passengers enjoying life on deck. When the ship is docked, passengers may drift ashore to take in the local scene, such as outdoor cafe life at Calvi on Corsica, or make the short climb to the cliffs overlooking the harbor at Bonifacio at the south end of the island.

On board, wines and spirits are complimentary in the bars and at meals. Freshly prepared Mediterranean seafood and fruits are menu highlights served in the lovely main restaurant or at the partly enclosed cafe up on deck. The chef may buy from a local market, and you can join in the shopping adventure. For a private dinner, or any meal at any hour, the cabin staff will serve you course by course in your quarters, either at the raised coffee table or at a proper table supplied for the occasion. On every cruise, one dinner is served poolside, and more often there are beach-party–style lunch barbecues and picnics. Cocktail hour features caviar, smoked salmon, shrimp, and hot and cold hors d'oeuvres in the main

lounge with musical accompaniment for dancing before and after dinner. A pianist plays at a grand piano in the dining room at night, and movies are shown out on deck under the stars.

The library has a good selection of books and videos and Internet access at moderate rates, and there is a small casino and open bridge policy.

Water sports and Asian spa treatments are popular activities, and while at anchor in some ports, passengers can swim, snorkel, Jet Ski, sail, or kayak from the stern marina. A golf simulator offers play at fifty championship courses. For the more sedentary, the outdoor pool is always open, and soaking in the whirlpool is a social event.

On this democratic, if high-end, ship, the minisuite-size cabins are nearly identical with windows in most and portholes for others, and a number may be combined to create a separate bedroom and lounge. The blond-wood cabinetry and furnishings are all new, and the elaborate amenities include refrigerator, soft-drink–stocked bar, safe housed in a vertical enclosure, and an entertainment center with a 20-inch flat screen TV, CD and DVD player, and an MP3 audio player. The beds, or bed if pushed together, are set before the window and can be curtained off from the lounge. Bathrooms have all been renewed with fresh marble tiles and glass-enclosed showers with multiple jets.

The Itinerary
The *SeaDream* pair offer several different one-week itineraries, most centered in the Western Mediterranean, and the one described here has especially good small-port content. Touring can be on your own from the landing, by private car, taxi, or on the cruise line's shore excursion program. Arrival and departure times are flexible

depending on the weather and touring factors.

Embarkation is at the commercial port of **Civitavecchia**, a ninety-minute drive from Rome, and the ship then sails overnight to **Positano**, a picture-postcard coastal town at the south end of the **Amalfi Drive**. The narrow streets don't permit buses, so touring is by foot or private hired car to **Pompeii, Herculaneum,** or **Sorrento**. The ship then shifts across the bay to Capri, one of the most popular spots in all of Italy, so it is wise to take a tour by boat along the coast to one of the grottos or to a secluded beach. A good land destination is the island's second town, **Anacapri**, perched high above the sea, and from here a chairlift glides above the vineyards en route to the top of Mt. Solaro for a stupendous view of Vesuvius, the Bay of Naples, Amalfi Coast, and the nearby island of Ischia.

At the north end of **Sardinia**, the stop at **Porto Servo** puts you in the world of the Aga Khan, who developed the **Costa Smeralda** beginning in the 1960s. You can visit some of the upscale resort hotels and

nearby villages by bus or car. It's a short sail over to **Corsica**, where there are two scheduled port calls, the first at the medieval town of **Bonifacio**, sandwiched between steep white cliffs with a citadel to climb overlooking the harbor. Inland drives access hill towns and the rugged island's national park. On the north coast, **Calvi** is a gem of a yachting center, and the ship docks alongside a long line of cafes and restaurants.

The **Bay of Cannes** is set aside for enjoying the ship sports marina for sailing, kayaking, swimming, tubing, and boarding or simply never leaving the comfy sun lounger on deck. Shifting to **Cannes** itself, you are in a big city resort ideal for a long promenade or for taking the ship's tour inland to the sixteenth-century, fortified hill town at **St. Paul en Vence** with an attractive drive in both directions.

The port of disembarkation is **Monte Carlo**, in the principality of **Monaco**, a longtime playground for the rich, and the *SeaDream II* will look very much at home here, so linger before you head off to other parts.

Address/Phone: SeaDream Yacht Club, 2601 South Bayshore Drive, Penthouse 1B, Coconut Grove, FL 33133; (305) 856–5622 or (800) 707–4911; fax: (305) 856–7599; www.seadreamyachtclub.com

The Ships: *SeaDream I* and *II*, built as the *Sea Goddess I* and *II* in 1984 and 1985 respectively, have a gross tonnage of 4,260 tons, a length of 334 feet, and a shallow draft of 14 feet.

Passengers: 110; mostly Americans, some Europeans; ages thirty-five and up

Dress: Tastefully casual every night

Officers/Crew: Scandinavian officers and European and international hotel staff

Cabins: 55 one-room minisuites, all nearly identical; lowest deck cabins have portholes rather than windows. Sixteen

units can be combined to provide a two-room suite.

Fare: $$$$

What's included: Cruise fare, all wines and spirits, and gratuities

What's not included: Port charges, shore excursions, airfare

Highlights: One of the most indulgent travel experiences possible in an atmosphere that is more private yacht than cruise ship

Other itineraries: In addition to the *SeaDream I* and *II* making seven-day cruises throughout the Mediterranean, both ships undertake seven-night itineraries in the Caribbean, with spring and fall transatlantic crossings connecting the two seasons. Be advised that an advertised sailing may not be available as the ships are often chartered.

STAR CLIPPERS'
Royal Clipper
Circumnavigate Sicily aboard the World's Largest Sailing Ship

 On first sight, the *Royal Clipper* presents a most powerful appearance. Five tall bare poles rise above a shapely steel hull that sports a thick black stripe running its full length. Black gun-port squares below give the ship an extra sense of importance, and if one did not have a passenger ticket in hand, this ship might pass for a man-of-war, or at least a commercial cargo carrier.

The 228-passenger *Royal Clipper* is a full-rigged ship, with square sails on all five masts, while the earlier four-masters, *Star Clipper* and *Star Flyer*, are barkentine-rigged. At 439 feet, the *Royal Clipper* is 79 feet longer and qualifies as the longest and largest sailing vessel ever built, in overall size as measured in gross tons. She carries 56,000 square feet of Dacron sail, compared to 36,000 for the *Star Clipper* and *Star Flyer*. The twenty-member deck crew uses electric winches to angle the twenty-six square sails and electric motors to furl and unfurl the square sails stored in the yardarms and the eleven staysails, four jibs, and one gaff-rigged spanker.

On the Main Deck, an upward-sloping observation lounge gives a view out to the foredeck and is used for meetings, informal talks, and Internet connections. The main lounge, located amidships, has banquette, soft couch and chair seating, a sit-up bar, and a central well that looks down into the dining room two decks below. As you leave via the aft doors, the covered Tropical Bar and the paneled Edwardian library and its electric fireplace recall the earlier pair.

The handsome paneled dining room, reached via freestanding staircase from the lounge, has a large upper level surrounding a central well, the location for additional tables and the buffet. An omelet chef cooks to order at breakfast, and a carvery features roast beef, ham, and pork at lunch. Seating at tables and banquettes is open for all meals, and the lunch buffets are the biggest hit with the menu featuring such choices as jumbo shrimp, foie gras, artichoke hearts, herring, potato salad, lots of salad fixings, hot and cold salmon, meatballs, and sliced roast beef. The dining room is set low enough that in any kind of sea, the water splashes washing-machine–style over the portholes. For an actual underwater view, Captain Nemo, the combination gym, spa, tiled Turkish bath, and beauty salon, has lounge seating from where one can look out for the creatures of the sea.

The deluxe suites are reached by walking along a central mahogany-paneled companionway with a thick sloping mast penetrating the corridor at the forward end. These luxurious cabins, mahogany-paneled with rosewood framing and molding, contrast with an off-white ceiling and the wall's upper portion. Pale gold-framed mirrors enlarge the cabin space, and brass-framed windows bring in light to bathe the corner sitting alcove. Brass wall lamps and sailing ship prints lend the distinctive feel of a ship's cabin, upward sloping at that, not the more common cruise ship hotel-style room on a hull.

A heavy wooden door leads to a private furnished teak-deck veranda with shrouds passing upward from the ship's side. Nods to upscale cruise ship amenities include the huge marble bathroom with Jacuzzi and a TV and minibar, hidden from view. There are fourteen of these 255-square-foot deluxe one-room suites, plus two even larger 320-square-foot owner's suites located at the stern, and two 175-square-foot deluxe cabins that open onto the after-deck. The most numerous standard cabins (88) in categories 2 to 5 are 148 square feet and vary mostly by location. They have marble bathrooms with shower, TV, satellite telephone, radio channels, private safe, and hair dryers. Six inside cabins round out the accommodations. The real show takes place up on the Burma teak Sun Deck, its full length cluttered with electric winches, halyards, belaying pins, lines, shackles, ventilators, lifeboats, and, incongruously, deck chairs arranged around three swimming pools. The center pool, 24 feet in length, has a glass bottom that drops into the piano lounge and serves as a skylight to the dining room three decks below.

A hydraulic platform stages the water sport activities, and the ship offers banana boats, waterskiing, diving, snorkeling, and swimming from the 16-foot inflatable raft. An interior stairway gives access to the marina. Two 60-passenger tenders, resembling military landing craft, and two 150-passenger fiberglass tenders ferry passengers between the anchored ship and pier.

The Itinerary

The *Royal Clipper* offers two of the most offbeat itineraries in the Mediterranean, embarking in **Civitavecchia,** the port for **Rome,** and heading south to Tyrrhenian Sea islands and to Sicily. The one described here circumnavigates the island, and both routes offer a full day under sail.

Leaving port, the *Royal Clipper* sets sail for the western tip of **Sicily,** pointing in the direction of the Tunisian coast. **Mazara del Vallo** has many layers of history—from Greek, Roman, and Arab, up to the present day. The town has an Arabian Kasbah with nearby Greek ruins, and an excursion visits the village of **Marsala,** established in the sixteenth-century and known for its sweet dessert wine often used in cooking.

To the south of Sicily, calls are made at the tiny island of **Gozo,** where you can visit the beautiful spot above a lagoon where Ulysses is said to have tarried with Calypso. **Valletta,** the handsome harbor capital of **Malta,** reveals how many centuries of trading have left multiple layers of history and architecture. Walk the streets overlooked by bay-windowed apartments and visit the

Address/Phone: Star Clippers, 4101 Salzebo Street, Coral Gables, FL 33146; (305) 442–0550 or (800) 442–0551; fax: (305) 442–1661; www.starclippers.com

The Ship: The *Royal Clipper* was built in 2000, has a gross tonnage of 5,000, a length of 439 feet, and a draft of 18.5 feet.

Passengers: 228; all ages, Americans and Europeans; English is the lingua franca

Dress: Casual at all times

Officers/Crew: European captain, European officers and international crew

Cabins: 114; all but 6 outside, 14 with verandas

Fare: $$

What's included: Cruise only

What's not included: Airfare, port charges, tips, drinks

Highlights: The ultimate in a sailing ship experience; social bonding aboard

Other itineraries: Besides these two Mediterranean itineraries offered between May and September, the *Royal Clipper* makes two annual transatlantic crossings in spring and fall. Star Clippers offers other sailing ship cruises aboard the *Star Clipper* and *Star Flyer* in the eastern or western Mediterranean, bases two ships in the Caribbean, and in fall the *Star Flyer* sails through Suez to cruise Malaysia and Thailand, returning via the Indian Ocean in April.

Palace of the Grand Knights of St. John and Caravaggio's paintings in St. John's Cathedral.

Sailing east around the bottom of Sicily, the next port is **Syracuse.** Ancient Syracuse, once the most powerful city-state in Sicily, with origins that date back to Corinthian colonists in 733 B.C., was involved in wars with Athens, Carthage, Rome, Byzantium, and the Arabs, Normans, and British. The city is a treasure trove of ruins that include the remains of the Temple of Athena seen embedded in the walls of the Norman-era duomo, plus fortifications, aqueducts, a Roman amphitheater, and catacombs.

Aiming northward, the *Royal Clipper* sails through the Strait of Messina, then calls in at **Panarea,** one of the smallest **Aeolian Islands,** known for their volcanic activity. The pretty village is a retreat for business types from Rome and Milan. Then the last call is at **Ventotene,** a tiny village in the **Pontine Islands,** located just off the coast of Italy, where there is a volcanic sand beach and the ruins of a Roman villa. Then it's an overnight sail back to Civitavecchia.

The alternative week calls at **Ponza,** also in the Pontine Islands, the coastal resort of **Sorrento** for **Pompeii,** the **Isle of Capri, Amalfi** for the famous drive, the Sicilian resort hill town of **Taormina,** and **Lipari** in the volcanic **Aeolian Islands.** After a close look at the still-active cone of **Stromboli,** enjoy two nights and a full day under sail en route to Civitavecchia for disembarkation.

ROYAL OLYMPIA'S
Olympia Explorer
The Concorde of Mediterranean Cruise Ships

Royal Olympia Cruises, a Greek-based line, was formed by a merger of Epirotiki Lines and Sun Line, both firms longtime specialists in Mediterranean cruising. Traditional owners of second-hand tonnage, ROC shot into the forefront of operating port-intensive itineraries with the introduction of the speedsters *Olympia Voyager* in 2000 and the *Olympia Explorer* in 2002.

The 836-passenger *Explorer* is an almost exact sister of the *Voyager,* differing only in having twelve balcony cabins replace the earlier ship's bay windows rooms. With a service speed of 28 knots, the pair qualifies as the world's fastest cruise ships, outpacing even the mighty liner *Queen Elizabeth 2,* which now normally cruises at a more leisurely 25 knots.

The public spaces are cherry-wood paneled with the smooth surfaces giving off a rich, soft glow. The fabric colors are Mediterranean blues, greens, and pottery-tile red, but not as dark as aboard the more traditional *Stella Solaris* and *Stella Oceanis.* The piano bar, observation lounge, smoking room, and library are all most inviting spaces and well used during the transits between ports.

Afternoon tea is served in the light-filled forward observation lounge, which triples as a quiet reading room during the day and a popular disco at night. A Romanian pianist and vocalist draw good crowds to the medium-tone veneered piano bar, and the show lounge offers typical musical reviews, specialty performers, such as a crew-staged Greek night, and usually a fine enrichment lecturer. The *Explorer* also offers a casino, gym, spa, small outdoor pool, boutique, cigar lounge, card room, and library.

Dinner aboard the *Olympia Explorer* is at two sittings, usually 7:00 and 9:00 P.M., but meal times often respond to varied port arrival and departure times. The food is good international fare featuring Greek specialties such as moussaka, souvlaki, marinated octopus, stuffed vine leaves, Greek feta cheese salads, and baklava. The Greek crew, numbering forty-seven, serve as navigating officers and dining stewards, while the remainder hail mainly from the Philippines and Eastern Europe. The lido is open for breakfast, lunch, and some dinners and has indoor and outdoor seating, and an outdoor grill produces excellent varieties of pizza.

Most cabin arrangements are similar, of average size (140 square feet), but with all the features that one comes to expect—TV, safe, fridge, telephone, decent stowage, and roomy bathroom. With a high service speed, the balcony cabins are not used as often as they might be aboard a ship sailing at a more leisurely pace, so think before paying a premium for one.

The popular deck space aft on three levels is usually protected from the wind, but in calm conditions the roomier port and starboard sides on the pool deck are also pleasant outdoor spots.

The Itinerary

The speed of the *Olympia Explorer* permits a most ambitious itinerary, adding up to the draw that attracts most passengers, both first-timers and those who cannot get enough of the culturally rich Eastern Mediterranean. The passenger mix for Royal Olympia has changed over the years to one in which Europeans are now in the majority, especially Italians, French, and Spanish. Ports of embarkation for this cruise are Piraeus, port for Athens, Venice, and Istanbul, and in addition calls are made at Corfu, Dubrovnik, Katakolon (Olympia), Mykonos, and Santorini. It should be noted that only Piraeus and Venice offer a full day in port.

To avoid haggling with local taxi drivers for sites too distant to reach on foot, the shore excursion program splits passengers

Address/Phone: Royal Olympia Cruises, 805 Third Avenue, New York, NY 10022; (800) 872–6400 or (212) 688–7555; fax: (888) 662–7555; www.royalolympia cruises.com

The Ship: *Olympia Explorer* began sailing in 2002 and has a gross tonnage of 25,000, a length of 590 feet, and a draft of 24 feet.

Passengers: 836; Europeans and Americans, all ages and lots of families in the summer

Dress: Casual most nights; jacket requested on two nights

Officers/Crew: Greek officers and dining room staff; otherwise international

Cabins: 422; most average size, of which 282 are outside and 24 have balconies

Fare: $$$

What's included: Cruise fare and port charges

What's not included: Airfare, tips, drinks, shore excursions

Highlights: For first-timers to the Mediterranean, a speedy itinerary and lots of ports

Other itineraries: In addition to this one-week Eastern Mediterranean cruise that operates between mid-April and the end of October, sister *Olympia Voyager* sails from France and Italy to Greece and Turkey. Royal Olympia's older ships offer a rich variety of trips in the Eastern Mediterranean and northern Europe, and in the winter months, the *Olympia Explorer* and *Olympia Voyager* cross the Atlantic to cruise the Caribbean and down to South America, including trips up the Amazon.

into about a half-dozen language groups, and the English-speaking guides are usually excellent for the genuinely interested. Be prepared for major crowds in the height of the summer, while the numbers drop off in the fall as families return home.

If embarking at **Piraeus,** it's an overnight sail around the bottom of the Peloponesus to **Corfu,** a popular Greek island resort with Corfu Town the main attraction for the cruise passenger. The narrow lanes are fun to explore, and a long arcade of cafe restaurants provides an excuse to linger and ogle the passing scene.

Several ports provide not-to-be-missed arrivals and departures by sea, and sailing into **Venice** past San Marco Square, the Doges Palace, and the entrance to the Grand Canal is certainly one of them. A day pass for the city's vaporettos (steamers) gives access to the city's twisting waterways, to **Murano Island** to observe the famous glass being made, and out to the **Lido,** the city's own resort town.

One of the most heartening sights of all is to walk the walls of **Dubrovnik** and look down into a handsomely rebuilt port city, nearly fully recovered from the devastating war with Serbia. For a comprehensive view of the city and its setting, the road passing above town is also a spectacular experience. The call at **Katakolon** is a short drive from **Olympia,** the origin of the ancient games that will be held at Athens in 2004. For the athletic, it's a thrill to sprint off the mark as the ancient Greeks did.

The route to and from **Istanbul** passes through the **Dardanelles, Sea of Mar-**mara, and the **Bosphorus.** Istanbul, an energetic harbor city straddling two continents, is a sheer delight for urban walkers, but for first-timers, the most efficient way to see the major sites—Topkapi Palace, St. Sophia, the Blue Mosque, the Grand and Spice Bazaars—is to take a tour. The ship's departure coincides with the sun setting over the city's spiky minarets.

Wind down on the final day with a stroll through the narrow streets of **Mykonos.** The lanes were designed to foil thieves, but now the only hazard is getting lost, never for long, as the sea laps at much of the perimeter. A few hours later the ship anchors in **Santorini**'s deep blue caldera beneath the white frosted villages perched high above. The dramatically situated island has remnants of a once important civilization that literally exploded into the atmosphere about 1500 B.C. There are unearthed ruins to pick over and the precariously clinging, white-washed village of **Oia** to explore. Because the ship doesn't sail until late evening, seek out an outdoor restaurant for a last meal in the main town of Santorini, and order a plate of calamari washed down with an ever-so-lightly-sparkling Santorini white wine. The final activity is the steep descent to the harbor landing by aerial tramway, mischievous mule, or more wearily on foot, avoiding the dotted piles of night soil.

After an overnight sail, the *Olympic Explorer* returns to Piraeus. And mercifully, the busy week includes four half days at sea to read, relax, socialize, and watch the wide wake trail off to the horizon.

WINDSTAR CRUISES'
Wind Spirit
Greek Islands and Coastal Turkey

Launched in 1986, Windstar Cruises combines the best of nineteenth-century clipper-ship design with the best of modern yacht engineering aboard its fleet of four- and five-masted sailing ships. While the *Wind Spirit*'s proud masts and yards of white sails cut an ever-so-attractive profile, the sails unfurl at the touch of a button. Windstar cruising is a top-of-the-line, ultra-comfortable experience, and a no-jackets-needed policy is appreciated by the stylish, formality-eschewing guests,

Onboard, stained teak, brass details, and lots of navy blue fabrics and carpeting and caramel-colored leathers lend a traditional nautical ambience. Passengers can visit the bridge at any time to watch the computerized sails at work. Intentionally, there are few organized activities offered, and the pool deck, with its hot tub, chaise longues, and open-air bar, is conducive to conversing, sunbathing, or just peaceful repose. The video library and CD collection are popular pastimes for in-cabin entertainment.

In the vaguely nautical-looking lounge, passengers congregate for port talks, pre- and post-dinner drinks, and dancing and listening to the pianist and vocalist. Local entertainment may come aboard at a port of call, and a modest casino offers slots, blackjack, and Caribbean stud poker. In addition, a tiny gym is housed in a cabin-sized room, with an adjacent coed sauna.

The food is inventive and imaginative, as reflected by an appetizer such as a corn risotto with wild mushrooms and basil, perhaps followed by an artfully presented potato-crusted fish with braised leeks and apple-smoked bacon, or a salmon tournedos with an herb crust served with stewed tomatoes and garlicky broccoli rabe. Irresistible desserts like banana pie with rasp-

berry sauce and French profiteroles with hot-fudge sauce are beyond tempting. The once-a-week evening pool-deck barbecue is a grand party under the stars. There are two open-seating dining venues: The Restaurant, accented with teakwood trim and wood paneling and pillars wrapped in hemp, is used for dinner only; and The Veranda, a sunny, window-lined room with additional tables under umbrellas, serves breakfast and lunch.

All twin-portholed cabins are similar wood-tone outsides measuring 188 square feet and equipped with a VCR and a TV showing CNN and lots of movies, a CD player, a minibar, bathrobes, fresh fruit, and a compact closet. Roomy teakwood-decked bathrooms are well laid out and come with hair dryer and circular shower stalls.

The Itinerary

The weekly departures alternate between the Athenian port of **Piraeus** and **Istanbul.** When sailing from Greece, the first call is **Mykonos,** where, as in most ports, there is no need to take an organized excursion. Hop the shuttle provided by the ship and walk the town from end to end, enjoying the classic whitewashed, blue-domed chapels and maze of streets; then choose a seaside restaurant for a Greek salad and plate of calamari.

The approach to **Santorini**'s cliff rim is nothing short of spectacular, and to reach the town 1,000 feet up, hire a donkey, take the cable car, or, if fit, use the zigzagging stairs. Besides the bird's-eye views, browse the cobbled streets and sample the fresh fish and Santorini white wines. Sailing eastward to **Rhodes,** the medieval city is a short walk from the ship, and within the walls are bustling squares, cobblestone side streets leading to small shops and some wonderful

Address/Phone: Windstar Cruises, 300 Elliott Avenue West, Seattle, WA 98119; (206) 281–3535 or (800) 258–7245; brochures: (800) 626–9900; fax: (206) 286–3229; www.windstarcruises.com

The Ship: *Wind Spirit* was built in 1988, has a gross tonnage of 5,350, a length of 440 feet, and a draft of 13 feet.

Passengers: 148; mostly American, thirty and up

Dress: Casual at all times

Officers/Crew: British officers; Filipino and Indonesian crew

Cabins: 74; all similar cabins, all outside, and no verandas

Fare: $$$$

What's included: Cruise fare, port charges, water sports, basic tips

What's not included: Airfare, drinks, shore excursions, extra tips

Highlights: Cuisine, ship itself, intimate atmosphere, service; Mediterranean itinerary

Other itineraries: In addition to these seven-night Eastern Mediterranean cruises, which operate between May and October, the three-ship fleet offers other Mediterranean itineraries, transatlantic positioning voyages, Caribbean programs, and a one-week program in Tahiti.

restaurants, perhaps for dinner, as the ship stays until nearly midnight. One excursion visits historic **Lindos,** perched high on a steep cliff above the sea.

Bodrum, a Turkish yachting and holiday port, has a Crusader past with fortified towers dominating the town and lots of resort-style shops and fish restaurants, where you choose the fish displayed whole for cooking. Weather conditions permitting, passengers may be able to go kayaking, sailing, windsurfing, and swimming from the

water-sports platform lowered at the stern. Then up the coast at **Kusadasi,** first-timers should take the tour to **Ephesus** to stand before the towering Library of Celsus and climb the steps of the great theater—but be prepared for hordes of other tourists. The pièce de résistance is the arrival in **Istanbul,** a breathtaking finale, with minarets rising up all around, with Topaki Palace and the Galata Tower adding considerable character to the skyline.

SILVERSEA CRUISES'
Silver Whisper
Unusual Eastern Mediterranean

The Silversea's fleet numbers four, one pair taking 296 passengers and a second newer pair carrying 388. The *Silver Whisper* is the latest of the four, completed in Italy in mid-2001. Like her fleetmates, she is designed to roam the globe offering high-end, virtually all-inclusive cruising.

Registered in the Bahamas, this beautiful ship measures 28,258 tons, and her passenger-space ratio is among the highest afloat.

The design has the cabins placed forward and the public rooms aft on six of the seven passenger decks, so be prepared for a lot of vertical movement during the day. The elevators are very efficient and respond quickly, and for some, stair climbing is simply sensible exercise. As with the smaller pair, the show lounge faces aft and is entered via both wings from a ship-wide bar, the vessel's social center. Passengers gravitate here before lunch and before and after dinner to the sit-up bar, the conversational seating, and for dancing to a small band. While the majority of passengers are usually American, there are likely to be many nationalities aboard drawn to the sophisticated European-style service.

For viewing the scenery within, the Panorama Lounge is well named with large-view windows on three sides. For pint-size places to roost, The Humidor draws the cigar smokers and brandy sippers to an English club setting, and the paneled wine bar caters to grape aficionados.

Dining is always open seating in a large but nicely divided main restaurant on the lowest deck, and at the Terrace Café for theme dinners by reservation but at no extra charge. The cafe also serves breakfast and lunch and has a delightful covered afterdeck usually protected against the wind. Table wines are served without charge at lunch and dinner. Le Champagne offers intimate dining for thirty on selected evenings. A grill

poolside allows bathers and sun worshippers to ward off hunger without having to change for the indoor venues.

The casino, located off the main lobby, is small, and the fitness center and spa, operated by Mandara, are far more elaborate than on the older pair. A computer center provides Internet access, which is also available in the suites.

Deck space is adequate for a crowd that takes the sun in small doses. Deck chairs surround the pool out in the sun and under the covered side deck, above which is also additional seating. The whirlpools become instant social centers.

The suites put the Silversea ships at the top of the high-end pack, and the smallest Vista suites are 287 square feet; the next and most numerous category, the Veranda suites, measure the same area but boast the addition of a balcony. The top accommodations fall into four more categories and range from 701 feet to 1,435 feet.

All accommodations come with sofas, cocktail tables that rise to become suitable for in-suite dining, TVs and VCRs, refrigerators, cocktail cabinets, arched curtain dividers, walk-in closets with good storage, and two-basin marble bathrooms with tubs

---

Address/Phone: Silversea Cruises, 110 East Broward Boulevard, Fort Lauderdale, FL 33301; (954) 522–4477 or (800) 722–9995; fax: (954) 522–4499

The Ship: The *Silver Whisper* was completed in 2001, has a gross tonnage of 28,258, a length of 610 feet, and a draft of 19.6 feet.

Passengers: 388; many Americans, some Europeans, forty-five and up

Dress: Formal, informal, and casual nights

Officers/Crew: Italian officers and a European and Filipino crew

Cabins: 194 spacious one-room suites, all outside, and 157 with balconies

Fare: $$$$$

What's included: Cruise fare, port charges, often a hotel stay, drinks and wines at lunch and dinner, gratuities, and usually a special shore side event

What's not included: Airfare, shore excursions

Highlights: Stylish atmosphere, unusual itineraries

Other itineraries: Besides this *Silver Whisper* warm-weather cruise in the Eastern Mediterranean, Silversea's four-ship fleet, including the *Silver Cloud, Silver Shadow,* and *Silver Wind,* covers virtually the entire world.

and stall showers, hair dryers, robes, and slippers.

Understated sophistication with an Italian flair marks the Silversea experience wherever the ships go, and the quartet sails the seven seas.

The Itinerary

Silversea offers a huge range of itineraries within the Mediterranean, and the nine-day Eastern Mediterranean cruise described here features more unusual range ports.

Embarkation is at **Piraeus,** port of **Athens,** with an evening departure for an overnight sail to **Aghios Nikolaos,** an attractive and now well-established resort on the north coast of the island of **Crete** to the east of Heraklion, Crete's main port city. Some will enjoy a day on the beach, while the organized excursion takes the coastal road to **Heraklion** to visit the ruins of the palace of King Minos at **Knossos,** one of the earliest restorations in the Mediterranean world, and the Heraklion Museum.

Following a late-night departure, the passage to Beirut involves two nights and a day sailing eastward through the Mediterranean. Once the Paris of the East or the Pearl of the Middle East, **Beirut** was heavily influenced by the French and has a nightclub life that draws Arabs from all over the region. Much of the city has been rebuilt since the long period of strife, and Western cruise ships are just beginning to resume calling there. In the city itself, there is vibrant street life at Souk el Barghout, the main marketplace, artifacts on display at the National Museum, which reopened in 1999, restored ruins at the Roman baths, and great views of the coastline while driving the Corniche. Trips may be organized to Biblical trading cities at Baalbeck, Byblos, and Sidon.

Sailing overnight to **Limassol,** the main port for the Greek side of **Cyprus,** excursions head inland to small villages nestled in the **Troodos Mountains,** the Monastery at

Savros, and the port city of **Nicosia.**

Antalya on the south coast of Turkey is the gateway for visiting some of the greatest archaeological sites in the Mediterranean world. **Perge** is known for its 1000 B.C. theater, remains of a marketplace with a floor of beautiful mosaics, and substantial Hellenistic and Roman gates. **Aspendos'** theater has a spectacular two-level stage and acoustics that are still so good that no microphone is needed for today's performances.

The call at **Rhodes** reveals many layers of history, as the strategic island was on the sea route between the Mediterranean world and the Holy Land.

The approach to **Istanbul** is incomparable, and the schedule calls for a daylight passage through the **Dardanelles** and into the **Sea of Marmara** before the spiky minarets of the Blue Mosque and Hagia Sophia appear above the cityscape. The city, divided between two continents and, in turn, the European side separated by the Golden Horn, has as much energy as any place on Earth.

First-timers may wish to take a guided tour to negotiate the crowds and complexities of Topkapi Palace and the Grand and Spice Bazaars. Istanbul is also walkable, but sometimes it is best to get to a certain area first by taxi to then find that several of the main mosques, churches, and former churches are located within a reasonable distance of each other. Be sure to take a ferry to Uskudar on the Asian side or Kadikoy for an additional Bosphorus view, both locations affording a visit to another continent within the space of an hour or so.

Although the ship remains docked at Istanbul for two nights, you may wish to extend your stay at one of the restored Victorian house-style hotels near Topkapi Palace or one of the large international hotels clustered near Taksim Square.

MINOAN LINES'
Ikarus Palace and *Pasiphae Palace*
A Minicruise from Venice to Greece

 Few ports are more enchanting from which to sail than Venice, and following a stay in this wonderful city, consider taking a minicruise south through the Adriatic to Greece, to linger on there or come straight back. Up to six times each week, a Minoan "Palace" ferry makes the 650-nautical-mile transit, calling in at two ports en route to Patras on the Peloponnese.

Dispel from your mind any preconceptions of Greek ferries, as Minoan Lines operates one of the most modern cruise ferry fleets in the Mediterranean. This Crete-based company was founded in 1974 to link that island with the Greek mainland, later branching out to the Adriatic Sea in 1981 where seven of its ten ships operate.

The *Ikarus Palace* and her sister the *Pasiphae Palace,* the pair featured here, were built in Norway for the company in 1997 and 1998 and, with streamlined superstructures, look both sleek and fast. A third ship on the route, the 2002-built *Ariadne Palace,* is marginally smaller.

Foot passengers (those traveling without a car) board via the stern ramp and use escalators to reach the passenger accommodation on Deck 6. Most of the compact two- and four-berth cabins with private facilities are on this deck, and once you are checked in at the reception desk, a smartly uniformed steward will show you to your cabin. The full range of accommodation includes inside and outside cabins, minisuites, aircraft-type reclining seat lounges, and even bedding down in your sleeping bag in designated areas on the open decks. Round-trip passengers might wish to consider paying the supplement for a minisuite on Deck 8, including sitting area, television, minibar, and room service.

The public rooms on Deck 7 feature an elegant self-service restaurant overlooking the bow for a wide range of freshly prepared hot and cold food at reasonable prices and a beautiful à la carte restaurant paneled with wood veneers and furnished with tasteful fabrics and wooden flooring. The restaurant on the *Ikarus Palace* may be one of the best at sea, rivaling some of the famed cruise liners for tasteful decoration. With excellent service and good food, complemented by mostly Greek wines, it's a splendid place for breakfast, lunch, or dinner. Be sure to try the shrimps Saganaki, Smyrna patties, and the Greek yogurt with honey.

Just aft is the ship's main bar, arranged with pleasant alcoves in which to enjoy a quiet drink. Other places on this deck are the shopping arcade, casino, and a pub-style bar. Up on Deck 8, an observation lounge during the day becomes a discotheque at night.

Outside, spacious open decks extend over four levels, and at the stern there is a swimming pool and whirlpool, a bar serving drinks and snacks, and seating both in the open and under cover.

The Itinerary

Boarding commences two hours prior to sailing, and the ship departs **Venice** at 3:00 P.M. The route along the Guidecca Canal affords a wonderful opportunity to view the city's outstanding architecture, and in about twenty minutes, the ship passes the entrance to the Grand Canal and then Piazza San Marco, the Cathedral, and the Doge's Palace. Ahead are the Lagoon, the Lido, and the open sea. The busy waterway transit to the broad **Adriatic,** shared with ferries, launches, yachts, and freighters, takes about one hour.

Have a drink, dinner about 8:00 P.M.,

and then listen to some music. After a night's rest and a leisurely breakfast, the ship will be sailing at 27 knots along the Albanian coast to then pass between the island of Corfu and the Greek mainland before calling at the little Greek port of **Igoumenitsa.** A good deal of freight and some tourist traffic leaves here for the 300 road miles to the industrial city of Thessalonika and for Istanbul about 750 miles distant. The call is brief, and the ship is soon under way, heading for **Corfu Town.** If there are other ships loading in the small harbor, the apparent chaos on the quayside can be quite entertaining. Heading south during the afternoon through the Ionian Islands, the ferry meets a steady stream of ships bound from **Patras** to various Italian desti-

nations, and by early evening she crosses the mouth of the Gulf of Patras to be berthed by 8:30 P.M.

Three times a week, the same ship sails again at midnight, while on other days it will be a different vessel. If booking a round-trip on the same ship, it is possible to retain the same cabin and leave luggage aboard, but disembarkation and check-in is compulsory. Consider having dinner ashore.

Sailing north, the call at Corfu is 6:30 A.M. the next morning, Igoumenitsa about 8:00 A.M., and arrival at Venice at 7:30 A.M. local time the following day. A free shuttle bus operates to the Piazzale Roma for the main bus terminus, and it's a short walk to Santa Lucia railway station.

As an alternative to returning immedi-

Address/Phone: Minoan Lines, Central Reservations Office 26, Akti Possidonos Street, GR 18531 Piraeus, Greece; +30 210 414 5700; fax: +30 210 414 5755; e-mail: booking@minoan.gr; www.minoan.gr (English pages available)

The Ships: *Ikarus Palace* and *Pasiphae Palace* were Norwegian-built in 1997 and 1998 and have gross tonnages of 30,010 and 30,018, respectively, and are 656 feet long. *Ariadne Palace* was built in South Korea in 2002, has a gross tonnage of 28,007, and is 693 feet long. All ships have a draft of 21 feet.

Passengers: *Ikarus Palace* and *Pasiphae Palace* 1,500 total; *Ariadne Palace* 1,250; predominantly German, then Austrian and Italian, and other Europeans plus backpackers from all around the world. Announcements are in Greek, English, Italian, and German.

Dress: Casual at all times

Officers/Crew: Greek

Cabins: *Ikarus Palace* and *Pasiphae Palace* have 700 beds in 200 cabins; *Ari-*

adne Palace has 412 beds in 120 cabins

Fare: $ to $$

What's included: Cruise only including port charges; deluxe cabins (minisuites) include breakfast

What's not included: Meals, drinks, tips

Highlights: Wonderful ferry ships, excellent service, the spectacle of departing from and arriving back at Venice, great scenery from Albania all the way down to Patras

Other itineraries: Minoan Lines operate an older ship between the northern Greek port of Thessalonika and Heraklion, Crete, calling at the islands of Skiathos and Tinos (or Syros), Mykonos, Paros (or Naxos), and Santorini during the peak summer season. The company also operates modern fast ships between Piraeus and Heraklion, Patras and Ancona (Italy), and Patras and Bari (Italy) seasonally. Ancona and Bari are connected to the Italian State Railway system.

ately, Minoan Lines operates a connecting bus to Athens and Piraeus, but given the after-midnight arrival, a night in Patras might be preferable. Patras is a fairly modern city laid out on a grid system with some stylish shops and attractive squares, but it is also quite scruffy in parts. A good place to stay is the Astir Hotel, a slightly faded, grand hotel from the 1960s that is clean and offers good service. Ask for a room on the fifth or sixth floors overlooking the harbor. The hotel's à la carte restaurant is particularly good, and between June and September a harbor-view rooftop restaurant serves dinner.

If moving on to other destinations in Greece, the Peloponnese narrow-gauge railway takes you from Patras along the coast and over the Corinth Canal to **Athens** in four hours and to **Piraeus** in four and a half hours. The express coach is faster but travels over a less interesting route, reaching the western bus station in Athens in about three hours depending on traffic. Piraeus is a major cruise and ferry port for accessing much of the Mediterranean.

AFRICA AND THE
MIDDLE EAST

ST. HELENA LINE'S
RMS *St. Helena*
Into the Remote South Atlantic via Royal Mail Ship

In 1978 Curnow Shipping of Falmouth, Cornwall, began operating a passenger, mail, and cargo service under a contract with the British government between Britain, the Canary Islands, Ascension, St. Helena, and Cape Town to replace the one hundred years of liner service operated by the Union-Castle Line. Now Andrew Weir Shipping holds the five-year contract.

Purpose-built in a Scottish shipyard in 1990 to serve the islands, the present RMS (for Royal Mail Ship), as she is affectionately known, undertakes four round-trip sailings a year from Portland, Dorset, to the island and makes additional sailings north from Cape Town, offering the comfortable facilities of a small liner for 128 passengers and a British and St. Helenian crew of sixty-five.

The homey public rooms include a two-section forward observation lounge with a bar, a video for screening films, and a reading area. Aft the Sun Lounge looks onto the open lido with outdoor pool, and a light breakfast and lunch are served here daily. The dining room, on a lower deck, operates with two reserved sittings at dinner, and the food is good British fare, such as tasty soups, lunchtime curries, dinner roasts, and well-prepared fish. The plainly furnished cabins are outside, with windows or portholes, twin beds, uppers and lowers, and private shower and toilet. Budget accommodations, reserved for the "Saints"—a people of mixed British, South Asian, East Indian, and Madagascar origin—are sometimes available for nonisland passengers.

The Itinerary
The ship embarks at Portland, Dorset, on the south coast of England for the two-week voyage to St. Helena, and following a week on the island, onward passage to Cape Town, South Africa. On our voyage, among the passengers were the Saints, who make up about half of the complement—students returning from university, persons on leave from jobs abroad, and others planning to resettle in their island home. The visitors came from Britain, Germany, France, South Africa, and the United States. Stored below decks were ninety-three bags of mail and parcels, refrigerated and frozen food, medical equipment and drugs, planks of a West African wood resistant to white ants, educational textbooks, nine automobiles, and one-fifth of a ton of stamps, one of the island's few sources of income.

During the cycle of gradually warming days, we established a daytime routine of reading and socializing on deck, visiting the bridge, and taking a swim or playing deck tennis with the officers atop the forward cargo hatch. In the evening the purser had an uncanny knack of getting everyone involved in creative activities: frog racing, quizzes, and pantomime, all old-fashioned shipboard fun. Such is the atmosphere aboard a purposeful ocean liner.

After a six-hour call at **Tenerife,** the Canary Islands, the RMS leaves the main shipping lanes for the remote South Atlantic. The sea remains placid and quite empty, erupting occasionally when flying fish and porpoises break the surface. A dozen days after leaving Cardiff, **Ascension** comes into view, a desolate and forbidding volcanic island rising 2,800 feet above sea level from the mid-Atlantic ridge. The ship anchors to take on passengers while the purser gives a tour ashore, weather permitting.

Two days later, **St. Helena** spreads across the horizon beneath a low cloud clinging to the mountain peaks. Brown at the edges and green in the center, the island's steep cliffs provide a natural fortress. The RMS anchors off Jamestown, a pastel-colored nineteenth-century Georgian town, sandwiched into a deep valley that slices inland to the island's incredibly beautiful central highlands.

Through passengers get the bonus of a week on the island while the RMS discharges her cargo and makes a passenger run to Ascension and back. Most visitors stay at two small hotels in Jamestown, whereas others choose self-catering cottages up in the hills, which means hiring a car and negotiating twisting, one-lane tracks and blind hairpin curves for touring and grocery shopping.

Napoleon spent six years here from 1815 until his death in 1821, and Longwood, his permanent residence and gardens, is open to visitors; nearby, Deadwood Plain is home to the island's indigenous wirebird. Transit passengers may be invited for a tour of Plantation House, a handsome 1791-built mansion and grounds that is home to a giant Seychellois tortoise named Jonathan, who is reputed to be nearing his 175th birthday. There are miles of walking trails around the coast and down to secluded bays, with rewarding mountain vistas and seascapes of pounding surf. Jamestown offers a small museum, a pretty Anglican church, a few shops, and a couple of restaurants, but the main attraction is Main Street, the island's social center, where everyone gathers to talk.

After a week the RMS returns and embarks passengers for **Cape Town,** a five-day voyage; then, just short of four weeks after departing England, the little ship sails into Table Bay as dawn breaks behind Table Mountain. Loading fresh food, supplies, cement, and coal takes three days; then the ship returns northward. Port calls in Namibia may be added to sailings to and from Cape Town.

Address/Phone: St. Helena Line, Andrew Weir Shipping Ltd., Dexter House, 2 Royal Mint Court, London EC3N 4XX, England; (011) 44 207 265 0808; fax: (011) 44 207 816 4992; www.aws.co.uk

The Ship: RMS *St. Helena* was built in 1990, has a gross tonnage of 6,767, a length of 344 feet, and a draft of 19.6 feet.

Passengers: 128 in all berths. Passengers of every age travel in the ship, with St. Helenians, British, and South Africans predominating, plus Europeans and some Americans.

Dress: Jacket at dinnertime only

Officers/Crew: British and St. Helenian officers; St. Helenian crew

Cabins: 49; mostly outside with two to four berths, plus a few inside without facilities sold at subsidized fares for St. Helenians

Fare: $$

What's included: Sea fare only unless you purchase an air-sea package

What's not included: Shore excursions, tips, drinks, and the hotel or cottage stay on the island, which must be arranged in advance through the line or done independently by fax or e-mail

Other itineraries: In addition to the one-month southbound voyage described here, the RMS *St. Helena* makes similar northbound trips, round-trip voyages that sail from Cape Town to St. Helena, where passengers go ashore for the week, while the ship sails to Ascension and returns via St. Helena to embark passengers for Cape Town. Once a year, the ship also makes a two-week round-trip voyage to the even more remote island of Tristan da Cunha, located about halfway between South Africa and South America. This one sells out well in advance.

ABERCROMBIE & KENT'S
Sun Boat III
Egypt's Nile Valley

 Abercrombie & Kent, one of the top expedition tour companies, operates an Egyptian program that uses luxury-level riverboats and forms groups for touring on land that do not exceed twenty-four participants. Well-educated Egyptologists, whose biographies appear in the brochures, provide a clear and highly palatable enrichment program that ferrets out a highly complex country's incredibly long history.

The *Sun Boat III*, one of the smallest on the Nile with just thirty-six berths, is a sleek-looking, well-maintained, four-deck riverboat with lots of outside space, both awning covered for reading, socializing, and taking in the riverbank sights and open for sunbathing and dipping in the Sun Deck pool. Tower Deck houses a lounge for lectures and showing videos, a separate lounge and bar for drinks, space for a barbecue lunch, and a comfy covered afterdeck with cane furniture. Additional amenities include a small gift shop, gym, massage room, card and board games, and laundry facilities.

The window-lined, no-smoking restaurant on Promenade Deck offers spectacular Nile views, so you miss nothing during meals. Seating is open and unassigned, and the menu includes excellent Egyptian/Middle Eastern dishes and nights with French and Italian themes. Fresh fruit is in abundance, and excellent local beer and palatable light wines are complimentary. Breakfast is an American-style buffet with eggs to order, lunch is a buffet, and dinner is served. The Egyptian staff is attentive and experienced.

The roomy, well-appointed cabins, located forward on three decks, are all windowed outsides with individually controlled air-conditioning, minibars, TVs, CD players, music channels, internal and international phone access, and bathrooms with showers and hair dryers. The lounges and cabins are delightful retreats after a long and sometimes hot day exploring the archaeological sites.

The Itinerary

The fourteen-day cruise tour described here, more comprehensive than most, sails downriver to Dendera and allows extra time in both Aswan and Luxor. When the number of passengers exceeds twenty-four, the group is split into two for the land tour portion and shore excursions. The initial **Cairo** stay visits the Egyptian Museum of Antiquities and includes a drive across the Nile to Memphis and the Step Pyramid at Sakkara, the Great Pyramids, Sphinx, and the Solar Boat Museum.

Leaving Cairo, the flight south lands at **Abu Simbel** for a visit to the Temple of Rameses II, four 65-foot statues flanking the entrance where inside, vivid reliefs depict Rameses' battle triumphs. Adjacent is the equally impressive Temple of Nefertari, Rameses' favorite wife.

Boarding the *Sun Boat III* at **Aswan,** the vessel becomes a hotel moored at the riverbank, with plenty of time for browsing ashore and shopping at both Aswan and Luxor. A boat boarded from a landing behind the Aswan High Dam heads to the island Temple of Philae with a stop to see an enormous unfinished obelisk lying on the ground. Leaving Aswan, the *Sun Boat III* first makes a stop to see **Kom Ombo**'s unique features—double portals and double sanctuaries containing mummified crocodiles and a painted ceiling panel with the wings of Horus in a fine state of preservation. Farther downstream at **Edfu,** horse and carriage clip-clop out to the Temple of Horus, the falcon god, with its remarkable storytelling reverse reliefs. The entry to a passageway is decorated with two guardian Horuses.

Sailing on, the small temple at **Esna,** located in the middle of a lively town, is 30 feet below grade and is threatened by the rising water table, one of the many (and this time negative) consequences of the **Aswan Dam.** Unfortunately, it can't be moved; every inch of its twenty-four columns is covered with wonderful inscriptions and topped by unique capitals, several with stone frogs perched, peering over the edges.

At **Luxor,** visits are made to the **Temple of Karnak** with its great hypostyle hall, a forest of 134 high columns that rise 70 feet. On the Nile's West Bank opposite Luxor, the tombs in the Valleys are constantly being opened and closed, but you will see the Colossus of Memnon, the Rameseum and the mortuary Temple of Hatshepsut. In the **Valley of the Kings,** our group saw the burial chambers for Rameses III and VI, the latter with vividly painted scenes in a remarkable state of preservation. Our energetic guides got their groups to the ticket kiosk early enough to get the very limited number of first-come, first-served tickets for the tomb of Tutankhamon. The dramatic story of its discovery lost nothing in the retelling at the site.

The **Temple of Dendera,** up the map and down the Nile north of Luxor, is isolated at the edge of the desert, and the Roman-era structure, unique because of its intact roof and excellent overall condition, has a depiction of Cleopatra. There's even graffiti from a 1799 Napoleonic expedition. The boat then returns to Luxor for visits to the Temple of Luxor, and to the excellent Luxor Museum for statuary found in the area and the mural from the Temple of Aton.

Returning by air to **Cairo,** the sightseeing encompasses Old Cairo's Coptic Christian Church, the Ben Ezra Synagogue

Address/Phone: Abercrombie & Kent, Inc., 1520 Kensington Road, Oak Brook, IL 60523; (800) 323–7308 or (630) 954–2944; brochures: (800) 757–5884; fax: (630) 954–3324; e-mail: info@ abercrombiekent.com; www.abercrombie kent.com

The Ship: *Sun Boat III* was built in 1993 and has a shallow draft.

Passengers: 36 passengers; Americans and British, forty-five and up

Dress: Casual at all times

Officers/Crew: Egyptian

Cabins: 18 cabins; all outside, 14 are doubles and 4 are suites

Fare: $$$$

What's included: A complete package, including hotels; meals on land; transfers; excursions; beer, wine, and soft drinks at meals; tips at hotels and on the riverboat

What's not included: International and internal Egyptian airfares, bar drinks, and tips to Egyptologists

Highlights: Seeing some of the greatest sights in the Ancient World, with terrific guides, and accomplished in considerable comfort

Other itineraries: Besides this eight-day Nile cruise, plus a land portion that includes Cairo and area and Abu Simbel, which operates between mid-September and the end of May, A&K operates the larger eighty-passenger *Sun Boat IV* on shorter five-day Nile cruises plus land packages. In addition, A&K operates expedition-style cruises and tours worldwide.

and Hanging Gardens, and a nighttime Sound and Light performance at the Pyramids and Sphinx. Then on the last day, it's Islamic Egypt, with visits to the medieval Citadel of Salah-el-Din and Mohammed Ali's Mosque, and modern Egypt with a foray into the Khan el-Khalili bazaar.

It's a full program, but if one comes reasonably well informed, interest is not likely to flag, especially when the guides are as good as they usually are. Aboard ship, in the coaches, and at the sites, security was both conspicuous and unobtrusive. A shorter cruise tour is also available.

SOUTHEAST ASIA AND
THE FAR EAST

STAR CLIPPERS'
Star Flyer
Thailand's Islands in the Andaman Sea

 Seemingly a vision from the past, the tall ship *Star Flyer* faithfully recreates the lure and romance of sailing on a true clipper ship. Cruising the idyllic and virtually undiscovered Andaman Sea islands off Thailand, passengers enjoy a delightfully social week of sailing and water sports without sacrificing too many cruise ship comforts.

It is impossible to prepare yourself. No matter how many pictures you've seen, your first glimpse of the *Star Flyer*, with her graceful bow stretching into a lengthy bowsprit and her three masts stretching 226 feet into the air, will literally send shivers down your spine.

Launched in 1991, this 360-foot vessel is one of the most beautiful sights on the ocean and delights both sailing purists and those seeking a reasonably priced alternative, ages apart from the Caribbean megaships. The culmination of a lifelong dream by Star Clippers owner Mikael Krafft, the *Star Flyer* is infused with the owner's zeal for sailing, and passengers take an active interest in their ship, often chatting with the captain on the bridge or listening to his morning navigational talks.

While not as luxurious as the Windstar vessels or as party-oriented as Windjammer Barefoot Cruises, these ships fall neatly in between and are the most authentic of the sailing cruise lines. Make no mistake—these are true sailing ships. Walk around and marvel at the myriad of rigging stretching skyward like a vertical spiderweb. Winches, cleats, and lines are scattered on all open decks, and whenever possible, the sails are used as the vessel's main propulsion.

Passengers come from around the world, with Americans often representing 10 percent or less of those onboard when in Asia. The spoken language is English,

and most passengers are in their forties and fifties, with several honeymooners on each trip. As is common on a small ship, meeting and bonding with others onboard becomes a valued and integral part of the experience.

Life onboard is low-key, unplanned, and casual, with a heavy emphasis placed on a popular water-sports program. Upon anchoring offshore in the morning, a flotilla of boats and kayaks is dispatched to the beach, and a Zodiac takes divers directly from the ship to the dive spot. Toward sunset, everyone mingles around the open-air bar and chats with the ship's resident parrot before heading one deck up to watch the sails being set and the ship begin to heel to the breeze.

Happily, Star Clippers still lets passengers roam almost anywhere, including the bowsprit stretching 30 feet forward of the bow with its hammocklike netting suspended over the ocean, affording probably the most unique and delightful setting on any cruise ship afloat. Passengers are also given the opportunity to climb into a harness and scramble up the ratlines to a platform partway up the mast. It is an amazing experience, to be lost high up amidst the sails, looking at your ship below being driven through the waves by the wind.

Although rarely used, the ship's public rooms are pleasantly nautical and offer a nice respite for those who have had too much sun. The Piano Bar is centered underneath one of the two splash pools and is comfortable with round banquettes and sailing ship paintings and prints hung on the bulkhead. Aft of the outdoor bar is a small Edwardian-style library, complete with faux fireplace, where the cruise director may hold nightly talks on sailing history.

Nightlife tends to be a bit hokey, with

the water sports staff often putting on a fashion show or organizing silly deck games. Although hardly sophisticated, it does gather everyone outdoors by the bar after dinner, with dancing and socializing sure to follow until 1:00 A.M. or so. Occasionally, a movie will be shown on deck, and passengers might stop by the open bridge and enjoy the quiet sounds of rustling canvas found only on a ship under sail at sea before retiring to their cabin.

Breakfast and lunch are served buffet style in the restaurant, and all meals are open seating without an assigned table or set time. Service, while always friendly, can be rushed and occasionally forgetful, and the food could stand to be somewhat improved. Still, passengers come for the casual sailing atmosphere, not luxury, and hence rarely complain about anything. In keeping with the casual atmosphere, a Polo shirt is sufficient for dinner, with passengers donning a button-down shirt for the captain's dinner.

Cabins themselves are attractive and atmospheric and, with some shaped by the hull's curvature, can be authentically cozy, with the smallest accommodations measuring only 97 square feet. Although the bathrooms are generally tight, the cabin layout makes the rooms feel homey rather than cramped.

For those eager for a social, unique week at sea, there are few more appealing or invigorating cruise experiences available. Spotting your ship at anchor each day, you will be amazed that such a sight still exists and then feel privileged to be lucky enough to experience it.

The Itinerary

Star Clippers tends to shun the larger, more developed ports, and on the northern **Andaman Sea** itinerary, the *Star Flyer* is the only foreign commercial vessel allowed to stop at some islands. Sailing from the resort city of **Phuket, Thailand,** the *Star Flyer* sails north to the **Surin Islands** near the

---

Address/Phone: Star Clippers, 4101 Salzebo Street, Coral Gables, FL 33146; (305) 442–0550 or reservations: (800) 442–0551; fax: (305) 442–1661; www.starclippers.com

The Ship: *Star Flyer* was built in 1991, has a gross tonnage of 2,298, a length of 360 feet, and a draft of 18.5 feet.

Passengers: 168 double occupancy; all ages, including Americans and Europeans; English is the lingua franca.

Dress: Casual at all times

Officers/Crew: European officers and international crew

Cabins: 78 of 84 are outside and most are relatively compact; no verandas

Fare: $$

What's included: Usually cruise only, although cruise tour rates will include air, hotels, some meals, some sightseeing, and transfers

What's not included: For cruise only, airfare, port charges, shore excursions, tips, drinks

Highlights: The ship is very much the destination, making one feel adventurous and recalling the sailing ship past; exotic itinerary for an exotic ship cruising with newfound friends

Other itineraries: Besides these seven-night alternating itineraries from Phuket, Thailand, along the west coast of Thailand and Malaysia, which are offered between November and April, the *Star Flyer* returns through the Indian Ocean to cruise the Greek islands and the Turkish coast from May to October. Between May and September, the *Star Clipper* and larger *Royal Clipper* offer alternative Western Mediterranean cruises, spring and fall transatlantic positioning voyages, and winter Caribbean itineraries.

Burmese border, anchoring offshore of this national park around noon. Other than the local Thai families staying at the campground and the sea gypsies that still live on a neighboring island, you can expect a deserted island and great diving.

The next day the ship sails south to the **Similan Islands,** another uninhabited cluster of islands also known for their fantastic diving and tranquil beaches. Snorkeling, diving, waterskiing, and hiking to the top of the island round out another day in the sun.

The rest of the cruise continues this pattern—sailing for a few hours in the morning before anchoring off a beach until sunset. Although the islands farther south become slightly more discovered with day tourists from Phuket, there are hardly crowds to speak of. With beautiful islands strung closely together, the Andaman Sea seems to be the Caribbean long before it

was discovered by the megaships—or even before chartered sailboats—and at a fraction of the cost.

The only disappointment with this itinerary is the lack of a consistent breeze, and although the crew will put on a brave face and often sail out of anchorages under sail alone, the engines come on at night far more frequently than on Caribbean or Mediterranean sailings.

The last day is spent sailing amidst the mesmerizing rock formations of **Phang Nga Bay.** Climbing into Zodiacs, you'll set off to explore sculpted, colored rock masses jutting straight out of the sea before returning to circle and photograph the ship under full sail. Having seen a sight you won't soon forget, you'll climb back aboard and settle in for one last night of being rocked to sleep before arriving in Phuket the next morning.

SEABOURN CRUISE LINE'S
Seabourn Spirit
Coastal Vietnam Sojourn

The *Seabourn Spirit,* one of three roughly 10,000-gross-register-ton, 200-passenger sisters, provides the ultimate in quiet, luxurious shipboard living, albeit at a high price. Passengers are well-traveled couples or friends traveling together, and few will be making a first cruise. Socializing is a major part of life aboard. Decorated in an understated Scandinavian style, the Club, a glass-partitioned complex, includes a lounge, a cocktail bar, and a casino. Drinks with music take place here before and after dinner, plus dancing and a cabaret show. During the days at sea, in the Amundsen Lounge, guest lecturers will give talks relating to East Asian history, relations with the United States, and economic issues.

With open seating for all meals, one has the choice of sitting alone or sharing a table. The menus are designed to encourage sampling five or six courses, and big eaters can order larger portions. The cold soups, rack of veal, saddle of venison, and broiled salmon were particularly memorable entrees, and, overall, the food and service are some of the best afloat. Poured wines are complimentary, as are all drinks. The Veranda Café offers both indoor seating and a single line of tables under a canvas awning at the stern, and breakfast time is a particularly friendly hour to meet other passengers. A chef takes special orders for eggs Benedict, Belgian waffles, and blueberry pancakes. Lunch is also served here and even more informally at the Sky Bar above the pool. Other than on hosted evenings, the Veranda Café serves dinner by reservation, with an Italian or Oriental theme.

Most passengers occupy similar 277-square-foot, one-room suites with a large sitting area next to a picture window. Thirty-six suites have been refitted with French balconies, in place of the large windows. Amenities are minibar and refrigerator, TV/VCR, radio, walk-in closet with a safe, and marble bathroom with double sinks and a tub.

On a warm-weather cruise, the lido provides protection from the sun and two popular Jacuzzis for cooling off after a steamy day ashore, plus an awkwardly sited outdoor pool. The spa offers an exercise room, two saunas, steam rooms, and a masseuse.

The Itinerary

On this cruise, the *Seabourn Spirit* embarks in **Bangkok** and sometimes in Hong Kong, reversing the order of ports. Sailing south into the Gulf of Thailand, the ship's first call is at the island of **Ko Kood,** followed by a full day at sea. Sailing out of the South

China Sea into the broad Mekong Delta, the ship follows the Saigon River channel to **Saigon,** now officially **Ho Chi Minh City.**

During the overnight stay docked next to the city center, visits include the former South Vietnamese presidential palace. Legacies from nineteenth-century French colonial days are Notre Dame Cathedral, the General Post Office, and the former City Hall. At the National Museum, a repository of Vietnamese and Chinese art, the Vietnamese water puppet show has unseen performers who maneuver colorful representations of fish, serpents, frogs, and humans.

A two-hour drive takes you to the Cu Chi Tunnels, a maze of underground passages and chambers started after World War II; from their well-concealed entrances, the Viet Cong sniped at the enemy and quickly retreated underground, where they could remain for weeks at a time. Several hundred feet of tunnels at three levels have been enlarged to allow tourists to explore, though it's not recommended for the claustrophobic.

Following two nights and a day at sea,

Address/Phone: Seabourn Cruise Line, 610 Blue Lagoon Drive, Suite 400, Miami, FL 33126; (305) 563–3000 or (800) 929–9391; fax: (305) 463–3010; www.seabourn.com

The Ship: *Seabourn Spirit* was built in 1989 and has a gross tonnage of 9,975, a length of 440 feet, and a draft of 17 feet.

Passengers: 204; mostly Americans, age fifty and up

Dress: Formal, informal, and casual nights

Officers/Crew: Norwegian officers; mostly European crew, plus some Filipinos

Cabins: 102; all outside suites, the majority identical except for location; six

with verandas. Thirty-six French balconies (window-type double doors set before a railing) have been added to some suites in the place of sealed windows.

Fare: $$$$$

What's included: Cruise, port charges, three nights in Bangkok, wine and drinks, tips

What's not included: Airfare, transfers, shore excursions

Highlights: A luxurious and enriching way to visit Vietnam

Other itineraries: In addition to this fourteen-day cruise tour between Bangkok and Hong Kong, Seabourn offers global itineraries, including *Seabourn Pride* in South America.

the ship calls at **Danang.** From here a three-hour scenic drive north along Route 1 crosses the Cloud Pass and descends to hug the low coastline into **Hue.** The city, located along the Perfume River, offers a glimpse at what formerly was a grand imperial palace virtually leveled during the 1968 Tet Offensive.

For the visit to **Hanoi,** this cruise calls at **Hongai,** but other cruises may use **Haiphong Harbor.** Regardless, the drive inland passes through a timeless landscape of rice paddies. Hanoi, a low-rise city built around Chinese-style lakes, presents a far slower pace than Saigon. A somber mausoleum, guarded by smartly uniformed soldiers, holds the embalmed body of Ho Chi Minh, the country's much-loved patriot who

died in 1969. There may be time to explore the Quarter of 36 Streets, each block specializing in some commodity such as paper goods, silver, silk, flowers, or hardware.

Entering **Halong Bay,** a national park made up of 3,000 towering limestone islets, you cruise through a fantastic natural wonder, similar to the conical peaks that dot the River Li at Guilin in China. After a final day at sea, the ship sails into **Hong Kong** harbor. Most visitors stay a few days to ride the incline railway for the view from Victoria Peak, or cross the island to seaside Repulse Bay and Aberdeen's typhoon shelter. On the **Kowloon** side there are visits to a Taoist temple, the jade and bird market, and Nathan and Canton Road shops.

VICTORIA CRUISES'
Victoria Star and *Victoria Queen*
Cruising the Yangtze

In 1994 Victoria Cruises, a Sino-American joint venture, brought international standards to Yangtze River travel when the 154-passenger *Victoria I* entered service, followed by *Victoria II, III, V,* and *VI,* and six additional ships. First-time visitors to China will want to visit several destinations such as Beijing, Shanghai, Suzhou, Xian, and Guilin, so Victoria Cruises concentrates on the Yangtze's most scenic portion, the 870 miles between Wuhan and Chongqing, a trip of four nights downstream and five nights upstream.

Victoria Cruises has introduced a new generation of larger and more sophisticated ships for more than 200 passengers with the addition of three vessels in 2003—the *Victoria Star,* the *Victoria Queen,* and the *Victoria Katarina*—and two more in 2004—

the *Victoria Jenna* and the *Victoria Emperor.* In addition, the *Victoria Prince,* which recently joined the fleet, got rebuilt in 2003 to handle additional passenger capacity in line with the others. The fleet will then number thirteen vessels.

The *Victoria Katarina,* completed in 2004 and the company's largest vessel, has 124 cabins (116 standard rooms and 8 suites to take up to 250 passengers). All cabins are roomy and have bathtubs, balconies, and closed-circuit films. The ships have atriums with chandeliers and walls of gleaming woods; overall decor features European influences and Asian accents.

The single-seating Dynasty Dining Room serves American breakfasts and lunch buffet style and serves dinner banquet style with both Western and Chinese fare. The Yangtze Club, with a small and the only smoking section on the ships, hosts cultural presentations, fashion shows, and traditional Chinese music. Additionally, Tai-chi, calligraphy, Chinese language, and kite flying lessons are offered. Additional amenities and services are a beauty salon, traditional massage, facials and acupuncture, fitness room, library, and gift shop. Outdoor space is generous for viewing the sometimes outstanding scenery.

The Itinerary

The **Yangtze** is south China's principal highway, and tugs, barges, cargo ships, ferries, passenger steamers, and cruise boats maneuver along the constantly shifting channel. This cruise shows the many aspects of this complex country and includes a visit to the world's largest dam.

At the smoky industrial town of **Yichang,** the boat passes through the Gezhouba Dam, China's largest, rising 65 feet in a single lock. This dam is nothing compared to the 600-foot-high **Three Gorges Dam** just upriver at **Sandouping,** which is beginning to flood many historical sites. If everything goes as planned, by 2009 a reservoir will stretch back 370 miles, submerging 1,500 towns and villages and 72,000 acres of agricultural land, forcing the resettlement of 1.3 million people. The project is expected to supply 15 percent of China's electricity, control flooding, facilitate navigation by eliminating rapids, and boost national pride.

Address/Phone: Victoria Cruises, 57-08 Thirty-ninth Avenue, Woodside, NY 11377; (800) 348–8084 or (212) 818–1680; fax: (212) 818–9889; e-mail: contact@victoriacruises.com; www.victoriacruises.com

The Ships: *Victoria Star* and *Victoria Queen,* rebuilt in 2003, are 3,424 gross tons, 289 feet in length, and have drafts of 8.5 feet. The other vessels are similar in size and standards.

Passengers: 210; age range is forty and up, Americans mostly on China tours; also many Chinese Americans, Chinese from all over Asia, and some Europeans

Dress: Casual

Officers/Crew: All Chinese, plus American cruise and enrichment staff

Cabins: 105 cabins; all outside with balconies, 93 standard rooms, 6 junior suites, 4 deluxe suites, and 2 Shangri-la suites

Fare: $$

What's included: For independent travelers (those not part of a tour), the cruise fare includes port charges and tea, coffee, and soft drinks with meals

What's not included: Airfare, tips, drinks not served at meals, and shore excursions

Highlights: The Three Gorges, plus a terrific insight into rural and industrial China

Other itineraries: In addition to the above cruise between Wuhan and Chongqing, which is offered between March and December, the company operates longer Yangtze River trips between Nanjing and Chongqing, nine days up and eight days downstream. The best travel months are May and June and September and October; July and August are unpleasantly hot and humid; fog descends on the river in winter. Several of the many tour operators that include the Yangtze in their programs are General Tours/TBI tours, (800) 223–0266; Maupintour, (800) 255–4266; Travcoa, (800) 992–2003; and Uniworld, (800) 733–7820.

During the stop at **Wushan,** make your way up a lively main street of shops and food stalls to high ground overlooking the junction of the Yangtze and **Daning** Rivers. At the far end of town, you board longboats that sputter up through the Daning River rapids into the **Three Little Gorges,** and when the strong currents threaten to stop progress, two men pole mightily to maintain headway.

The main event, the passage through the **Three Gorges,** extends over two days. The 47-mile **Xiling Gorge** at one time was considered the most dangerous of all. Numerous steamers came to grief in the rock-strewn rapids before a safe channel was blasted through in the 1950s. A temple, built 1,500 years ago, is silhouetted against the sky. The 35-mile **Wu Gorge**'s sheer cliffs rise to green-clad limestone peaks often enshrouded in swirling mists, and the highest, Goddess Peak, resembles a woman kneeling in front of a pillar. **Qutang Gorge** is dramatically flanked by 4,000-foot mountains that squeeze the river into a narrow canyon, inhibiting two-way traffic.

Beyond the attractive walled city of **Fengjie,** where stone steps lead up from the river landings to Ming Dynasty gates, hundreds of porters load coal into baskets and with rapid steps file down to ships at the water's edge. At **Fengdu,** known as the City of Ghosts, a temple complex, which dates back to the Han Dynasty (206 B.C. to A.D. 220), has undergone extensive reconstruction. Disembarking at **Chongqing,** passengers will see that the city is usually enveloped in fog, a natural phenomenon exacerbated by industrial pollution.

POLAR REGIONS

CLIPPER CRUISE LINE'S
Clipper Adventurer
Cruising the White Continent

 St. Louis–based Clipper Cruise Line, in business since 1983, operates four small ships, one of which is the 122-passenger *Clipper Adventurer*, introduced in 1988. Rebuilt from the Russian-flag *Alla Tarasova,* the ship operates in the style of a seagoing club and is a graceful, stabilized beauty within and without.

The public rooms, paneled with mahogany-wood grain, include a forward lounge and bar, seating all passengers for talks, films, and light breakfast and lunch buffets. The Clipper Club, a second bar with card tables and settees, leads aft to an open-seating restaurant with wraparound windows. The menus feature grilled salmon, sea bass, roasted duckling, prime ribs, tasty wild mushroom and roasted pepper soups, fresh salads, and freshly baked cakes and pies. The library, one deck above, is a warm and quiet retreat for readers, puzzle addicts, and board-game players. With an open-bridge policy, the ship provides passengers with another popular social center, and it's just a few steps down to the forward observation deck.

The all outside cabins (portholes or windows) fall into seven categories and have parallel or L-shaped twin beds, good closet space, and bathrooms with showers. Promenade Deck cabins look through two sets of glass to the sea.

The Itinerary

Following two days experiencing the cafe, restaurant, and street life of **Buenos Aires,** embarkation takes place at the southern Argentinean port of **Ushuaia.** Orientation talks are scheduled during the two nights and a day en route to the **Falklands,** the British islands invaded by Argentina in 1982.

The first wet Zodiac landing visits a cliff-side rookery of nesting rockhopper penguins, black-browed albatross, and blue-eyed cormorants. Seated on a nearby rock, I watched a well-ordered line of 2-foot-high penguins literally hop their way up the steep path from the beach, bellies full of fish and krill (shrimplike crustacean) for regurgitating into the mouths of their fluffy chicks. A second landing provided a gentle 3-mile walk through an active hillside colony of burrowing Magellanic penguins, who pop up to have a look as we pass. **Port Stanley,** the island capital, is a sleepy bit of old England transferred to the South Atlantic. Here you can visit with the world's most southerly Anglican cathedral and an eccentric museum packed with historic and natural-history exhibits overseen by a delightful curator.

During the forty-eight-hour crossing of the **Drake Passage,** which can be extremely rough, the naturalists might spot Wilson's storm petrels, Antarctic terns, and the huge wandering albatross, which boasts a wingspan of up to 9 feet. Landings on the Antarctic Peninsula may vary from cruise to cruise because of high winds and weather, but you see Adélie penguins in several locations and, on **Half Moon Island,** colonies of chinstrap penguins, Weddell seals, and fur seals. Stay ashore as long as you can to enjoy their antics. The Antarctic summer comes with almost twenty-four hours of daylight and temperatures that may rise into the 50s.

Cruising into the drowned caldera of **Deception Island,** the *Clipper Adventurer* drops anchor for a walk among the eerie ruins of a whaling station and British research base, quickly abandoned just prior to a volcanic eruption in 1969. Steam and the smell of sulfur percolate through the black sand. Continuing south, towering icebergs with fantastic shapes and shades of blue and green often generate their own strong winds even when it otherwise seems calm. Other landings add the sight and

smell of molting young elephant seals, weighing up to 4,000 pounds, a gentoo penguin rookery, and a Russian research station. Northbound, hold on for a second crossing of the **Drake Passage,** understandably feared by the legendary Cape Horners battling monstrous seas for days on end, until the ship reaches lee of **Tierra del Fuego,** finally docking at **Ushuaia.**

Address/Phone: Clipper Cruise Line, 11969 Westline Industrial Drive, St. Louis, MO 63146; reservations: (800) 325–0010; brochures: (800) 282–7245; fax: (314) 727–6576; e-mail: clipper@clippercruise.com; www.clippercruise.com

The Ship: *Clipper Adventurer,* built in 1975 as the Russian-flag *Alla Tarasova* and rebuilt in 1998, has a gross tonnage of 4,575, a length of 330 feet, and a draft of 16 feet.

Passengers: 122; age fifty and up, nearly all American

Dress: Casual at all times

Officers/Crew: Scandinavian; Filipino officers; American bar staff; Filipino wait staff, deckhands, and cabin stewardesses

Cabins: 61; all outside, average size

Fare: $$$$

What's included: Cruise, port charges, all shore excursions, connecting flights between Miami and the ship, hotel nights in Buenos Aires and Santiago

What's not included: Airfare between home and Miami, drinks, tips

Highlights: Incredible beauty of Antarctica, icebergs, many types of penguins, remote research stations, British colony of the Falklands, excellent enrichment program

Other itineraries: In addition to this fifteen-day Antarctica and the Falklands winter cruise itinerary, several longer cruises also including South Georgia, the *Clipper Adventurer* offers late spring and summer trips in the Mediterranean, Northern Europe, Iceland, Greenland, and Eastern Canada; and in fall south along the U.S. East Coast to South America and the Amazon. The *Yorktown Clipper* cruises California's rivers, and the *Nantucket Clipper* cruises the East Coast.

LINDBLAD EXPEDITIONS'
Endeavour
Antarctica, Falklands, and South Georgia

 Originally built for the North Sea fishing industry, the *Endeavour* is an extremely well-built and well-maintained expedition ship that was very recently refitted. The Scandinavian officers and Filipino crew provide a disciplined yet happy ship, and they mix well with the older, well-traveled, and mostly American passengers. The ship has an open-bridge policy, a very popular feature. With a hull hardened for ice and a deep 21-foot draft, she can take the pounding seas of the South Atlantic and upon occasion has seen the worst weather that nature can produce.

On the Bridge Deck, a small, large-windowed library offers comfortable seating and lots of books on history, ecology, geography, and fauna and flora, plus twenty-four-hour coffee- and tea-making facilities. Aft is a cluster that includes a small gym with treadmills, bikes, a sauna, and an e-mail station. The Veranda Deck below houses the spacious lounge and bar where evening recaps take place, plus the lecture program—up to three on a sea day—that often includes slides and videos screened on TV monitors.

One naturalist is a diver who will show footage taken that same day of undersea marine life such as shrimp, octopus, dolphins, and acrobatic seals. A professionally produced ninety-minute trip video, with music and commentary, is available for purchase at the end of the cruise.

Forward on the Upper Deck, the restaurant has an open-seating policy, with tables for two to eight, buffet-style meals for breakfast and lunch, and table service from a menu for dinner. The food gets good

marks for variety, preparation, and presentation.

The cabins are comfortable, all outside with windows or portholes, and most have beds placed athwartships to minimize rolling. The cabin radio airs announcements and music, and the closet and drawer space is adequate for a casual cruise. There is a lock drawer. As on Lindblad's other ships, there are no cabin keys. Viewing is excellent from the forward observation deck, the bow, the bridge wings, and the port and starboard sides and aft. Some of the deck space is sheltered.

The Itinerary

This twenty-two-day cruise-tour begins in **Santiago,** Chile, with a night's hotel stay and sight-seeing, then a flight south to **Ushuaia** for boarding the ship. Depending on the weather, the *Endeavour* may or may not stop at Cape Horn before making the two-day **Drake Passage** to the **Antarctic Peninsula.**

The ship first sails into **Deception Island**'s water-filled extinct volcano, with whaling station ruins to explore. At **Paradise Island,** two-person kayaks provide some close-up penguin and iceberg inspections. **Palmer Station** is a U.S. research center that welcomes only a very few ships each year, and the scientists offer a tour to show how the base operates and to give you a look at the marine life under study in tanks. The ship also visits **Port Lockroy,** a landlocked harbor and location for a British station, for a tour and to pick up mail.

In the **Weddell Sea,** the *Endeavour* may experience pack ice, with slabs large enough to climb over, while the captain keeps watch to see that the ship does not get caught should the ice shift with a change of wind direction.

Ernest Shackleton and his crew made their longest stay on **Elephant Island** before he and a handful of men set out in a very small boat for **South Georgia.** The *Endeavour* will make up to eleven landings here at such places as **King Haakon Bay** on the west coast, where Shackleton landed, and **Peggotty Camp,** where he began his march across island to rescue his stranded crew. At **St. Andrews Bay,** on the lee side of the island, passengers may have a beach reception committee of literally thousands of king penguins, plus a herd of elephant seals that deserve a wide berth.

Grytviken is an abandoned whaling station, and the naturalists offer a 2-mile hike over the mountain. The settlement has a museum of South Georgia island history, remnants of the whaling activities, and the cemetery where Shackleton is buried.

Between here and the Falklands, Shag Rocks, cone-shaped protrusions rising from the sea, swarm with bird life, and here on one cruise eight right whales were sighted. On the Falklands, Port Stanley is a charming British town deep in the South Atlantic, while nearby Carcass Island offers a scenic 2.5-mile trek, at the end of which a farming family serves afternoon tea.

This is the ultimate in a South Atlantic cruise, and the passengers who come aboard are in for the best that Lindblad has to offer—the fine ship, its personnel and the expedition leader, and naturalists who share their knowledge and enthusiasm at informal presentations, meals, in Zodiacs, and ashore.

Address/Phone: Lindblad Expeditions, 720 Fifth Avenue, Sixth Floor, New York, NY 10019; (212) 765–7740 or (800) 397–3348; fax: (212) 265–3370; e-mail: explore@expeditions.com; www.expeditions.com

The Ship: *Endeavour* was originally built in 1966 for the fishing industry. It was rebuilt as a cruise ship and renamed *North Star* and *Caledonian Star* before taking on the current name. The gross tonnage is 3,132, the length is 295 feet, and the draft is 21 feet.

Passengers: 113, mostly Americans, age fifty-five and up

Dress: Casual

Officers/Crew: Scandinavian officers; Filipino crew

Cabins: 61; all outside, twin beds, no verandas

Fare: $$$$

What's included: Cruise, port charges, airfare between Santiago and the ship, shore excursions

What's not included: Airfare between home and Santiago, tips, drinks

Highlights: In-depth tour of Antarctica, the Falklands, and South Georgia; Shackleton connections, naturalist staff, ambience on board

Other itineraries: Apart from this twenty-two-day cruise to Antarctica, the Falklands, and South Georgia, the *Endeavour* also makes twelve-day cruises to Antartica, sails along the South America coast, and in Northern Europe and the Mediterranean. The *Polaris* cruises within the Galápagos, and the *Sea Lion* and *Sea Bird* cruise to Alaska, along the Columbia and Snake Rivers, along California rivers, and in the Sea of Cortez.

CIRCUMNAVIGATIONS

CUNARD LINE'S
Queen Elizabeth 2
Around the World in 111 Days

 Cunard initiated annual world cruises in the 1920s, and the *QE2* has carried on the grand tradition for more than two decades. Her speed, up to 28.5 knots, means she can include more ports and stay longer than any other ship. Designed as an ocean liner, she takes the seas as well as any ship afloat, an important consideration when facing every season and type of weather.

A world cruise is a highly social experience, and the *QE2* offers so many venues for a good time. Looking to join friends for a drink before lunch or dinner? Well, there are no fewer than ten watering holes from which to choose. My favorite is the Chart Room, a nicely divided room where you can choose between a seat along the enclosed promenade to people watch or, more privately, away from the foot traffic. Either way, a harpist or a pianist using the *Queen Mary*'s old grand piano is there to add to the atmosphere. For something more informal the Golden Lion pub stocks more types of British, European, and North American beers than most people know exist.

Formal afternoon tea, including those crustless sandwiches and pastries, is served in the elegant Queens Room, which later is transformed into a proper ballroom for dancing to a full orchestra. Those old photographs showing couples bundled in steamer rugs sipping bouillon and afternoon tea come to life high up on the Sun Deck, in the shadow of the tall funnel that sports the famous Cunard Red. The library is the most elaborate for any ship, with two professional librarians in charge of the reading room and a library shop that sells shipping books, videos, postcards, and posters.

Cunard Line represents history at sea, 165 years of it. Upon boarding, a circular mural in the Midships Lobby evokes that sense of embarking and being at sea. Artists Stephen Card and Hanley Crossley have painted the Cunard fleet in all sorts of settings on "G" Stairway, and a wonderfully cluttered case of memorabilia displays menus, brochures, souvenir spoons, and ashtrays. Passengers enjoy studying the montage of unlabeled celebrity photos and guessing who's who with others.

The *QE2* has a proper big-screen movie theater with a cozy balcony, a grand space that also hosts lectures by a well-known author, a financial analyst, or an astute Washington correspondent. On Sunday morning the captain leads an interdenominational service. For active passengers the *QE2* Spa is as good as any afloat, and an indoor pool invites you to continue your exercise if the weather is not conducive to taking an open-air dip. You can hit a golf ball, play Ping-Pong, jog into head winds, and be pushed by tail winds on the Boat Deck.

Cabins come in every imaginable configuration, but if you want the most evocative accommodations afloat, choose one of the wood-paneled rooms on One Deck, which have a large elliptical window, satin walls, a walk-in closet, and a corner in which to place your standing steamer trunk. Higher up are balcony suites reached by a private entrance, and single passengers will find a selection of 105 dedicated inside and outside single cabins.

Your cabin choice determines your restaurant. Starting at the top of the ship, the two-level Queens Grill allows ordering off the menu, as do the more intimate side-facing Britannia and Princess Grills. An extra-high ceiling is a feature of the mahogany-paneled Caronia Restaurant, whose entrance is flanked by portraits of the royal family and a huge model of the 1907 Cunard speedster *Mauretania*. That great name is also the name of the ship's fifth restaurant, but the dining options do not stop there. The Lido Restaurant serves all three meals, and the Pavilion, one deck down, satisfies diners who want to stay by the pool and pair of whirlpools.

The Itinerary

Every year the itinerary changes, but usually the *QE2* sails from New York and Fort Lauderdale then via Panama and westward around the world, with the main variation being the return to Southampton and New York via South Africa or the Suez Canal. In 2004 the world cruise begins in **New York** on January 5, and the complete global voyage lasts an ambitious 111 days.

The route's outline sees the ship pausing to embark at **Fort Lauderdale,** then transiting the **Panama Canal,** calling at two Mexican ports en route to **Los Angeles,** then into the **South Pacific** via **Honolulu** to four ports in **New Zealand** and four in **Australia,** with overnights in **Melbourne** and **Sydney.** Sailing northward along the Barrier Reef, the ship makes a couple of Pacific island calls en route to **Japan,** then turns south to **Taiwan** and **Hong Kong,** where the ship ties up for three days.

Southeast Asia has the ship calling in **Thailand** and **Singapore,** then west across the **Indian Ocean** to **Colombo** and two days docked at **Mumbai (Bombay).** Aiming southwest to the **Seychelles** and **Mauritius,** the ship calls in at **Durban, Cape Town,** and **Walvis Bay** in Southern Africa, then lots of sea time en route to **Las Palmas, Lisbon,** and to **Southampton** and a transatlantic crossing to New York.

Address/Phone: Cunard Line, 6100 Blue Lagoon Drive, Suite 400, Miami, FL 33126; (800) 7–CUNARD; fax: (305) 463–3010; www.cunardline.com

The Ship: *Queen Elizabeth 2* was built in 1969, has a gross tonnage of 70,327, a length of 963 feet, and a deep draft of 33 feet.

Passengers: 1,740; American, British, and Europeans, age fifty and up

Dress: Formal attire on many nights at sea, also theme, semiformal, and casual nights

Officers/Crew: British officers; international staff

Cabins: 925, sold in twenty-one wide-ranging categories; 689 outside, 150 single, and 30 with verandas. Cabin determines restaurant allocation.

Fare: $$$$

What's included: For full world-cruise passengers—first-class airfare, port charges, one precruise hotel night

What's not included: Shore excursions, drinks, tips

Highlights: The ultimate ocean voyage on the world's best-known ship

Other itineraries: In addition to the world cruise, which operates between early January to just after the middle of April, the *QE2* makes an occasional transatlantic crossing and is otherwise based in Southampton, cruising to the British Isles, Northern Europe, Iberia, Mediterranean, and the Caribbean.

HOLLAND AMERICA LINE'S
Prinsendam
Circumnavigating the Globe

 The *Prinsendam,* Holland America's new world cruiser, has a past dating back to 1988, when she entered service for the Royal Viking Line as the *Royal Viking Sun*. The ship was designed to bring back roominess and space, which had been lost when the original early-1970s 22,000-ton Royal Viking trio had midsections inserted and tonnage increased to 28,500 and passenger capacity got upped to 750. The *Royal Viking Sun* carried 758 passengers within a ship of 37,845 gross tons. When Royal Viking was disbanded, the *Royal Viking Sun* became the *Seabourn Sun* for Cunard's Seabourn division, an awkward fit as she was so much larger than the original Seabourn trio and the Sea Goddess pair. Then in May 2002 she was transferred to Holland America and, after a makeover, reemerged as the *Prinsendam* to cruise Alaska and make a global voyage, taking over the latter role from the *Amsterdam* and *Rotterdam*.

With a roomy passenger space ratio of 47.6, she has taken on many familiar Holland America Line features, yet with half the passenger capacity of the rest of the fleet, she has a clubby atmosphere and is distinctive and well suited to take on ambitious worldwide itineraries. The officers are European, and the crew includes some Dutch but mostly Indonesians and Filipinos.

Approaching the ship, she sports a blue hull and once aboard, a curved double staircase rises through the five-deck atrium, decorated with handsome glass bas reliefs, tubular glass sculpture and Dutch maritime art. Promenade Deck is Grand Central, and from the atrium public rooms, renamed to coincide with the HAL fleet, range fore and aft.

Forward, the Queens Lounge, the ship's 424-seat show room, mounts five new productions each cruise on a new stage. Walking aft past the Erasmus Library, furnished with four leather chairs, the angled corridor becomes a shopping arcade leading to the 100-seat Wajang Theater, used to screen films and host lectures. The clubby Java Bar and Cafe connects to the Oak Room, a largely original smoking lounge with electric fireplace, and to the moderately small casino, offering roulette, poker games, blackjack, dice, and slot machines. On the starboard side, the former Compass Rose has been freshly transformed into the Explorer's Lounge, a walk-through piano bar furnished with tan leather chairs, dark veneer paneling, and a patterned wine-red carpet. The artwork is a traditional-style Dutch maritime painting on aluminum and a set of drawings touting early Dutch exploration.

Lower Promenade features a continuous wraparound walking deck where four laps equal a mile and the width permits easy passing, but not a line of lounge-style deck chairs as with the rest of the fleet. Within are the restaurants, and it is here that there are significant changes.

The main restaurant aboard the ship as built could handle all passengers at one seating, but to match the rest of the fleet, it has been downsized for two seatings. Most passengers will want to secure a table in the after big-window section rather than the starboard side passage. Tables are set with Rosenthal china and Holland America–embossed silverware, and for dinner the chairs are covered with a white drapery, giving the otherwise handsome room a sterile look.

The former midships section of the

restaurant has been converted into Holland America's trademark Ocean Bar, the ship's social center. The fore-aft varnished wood deck passage runs through the lower lounge section parallel to the promenade deck windows and to the bar, dance floor and bandstand recessed on the raised interior portion.

The pièce de résistance is this ship's Pinnacle Grill, formerly the Odyssey Restaurant, an alternative dining venue offering a Pacific Northwest menu at an extra charge. It looks out onto the Lower Promenade, and it offers just forty-eight seats in a lovely paneled setting with Murano glass wall scones set against a wine red and pale yellow fabric, the rich colors also matching the carpet. Suite passengers get the first shot at reservations.

Moving to an altogether different part of the ship, the Crow's Nest high up on Sports Deck is a lovely blue, green, and aquamarine observation lounge, bar, and piano bar. Its scale is much more intimate and better arranged for viewing than the vast three-sectioned Crow's Nests on the bigger ships.

The outdoor spaces are many, including cozy fore and aft sections on several decks and the standard lido-style pool deck. This ship does not have a Magrodome, and the oversized whirlpool is almost as large as the small swimming pool. A larger pool is tucked aft behind the spa, gym, and beauty salon complex. The lido restaurant is designed with double lines, plus a terrace grill, ice-cream bar and sit-up bar, and a most attractive awning-covered seating area aft. Other spaces are an eleven-station Internet Cafe, meeting and card rooms, art gallery, practice tennis, volleyball/basketball court, and golf driving range.

There are 398 cabins in seven categories, including just twenty-five insides and 145 with private verandas. A new block of ten poorly designed balcony cabins are in a cluster aft in a private section of promenade deck. Eight have balconies that those on the deck above can look down into, and two have smoked glass enclosures jutting out onto the aft deck. The Midnight Sun Lounge was sadly sacrificed to up the passenger capacity. The nineteen suites on Sports and Lido Decks have use of the Nep-

---

Address/Phone: Holland America Line, 300 Elliott Avenue West, Seattle, WA 98119; (800) 426–0327; fax: (206) 281–7110; www.hollandamerica.com

The Ship: *Prinsendam* was completed in 1988, originally sailing as the *Royal Viking Sun*, the *Seabourn Sun*. She now measures 37,845 gross tons, has a length of 674 feet and a draft of 23.6 feet.

Passengers: 794, mostly Americans, fifty-five and up on the World Cruise

Dress: Formal, informal, and casual nights

Officers/Crew: Officers are Dutch and European, and the crew is Indonesian and Filipino

Cabins: 396, of which 368 are outside and 145 have balconies

Fare: $$$

What's included: Cruise fare only, and tips included but most will add to these

What's not included: Airfare, port charges, drinks, shore excursions, additional tipping

Highlights: Sailing aboard a ship built for world cruising

Other itineraries: Besides this world cruise that operates between January and April, the *Prinsendam* operates to Alaska in the summer, and the combined Holland America fleet covers North and South America and Europe plus some long circle Pacific cruises.

tune Lounge with veranda for reading, snacks, and concierge services. All cabins have telephones with computerized wake-up service, multichannel music system, and closed circuit television. All but the insides have full tub baths.

Holland America's newly acquired *Prinsendam* shows how an outclassed dowager can be transferred into a clubby world cruiser.

The Itinerary

The world cruise, an annual staple for Holland America Line for more than forty years, adjusts its itinerary every year to freshen up the route and respond to world hot spots, so what follows is simply an example of the 2004 circumnavigation. The official world cruise begins in **Los Angeles** on January 20 and sails westward to end in **Fort Lauderdale** or **New York,** the latter on Day 108. However, passengers may board in Fort Lauderdale on January 4 for the trans-canal portion to Los Angeles, making a 121-day global voyage. As with all world cruises, three- to five-week segments are also sold.

The trans-Pacific portion sails via **Honolulu,** then south to **New Zealand** and **Australia,** where the ship heads along the east coast to **Darwin.** In **Indonesia,** the home of many crewmembers, there are calls at **Komodo Island** for the famous dragons, then **Bali** and **Sandakan** for orangutans. **Manila** will delight the Filipino crew, followed by **Hong Kong, Vietnam**'s island-studded **Halong Bay,** then **Singapore, Bangkok, Malaysian** ports, and **Myanmar (Burma).** Westward across the **Indian Ocean,** calls are made at **Cochin, Mumbai (Bombay),** and **Muscat** in the Persian Gulf, then into the Red Sea for the **Suez Canal, Egypt,** and four Mediterranean ports, then **Funchal (Madeira)** and transatlantic to Fort Lauderdale and New York.

P&O CRUISES'
Aurora
Sailing around the World: British Style

The official name of the line is a mouthful—The Peninsular and Oriental Steam Navigation Company—but people in the know simply say "P&O." The company dates back to 1837, three years before Samuel Cunard launched his transatlantic mail and passenger service. P&O expanded with the British Empire, east via Suez to India, to colonies in Asia, Australia, and New Zealand. London-based P&O is now owned by Carnival Corporation.

The 76,152-ton *Aurora* entered service in 2000, maintaining the tradition of offering a wide range of public rooms (seven-teen) to satisfy all tastes and lifestyles. If your preference is for after-dinner coffee and a liqueur in genteel surroundings, the living-room atmosphere of Anderson's, named after one of P&O's founding fathers, will suit. Evening classical concerts take place in the Playhouse, which also serves as the cinema, while extravaganzas debut in the Curzon Theatre and nightclub acts come alive in Carmen's. Monte Carlo is the casino, small by American standards, and Masquerade is the disco. For a pint of ale, Champions has a sporting theme, and for readers and dozers, the library has comfortable armchairs, some equipped with CD players, and lots of books. Vanderbilt's is one of the largest card rooms at sea, and bridge instruction, dance classes, and special-interest lectures are always offered.

My favorite room has always been P&O's Crows Nest, and on the *Aurora,* it is a superb, spacious observation bar lounge with a trio playing and singing before and after dinner. The centerpiece is a lighted builders' model of the *Strathnaver,* the first of P&O's 1930s White Sisters, built for the long run to Australia. P&O owns an outstanding art collection, and oil paintings, watercolors, needlepoint tapestries, and historic documents are to be found throughout the ship.

British food has its own reputation, but it has come a long way in the last decade, and the *Aurora's* menus and presentation are no exception. The great British breakfast has never been criticized except for offering too much to eat so early in the day. Don't count on lots of pasta dishes, as on Princess ships, or even dinner salads, as the British eat rabbit food at lunch. The cream soups are excellent, and so is the roast beef and lamb, as one might expect. Desserts are delicious, and the daily lunchtime curry is a great favorite. On formal nights nearly every British male dons a dinner jacket, and the women appear in all manner of ball gowns. Officers are British and host tables at dinner, whereas the well-trained service staff is mostly Indian, many from Goa. Besides two main restaurants, breakfast and lunch are also available in the Conservatory, which has both indoor and outdoor seating.

With the company's long history of taking families to jobs and new lives overseas, the children's facilities are outstanding. An entire area, devoted to various age levels, includes a large indoor and outdoor playroom, a games arcade, a cinema, a paddle pool, a swimming pool, a Jacuzzi, and even a night nursery for late-night parents.

A wide range of cabin types features 114 dedicated single cabins—a rarity in the modern cruise industry but a P&O tradition—that are available on six passenger decks. For example, a B-category double has a balcony, a sitting area, lots of storage space, a generous-size bathroom with tub,

Address/Phone: P&O Cruises, Richmond House, Terminus Terrace, Southampton SO14 3PN England; (011) 44 845 555 333; www.pocruises.com

The Ship: *Aurora* was built in 2000, has a gross tonnage of 76,152, a length of 885.8 feet, and a draft of 25.9 feet.

Passengers: 1,868; all ages, but older on longer cruises; a mix of British, Australians, Americans, and some Europeans

Dress: Formal and informal nights onboard; casual in port

Officers/Crew: British officers; mostly Indian hotel staff; Pakistani deck and engine crew

Cabins: 934, with a wide range of configurations; 406 verandas

Fare: $$$

What's included: Cruise only unless part of a package

What's not included: Airfare, port charges, shore excursions, drinks, and tips

Highlights: Very British atmosphere, lots of activities, and a beautifully operated ship

Other itineraries: In addition to the annual world cruise, the *Aurora* and the similar *Oriana* offer nonrepeating cruises of from nine days to three weeks from Southampton, England, to northern European ports, the Atlantic islands, the Mediterranean, and to the Caribbean and South America. P&O operates the *Adonia,* an adults-only ship, and the *Oceana* to cover the seven seas mainly from Southampton.

plus amenities such as TV and refrigerator. Economical four-berth cabins are booked by families.

The *Aurora* offers acres of open-deck space plus golf, cricket, and football (read soccer) nets, deck tennis, deck quoits, shuffleboard, and two adult pools and Jacuzzis. On every voyage the British officers take on the passengers at a cricket match. The wide promenade offers deck chairs, with lifeboats above giving shade and a view of a steady stream of humanity doing counterclockwise constitutionals before and after breakfast.

The Itinerary

Round-the-world cruises alter itineraries every year to keep loyalists happy, and on this ship, ports often take second place to life onboard. Every cruise carries a port lecturer, an entertaining type with a British sense of humor. Some passengers take the entire voyage, three months plus, although most book segments of a couple of weeks to a month or more.

In 2004 the *Aurora* leaves **Southampton** on January 11 to sail southwest across the Atlantic with increasingly warm temperatures and three island calls en route to the **Panama Canal** and the blue Pacific. Northbound now, the ship calls in at **Acapulco** and **San Francisco,** then sails southwest across the Pacific via **Honolulu** to **New Zealand** and **Australian** ports. There is usually a large turnover of passengers at **Sydney,** as many still use the ship to sail between the UK and Australia.

The route skirts the Great Barrier Reef, pauses at **Darwin,** then aims for **Manila, Hong Kong, Bangkok,** and **Singapore** before a westward track to **Mumbai (Bombay),** and **Safaga** for **Egypt's Nile Valley.** Passing through **Suez,** the last two ports are **Piraeus (Athens)** and **Lisbon** before arriving back at Southampton on April 1.

PETER DEILMANN'S
Deutschland
A National Flagship in the European Tradition

 The name of this handsome German flagship, *Deutschland,* simply means Germany. Unlike the multinational crews found aboard most ships today, the *Deutschland's* 260-member crew, and most of the passengers, are largely from the German-speaking countries of Germany, Austria, and Switzerland. The staff's standard of speaking English is as good or even better than on many internationally crewed ships catering to North American passengers.

Within, the *Deutschland* is, without qualification, absolutely beautiful, extremely well designed, and has a public-room layout that suits many different occasions and moods. The decor is richly Edwardian, with art nouveau and art deco flourishes. Public rooms are varied and spacious with never a feeling of crowding, and they run the gamut from light and airy with large windows to one that opens onto side galleries to another that's cozy and enclosed for late-night conversation.

The materials are high quality and carry off the effect better than I have seen on any ship—real marble and faux marble; real wood, wood veneers, and faux burled paneling; some real brass that tarnishes and needs constant polishing and some metal that is brass in color; molding and pilasters that appear to be plaster; excellent Tiffany-style stained glass especially in the ceilings; and very tasteful furnishings.

For quiet reading, playing games, and having afternoon tea, the Lido Terrace, an observation lounge, provides a wonderful light-filled atmosphere with views outside to the surrounding open decks. The furnishings are comfortable white and tan wicker chairs with green and gold patterned cushions.

For a drink before meals, with music provided by a trio, the Lili Marleen Salon, dedicated to Marlene Dietrich, is a cozy space with polished medium-dark paneling, a beamed ceiling with plaster decoration, opaque cut-glass globes, and additional indirect lighting from stately floor lamps. Zum Alten Fritz replicates a dark paneled taverna with its etched glass mirrors and button leather curved banquettes. It offers live music, hot snacks such as bratwurst (frankfurters) and weiss wurst (white veal sausage), and beer by the stein.

The deck space is so good and varied that one needs a very long voyage to enjoy all the outdoor, covered, and enclosed venues furnished with high-quality varnished wooden deck chairs and royal blue cushions. Happily, the ship offers extended cruises.

Dining takes place in a two-sitting main restaurant, the Berlin, in the more private Vierjahreszeiten (Four Seasons) with reservations but no extra charge, and the Lido Gourmet, a buffet offering indoor and outdoor seating, The menus are continental with German specialties, and the preparation is good to excellent.

Some of the courses that we enjoyed were air-dried beef with fresh horseradish; mild French goat cheese with grape seed oil and a baguette; cream of asparagus with baby shrimps; black noodles with lobster and scallops; grilled lemon sole with lime sauce; veal loin with morels and dates in a cream sauce; and white chocolate mousse with basil.

The lunchtime buffets offer hot and cold meats, a fair variety of salad fixings, lots of cheeses, and excellent desserts. From the grill, one could order freshly prepared shrimp, lamb chops, rib eye steaks, and chicken. At breakfast, the menu caters to European and American tastes. The service in the main dining room is relaxed and professional, and in the Vierjahreszeiten, the dinner sessions are scheduled for up to three hours.

The Kaisersaal is an extraordinarily opu-

Address/Phone: Peter Deilmann Cruises, 1800 Diagnoal Road, Suite 170, Alexandria, VA 22314; (703) 549–1741 or (800) 348–8287; fax: (703) 549–7924; www.deilmann-cruises.com

The Ship: *Deutschland* was completed in 1998. It has a gross tonnage of 22,400, a length of 574 feet, and a draft of 18.4 feet.

Passengers: 513, age forty-five and up; German-speaking, plus some Americans on some cruises (inquire when booking)

Dress: Formal, informal, and casual nights

Officers/Crew: German officers; largely German-speaking crew

Cabins: 286, with 224 outside; 17 outside and 50 inside singles

Fare: $$$

What's included: Cruise fare and port charges

What's not included: Airfare, shore excursions, tips, and drinks

Highlights: Splendid art nouveau and Edwardian decor; German-speaking European atmosphere

Other itineraries: The *Deutschland* travels all over the world. Deilmann riverboats cruise European waterways.

lent cabaret lounge furnished in a 1920s bordello style, with comfortable chairs, small table lamps, and a mezzanine with tables for two set next to the railing. Of the 286 cabins, 224 are outside and seventeen outside are singles, and all have white wood-tone paneling, handsomely framed reproduction oil paintings, decent closets, storage, and counter space, color TVs, radios, safes, and stocked refrigerators with charges for their use. Most cabins are moderately sized with less attention paid to elaborate decorative details than in the public rooms.

The prevalence of smoking is as you would find in any European setting. Any American who likes European travel or more specifically travel to Germany will find this ship a most appealing and certainly a most distinctive experience.

The Itinerary

The *Deutschland* explores most of the world's seas, making lingering cruises in the Mediterranean and North Europe in spring and early summer and for a shorter period in the Caribbean in winter. In early 2004 the ship passes through the **Panama Canal,** calling in **California** en route to **Hawaii,**

then across the Pacific southwest to **New Zealand** and **Australia.** Then from **Darwin,** the ship runs north to **Japan,** then south along the China coast to **Hong Kong, Singapore,** and across the Bay of Bengal to **Mumbai (Bombay)** and the Indian Ocean to **Suez** and the **Mediterranean** by early April.

After a month in the Mediterranean, based at **Piraeus (Athens)** and **Civitavecchia (Rome),** the *Deutschland* aims for **Kiel, Germany,** to begin a series of cruises to the Baltic, **Norway,** and northern isles before crossing the Atlantic to **Halifax** and **Montreal,** then down the St. Lawrence and out to sea again to **New York,** arriving by the last part of October.

Heading to warm weather again, the ship sails from **Santo Domingo** to Caribbean ports, at year's end makes a partial circumnavigation of **South America,** out by the West Coast and via **Cape Horn** to **Buenos Aires, Rio de Janeiro,** and from **Belem** across to **Lisbon,** arriving by February 2005.

North Americans are offered specific segments that include low-cost or free air and a low-cost package of shore excursions.

RESIDENSEA'S
The World
Apartment Living at Sea

 We might like to cruise for a week or so, but would we want to live on a ship for weeks or months at a time?

Some years back Norwegian visionary Knut Kloster Jr. came up with the idea of a megasize condo ship, one where people with large disposable incomes would buy a complete apartment to inhabit whenever they wished and perhaps rent it out to help

defray the carrying costs. Gradually the vessel's size decreased to what was thought to be the optimum size, and she finally got delivered from a Norwegian yard in spring 2002. The ship and its operation are owned by the condominium owners like a land-based resort.

The World of ResidenSea measures 43,000 tons and has 110 two- and three-bedroom fully equipped apartments and eighty-eight studio residences, the first batch for sale and the second for rent, though now all remaining unsold units are both for sale or for rent. The studios are similar to a good-size cruise ship cabin, some with balconies and some not. Beginning in spring 2003, some studios got combined into one-bedroom apartments by removing part of the divider at the seaward end. One unit remains the bedroom, and the adjoining unit becomes a larger lounge with kitchenette facilities and a second bathroom. The apartments are mostly two and three bedrooms, each with its own bathroom, fully equipped kitchen, terrace, and audiovisual equipment. There are five standard floor plans from which to choose and four design styles.

Current owners are 40 percent American and 40 percent European, and the remaining 20 percent are from the rest of the globe; most are still working. Net worth must be $5 million to qualify for purchasing a condo. Some residents like privacy, as one might expect, and pretty much hole up in their apartments, with perhaps an appearance in the lobby and piano bar before dinner or to use the sports facilities and enjoy a stroll on deck. More social types say they look forward to short-stay renters to bring new blood aboard and pep up the social life.

Personally, and fantasizing just a bit, I would like to try shipboard home living because my wife and I enjoy cooking and would look forward to having the ship's concierge direct us to the best markets and food stores in the next port. I think this would be a great way to sample the local culture. When *The World* arrived in New York, I would take a taxi to Upper Broadway where within a few blocks you can find everything you could ever want in the food departments at Citarella, Fairway, and Zabar's.

Owners who do not wish to cook a meal in their quarters can have it ordered in, have a traveling chef come in to prepare it, or eat out at one of the four onboard restaurants. Owners may buy coupons for breakfast, lunch, and dinner to maintain the cashless society.

Address/Phone: ResidenSea Ltd.; for residential purchase inquiries: (305) 264–9090, vacation stays: (800) 970–6601, outside U.S. and Canada: (305) 779–3399; www.residensea.com

The Ship: *The World* was built in 2002, has a gross tonnage of 43,000, a length of 644 feet, and a draft of 22 feet.

Passengers: 40 percent American, 40 percent European, 20 percent other

Dress: Country club style

Officers/Crew: Norwegian officers, European and Filipino crew

Cabins: 110 apartments; 88 studio residences (some being combined into one-bedroom apartments), all outside with tub baths and all but 16 with balconies

Fare: $$$ to $$$$

What's included: For renters: cruise fare, port charges, meals, drinks, wines, and gratuities; for owners: cruise fare, port charges, gratuities

What's not included: For renters: airfare; for owners: maintenance charges, airfare, meals in restaurants (coupons can be purchased)

Highlights: Owning a piece of a floating resort that sails the world. Attractive surroundings and excellent restaurants and sports facilities. For renters: a chance to be a part of a seagoing condominium community.

Other itineraries: *The World* continually cruises the world and spends multiple days in the more interesting ports.

Owners may rent out their units, and those not sold can also be rented at varying per diems depending on the size of the unit and the itinerary. The per diem rates include gratuities, three meals a day, selected drinks in the bars, and wines and dinner. The ship continually cruises around the world and remains for two to five days in some of the most popular ports. In summer *The World* may divide its time between northern Europe and the Mediterranean, lingering at Greenwich for London, Rouen on the Seine not far from Paris, or Barcelona and Venice.

Then in the cooler months, the ship will cross the Atlantic to circumnavigate South America and then cross the Pacific to New Zealand and Australia with multiple-day stays in Auckland and Sydney. Shore excursions are operated by Abercombie & Kent on a group or individual basis. Some owners keep bicycles aboard for touring ashore.

The ship has a full-size tennis court (unique), paddle tennis, a highly sophisticated golf simulator with forty courses to play, putting green, a pro shop, sports marina, indoor and outdoor pool, jogging track, a high-end spa run by Swiss Clinique La Prairie, several tastefully decorated lounges, casino, an Internet cafe, library, and a cinema. Services include a medical facility, catering, business center, secretarial services, hair salon, laundry, dry cleaning, travel agency, and twenty-four-hour concierge. Besides a resident band, often jazz, there is a pianist and vocalist, local entertainers in ports, and port information and special-interest lecturers. Typically, there might be about 250 owners and renters on board at any one time, but this number varies widely depending on the ship's locale.

Dining is of course a major attraction, and there are a half-dozen locales to enjoy varied meals. The most formal is Portraits, an intimate French restaurant for a special dinner. East serves Asian food at tables nicely separated by partitions and at a sushi bar. Tides is Mediterranean with an Italian slant, located high up with great sea views,

and the Marina is a steak and seafood venue where diners can watch the rotisserie preparation and look down onto the indoor pool and sports marina. Depending on how many people are aboard, the restaurants are open on a rotating basis, but there are always at least two from which to choose. For a continental breakfast or a light lunch, the ship's delicatessen has table and counter seats as well as provisions to buy for eating in, and the pool has a grill.

The World has cruise ship amenities, but it is unlike any other on the high seas in that many of those aboard are owners of their accommodations and take the same pride one might have in a land-based condominium ownership. Guests or renters can also enjoy this atmosphere at rates that range from a tremendous value to very high-end depending on the apartment size and the specific itinerary.

The Itinerary

The World is constantly on the move to ports around the world, and the company projects itineraries well in advance, though occasionally world events may cause a shift in locale. For 2004 into 2005, here is a route outline; be sure to check the Web site for changes and schedules. Only the major ports and regions are listed here.

Beginning in January 2004, *The World* will be northbound along the west coast of **South America,** then via the **Panama Canal** into the Gulf of Mexico and the **Caribbean** calling at **Houston** for two days and **New Orleans** for three. Leaving **Barbados** in early March, the ship crosses the Atlantic to the **Canaries** and into the **Mediterranean** with three-day stays at **Barcelona, Civitavecchia (for Rome),** and **Venice.** Leaving the Mediterranean, the ship ties up at **Rouen (for Paris)** in early June for three days, then crosses the Channel to **Falmouth** and **Greenwich (for London),** England. By the end of the month, and into July, the ship visits the coast of **Norway** for the midnight sun and makes three-day calls at **Stockholm, St. Petersburg,** and **Copen-**

hagen. In August, it's the **French Riviera** with extended stays at **Monte Carlo, Nice,** and **St. Tropez** and in September, eastward to **Greece, Turkey,** and into the **Black Sea.** A call is planned at **Ashdod, Israel,** for early October, then it's via **Suez** to the **Seychelles** and **East** and **South Africa** with four days in the shadow of Table Mountain at **Cape Town.** By November 2004, *The World* has crossed the South Atlantic and works its way up the East Coast of **South America** into the **Caribbean,** and at year's end makes U.S. port calls at **Fort Lauderdale** and **Key West.**

Then for 2005, in summation, *The World* spends the year encircling the globe by way of the Panama Canal into the South Pacific, down to New Zealand and Australia, up to Southeast Asia, and across the Indian Ocean via India to the Mediterranean via the Suez Canal. May, June, and July are spent in European waters, then in August she crosses the Atlantic to Canada and New England followed by calls at Boston, New York, Bermuda, and Fort Lauderdale, reaching the last named by October. The Caribbean is then the principal cruising ground to year's end.

APPENDIX

SHIPS BY SIZE

Small Ships take up to 400 passengers, double occupancy, and include all the expedition-style vessels, riverboats (except the two largest Mississippi sternwheelers), and coastal cruise vessels and most of the super luxurious boutique ships:

American Eagle 32
Aranui III 140
Arca 120
Canada Maritime (container ships) 72
Canadian Empress 54
Clipper Adventurer 216
Delta Queen 38
Emita II 31
Endeavour 218
Frederic Chopin 174
Galapagos Explorer II 122
Grande Caribe 29
Grande Mariner .36
Hebridean Princess 157
Kawartha Voyageur 56
L'Abercrombie 176
Legacy 101
Mozart 171
Nantucket Clipper 34
Niagara Prince 40
Pacific Explorer .110
Paul Gauguin 142
Polaris 124
Queen of the West 52
Radisson Diamond 181
Reef Endeavour .134
Rio Amazonas 120
River Explorer 46
Royal Clipper 70, 188
St. Helena 202
Sea Bird 50
Sea Cloud 95
Seabourn Pride .125
Seabourn Spirit .210
Sea Dream I and II 186
Sea Lion 50
Sea Voyager 112

Silver Shadow 136
Silver Whisper 194
Silver Wind 130
Spirit of Endeavour 104
Spirit of '98 22
Star Clipper .99, 183
Star Flyer 208
Sun Boat III 204
Taku (ferry) 25
Victoria Star and Victoria Queen 212
Viking Neptune and Viking Pride 169
Wind Spirit .97, 193
Yorktown Clipper 48

Midsize Ships, taking from 400 to 1,000 passengers, are relatively few in number and include some of the ferry liners (total passenger capacity) and a few of the top luxury ships:

American Queen 42
Caronia 150
Columbia (ferry) 25
Crystal Harmony 114
Crystal Symphony 2, 146
Deutschland 228
Hjaltland and Hrossey (ferries) 159
Kennicott (ferry) 25
Malaspina (ferry) 25
Marco Polo 127
Matanuska (ferry) 25
Minerva II 155, 167
Mississippi Queen 44
Nordkapp 162
Olympia Explorer 190
Prinsendam 224
Queen of the North (ferry) 27
Queen of Prince Rupert (ferry) 27
Seven Seas Mariner 19
Seven Seas Navigator 62
The World 230

Large Ships carrying more than 1,000 passengers include most of the megaships that also appear in the City at Sea category, those that will appeal to families, and several of the largest Scandinavian ferry liners.

The largest, including more on order, exceed 2,500 passengers when all berths are occupied, and a few even top 3,000 (not including crews numbering 1,000).

TYPES OF CRUISES

Expedition-style Cruises
Some of the best destination-oriented cruises take place aboard small expedition vessels offering what are often called soft adventure or naturalist cruises. These explore remote and exotic parts of the globe such as the Arctic, Antarctica, the Upper Amazon, and Australia's Great Bar-

rier Reef. Some incorporate a distinctive interest in the local culture, and often the lines invite experts in natural history, ecology, anthropology, and wildlife to give enrichment talks aboard ship and to accompany passengers ashore.

Cultural Enrichment Cruises
While a number of expedition-style cruises carrying a lecture staff have some cultural orientation, the list here includes those that emphasize the region through which they are sailing, with onboard experts in the fields of history, politics, and archaeology.

Cruising under Sail

Sailing ships often draw people who would not otherwise take a standard big ship cruise. These ships also operate with diesel engines when winds are not favorable and for maneuvering in port.

Super Luxury

Some high-end ships offer all-suite accommodations and the very best food and service afloat. Most are relatively small and take 300 passengers or fewer, but there are exceptions in the midsize category and aboard the *Queen Elizabeth 2* when booking grill-class accommodations.

Cruising with Children

Families traveling with children can enjoy a wide variety of activities, including separate supervised areas catering to several age levels. Most lines provide babysitting services, and some British ships have matrons to look after very small children and an early sitting for supper. Overnight ferry cruises are fun for children, offering informal dining and playrooms and games arcades aboard Scandinavian ships. A few soft adventure-type cruises are included for their orientation toward water activities.

Honeymooners and Romantics

Many lines have honeymoon packages, and the captains of the *Grand Princess* and the *Golden Princess* can perform civil marriage ceremonies. The hopelessly romantic will also enjoy the sail cruisers.

Cruising with Foreigners

Sailing with different nationalities can be an enriching experience, especially in European waters. On a few ships, Americans may be in the minority, but all languages will be equally catered for. Some ships, as indicated, may carry mostly British or German-speaking passengers, and a few may be English-speaking unions (ESU) of Americans, British, Australians, New Zealanders, and South Africans.

Cities at Sea

The largest ships afloat are virtual urban centers with many activities, varied entertainment, large casinos,shopping malls, acres of deck space, several outdoor pools and whirlpools, elaborate health and fitness spas, and multiple dining options.

No Mal de Mer

Seasickness does affect some passengers and is a worry for others, so we are listing those ships navigating rivers and inshore waters that are less likely to cause any upset stomachs. Those marked * also offer some itineraries with short open sea stretches.

INDEX

Granada, Spain, 169
Grande Mariner, 36–38
Great Barrier Reef, Australia, 134–35
Greece, 180, 192–93, 196, 198–99
Grenada,Windward Islands, 97
Guernsey, Channel Islands, 157
Gulf of Alaska, 14

H
Haines, Alaska, 26
Halifax, Nova Scotia, 4
Hamilton, Bermuda, 60–61, 64
Hawaii (Big Island), 139–40
Hawaiian Islands, 138–40
Hebridean Island Cruises, 157–59
Hebridean Princess, 157–59
Hells Canyon, Id., 51, 53
Helsinki, Finland, 146, 154, 167
Hjaltland, 159–60
Ho Chi Minh City (Saigon), 211
Holland America Line, 4–6, 11–13, 116–17, 138–39
Hong Kong, 212, 223, 226, 228, 230
Honolulu, Hawaii, 139
Horizon, 60–61
Hrossey, 159–60
Hudson River, N.Y., 30, 35
Hue,Vietnam, 212
Hungary, 169–71, 173

I
Ikarus Palace, 197
Illinois, 40–41
Infinity, 17
Intracoastal Waterway, 37, 41, 47
Iquitos, Peru, 120
Istanbul,Turkey, 192–94, 196
Italy, 180, 183, 185, 187, 189–90, 192, 197

J
Jamaica, 95
Jost Van Dyke, British VI, 99–101
Juneau, Alaska, 11, 13, 16, 18, 21, 24, 26–27

K
Kauai, Hawaii, 140
Kawartha Voyageur, 56–57
KD River Cruises, *see* Viking River Cruises

Kennebunkport, Maine, 6
Kennicott, 25–27
Kentucky, 41
Ketchikan, Alaska, 11, 13, 16, 18, 21, 23, 25, 27
Key West, Fla., 80, 90, 233
Kiel Canal, 153
Kingston, Ont., 56
Kusadasi, Turkey, 194

L
L'Abercrombie, 176–78
Laguna San Rafael, Chile, 132
La Paz, Mexico, 104
Lake Llanquihue, 128, 131
Lake Ontario, 30
Las Palmas, Spain, 72
Legacy, 101–2
La Havre, France, 74
Lerwick, Shetlands, 160
Leticia, 121
Lima, Peru, 129
Limassol, Cyprus, 196
Lindblad Expeditions, 50–51, 112–13, 124–25, 218–19
Lindos, Rhodes, 194
Lisbon, Portugal, 169, 228
Little Falls, N.Y., 31
Livorno, Italy, 180, 183
London, 74
Long Beach, Calif., 107
Los Angeles, Calif., 109, 115
Louisiana, 41, 44–47, 115
Los Seuños, Costa Rica, 110

M
Maasdam, 4–6
Maine, 3, 6, 10
Malaga, Spain, 72, 169
Malaspina, 25–27
Malaysia, 209
Majorca, Spain, 72
Manaus, Brazil, 126, 127
Marco Polo, 127–30
Margarita Island, Venezuela, 93
Marietta, Ohio, 43
Marquesas, South Pacific, 140–42, 143
Marseille, France, 182
Martha's Vineyard, Mass., 5, 33

ABOUT THE AUTHOR

Theodore W. Scull has spent more than four years on ocean liners, cruise ships, expedition vessels, sailing ships, riverboats, barges, and overnight ferries plying the seven seas to and from such diverse ports as Juneau, Valparaiso, Auckland, Singapore, Aswan, Prague, and his own homeport—New York. Besides *100 Best Cruise Vacations,* he has had seven other books published on travel, transportation, and New York topics. He writes for nearly every issue of *Cruise Travel;* U.S. newspaper travel sections and cruise industry publications; British cruise magazines and newspapers; and Internet Web sites. On the lecture circuit, he speaks on travel and maritime subjects aboard ships and to general and special interest groups. He and his wife, Suellyn, are longtime residents of Manhattan, now and forever.